THE
EUROCURRENCY
MARKET
HANDBOOK

THE GLOBAL EURODEPOSIT AND RELATED MARKETS

DR. EUGENE SARVER

NEW YORK INSTITUTE OF FINANCE
PRENTICE-HALL

Library of Congress Cataloging-in-Publication

Sarver, Eugene.
   The Eurocurrency market handbook.

   Includes index.
   1. Eurodollar market.   I.   Title.
HG3897.S27   1987   332.4'5   87-7739
ISBN 0–13–296161–X

This publication is designed to provide accurate and authoritative information in regard to the subject matter covered. It is sold with the understanding that the publisher is not engaged in rendering legal, accounting, or other professional service. If legal advice or other expert assistance is required, the services of a competent professional person should be sought.

—*From a Declaration of Principles jointly adopted by a Committee of the American Bar Association and a committee of Publishers and Associations*

Printed in the United States of America

10   9   8   7   6   5   4   3   2   1

New York Institute of Finance
(NYIF Corp.)
70 Pine St.
New York, New York 10270-0003

To María Teresa,
for whom *libros* mean so much

Contents

3
Eurocurrency Banking Centers, 39

4
Principal Nondollar Eurocurrency Markets, 163

5
Interbank Eurocurrency Trading, 203

6
Eurocurrency Market Instruments, 221

7
Syndicated Eurocurrency Bank Credits, 249

8
Eurocurrency Market Supervision, 285

9
The Eurobond Market, 299

Appendixes, *321*

Annotated Bibliography, 358

Index, 365

Preface

     This book integrates in convenient form various reports covering the major aspects of the Eurocurrency market. The materials were initially developed in conjunction with my teaching responsibilities in Chemical Bank and Credit Lyonnais financial training programs, as well as in teaching positions at the New York Institute of Finance, the American Institute of Banking, and Pace University.

     I would like to express my gratitude to Morgan Guaranty Trust, Chemical Bank, and Salomon Brothers for their permission to reprint various tables. Likewise, I am grateful to *The Journal of Commerce — International Edition* for its permission to reprint four of my articles that it originally published.

     I am especially grateful to the secretarial staff of the New York Institute of Finance, including Ms. Ann Marie Leitch, the Manager of Administrative Services, as well as Virginia Irvin and Dawn Bushey for their exemplary assistance in the word processing of this book. Finally, a special note of appreciation is extended to Fred Dahl, who oversaw the production of this book, and to John Goddard who did the computerized typesetting.

EUGENE SARVER

Introduction

In this dynamic era of global banking and brokerage networks, woven ever more tightly together by S.W.I.F.T., CHIPS, Reuters, and Telerate, banking increasingly means international banking. In turn, *international banking* means not the traditional foreign banking of accepting deposits from and extending loans to nonresidents in a bank's domestic currency; rather, it usually means banking activities conducted in foreign currencies, that is, Eurobanking, or more broadly, the Eurocurrency market.

A *Eurocurrency* is simply a currency on deposit outside its country of origin. Such deposits are also called *external currencies, international currencies*, and *xenocurrencies* (*xeno* meaning "foreign" in Latin, as in xenophobia). However, the term "Eurocurrency" is preferred, its etymology being that one of the original banks in the market was the Banque Commercial pour l'Europe du Nord, best known by its cable code, EUROBANK. Also, the original locus of the Euromarket was in Europe (especially London), reinforcing use of the term "Eurocurrency."

Reflecting the preference to conduct banking as free as possible from reserve requirements, interest rate ceilings, deposit insurance fees, capital export controls, legal lending limits, limits on bank assets growth (such as the U.K. corset), mandated credit allocations, capital: asset ratio requirements, liquidity ratios, and multiple tax authorities, the gross size of the Eurocurrency market has grown to the equivalent of $2,764 billion, nearly four times its size as recently as 1977. The Eurodollar market accounts for 78% of it, and much of the balance is Euro-Deutschemarks (11%) and Euro-Swiss francs (5%). However, Euro-yen is rapidly growing in importance, and there are also significant Euromarkets in British pounds, French francs, Dutch guilders, Canadian dollars, Belgian francs, Italian lira, ECUs, and Australian dollars.

While domestic banking and Eurobanking inevitably have much in common, their asset and liability profiles are nevertheless so distinct that Eurobanking must be considered a separate market. Exemplifying the distinctions are the U.S. dollar domestic and Euromarkets.

Domestic banking *liabilities* tend to be rather diverse, often of indeterminate maturity and noninterest-bearing (demand deposits), and emphasize negotiable CDs (not term Fed funds) for maturities beyond a few weeks. Eurodollar liabilities are predominantly time deposits (to a moderate extent, negotiable CDs) and are all interest-bearing, with fixed maturities.

Concurrently, domestic bank *assets* are generally loans priced on a floating prime rate (or money market) basis, extended by a single bank to a corporate borrower. Typically, Eurobanking assets are syndicated loans, repriced on a three- or six-month rollover basis (LIBOR), offered by an international group of banks to a sovereign borrower or multinational corporation. Multicurrency funding and lending options, with the associated foreign exchange risks, further widen the differences between the domestic and Eurocurrency markets.

The Eurocurrency Market Handbook sequentially treats the principal aspects of that central sphere of international finance. Section 1 statistically presents the immense scope of the Eurocurrency market, its remarkable growth over the last 22 years, its major currency segments, and other key characteristics, such as participant and maturity profiles. Section 2 chronicles the historical development of the Eurocurrency market, focusing on the factors that have promoted its unprecedented expansion.

Next, Section 3 scrutinizes the critical and ancillary factors that have propelled certain financial centers to global banking significance. Complementing that theoretical perspective is an examination of several major centers such as London, Luxembourg, Paris, New York, Cayman, Nassau, Panama, Tokyo, Singapore, Hong Kong, and Bahrain.

Section 4 then focuses on the principal Eurocurrency markets in terms of their disparate characteristics, highlighting their distinct interest rate levels and structures. Additionally, the Eurocurrency markets are compared with their corresponding domestic markets, especially from the perspective of impediments to arbitrage. Finally, the eleven major non-U.S. dollar Eurocurrency markets are studied in terms of their historical development, market participants, interest rate factors, and interest rate movements from 1976 to 1987. The Eurocurrency markets examined include those in Deutschemarks, Swiss francs, Japanese yen, ECUs, pounds sterling, French francs, Dutch guilders, Belgian francs, Italian lira, Canadian dollars, and Australian dollars

Next Section 5 details interbank Eurocurrency trading and related brokering, both in terms of intracenter and intercenter transactions. While Section 6 presents a complementary look at the principal Eurocurrency market instruments (aside from the dominant one of non-negotiable time deposits), including fixed and floating rate negotiable CDs, Eurodollar futures contracts, and Euronotes (including Eurocommercial paper).

Section 7 then details the principal ultimate asset of the Euromarket, the syndicated Eurocurrency loans. An exposition of the syndication process is followed by a detailing of the elements of Eurocurrency credits, and a statistical breakdown, by region and individual countries, of such bank credits, as well as international bonds from 1983 through May 1986. Finally, a description of the global debt crisis and the *watch group* for the syndicated loans spawned by the crisis, the Institute of International Finance, is included.

Section 8 provides insight into the elusive concept of Eurocurrency market supervision with the full 1975 and revised 1983 *BIS Reports on the Supervision of Banks' Foreign Establishments*. Especially noteworthy are the distinctions between branches, subsidiaries, and joint ventures (consortia), as well as the concern with the related but separate problems of liquidity, solvency, and prudent foreign exchange management. Also, the historic 1980 communique by the Bank for International Settlements on the Eurocurrency market is included.

Finally, Section 9 provides current statistical information (through end-1985) comparing the Eurobond and Eurocurrency bank credit market. While the Eurobond market has been traditionally secondary to the Eurocurrency bank credit market, it made a strong showing in 1983 ($49 billion vs. $74 billion) and 1984 ($80 billion vs. $113 billion) and surpassed it in 1985 ($137 billion vs. $110 billion), as it offers lower costs to qualified borrowers. A description of the Eurobond market is provided, as well as tables analyzing the market in 1984 and 1985 in terms of type of issue (such as fixed rate), currency, and issuers by nationality. The section concludes with a description of the secondary Eurobond market, including the recent problem with perpetual FRNs.

1
Eurocurrency
Market Size and Profile

The Eurocurrency market, by virtue of its $2.8 trillion size, plays a major role in international finance. Thus, this unit begins with a discussion of its current size. Complementing its size, both in gross and net terms, it is useful to know as well the relative role of different leading participants (banks, corporations, central banks), which is shown as well.

Due to the Eurocurrency market's sensitivity to exogenous events, such as the two oil price shocks (1973, 1979-80) and the global debt crisis (1982-84), historical perspective on the market's growth is invaluable, which is addressed in the second subsection. The changing global situation affects not only the market's growth rate, but also the relative role of the dollar, also shown.

Besides the dollar, the Deutschemark, the Swiss franc, and some other leading currencies play an important role in the Eurocurrency market. The third section of this unit details the current currency profile of the market.

Complementing its currency profile, the market's maturity profile also greatly impacts its essential character. In particular, as demonstrated in the fourth section, the market is composed of rather short-term liabilities, but longer-term assets, accomplishing a maturity transformation. That function is the source of much of its profits, especially given the usual positively sloped yield curve of dollar-denominated interest rates.

Another key characteristic of the Eurocurrency market is the considerable role of interbank deposits, as opposed to lending to ultimate borrowers (such as multinational corporations). In the fifth section, the unusually large role of interbank depositing is detailed.

Finally, it is useful to have direct look at the mighty engine that drives the Eurocurrency market's speeding locomotive. It is the significantly greater competitiveness of the Eurodollar market, its dominant currency, relative to the U.S. domestic market. The sixth section graphically demonstrates that critical characteristic of the Eurodollar market.

Current Eurocurrency Market Size and Participant Profile

As Exhibit 1-1 shows, the gross size of the Eurocurrency market was $2.8 trillion at the end of 1985. In net terms, excluding interbank deposits, it totaled $1.7 trillion. An examination of the end-1985 depositor profile shows that *other banks*, meaning commercial banks, dominated the market, representing 76% of deposits. Concurrently, *nonbanks*, largely corporations, represented 21% of the market, and *official monetary institutions*, largely central banks investing their countries' international reserves, constituted the remaining 4% of the market.

The current depositor profile represents a substantial change over earlier periods. In particular, comparing 1985 with 1977 shows that the dominant role of *other banks* has become even more so, with their current 76% share of the market well up from 68% in the earlier year. Concurrently, the share of *nonbanks* has increased more moderately during 1977-1985, from 18% to 21%. Offsetting the enhanced share of the *other banks* and *nonbanks*, the share of *official monetary institutions* has dropped sharply to 4% from 14% over the same period.

Eurocurrency Market Size and the Dollar Role During 1964-1985

The gross and net size of the Eurocurrency market have both grown considerably over the 1964-1985 period, as shown in Exhibit 1-

2. From $20 billion and $14 billion, respectively, in 1964, it grew 140 times larger gross, and 120 times larger net, in just twenty years. In particular, the gross size of the Eurocurrency market grew to $2,764 billion as of end-1985, nearly four times the level of 1977 ($740 billion) and nine times the level of 1973 ($315 billion). At $2.8 trillion, it corresponds closely to the level of M-2 in the United States.

While 25% compounded rates of growth were common in the 1970s, in the peak years of gross market growth, it hit rates as high as 53% in 1973 and 33%/36% in 1979/1980, both periods representing the recycling of petrodollars in response to oil price shocks, as well as high inflation.

In 1983 and 1984, the Eurocurrency market grew at only about 5% (little above the corresponding inflation rate). That slowdown was caused principally by the global debt crisis, which made investors wary of depositing in Eurobanks, as well by Eurobanks wary of lending to third world borrowers. The global economic slowdown, which affected the industrialized countries as well, caused in the latter case by the loss of third world markets plus deflationary monetary and fiscal policies despite high unemployment, was also a major contributing factor to the sluggish pace of market growth during 1983-1984. However, in 1985, with the global debt crisis largely contained (such as, Brazil, the largest debtor at $109 billion, showed significant improvement with a 1985 merchandise trade surplus of $12 billion), aside perhaps from oil-dependent countries like Mexico, and global GNP growth accelerating, the Eurocurrency market grew at a much faster 17%.

One notable change from the mid-1960s to the mid-1980s is the increased role of interbank depositing. As Exhibit 1-2 shows, the relative net size of the Eurocurrency market, exclusive of interbank deposits, declined from approximately 70% of the gross market size in the mid-1960s to only 60% of the gross market size in the mid-1980s.

A final notable factor is the relative role of the Eurodollar, as opposed to other major Eurocurrencies, such as the Euro-Deutschemark and the Swiss franc, which, like the growth rate, has fluctuated considerably. Since 1964, it has fluctuated, as Exhibit 1-2 shows, within a range of 72% (1979) to 84% (1967 and 1969), averaging around 77%. Basically, due to investor preferences for depositing strong currencies, it covaries with the spot dollar. With the large drop in the trade-weighted value of the spot dollar in 1985, it fell dramatically in that year to only 75% of the market.

Exhibit 1-1
INTERNATIONAL BANKING MARKET SIZE
(At end of period, billions of dollars)

	1981	1982	1983r	1984 Sept.	1984 Dec.	1985 Mar	June	Sept.	Dec.
Gross claims									
Eurocurrencies, on residents and nonresidents	**1,929**	**2,146**	**2,253**	**2,322**	**2,359**	**2,473**	**2,459**	**2,622**	**2,764**
On non banks	557	634	665	676	694	722	735	761	789
On banks	1,372	1,512	1,588	1,646	1,665	1,751	1,724	1,861	1,975
In dollars	1,504	1,694	1,797	1,857	1,894	1,960	1,924	2,002	2,039
In other currencies	425	452	456	465	465	513	535	620	725
Domestic currencies, on nonresidents	**365**	**398**	**398**	**397**	**402**	**409**	**422**	**451**	**503**
On nonbanks	128	132	136	142	142	147	150	165	185
On banks	237	266	262	255	260	262	272	286	318
In dollars	188	211	217	208	215	208	209	205	215
In other currencies	177	187	181	185	187	201	213	246	288
Total	**2,294**	**2,544**	**2,651**	**2,719**	**2,761**	**2,882**	**2,881**	**3,073**	**3,267**
On nonbanks	685	766	801	818	836	869	885	926	974
On banks	1,609	1,778	1,850	1,901	1,925	2,013	1,996	2,147	2,293
In dollars	1,692	1,905	2,014	2,069	2,109	2,168	2,133	2,207	2,254
In other currencies	602	639	637	650	652	714	748	866	1,013
Gross liabilities									
Eurocurrencies, to residents and nonresidents	**1,954**	**2,168**	**2,278**	**2,349**	**2,386**	**2,489**	**2,471**	**2,641**	**2,796**
To nonbanks	372	432	479	492	497	508	520	546	572
To official monetary institutions	112	91	88	94	96	96	106	109	112
To other banks	1,470	1,645	1,711	1,763	1,793	1,885	1,845	1,986	2,112

In dollars	1,539	1,741	1,846	1,912	1,950	2,010	1,969	2,045	2,099
In other currencies	415	427	432	437	436	479	502	596	697
Domestic currencies, to nonresidents	**263**	**250**	**260**	**277**	**280**	**293**	**310**	**341**	**377**
To nonbanks	74	70	73	75	80	82	89	103	109
To banks	189	180	187	202	200	211	221	238	268
In dollars	126	116	135	143	146	147	154	159	169
In other currencies	137	134	125	134	134	146	156	182	206
Total	**2,217**	**2,418**	**2,538**	**2,626**	**2,666**	**2,782**	**2,781**	**2,982**	**3,173**
To nonbanks	446	502	552	567	577	590	609	649	681
To banks and official institutions	1,771	1,916	1,986	2,059	2,089	2,192	2,172	2,333	2,492
In dollars	1,665	1,857	1,981	2,055	2,096	2,157	2,123	2,204	2,268
In other currencies	552	561	557	571	570	625	658	778	905
Net market size	1,155	1,285	1,382	1,411	1,430	1,470	1,497	1,578	1,668

Source: *World Financial Markets* (June/July 1986). Reprinted with permission of the Morgan Guaranty Trust Company of New York.

Exhibit 1-2
EUROCURRENCY DEPOSIT MARKET: 1964-1985
(At end of period, billions of dollars equivalent)

	1964	1965	1966
Estimated size	**1964**	**1965**	**1966**
Gross	20	24	29
Net	14	17	21
Eurodollars as % of all Eurocurrencies—gross	83%	84%	83%

	1972	1973	1974
Estimated size	**1972**	**1973**	**1974**
Gross	200	305	375
Net	110	160	215
Eurodollars as % of all Eurocurrencies—gross	78%	73%	77%

	1980	1981	1982
Estimated size	**1980**	**1981**	**1982**
Gross	1,515	1,954	2,168
Net	755	1,155	1,285
Eurodollars as % of all Eurocurrencies—gross	74%	79%	80%

Source: *World Financial Markets*, various issues.

Eurocurrency Market Currency Profile

As shown in Exhibit 1-2, the share of the Euro-dollar relative to other Eurocurrencies has fluctuated from a low of 72% to a high of 84%, although 82% has been the high in over the last fifteen years. When the spot dollar was very weak, such as the 1979 "Carter dollar," the share hit the 72% trough. When the spot dollar was strong, such as the 1984 "Reagan fiscal deficit dollar," the share hit the 82% peak. The complementary aspect to the dollar's role is that of the other Eurocurrencies, whose share has fluctuated from 18% to 28% over the past fifteen years.

The only detailed reporting on the currency profile of the Eurocurrency market is provided by the *Annual Report* of the Bank for International Settlements and it, unfortunately, frequently changes the content of this important series. For example, from 1984 to 1985, it

1967	1968	1969	1970	1971
36	50	85	110	145
25	34	50	65	85
84%	82%	84%	81%	76%

1975	1976	1977	1978	1979
460	565	695	835	1,111
250	310	380	475	600
78%	79%	76%	74%	72%

1983	1984	1985
2,278	2,383	2,796
1,377	1,415	1,668
81%	82%	75%

changed both the scope of banks covered (from *BIS Reporting Countries in Europe* to *Industrial Reporting BIS Countries*) and the number of individual Eurocurrencies covered (from ten to only six).

Nevertheless, certain patterns can be identified. First, the Euro-Deutschemark's domination of the nondollar Eurocurrency market remains unchallenged (at a steady 11% of the overall market). Yet slower growth than some other Eurocurrencies has caused its relative share to drop to about a third in 1985 from roughly half of the residual market (Exhibit 1-3 is indicative).

Likewise, the Swiss franc has held onto its 5% share of the overall market, but with the drop in the Eurodollar's share, its slower relative growth has enabled the Euroyen to almost overtake it in 1985. In particular, investor demand for the Euroyen, boosted by Japan's mammoth merchandise trade surpluses, low inflation, and financial market deregulation, pushed its 1985 share of the market to 5%, twice its 1984 share.

However impressive the jump in the Euroyen's share, the share of the Euro-British pound grew in 1985 at a faster rate of 125% to represent 4% of the market. Boosting its growth were very high interest rates, both in nominal and real terms, amidst confidence inspired by the Thatcher government's conservative economic policies (despite 13% unemployment) and by firm oil prices until late in the year. Finally, ECU deposits were steady at 1.8% of the market in 1985, reflecting a maturing of that relatively new market.

Exhibit 1-3
THE EUROCURRENCY MARKET CURRENCY PROFILE
(Foreign currency liabilities of banks in
industrial reporting BIS countries at end-1985)

Eurocurrency (billions of U.S. dollars equivalent)		% of Euromarket
1. U.S. dollar	$1,287.3	67.5%
2. German mark	208.3	10.9%
3. Swiss franc	101.5	5.3%
4. Japanese yen	97.0	5.1%
5. British pound	77.5	4.1%
6. ECU	34.3	1.8%
7. Other currencies*	101.8	5.3%
Total	$1,907.7	100.0%

*French francs, Dutch guilders, Belgian francs, Italian lira, and so on.

Source: Bank for International Settlements, *Fifty-Sixth Annual Report, 1 April 1985– 31 March 1986* (Basle, 10 June 1986).

Maturity Profile of Eurocurrency Liabilities and Claims

Besides its currency profile, a key characteristic of the Eurocurrency market is its maturity profile. As is evident from Exhibit 1-4, most Eurocurrency liabilities are of short duration, while claims tend to be of a significantly longer duration. The resulting maturity transformation is one of the market's most important functions.

In particular, in observing two paramount but geographically disparate centers, London (the world's leading Eurocurrency center) and Singapore (the center of the Asian dollar market), one finds very similar maturity profiles that bear out the short-liabilities, longer-claims pattern. In London, 72% of the liabilities are three months or less, while the comparable number for Singapore is 77%; concurrently, only 4% of the liabilities in London, and 3% in Singapore are over one year. Conversely, only 54% of the claims in London and 62% in Singapore are three months or less, while 24% of the claims in London and 17% in Singapore are over one year.

The resultant short funding in the Euromarket entails more risk than in the U.S. domestic market, where short funding is also common. This is because Euroloans are generally fixed in rate for a three- or six-month rollover period, while domestic loans are based on a floating prime rate that rises in response to tightening money market conditions. As compensation for the greater risk, Eurobanks generally demand a wider spread on their Euroloans during periods of risky interest rate volatility. (This problem is discussed in Chapter 7.)

Exhibit 1-4
MATURITY ANALYSIS OF LIABILITIES AND CLAIMS
IN EUROCURRENCIES
(Percent, December 1981)

	Claims	
Maturities	**London**	**Singapore**
One month	31.2	35.0
One to three months	23.0	27.0
Over three months to twelve months	21.8	21.0
Over one year to three years	7.4	4.0
Three years and over	16.6	13.0

	Liabilities	
Maturities	**London**	**Singapore**
One month	42.9	46.5
One to three months	28.9	30.0
Over three months to twelve months	24.5	20.0
Over one year to three years	2.3	2.0
Three years and over	1.6	1.0

Source: Federal Reserve Bank of San Francisco, *Economic Review* (Winter 1983).

Depositor Profile of Active Eurobanks

Besides the Eurocurrency market's currency and maturity profile, a key characteristic of the market is the considerable role of interbank deposits as opposed to deposits by nonbanks. As is evident from Exhibit 1-5, the liabilities of Eurobanks in eight BIS European countries to other banks were for one representative period a preponderant 86% of total liabilities. Concurrently, their assets vis-a-vis other banks were nearly as preponderant at 72%.

The interbank deposit and loan activity reflects not only interbank loans to offset corporate deposits, and borrowings to offset corporate loans, but it also involves pure speculation based on a view of the future interest rate movements, and implemented by either long-funding or short-funding strategies. Some interbank activity, moreover, is driven by arbitrage activity, such as that of issuing negotiable CDs at a relatively low rate, and investing the proceeds in the higher-rate interbank (non-negotiable) time deposit market. Finally some interbank activity is driven by the simple necessity of keeping the bank's name in the market. Such activity is often done at little profit (such as just the bid-ask spread) or no profit, but an image of responsiveness to other banks' bids assures a more favorable reception when one's own bank is actively bidding for funds. As in so many other spheres of human activity, *reciprocity* is the name of the game.

Exhibit 1-5
BALANCE SHEET OF EUROBANKS, FOREIGN CURRENCY
(December 1980)

Assets		Liabilities	
Vis-a-vis other banks	71.6%	Vis-a-vis other banks	86.1%
Vis-a-vis nonbanks	28.4%	Vis-a-vis nonbanks	13.9%
Total	100.0%	Total	100.0%
Total in billions of U.S. dollars	681.2	Total in billions of U.S. dollars	800.5

Note: Based on banks in eight European countries whose figures are reported to the Bank for International Settlements (BIS). The asset and liability totals are not equal because the reporting banks do not necessarily match deposits and liabilities denominated in foreign currency.

Source: Bank for International Settlements, Monetary and Economic Department, *International Banking Developments: Third Quarter 1981* (February 1982).

Greater Competitiveness of
the Eurodollar Market vs. the U.S. Domestic Market

Despite the greater inherent difficulties, transaction expense, and risk of the Eurodollar market, over the last twenty-five years, it has grown at a much faster pace than the corresponding U.S. domestic market. That achievement is the direct result of its greater competitiveness than the domestic American market, a final key characteristic of the Euromarket.

In a word, as is shown by Exhibit 1-6, it offers depositors higher deposit rates and borrowers lower lending rates, thereby operating on a much narrower spread than the U.S. domestic market. Otherwise, obviously, those market participants would not overlook the market's greater transaction expenses (both money and time) and higher risks.

Due to the absence of reserve requirements, FDIC insurance fees, and interest rate ceilings or controls, as well as generally lower or no taxes, the Eurodollar market can offer high deposit rates. (The effective rates are even higher for most depositors as they decline to reveal their interest earnings to their national tax authorities, while conversely domestic interest earnings are reported by the banks to their national tax authority.) In fact, the Eurodollar market must offer higher deposit rates to induce depositors to forsake the safer domestic market with its clearcut lender of last resort (the central bank), FDIC deposit insurance coverage (de jure $100,000, but de facto generally all deposits, as exemplified by the Continental Illinois rescue), tighter regulation and supervision, and so on.

On the lending side, the Eurodollar market offers lower rates than the U.S. domestic market. Practically this means that the Eurodollar loan rates of LIBOR plus spread are significantly lower than the effective U.S. domestic loan rates of prime plus the effect of compensating balances. For example, if six-month LIBOR is 6% and a standard spread is 1%, the lending rate is 7%. The corresponding domestic rate would be 7½% prime. This is a relatively high rate reflecting a cartelized industry with the largest banks establishing an administered prime rate that the other banks follow, reinforced by the geographic segmentation of markets, due to the McFadden Act, etc. Add to the domestic rate a 20% compensating balance requirement, for an effective domestic lending rate of 9.375%, or a margin of 2.375% over the corresponding Eurodollar lending rate. A minor qualification would be that compensating balances do not have to be maintained every day, as long as they average out the required amount; that is, the corporate borrower can use an optimal cash management strategy that minimizes the impact of the compensating balance requirement, so that the effective cost to the corporation is somewhat less than it appears.

While the latter comparison accurately describes the traditional situation of the relative competitiveness of the Eurodollar and domestic U.S. market, over the last several years the competitiveness of the U.S. domestic market has significantly increased. Buffeted by the collective impact of a fast growing commercial paper market (now $335 billion) and aggressive price cutting foreign banks in the U.S. (20% of commercial and industrial loans in the U.S., including 40% in New York) and commercial finance companies, as well as the competition from the Eurobank loans (plus the Euronote and the Eurocommercial paper markets), American banks now offer cost plus loans (such as 90-day CD plus, 90-day commercial paper plus, overnight Fed funds plus) to their

Exhibit 1-6
THE NARROWER LENDING-DEPOSIT SPREAD OF THE EURODOLLAR MARKET AS OPPOSED TO THE U.S. DOMESTIC MARKET

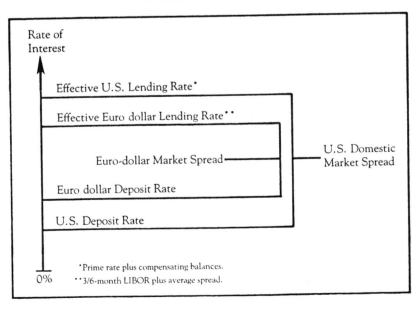

large corporate customers, reserving the much pricier prime-rate-based loans for the middle market and smaller customers.

Nevertheless, the Euromarket is still a cheaper market, with lower lending rates resulting from historically lower loan loss rates (due to lending only the blue chip multinationals and sovereign borrowers), lower relative administrative costs due to larger loan sizes, freedom from governmental credit allocation policies, possibly lower or no corporate income taxes, and tougher competition fostered by the *arm-length* banking culture as opposed to the *relationship banking* that has traditionally characterized the U.S. domestic market.

2

Historical Development
of the Eurocurrency Market

This section begins with "A Short History of the Eurocurrency Market." Reviewing the thirty-five-year history of the market is important for two reasons. First, by knowing the history of the market, one is able to enter the mindset of a seasoned Eurocurrency trader or analyst. Instead of being unduly influenced by the current ascendance of Japan and Western Europe and the corresponding decline of the United States and OPEC, one is able to judge current conditions against the broader perspective of history—to see highly reversible cycles instead of extrapolating current trends. Traders and others who "bet" long-term on what seemed an overwhelming trend at the time are generally pursuing other lines of work these days. (Corporate treasurers who borrowed medium to long-term Swissy around 1970 are a good example of such myopia.)

A second reason besides a good macroeconomic perspective is a greater microsensitivity; specifically, what have been the responses of commercial banks, multinational corporations, and central banks to the Euromarket challenges in the past, as analogous difficulties can be expected in the future. Successful responses can be expected to be repeated and refined, while less fruitful reactions can be expected to be dropped from the armory of those institutions.

Complementing the history of the market is a brief recapitulation of "Factors Promoting the Initiation of the Eurodollar Market" and "Factors Promoting the Rapid Growth of the Eurodollar Market." Understanding those two sets of factors provides considerable insight into the great success that the Eurodollar market and the broader Eurocurrency market have enjoyed.

A Short History of the Eurocurrency Market

ORIGINS OF THE EUROCURRENCY MARKET

While the Eurocurrency market dates from the 1950s, it was anticipated by the availability of dollar deposits at European banks in hyperinflationary countries in the 1920s. However, salient characteristics of the contemporary Eurocurrency market, such as the interbank deposit market and syndicated loans, were absent.

The subsequent successful initiation of the Eurodollar market in the 1950s owes much to the central role granted the U.S. dollar by the Bretton Woods conference of 1944. It replaced the waning pound sterling as *the* international currency. Convertible into fine gold (.995 pure) at the rate of $35 per troy ounce, it was literally as "good as gold." Moreover, it was the currency of the world's strongest economic/political system, and one that had suffered little damage in World War II. Reinforcing its global role was the depth of America's money and capital markets, its use in pricing commodities (such as oil and wheat), its general global use in denominating exports, and its acceptance as a transaction currency everywhere. In short, the U.S. dollar was generally the currency of choice for investors worldwide, especially for those who had safety of principal as their primary goal. Finally, the dollar's stability and indeed ascendance were highlighted by the 30% devaluation of the pound sterling in 1949, which was followed by numerous similar devaluations.

Paradoxically, the creation of the Eurodollar market, one of the world's largest capitalist markets, was, to a significant extent, the work of Communist governments—those of the Soviet Union, Eastern Europe, and China. As their own currencies were inconvertible, those nations maintained dollar deposits in New York in order to conduct international trade—such as the exchange of Soviet gold, diamonds, furs, oil and natural gas for machinery and grain from the West.

Exhibit 2-1
FACTORS PROMOTING THE INITIATION OF
THE EURODOLLAR MARKET

INTERNATIONAL FACTORS

1. Investor confidence in the U.S. dollar due to its convertibility to gold (Bretton Woods), its being the currency of the world's strongest economic/political system, which suffered little World War II dam-

age, the depth of its money and capital markets, its use in denominating commodities (such as oil), its general global use in denominating exports and its acceptance as a transaction currency worldwide (virtually an international currency).

2. The fear on the part of the communist countries of China, the Soviet Union, and Eastern Europe that their U.S. dollar deposits (necessary for their external trade due to the inconvertibility of their own currencies) in New York would be subject to seizure due to Cold War tensions (as well as the "hot war" in Korea), their seizure of property (farms, houses, stores, factories) owned by U.S. citizens without compensation, and their defaulting on bonds issued by the previous governments, some of which were owned by U.S. citizens.

3. The fear on the part of some Arab investors that their U.S. dollar deposits in New York would be subject to freezing as was the case of belligerent assets (such as Egypt's) during the Suez War of 1956.

4. The existence of an unofficial but rigid lending rate structure in Italy for lira loans (monitored by the Bank of Italy) which caused aggressive banks seeking to enlarge their market share to bid for U.S. dollars to make dollar-denominated loans exempt from the lira interest rate structure.

5. The essential termination of foreign exchange controls in Western Europe in 1958 broadly encouraged Euromarket activity, such as multicurrency loans.

U.S. REGULATORY FACTORS

1. Reserve requirements on time deposits (Regulation D).

2. The requirement that no interest be paid on *demand deposits,* while *time deposits* were subject to a 30-day minimum; concurrently, time deposits were subject to interest rate ceilings (Regulation Q).

3. The de facto requirement that commercial banks have deposit insurance (FDIC) and pay the corresponding insurance premiums, which were based on the banks' total deposits as opposed to the actually insured amounts (that is, the first $40,000 of each account).

4. Federal, state, and local taxation of banks' net income (such as in New York City, the state and local marginal tax rate was 25.8%).

5. The "legal lending limits," which generally limited a bank's total loans to a single borrower to a maximum of 10% of its capital and undivided profits.

However, East-West relations had badly deteriorated in the late 1940s and early 1950s admidst the coup d'etat in Czechoslavakia, the Berlin blockade, the Chinese civil war, and ultimately the transformation of the Cold War into a hot war in the Korean peninsula. Given the strong anticommunist sentiments in America, highlighted by the Rosenberg trial and the McCarthy hearings, the Communist governments were apprehensive regarding "U.S. sovereign risk," the possibility that the U.S. government might freeze or seize their assets (that is, bank deposits).

Moreover, both the U.S. government and American private citizens had a legal basis for attaching the deposits for a variety of reasons. First, American citizens (represented by the Foreign Bondholders Protective Council) held bonds issued by the pre-Communist governments in Russia, Eastern Europe, and China, which the successor Communist governments were refusing to redeem. Secondly, American citizens owned houses, shops, factories, and farmland in the Communist countries which had been nationalized, but without compensation being given. Finally, the Soviet Union was in arrears with respect to lend-lease loan repayments (World War II loans granted by the U.S. government).

The Soviet Union confided its apprehensions to a financial advisor, a British bank in London, which advised it to transfer its dollar deposits to banks in Europe. The proposal was well received because, in addition to safeguarding Communist deposits, it fitted in with the Soviet strategy of enhancing its relationships with western European banks.

Thus, the Soviet Union initially transferred deposits to the bank it owned in Paris—the Banque Commercial pour l'Europe du Nord, known best by its telex code of EUROBANK. Hence, the dollars at Eurobank became known as Euro-dollars. The Soviet Union and its allies also transferred dollar deposits to the Soviet-owned bank in London—the Moscow Narodny Bank. Thus, two Communist banks spawned the ultimate capitalist financial market—the Eurocurrency market.

New impetus to the growth of the Eurodollar market came in 1956 owing to U.S. reaction to the outbreak of the Suez War of 1956. The conflict itself resulted from a joint British-French attempt to recapture the British-French investor-owned Suez Canal, which President Nasser had nationalized to help repay Soviet loans to build the Aswan Dam. Israel, alerted to the British-French paratrooper assault on Port Said, sent its army into the Gaza Strip to wipe out bases from which terrorists had preyed on its kibbutzim in the Negev Desert. The U.S., which had not been advised in advance of the coordinated invasion of Egypt, reacted by freezing the U.S. assets of all the belligerents, including Egypt. While British, French, and Israeli investors took the temporary measure in stride, many Arab investors reconsidered "U.S. sovereign risk" and transferred their dollar deposits to Europe.

Further impetus to the early growth of the market came from Italy, where growth-oriented Italian banks were being held back by a fixed lending rate structure for lira loans that resulted from interbank consensus. Thus, to expand their market share, they bid aggressively for dollar deposits in order to make dollar-denominated loans exempt from the lira interest rate restrictions.

While the Russians, East Europeans, Chinese, Arabs, and Italians were the charter members of the Eurodollar market, it awaited the active participation of the London bankers to give the market a sustained, dynamic guidance. Their aggressive involvement began in 1957, fostered by Bank of England regulations of that year that prohibited British banks from doing sterling financing of third country trade (that is, not involving the UK as either exporter or importer). While the regulations were an understandable reaction to Britain's balance of payments crisis (spawned by uncompetitive domestic prices and capital outflows), the bankers of "The City" were not about to give up a lucrative business in which they had developed a special expertise. So they started bidding for dollar deposits with which to finance the third country trade—dollar financing replaced sterling financing.

The final development that shaped the market's formative period was the termination of most West European foreign exchange regulations in 1958 (aside from capital controls in France, and the like). The lifting of the complex regulatory structure (exemplified by the European Payments Union) reflected the remarkable progress in the reconstruction of Europe in the thirteen years from the Nazi surrender to 1958.

Now admidst the stability of fixed (if adjustable) exchange rates of the Bretton Woods System, it was possible, indeed virtually mandatory, for prudent liability management to continuously shift the currency in which a corporation's debts were denominated to achieve the lowest possible borrowing costs. An active interbank Euromarket in all the major currencies developed to enable the banks to respond to the new corporate borrowing strategies. Now all the elements were in place for sustained, rapid growth of the Eurocurrency market.

The spectacular growth of the Euromarket reflected not only the Communist, Arab, Italian, and British factors cited, but six U.S. regulatory/tax factors which made use of the Eurodollar market highly advantageous. These included:

1. Reserve requirements on time deposits (Regulation D) of 1-6%;
2. The requirement that no interest be paid on demand deposits, while time deposits were subject to a 30-day minimum (Regulation Q);
3. All time deposits were subject to interest rate ceilings (Regulation Q);
4. The requirement that (Fed member) commercial banks have FDIC insurance coverage and pay the corresponding premium of 0.085%, of total deposits, which added 8.5 basis points to the cost of taking deposits—the premium applied to total deposits although only the first $40,000 (later $100,000) of each account was covered;
5. Federal, state, and local taxation of banks' net income—in New York the marginal state and local taxation rate alone was 25.8%.
6. The legal lending limit which limited a bank's total loans to a single borrower to 10% of its capital and reserves.

THE DOLLAR CRISIS OF THE 1960s

The flip side of European success and corresponding strong European currencies was a reassessment of the dollar. Indeed the "dollar shortage" had become the "dollar glut." Nevertheless, the U.S. was continuing to abuse its numeraire role in the Bretton Woods System by running massive, sustained balance of payments deficits (a "deficit without tears"). They were caused by huge capital outflows (direct investments by American multinationals, foreign loans by American banks, and America's growing purchase of higher-yielding foreign stocks and bonds), as well as by foreign military expenditures to contain Soviet expansion (NATO, CENTRO, SEATO) and by American tourists taking advantage of the strong dollar. These deficits were undermining investor confidence in the "almighty dollar."

Indeed some governments, notably the French, were taking advantage of America's dollar-gold exchange policy to convert greenbacks into shiny bars. (The French policy was due, in part, to their substantial international reserves loss in the 29% sterling devaluation of 1931.)

To restore investor confidence in the U.S. dollar, the central bank of the U.S. and those of six European nations (UK, Belgium, Italy, the Netherlands, Switzerland, and West Germany) created the Gold Pool. The Pool, operating primarily through the BIS, provided gold as needed to the London gold market, and thus kept the price of gold in the world market consistent with the gold price of the dollar.

The Gold Pool was helpful, but insufficient by itself to counter the effects of America's large, sustained balance of payments deficits; the deficits themselves were largely financed by the accumulation of dollar reserves by the surplus nations' central banks.

U.S. BALANCE OF PAYMENTS CONTROLS
AND THE BIRTH OF THE EUROBOND MARKET

To rectify the situation, President Kennedy in February 1961 initiated "Operation Twist," a combination of high short-term rates to attract capital inflows and thereby strengthen the spot dollar, concurrent with low long-term rates to promote investment and thereby "get the country moving again" toward the "new frontier." This "unnatural" inverted yield curve was inadequate to its mandate. It was thus followed by a major speech in February 1962 by Secretary of the Treasury Dillon exhorting Europeans to use their own capital markets, and by three balance of payments controls that greatly stimulated the growth of the Eurodollar market, while giving rise to the birth of the Eurobond market.

The first balance of payments measure was the imposition of the Interest Equalization Tax (IET) in mid-1963, which markedly reduced capital outflows by equating the U.S. and European (erstwhile higher due to faster growth rates) yields on stocks and bonds. Specifically a tax of 15% was put on foreign stocks, while foreign bonds were subject to a variable 0-15% tax. Securities of developing countries, international institutions, and later Canada were exempted.

Thus, European companies, accustomed to using the deep and relatively inexpensive U.S. capital market, had to find an alternative source of capital. That alternative turned out to be the Eurobond market, which was initiated on July 1, 1963 by Autostrade, the concessionaire and operator of toll motorways in Italy, and guaranteed by IRI, the principal industrial and financial holding corporation owned by the Italian state. It was unique in being lead-managed by a London-based bank (S.G. Warburg) and co-managed by banks in Belgium, West Germany, the Netherlands and Luxembourg (including Banque de Bruxelles, Deutsche Bank, Rotterdamsche Bank, and Banque Internationale`a Luxembourg).

Aided by the initiation of U.S. balance of payments controls, the Eurodollar market in 1964 grew to a gross size of $20 billion, and a net size (net of interbank deposits) of $14 billion. Eurodollars represented a hefty 83% of the Eurocurrency market.

The IET proved inadequate in stemming capital outflows from the U.S., so the American government next focused on the impact of U.S. bank acquisition of foreign assets (that is, foreign lending). The result was the Fed's initiating a Voluntary Foreign Credit Restraint Program (VFCRP) in February 1965, a virtually mandatory measure which prevented American banks from increasing their loans to European and Japanese companies. Thus, these companies began to look to the Eurodollar market in London and other centers to meet their financing requirements.

The VFCRP supplementation of the IET also proved inadequate in rectifying the U.S. balance of payments deficit, so the American government next focused its attention on the U.S. multinationals which domestically funded their foreign investments. The result was the Mandatory Foreign Investment Program, which began on a more modest basis in 1965, enforced by the Office of Foreign Direct Investments (OFDI). It forbade domestic financing of foreign investment by the U.S. multinationals, and thus caused those giant corporations to turn to the Eurodollar syndicated loan and Eurobond markets for their financing needs.

EUROMARKET GROWTH DURING THE 1960s

Also stimulating the growth of the Eurodollar market was Citibank's introduction of negotiable CDs in London in 1966. (Earlier in 1961 Citibank had introduced negotiable CDs into the U.S. domestic market.) With White Weld simultaneously creating a secondary market for such CDs, the market was an instant success, soon joined by many other banks.

Besides new instruments such as the Eurobond and the negotiable

CD complementing the traditional time deposit market, the Eurocurrency market received impetus from the proliferation of new centers. In the late 1960s, Singapore and Nassau-Cayman networked into the active Eurocurrency market in Europe, the Caribbean islands having especially convenient times zones for being booking centers (*shell* or *brass plaque* branches) for the New York banks.

As the 1960s drew to a close, a final factor stimulating growth of the market was tight monetary policy in 1969 in the U.S., which pushed market rates above Regulation Q interest rate ceilings. In response, American banks started borrowing massive sums from their branches and other banks in London—in November such borrowings peaked at $15 billion.

Factors slowing the growth of the Eurodollar market appeared as well. Declining confidence in the dollar caused the demise of the Gold Pool in 1968, to be replaced by a two-tier gold price (one for official and one for private sector transactions). Moreover, in September 1969, American banks were made subject to Regulation M, a 10% marginal reserve requirement on any increase in Eurodollar borrowings from their branches above the May 1969 level. Such borrowings began a rapid decline in December, reducing significantly the demand for Eurodollars.

Nevertheless, the Eurocurrency market grew rapidly, reaching a gross size of $85 billion by the end of the 1960s—in the five-year period from 1964 it grew 450%, and in 1969 alone, it grew 70%. For end-1969, the corresponding net size was $50 billion, a level representing a growth rate of 360% from 1964, and Eurodollars represented a peak 84% of the market.

THE SHOCKS TO THE EUROMARKET IN THE EARLY 1970s

The advent of the 1970s was dominated by concern for the deteriorating dollar—the decline in investor confidence in the spot dollar seemed more than matched by speculative demand for Euro-dollars. The latter were borrowed by currency speculators, who promptly converted their borrowings to hard currencies (marks, Swissy, and yen) in the hopes that at maturity they would be able to repay their loans with cheaper dollars.

Offsetting the latter factor, several regulatory factors moderated the demand for and supply of Eurodollars. In June 1970, Reg Q interest rate ceilings were suspended on "large CDs" ($100,000 plus) with maturities of less than 90 days, enhancing the competitiveness of the U.S. domestic market. Seven months later the marginal reserve requirement for American banks borrowing Eurodollars was doubled to 20% (Regulation M). Later that year, the central banks from the Group of 10 and Switzerland agreed to abstain from making further Eurodollar deposits to reduce the use of Eurodollar borrowings to speculate against the dollar.

The growing aversion to the dollar was vindicated in August 1971, when President Nixon suspended the convertibility of the dollar into gold, and even more so, in December when the dollar was devalued 8.6% by raising the dollar price of a troy ounce of gold to $38 from $35 (while the mark and yen were revalued) in a financial summit at the Smithsonian Institution. Despite that devaluation and the growing feeling that the dollar was still overvalued, incredibly, the resilient Eurodollar market continued to grow.

Upward pressure continued on the hard currencies, alarming those countries' central banks because of the resultant loss of export competitiveness. Germany imposed a Bardepot 40% cash deposit on foreign borrowing by German firms, while Switzerland imposed a negative interest rate on nonresident Swiss franc deposits. Then in February 1973, the dollar was devalued a second larger time of 11% (by raising the gold price to $42.22), effectively restoring equilibrium to the U.S. balance of payments and removing the black cloud of devaluation risk under which the dollar had labored since the 1960s.

FACTORS PROMOTING EURODOLLAR MARKET GROWTH

By the time of the second dollar devaluation, the Eurocurrency market had grown to over $200 billion. A major factor promoting the growth of the market had been the phenomenal growth of international trade and investment in the post-war period, even greater than the commendable global growth rate. A considerable amount of those activities had been financed in the Eurocurrency market.

Another factor had been the massive U.S. balance of payments deficits, which greatly expanded the pool of dollars abroad. While the deficits were a "helpful" condition, they were not a necessary one. Foreign holders could have deposited their dollars in the United States or alternately converted them to other currencies or gold, avoiding the Eurodollar market. Conversely, it should be noted that the Euro-mark and Euro-Swiss franc markets grew at vigorous rates despite those countries' balance of payments surpluses.

Another major factor promoting the expansion of the Eurodollar market was its greater competitiveness than the U.S. domestic market. It offered higher deposit rates (due to the absence of reserve requirements, FDIC premiums, and Regulation Q interest rate ceilings) and lower lending rates. In particular, the lending rates, composed of three or six months LIBOR plus a spread (of generally 0.75%-2%) to cover risk, administrative costs and profit, was consistently significantly less than the U.S. *effective prime rate* (the prime rate adjusted upward for the effect of 20% compensating balances). The uncompetitive prime rate reflected the prime-based cartelization of the American banking market, reinforced by the geographical delineation of markets (restrictions based on the McFaddon Act of 1927 and state laws and regulations), difficulty of entry (required a charter for which the applicant had to show the need for an additional bank as well as adequate financial and managerial resources), and an environment emphasizing *relationship banking* as opposed to *arm's length banking.* The former was more expensive, but generally involved the provision of some free services and a bank's obligation to make funds available to its good customers, even in difficult tight money periods.

Also contributing to the greater competitiveness of the Eurodollar market were its economies of scale—the lower administrative costs resulting from dealing in substantially larger (wholesale) deposit and loan sizes. A final factor keeping its effective lending rates lower was its lower loan losses relative to the U.S. market, as most Eurodollar loans were to blue chip multinationals, governments or government guaranteed corporations.

Also promoting the Euromarket was the proliferation of international banking centers. From its initial base in London and Paris, the Euromarket spread throughout Europe and then to Nassau and Cayman in the mid-1960s, to Singapore in 1968, and to Panama in 1970. Bahrain was added in 1975. In tandem with the proliferation of centers, the Eurocurrency brokerage system, based in London, spread around the world via branches and correspondents.

Also proliferating and thereby enhancing the attractiveness of the market were its asset and liability instruments. Initially, the Eurodollar market consisted of time deposits on the liability side and short-term trade financing on the asset side. In the 1960s such vital instruments as

Eurobonds, negotiable CDs, and syndicated loans (for project and balance of payments financing) were added, while in the 1970s new instruments included floating rate CDs, floating rate notes (FRNs), convertible Eurobonds, and Eurocommercial paper.

THE IMPACT OF THE FIRST OIL SHOCK

In the first half of 1973, the Eurodollar market was mildly hurt by changes in American regulations suspending Regulation Q interest rate ceilings on "large CDs" with maturities of more than 90 days and by subjecting, for the first time, the agencies and branches of foreign banks in the U.S. to reserve requirements on Eurodollar borrowings (previously their activity was erroneously viewed as "insignificant"). Conversely, the market greatly expanded in the wake of the Yom Kippur War in October (Egypt and Syria's attack on Israeli forces in the Sinai Desert and Golan Heights), due to the impact of a subsequent Arab oil embargo, which ultimately led to the quadrupling of oil prices to $12/barrel.

Oil-exporting countries such as Saudi Arabia and Kuwait quickly developed enormous current account surpluses, while non-oil-industrialized countries (such as France and Italy) and non-oil-developing nations (in Asia, Africa, and Latin America) developed enormous current account deficits just as fast.

The need of OPEC countries to invest their vast surpluses in conjunction with the need of the non-oil countries to borrow vast sums to cushion the deflationary impact of their new current account deficits provided the Eurocurrency market with its greatest challenge—the recycling of the petrodollars.

Much of the challenge resulted from the inevitable mismatching of liability and asset maturities, as the suspicious Arabs only provided short-term deposits, while the borrowing nations needed medium-term balance of payments financing. Despite a plethora of alarmist articles in the media which raised the spectre of bank liquidity crises, the Arabs rolled over their deposits, and as they became more confident and astute, started extending their maturities to enhance their yields. However, even if they had pulled their deposits from a politically targeted bank, that bank would have been ultimately able to "recapture" its lost deposits in the vibrant interbank market.

Exhibit 2-2
FACTORS PROMOTING THE RAPID GROWTH OF
THE EURODOLLAR MARKET

1. The especially rapid growth of international trade and investment in the post-World War II period.

2. The existence of a large pool of dollars outside the U.S. due to (a) the Bretton Woods Agreement requirement that central banks maintain large dollar reserves to intervene in the foreign exchange market when their respective currencies approached the maximum 1% deviation from par value; (b) the large and sustained U.S. balance of payments deficits in the post-war period due to massive capital outflows (investments and loans) as well as foreign military expenditures and tourism.

3. The greater competitiveness of the Eurodollar market than the U.S. domestic market (that is, "3/6-month LIBOR + spread" was less than "prime + compensating balances") due to the prime-based cartelization of the U.S. market, reinforced by its geographical delineation of markets, fewer new entries, and provision of free services for good corporate customers.

4. The lower administrative costs (economies of scale) of operating in the Eurodollar market due to substantially larger deposit and loan sizes.

5. The lower loan losses in the Eurodollar market as opposed to the U.S. domestic market as most Euroloans were to blue chip multinationals, governments, and government-guaranteed corporations.

6. The diversification of risk through frequent use by banks of the syndication mechanism.

7. The development of an efficient, international Eurodollar brokerage system spearheaded by the London-based brokerage firms.

8. The proliferation of Eurocenters exemplified by international banking centers such as London, Paris and Zurich, joined by Luxembourg, Nassau, Cayman, Singapore, Bahrain, Hong Kong, and New York.

9. The increasing variety of Euro asset and liability instruments, with the initial time deposits and trade financing enhanced by negotiable CDs (fixed and floating rate), Eurobonds, floating rate notes (FRNs), Eurocommercial paper and Euronotes as well as syndicated Eurocurrency credits for project and balance of payments financing.

10. The U.S. balance of payments controls, including the Interest Equalization Tax (1963-1973), the Voluntary Foreign Credit Restraint

Program (1965-1973), and the Mandatory Foreign Investment Program (1968-1973), which successively caused European and then U.S. multinationals to seek financing in the Eurobond and Eurodollar syndicated loan market as opposed to the U.S. bond market and U.S. commercial banks.

11. The dollar weakness in the late 1960s, and early 1970s which led to substantial Eurodollar borrowing to speculate against a dollar devaluation.

12. The first (1973) and second (1979) oil "shocks" (large price hikes), which led to huge balance of payments surpluses for the oil-exporting nations, much of which was invested in the Eurodollar market; while concurrently non-oil industrial and developing nations borrowed huge sums from the Eurodollar market as they struggled to adjust to the changed "terms of trade."

At any rate, 1973 was a spectacular year for the Eurocurrency market—the gross size of the market jumped 53% to $305 billion, while the net size of the market grew 45% to $110 billion. However, misgivings about the dollar, reinforced by the American economy sliding into recession in late 1973, caused the Eurodollar market's percentage of the Eurocurrency market to drop to a record low of 73%.

The American recession, which led the global recession by about a year, reflected, in part, the impact of the jump in energy prices on the energy-intensive U.S. economy. Confidence in the U.S. was further undermined by the televised Watergate hearings, which lasted from May to August (when President Nixon resigned). To the world, it seemed that the American government was out of business (of course, the bureaucracy kept things running smoothly in the best "Italian style"), and the spot dollar, which should have strengthened on the basis of the improvement in America's inflation and balance of payments performance, stayed soft.

THE FAILURE OF
THE FRANKLIN AND HERSTATT BANKS

Even more upsetting to the markets were the failure of two internationally active banks and large foreign exchange losses at others. In particular, America's seventeenth largest bank, the Franklin National Bank of New York, run by Sicilian financier Michele Sindona (subsequently convicted of major crimes by both the American and Italian courts) failed in May 1974 due, in part, to large foreign exchange losses involving substantial fraud. (It was merged into the European American Bank.) Much more devastating to the market was the collapse of Bankhaus Herstatt of Cologne in June with $600 million in foreign exchange losses. Its damaging impact resulted from its perverse bankruptcy style: For the day it chose to go under, it made considerable purchases of marks against dollars, taking delivery of the marks in the European morning but succumbing before the opening of the New York banks would have allowed the corresponding dollars to be paid. Finally, several other major banks had massive but not fatal foreign exchange losses. These included Lloyds Bank-Lugano, the Bank of Belgium, and the Westdeutsche Landesbank.

As a consequence of the Franklin/Herstatt failures, as well as the big foreign exchange losses at other banks, which generated a perception of greater risk, all banks reviewed their credit lines to other banks, cutting out many smaller banks and reducing their lines to the larger ones. In addition, a tiering of rates developed which was to become a permanent fixture of the Euromarket, especially pronounced in times of tight money. In November 1974, the nine levels of tiering included:

- Four prime U.S. banks.
- Rest of the top U.S. banks.
- Second-tier U.S. banks from major cities.
- Canadian and certain West Coast U.S. banks.
- London clearing banks and regional U.S. banks.
- Wholly owned U.S. banks in Europe.
- Medium-sized consortium banks.
- Italian banks.
- Japanese banks (owing to huge dollar borrowings).

Another consequence of Herstatt was that banks developed safe but cumbersome procedures to insure that all counter-payments due them were received as their payments were made. Naturally interbank trading volume fell substantially until confidence and the traditional efficient procedures were restored.

Finally, the combined impact of the jump in oil prices and related balance of payments crises, the U.S. recession and developing global one, and the failure of some key banks and large losses at others, was to greatly raise the perception of risk in the market. As a result in autumn, the total yield to lenders on the blended average of medium-term corporate/governmental credits reached a historic high of 1.60% over LIBOR. Despite everything, the gross size of the Eurodollar market grew 23% in 1974 and the dollar's share climbed to 77%.

MARKET STABILIZATION
AND RENEWED DOLLAR WEAKNESS

In 1975, the market restabilized after the traumatic developments of the previous year, exemplified by declining rates, narrowing spreads, and the promulgation of a BIS Concordat on guidelines for cooperation among central banks with regard to their banks' foreign establishments' activities. However, in November, the New York City fiscal crisis (caused by massive deficits resulting from overgenerous labor pacts) triggered the start of an extensive dollar decline, which was to last until 1980, and provoked many export-oriented countermoves by the *hard currency* countries.

The defensive measures began in November 1977 when the Bank of Japan imposed a 50% marginal reserve requirement on inflows into yen, which the following March was raised to 100%. A month after the initial Japanese move, the Bundesbank increased the *marginal* reserve requirement on DM deposits from abroad to 100%.

The American government and central bank viewed the slide of the dollar with increasing apprehension, as it was eroding confidence in America's leadership and stimulating inflation. In December 1977, America's countermoves began with a modification of Regulation M which reduced U.S. banks' reserve requirements on foreign branch (Eurodollar) loans to U.S. borrowers to 1%. Then the following August, Regulation M was modified again as U.S. banks' reserve requirement on foreign borrowings (Eurodollars) from their foreign branches and other foreign banks was reduced to zero from 4%. Both measures strengthened the U.S. balance of payments and thereby the spot dollar. Also, in August, the Fed began raising the discount rate in stages from 7.25% to further aid the dollar and contain inflation.

In November 1978, with the plunging dollar hitting an all-time low of DM 1.703, a joint Administration-Fed dollar defense package was announced. The Fed raised the discount rate 1% to 9.5%, while concurrently raising the "large CD" reserve requirement by 2% to 8% to encourage Eurodollar borrowings for balance of payments support. Also, the U.S. mobilized $30 billion in credits, and announced that it would issue $10 billion of foreign securities (DM bonds) to generate hard currency for dollar support interventions.

In May 1979, attention was temporarily diverted from America's problems by the Conservative Party victory in the UK, making Margaret Thatcher the UK Prime Minister. Emphasizing monetary control, she raised sterling interest rates sharply. Five months later in October, she terminated the foreign exchange controls on sterling, which propelled the Eurosterling market from insignificance to ranking just behind the "Big 3" of dollars, marks, and Swissy.

Meanwhile, the persistence of the related problems of excessive monetary growth, inflation and a weak dollar prompted President Carter to replace the inexperienced G. William Miller as Fed Chairman with the internationally reputed president of the Federal Reserve Bank of New York, Paul Volker. Concurrent with the July appointment, the U.S. discount rate was raised to 10%, followed by a further 1% rise in September.

U.S. conditions, however, continued to deteriorate leading to the famous "Saturday Massacre" of October 6, 1979 when the Fed switched from a Keynesian policy of interest rate targeting (that is, a relatively stable Fed funds rate at the expense of volatile and excessive monetary growth) to a monetarist policy of targeting the monetary aggregates (causing volatile Fed funds rates). Reinforcing the policy change, the Fed hiked the discount rate another 1% to 12% and instituted *marginal* reserve requirements (above banks' end-September borrowing level) on *managed liabilities*, including Eurodollar borrowings and "large CDs."

The resulting boost of the spot dollar prompted Germany, Switzerland, and Japan toward the end of October to all raise their bank rates by 1% and the Swiss National Bank to reduce its negative interest rate on nonresident Swissy deposits (from 40% to 10%). Moreover, a few weeks later, growing dollar strength prompted the UK to raise its minimum lending rate (MLR) by 3% to 17%, while Italy hiked its bank rate by 3%, the Swiss National Bank eliminated the negative interest rate on nonresident Swissy deposits, and Japan announced a yen support package.

THE SECOND OIL SHOCK AND RENEWED DOLLAR STRENGTH

In December 1979, OPEC imposed the second "oil shock" by raising oil prices 30% due to supply shortfalls caused by the chaotic Iranian situation. As in 1973, the global balance of payments profile was drastically altered and the Eurobanks were again in the petrodollar recycling business. Reflecting the pervasive uncertainties, with food as well as energy prices jumping, gold peaked at $850 per troy ounce in January 1980.

Tight monetary policy in the U.S. plus the oil price jumps caused Switzerland (which imports all its oil) in February to allow interest payments on nonresident Swissy deposits. At the same time, both Switzerland and Germany raised their bank rates by 1% in March.

Also in March, the U.S. tightened further, increasing the marginal reserve requirement on *managed liabilities* to 10% from 8%, while decreasing the exempt base (end-September borrowing level) by 7%. That action, as well as the oil situation (Japan was importing 99% of its oil for 70% of its energy requirements) prompted Japan to announce fiscal-monetary tightening and increased international credits in support of yen. The tight U.S. monetary policy succeeded in halting the excessive monetary growth, but at the cost of a severe contraction of business activity, especially the interest rate sensitive sectors such as construction and autos, which caused money market rates to fall from 20% in March to 8.75% by June. Promoting the drop in interest rates as well was the Fed's increasing of the exempt base on *managed liabilities* (including Eurodollar borrowings) by 7.5% and subsequently reducing the marginal reserve requirement to 5% from 10%. Finally, to abort the unexpectedly severe recession, the Fed, in July, finished lifting its credit restrictions, completely canceling the marginal reserve requirement on *managed liabilities*, while concurrently reducing the CD reserve requirement to 6%. Thus, the Fed reversed course, now charting an expansionary monetary policy.

Despite the volatility of developments in the U.S. markets, the dollar strengthened from mid-year until the mid-1981, aided by rising interest rates as the Fed has begun its expansionary monetary policy before inflationary pressures had been contained. To rectify that, the Fed retightened monetary policy in November after the Presidential election, in which Ronald Reagan soundly beat Jimmy Carter.

The last act of 1980 was played out later in November, when the monumental Depository Institution Deregulation and Monetary Control Act became effective. It applied (over a seven-year phase-in period) new uniform reserve requirements to *all* U.S. depository institutions— 12% on transaction accounts (demand deposits, NOW accounts), 3% on nonpersonal (that is, corporate) time deposits of less than 1.5 years and 3% on all types of Eurocurrency liabilities.

As a consequence of tightening U.S. monetary policy, exemplified by raising the discount rate to a peak 14% in May, the dollar strengthened through late summer of 1981. In response to the appreciating unit, Japan had at the end of 1980 relaxed controls on capital inflows into yen, while in February, Switzerland raised its bank rate by 1% and the Bundesbank suspended its Lombard credit facility, sending call rates over 20%. In May, Switzerland again raised its bank rate by 1%, and France began raising interest rates in stages from 13.5% to 22% (the latter related to the French presidential election in which Mitterand defeated Giscard d'Estaing, as well as the strong dollar). Euro-French franc rates climbed again in the autumn in front of an expected devaluation of "spot Paris," which occurred in October and amounted to an aggregate 8.5%.

SAME-DAY FUNDS AND IBFs

Also transpiring in October was an important change in the Eurodollar market—in particular, the clearing change from "next-day funds" to "same-day funds." Prior to October 1, all Eurodollar transactions for U.S domestic banks cleared not on the same day as Fed funds, but on the next business day, and were known as *clearing house funds* (related to the operational role of the New York Clearing House Association). This created aberrational rates for Thursday-Friday and weekend (Friday-Monday) Eurodollars.

Thursday-Friday dollars were actually received on Friday and returned on Monday; de jure, they were overnight (o/n) dollars, but de facto, they were three days' use as Fed funds. Hence, they traded for approximately three times the average overnight (o/n) Fed funds rate— actually somewhat less as the lucrative rate caused supply to somewhat exceed demand. Thus, if o/n Fed funds were trading at 9%, Thursday-Friday Eurodollars were around 26%. Weekend or Friday-Monday Eurodollars were actually received on Monday and returned on Tuesday; de jure, they were three-day dollars, but de facto, they were one day's use as Fed funds. Hence, they traded for approximately one-third the average o/n Fed funds rate; actually somewhat more, as the Fed allowed the weekend dollars—actually "cash items in the process of collection" (CIPC)—to count as three days' credit in meeting reserve requirements, causing demand to slightly exceed supply. Thus, if o/n Fed funds were trading at 9%, weekend Eurodollars were around 3.5%. Of course, if Monday were a U.S. bank holiday, then the Thursday-Friday rates would be around 35% and the weekend dollars around 2.5% (using 4/.25 factors instead of 3/.33 factors). Until terminated by the October 1 clearing change, the Thursday-Friday and weekend arbitrages were highly lucrative, especially to agencies and branches of foreign banks, which did high volume in such arbitrages.

December 1981 also marked a major change in the Eurodollar market, with the inauguration of International Banking Facilities (IBFs) in the United States. For the first time, Eurobanking free of reserve requirements, FDIC premiums, state and local taxation, and foreign currency restrictions could be conducted in America. In the first four weeks of market activity to December 31, IBF liabilities jumped from zero to $52.4 billion, most of it representing deposits shifted from shell branches in Nassau and Cayman. Concurrently, Japanese and Italian banks, which generally did not have Nassau or Cayman branches, shifted deposits from their New York agencies and branches.

GLOBAL RECESSION AND THE RISING SPOT DOLLAR

As the end of 1981 approached, global economic activity and corresponding inflation were both slowing. In response, Germany and Switzerland lowered their bank rates by 0.5%, while the Federal Reserve cut the discount rate by 1%. Despite the economic sluggishness, the Eurocurrency market grew by 29% gross and a much greater 53% net in 1981, with the strenghtening spot dollar considerably enhancing the dollar share of the market to 79%.

The year 1982 was a very difficult one for the Euromarket as global recession brought down commodity prices, causing massive balance of payments deficits, large currency devaluations and the global debt crisis. The recession also prompted credit easing, with the Fed cutting the discount rate in stages from 12% to 8.5% between July and December. Finally, it also was the year of the Falklands War (April), which prompted Britain to freeze Argentine assets in the UK, giving greater import to the concept of "sovereign risk."

Frequent currency devaluations during 1982 included the Mexican peso (throughout the year, falling from MP27/$ to MP150/$), the Belgian franc (8.5%), the Argentine peso (14.6%), the French franc (10%), the Chilean peso (17%), again the Argentine peso (22%), the Finnish mark (10%), the Swedish krona (16%), and the Spanish peseta (8%). The economic weakness substantially slowed Euromarket growth while currency uncertainties in conjunction with dollar strength prompted movements into dollar deposits. The Eurocurrency market grew only 11% in 1982, both gross and net, while the Eurodollar's share rose to 80%.

The global recession dragged on into 1983, further slowing Euromarket growth, while growing dollar strength and a continuing related rash of currency devaluations prompted further movements into dollars and related Eurodollar deposits. During the year, while the Eurocurrency market grew only 5% gross and 7% net, the Eurodollar's share of the market rose to 81%. Currency devaluations during January through June include the Greek drachma (15%), the Brazilian cruzeiro (23%), the Venezuelan bolivar (47%), the Indonesian rupiah (27.5%), the Australian dollar (10%), the French franc (8%), the Portuguese escudo (12.7%), and the Philippine peso (8.9%). During the balance of the year, the South African rand, the Hong Kong dollar and the Australian dollar all exhibited weakness, while the Philippine peso was devalued a further 21%.

Widespread economic weakness and the global debt crisis enhanced the importance for investors of safety of principal over interest rate differentials. This caused a decline in activity at the smaller Eurocenters, such as Bahrain and Panama, in favor of London, New York, and Tokyo. Moreover, Luxembourg's reputation suffered from the huge DM420 million losses of the local subsidiary of Schroder, Munchmyer, Heugst and Co.'s (Germany's largest private bank), just a year after the embarrassment of the $400 million failure of Banco Ambrosiano Holdings, SA (Luxembourg).

In an attempt to weaken the dollar, whose safety and high yields (due to the need to finance record fiscal and trade deficits along with a growing economy) were proving irresistible to investors, the U.S. participated in August 1983 in a concerted intervention to depress the dollar, which stood at a nine-year high versus the German mark. However, the effort representing a follow-through on commitments made earlier in May at the Williamsburg G-7 economic summit proved to no avail.

The year 1984 proved similar to 1983, with the Eurocurrency market, in the context of global economic stagnation, growing only 5% gross and 3% net, while the dollar's share, prompted by a strengthening spot dollar, rose further to 82%, its highest percentage since 1969. The weakness of many currencies was exemplified in June by the Philippine peso's devaluation of 22% and the Canadian dollar's record lows ($.75) in July.

However, the dollar was hurt by the May run on the Continental Illinois Bank, America's seventh largest bank, which required a $7.5 billion FDIC rescue package. Moreover, Bundesbank intervention from September held the strong dollar at DM 3.18 till the end of the year.

THE FALL OF THE DOLLAR
AND INTERNATIONAL INTEREST RATES

The year 1985 marked a sea change in the international financial markets. While the Eurocurrency market grew 17% gross and net, the Eurodollar's share fell to 74%. Prompting the change was a dramatic and substantial fall in the dollar; after peaking in February at DM 3.48 and Y264, and $1.035 against the pound, it fell by year-end to DM2.45, Y200 and $1.44 against the pound.

Depressing the dollar was the growing realization of America's massive and cumulative current account deficits (as well as the $200 billion fiscal deficits), which left the U.S. as the world's largest debtor country in their wake (the U.S. became a net debtor nation in May 1985 for the first time since 1919, and by early 1986, its net foreign debt equaled that of Brazil, the previous reigning debt champion at $109 billion). Factors behind the ultimately $170 billion merchandise trade deficits included the trade impact of the overvalued dollar, America's relatively high growth rate, weakness among America's traditional customers such as the debt-afflicted Latin Americans, and the liquidity effect of the vast capital inflows.

Two rounds of concerted central bank intervention against the dollar accelerated the unit's fall—one in the wake of the February peaking, and the other in the wake of the September G-5 (U.S., Japan, Germany, UK, France) meeting at the Plaza Hotel in New York (where depreciation vis-a-vis the particularly undervalued yen was emphasized). The latter involved a watershed policy change for the Reagan administration, which, despite its laissez faire orientation, chose to join in the intervention to avert growing protectionist sentiment among afflicted industries (steel, textiles, autos) and their vocal representatives in Congress.

The first half of 1986 represented a continuation of the previous year's trends, with the U.S. continuing to post huge monthly trade deficits, including a record $16.5 billion shortfall in January. The unexpected prolongation of the extreme American trade imbalance, despite the over 25% dollar depreciation vis-a-vis the yen and the major European currencies, was explained on the basis of the *J-curve* (the standard delay in volume adjustment to the higher import/lower export prices, which initially worsens matters), the fact that many of America's trade partners' currencies are pegged to the dollar (such as the "little dragons" of Asia, including Taiwan, Korea, Hong Kong, and Singapore) or had even depreciated against it (like the Canadian dollar and many Latin American currencies), such that overall dollar depreciation was only 6% (Fed-Dallas X-131 Bi-Lateral Trade Weighted Dollar Index), and sluggish global economic conditions. The continuing trade imbalance continued the dollar's slide, aside from an uptick in the spring. In line with the outlook for a weakening dollar, the Eurodollar's share of the Eurocurrency market continued to fall.

Deposit rates also continued to fall. In March, there were coordinated 0.5% discount rate cuts by Japan, Germany, and the U.S., followed in April by further 0.5% cuts by the U.S. and Japan. Finally, in July, the U.S. cut its discount rate another 0.5% after unsuccessfully trying to convince Japan and Germany to make similar cuts. That strategy of Fed Chairman Volker was to avoid the possibility of a sharp drop ("hard landing") for the spot dollar, which could considerably accelerate inflation in its wake, as well as discourage vital capital inflows.

Despite the dollar's weakness (at end-July, it stood at DM2.09, Y252, and the pound was $1.49), several other currencies suffered even greater value losses. In January, the Philippines peso fell 10% (in the wake of a controversial presidential election), while in March the Canadian dollar fell to an all-time record low of C$1.45 ($.69) in the aftermath of a budget statement preceived as inadequately addressing the fiscal deficit. Finally, in May, the Norwegian krone was devalued 12% and the Finnish mark by 2%.

All in all in the first half of 1986, the Eurocurrency market continued to grow and the Eurodollar's share, though declining, was supported by several factors. Although dollar interest rates had fallen considerably, other key Eurocurrencies offered even lower rates, and on an inflation-adjusted basis (real as opposed to nominal rates), the U.S. rates were quite high (for example, nominal rates around 7%, with CPI inflation around 2%, resulting in a generous 5% real rates).

In the second half of 1986, international interest rates generally declined (with the notable exception of sterling) until a moderate up-tick in December. Spearheading the drop were two 50-basis-point discount rate cuts by the Fed, in July and August. Prompting the monetary easing, which was facilitated by very low 1% inflation (aided by dropping oil prices), was Fed concern with a weak American economy. The Fed monetary easing, on top of mammoth U.S. trade, current account and fiscal deficits, weakened the spot dollar, which depreciated to DM 1.94 and Y 160 by the end of 1986. Concurrently, Germany and Japan only eased modestly as the Germans were fearful of stimulating inflation in the context of above-target monetary growth (7.9% vs. 3.5-5.5%); and the Japanese were skeptical of the benefits of cutting already very low rates, although they did cut their discount rate by 50 basis points to 3% in October (as part of a wider Treasury Secretary Baker-Finance Minister Miyazawa agreement prompted by a yen as strong as $ = Y 150 in 1986.3).

In January 1987, the Fed appeared to have tightened the Fed funds market to protect the faltering dollar, which nevertheless fell to DM 1.78 and Y 151 by the end of January. The strong DM provoked an EMS realignment in mid-January, which revalued it and the guilder 3% (and the Belgium franc 1%) against the other EMS members, while in late February, the strong yen encouraged a discount rate cut to 2½%. Rumors and ultimately the reality of a G-6 meeting subsequently lifted the dollar, to DM 1.86 and Y 154 in early March amidst the belief of *target ranges* for the dollar against the mark and the yen. However, a subsequent testing of central banks' resolve in late March depressed the dollar to Y 145, amidst rising dollar interest rates in the response to the dollar's depreciation and the related spectre of accelerated inflation.

3

Eurocurrency Banking Centers

Vital to the functioning of the Eurocurrency market is the availability of financial centers free of regulation especially reserve requirements and burdensome taxation especially withholding taxes on nonresident interest income). Moreover, they must offer a modern infrastructure in which the computerized, electronic dynamics of international Eurocurrency trading can smoothly function.

In "Desiderata Pertinent to the Formation of an International Banking Center," both the general and technical desiderata of such centers are detailed. The list was originally compiled by the author in 1975 in response to a research request by a major Egyptian bank questioning the viability of the newly established Bahrain Eurocurrency center. Using the list as a checklist for Bahrain yielded an optimistic outlook for that Persian Gulf nation, and the Egyptian bank went ahead with establishing Eurocurrency activities there, a decision completely vindicated by their subsequent profitability.

Complementing the *checklist,* a detailed description is offered of the major Eurocurrency centers. Noting each center's characteristics against the checklist is a useful way to understand both why a certain city has been able to emerge as a Eurocurrency center as opposed to proximate alternative cities, and also to measure a center's international competitiveness and thus its growth outlook.

For example, why have Luxembourg and Singapore become major Eurocenters, but not Frankfurt or Kuala Lampur? Or why have Tokyo and Zurich been growing lately at the expense of the so-called "offshore" centers, the smaller and previously dynamic centers, such as Panama City and Bahrain?

By way of introduction, the latest Bank of England international banking center table is included, showing the relative size and activity of the major such centers. Of note as well is the relative growth rate of the centers as reflected in their changing share of the total market during 1983-1985.

Following is a detailed description of the various Eurocurrency centers themselves, grouped by geographical region. The sequence of Europe, North America, and Asia reflects the general chronology of their joining the Eurocurrency market. In Europe, the centers included are London, Paris, Zurich and Geneva, Luxembourg, Brussels, Amsterdam, and the Channel Islands. While in North America, the centers include New York-Miami-Los Angeles-San Francisco, Toronto, Nassau, Cayman, the Netherlands Antilles, Panama, Bermuda, Barbados, and Antigua. Finally, in Asia the centers include Singapore, Hong Kong, Manila, Taipei, Vanuatu and Bahrain.

Desiderata Pertinent to the Formation of an International Banking Center

The desiderata can be categorized as *general* infrastructural elements or *technical* elements relating to specific bank operations.

GENERAL DESIDERATA

Strong Political Will to Establish Banking Center. Given the high political costs involved in creating a satisfactory legal infrastructure for the formation and growth of an international banking center, one desideratum is the strong motivation to create such a center. Such can be generated by a strong need for growth industry in a situation where an area's major industry is declining, and/or there is a high birth rate leading to numerous entrants into the labor force.

Political and Social Stability. A stable political system, reinforced by social stability, is necessary to attract the international financial companies and assure them of continuity in the legal environment necessary to the viability of international banking operations.

Stable Foreign Exchange Conditions. Reasonably stable foreign exchange conditions based in a sound balance of payments, related to economic stability, moderate inflation, and other related conditions, in conjunction with exchange rate flexibility to handle temporary stresses, are important if exchange controls and just the very threat of their imposition are to be avoided.

Substantial and Strong Domestic Economy. A strong and stable domestic economy promotes the growth of the country's financial sector, including generating favorable investment opportunities for it. However, it can likewise erode the political will to create the necessary legal and other conditions for an international financial center (that is, special privileges for foreign banks), which political priority can conversely be helped by the desire to offset economic weakness.

Traditional Regional Center. Helpful to transforming a city into an international financial center is its traditionally having served as a business center for its region, including such elements as handling *entrepot* trade, serving as regional headquarters, service centers, and so on.

Skilled Work Force. Development of an international banking center requires adequate numbers of skilled individuals, including those trained in business and finance, the skilled trades, such as electricians, and ancillary business vocations, such as multilingual secretaries. To develop such skilled people, a good educational system is an obvious necessity.

Facility with the English Language. As the language of Eurocurrency market dealings is generally English, having English as the national language, or widespread familiarity with it, is very helpful.

Office and Hotel Space. Development of an international banking center requires substantial, modern office space and adequate first-class hotel accommodations for the inflow of visiting business persons.

Communications. Immediate and direct telephone (including automatic dialers, etc.), telex, and cable connections are significant necessities in the operation of an international banking center, with such connections immeasurably improved by access to satellite systems.

Electronic News Services. The availability of electronic news services, such as Reuters, Telerate, Dow Jones, and the like, is necessary for effective trading in the international markets.

Transportation. Given the constant flow of business persons associated with an international financial center, convenient air connections are important, including a major airport, capable of handling large jets, and good regular service by international airlines.

Good Relations with Major Financial Powers. Cordial and reasonably close relations with the governments, central banks, and other institutions of the major financial powers, such as the United States, United Kingdom, and Japan, are obviously helpful in the development of an international financial center.

Optimum Geographic Location. The location of the banking center should be such that it is a "natural link" *(propitious longitude)* between other financial centers, while its time zone is such that its business hours overlap the business hours of other major financial centers.

Proximity to Major Depositors/Borrowers ("Localization Concept"). Proximity to such customers is desirable, especially where the regional/local markets are growing and there is ideological compatibility between the banking center and its clientele; the keeping of convenient business hours for its clientele is one particularly attractive element.

Convenient Work Week. A work week that articulates with that of other financial centers facilitates the growth of a banking center; however, a somewhat different work week, such as the Islamic tradition of observing Thursday afternoon and Friday as the weekend, but working on Saturday and Sunday, offers some advantage, as it makes possible financial operations when other major financial centers are closed.

Atmosphere of Trust. Important to the smooth functioning of an international financial center is an atmosphere of reasonable trust among the participants in financial markets (especially given the importance of verbal dealing, now strengthened by widespread tape recording), the absence of which leads to such cumbersome and slow dealing that the center's viability is eroded. Concurrently, an appropriate judicial system to deal with violations of trust and law is likewise desirable.

Quality of Life. A good quality of life, including reasonably temperate climate, adequate housing, access to consumer goods and recreation, is desirable as a new banking center must attract and retain a substantial number of foreign skilled business persons.

Reasonably Large and Diversified Financial Sector. The development of an international banking center can obviously be helped by its being situated in the midst of a large and diversified financial sector, with the expertise, services, investment opportunities, and so on that such entails. In particular, the presence of principals and risk-takers gives necessary depth to the financial markets.

Reliable Utilities. Operation of an international financial center requires reliable public utilities, especially power.

Efficient Freight Handling. Given the increasing importance of sophisticated electronic machinery, and the like in international financial operations, it is important that equipment deliveries be made rapidly and without significant complications as well from import licenses, tariffs, etc. In particular, good logistics requires an efficient port facility.

Receptivity to Foreigners. Given the substantial number of foreign business persons who work and visit international banking centers, receptivity to foreigners and their culture is necessary to create and assure the smooth social relationships that are important to the viability of such centers.

TECHNICAL DESIDERATA

The technical desiderata largely relate to creating an environment where there is no tax, penalty, or other interference with *intermediation,* the essential function of an international financial center.

Ready Acceptance of Foreign Banks. Ready acceptance of foreign banks includes actively soliciting their entry into the developing financial center, and ease and moderate fees for incorporation, licensing, and other administrative needs.

No Taxation. As taxes lower the effective yield of the banks' resources, no (or minimal) corporate taxation is desirable, which also eliminates the complications of withholding taxes on interest and dividends and other earnings. Concomitantly, no individual income taxation makes the center more attractive to foreign business persons. Finally, no taxation eliminates the need for "exchange control" related to tax enforcement.

A Well-Developed Domestic Banking System. Helpful to the development of an international banking center is the pre-existence of a well developed domestic banking system, including a term structure of interest rates and facilities for interest arbitrage, as well as an active two-way spot and forward foreign exchange market in at least one major currency (as opposed to a dominant role for the central bank).

Foreign Exchange/Eurocurrency Brokerage System. An efficient foreign exchange/Eurocurrency brokerage system, intelligently regulated, is quite helpful to the development of an international banking center.

Competent Central Bank. A competent, yet unintrusive, central bank carrying on functions such as statistical compilation, planning (such as optimum bank concentration), marketing, clearinghouse services, moderate regulation, such as receiving regular audited bank statements, and serving as an exchange market of last resort for major currencies, is highly useful to the development of an international banking center.

No Reserve Requirements. As reserve requirements (also "liquidity ratios") lower the effective yield of the banks' resources, having no reserve requirements is very helpful to the development of an international banking center. To prevent conflict with the domestic banking environment (which may well include reserve requirements on deposits in the national currency), "offshore banking facilities" can be used for international operations.

No Exchange Control. No exchange control or intelligently administered exchange control (as was conducted by the United Kingdom prior to its elimination in 1979) is vital to the operations of an international banking center, including no restrictions on convertibility or the repatriation of capital and profits. With no restrictions on current international payments or capital movements, the intermediation function can develop unimpaired.

Separation of International and Domestic Banking Operations Through "Off-Shore Entities." Intelligently administered separation of domestic and international banking operations is important so as not to interfere with the normal growth of the domestic money supply (with the related inflation and foreign exchange implications) and the domestic interest rate structure, as unfavorable financial pressures would generate support for restrictions on the international banking operations.

Availability of Financial Specialists. Important to the early growth of an international banking center is the availability of experienced financial specialists, such as discount and security specialists to develop "certificate of deposit" markets (primary and secondary).

No Deposit Insurance Requirement. As deposit insurance requirements (such as the Federal Deposit Insurance Corporation levy on American banks, which adds the equivalent of 8.5 basis points to the cost of deposits) lower the effective yield of banks' resources, the absence of such is helpful to the growth of an international banking center. Of course, the positive effect of no deposit insurance requirements is offset somewhat by the lower confidence, despite the fact that insurance applies usually only to relatively small amounts (such as $100,000 in the U.S.) as opposed to the multimillion dollar deposits associated with international money market participants.

No Legal Lending Limits. As legal lending limits, which limit the value of a bank's loans to a single borrower (currently to 15% of a bank's capital and undivided profits in the United States), interfere with a bank management's ability to maximize profits, their absence promotes an international banking center's growth.

No Mandated Credit Allocations. As government requirements to allocate credits to favored sectors (such as export industries) interfere with a bank management's ability to maximize profits, their absence promotes an international banking center's growth.

Bank Confidentiality. Regulations insuring the confidentiality of bank accounts (e.g. vis-a-vis foreign tax authorities) are very important for garnering deposits.

International Banking Centers: A Global Perspective

The changing size and profile of international banking centers are largely shaped by developments in the Eurocurrency market. While international banking includes domestic currency lending to nonresidents (traditional foreign banking), for all major Eurocurrency centers, as shown in Exhibit 3-1, with only the exceptions of the United States (which is not really an exception because the vast majority of such lending is Eurolending done out of onshore/offshore International Banking

Exhibit 3-1
INTERNATIONAL BANKING CENTERS AT
END-SEPTEMBER 1985
(billions of U.S. dollars)

	Foreign Currency lending to: Nonresidents	Residents
Gross lending	1,708	541
of which:		
United Kingdom	497	198
United States	15	393
Japan	109	147
France	128	49
Luxembourg	96	19
Swiss trustee accounts		
Belgium	83	27
Germany, Federal Republic	23	2
Netherlands	52	9
Switzerland	32	8
Canada	41	25
Italy	34	19
"Offshore" banking centers		

*The three components do not sum to the total, which also includes Swiss trustee accounts
**July 1985.
Source: Bank of England *Quarterly Bulletin* (March 1985).

Facilities, not domestic bank offices) and Germany, Eurolending to nonresidents and residents greatly exceeds domestic currency lending to nonresidents.

As of end-September 1985, London (United Kingdom), with a 24.4% market share, by far remained the leading international banking center with almost twice the market share of the second leading center (U.S.), but it was a clearly declining position. The U.S. (largely New York) market share, while strong at 13.6%, was also suffering erosion, accelerated by the 25% depreciation of its currency (the unit of denomination of 96% of its international banking loans) against the EMS currencies and the yen.

Domestic Currency lending to Nonresidents	Total*	SHARE TOTAL MARKET (percentages)		
		1983	1984	1985
639	3,003			
36	732	26.6	24.9	24.4
408		15.4	15.0	13.6
57	313	8.6	9.1	10.4
24	200	7.0	6.6	6.7
2	117	4.2	3.7	3.9
	115**	3.4	3.7	3.8
4	113	3.3	3.3	3.8
53	79	2.5	2.3	2.6
16	77	2.6	2.4	2.6
34	74	2.8	2.3	2.5
3	70	2.6	2.6	2.4
2	55	1.6	1.7	1.8
	533	18.1	18.9	17.7

Offsetting the erosion of the British and American market dominance was the growth of Tokyo, and to a lesser degree, Continental European centers in West Germany, Belgium, and Italy. Their growing role reflects both increasing depositor preference for nondollar currencies (such as the yen and DM) and their greatly improving current account balances (for example, Germany's was DM39 billion in 1985, and a DM78 billion in 1986).

Concurrently, "offshore banking centers," which function virtually solely as financial intermediaries as opposed to the initial depositor and ultimate borrower roles, suffered moderate erosion of market share in 1985. Such centers, which include Nassau, Cayman, Bahrain, and Panama, have been hurt by a number of factors, including the growing aversion of depositors to small Eurocenters in light of the global debt crisis, the current wave of deregulation in the major industrialized nations, the increasing use of American IBFs as opposed to Nassau and Cayman, and in the case of Bahrain, the unrest in the Middle East, epitomized by the seven-year Iran/Iraq war.

Eurocurrency Market Centers

EUROPE

- London
- Paris
- Zurich and Geneva
- Luxembourg
- Brussels
- Amsterdam
- Channel Islands

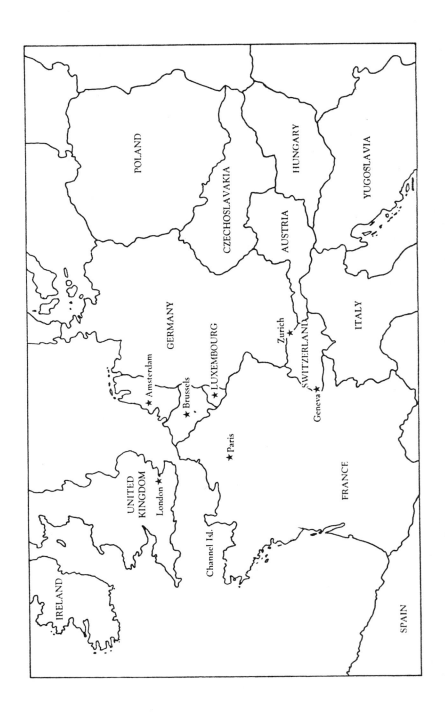

POLAND

CZECHOSLAVAKIA

HUNGARY

YUGOSLAVIA

AUSTRIA

GERMANY

LUXEMBOURG

Zurich ★

SWITZERLAND

Geneva ★

ITALY

Amsterdam ★

Brussels ★

★ Paris

UNITED
KINGDOM

London ★

Channel Isl.

FRANCE

IRELAND

SPAIN

LONDON

London is the capital and largest city of the United Kingdom, with a population of 6,696,008 (1981 census). It developed into the world's leading financial center on the basis of its being the financial heart of the global British Empire. In particular, it has always served as the center of trade finance, particularly for the discount and acceptance of trade bills. Moreover, its English language has enhanced its economic relationship to the United States and its role as the center of the Euro-dollar market.

Its financial role has been encouraged by the Bank of England's being relatively accommodating to the influx of foreign banks, while providing flexible regulation, emphasizing banks' own self-regulatory responsibilities; moreover, it imposes few formal limits on the structure of banks' balance sheets.

Activity has traditionally centered in London's four clearing banks (the $85-billion Barclays, the $83-billion National Westminster, the $71-billion Midland Bank, and the $51-billion Lloyds Bank), its large merchant banks (such as the $3 billion Hill Samuel and Company, N.M. Rothchild, Samuel Montegue, Klienwort Benson), discount houses, commodities and shipping (Baltic) exchanges and markets (especially gold with the twice-daily fixings at N.M. Rothschild), and insurance activities, clustered at Lloyds.

Complementing domestic financial institutions are 460 foreign bank representatives—391 directly and 69 via consortium banks (cf. 114 in 1967; 163 in 1970; 335 in 1975 and 403 in 1980). Countries with especially large banking representations in London include the United States (76), Japan (33), Italy (21), France (19), Switzerland (17), and Germany (16). The 391 directly represented banking groups include 225 full service branches, 142 representative offices and 24 subsidiaries. The foreign banks' activity is particularly important because of the inadequacy and poor distribution of British savings.

London conducted 24.4% of the world's international banking in 1985, down from 24.9% in 1984, and an even greater 26.6% in 1983. In 1985, Eurocurrency lending to nonresidents totaled $497 billion, while such lending to residents totaled $198 billion; sterling lending to non-residents totaled $36 billion, so total international lending was $732 billion.

London serves as the principal trading center for the Euro-dollar,

Euro-Swiss franc, Euro-yen and Euro-Canadian dollar, Euro-lira, and Euro-Australian dollar markets, and it is second only to Brussels and Luxembourg for Euro-French francs and Euro Deutschemarks, respectively. Euromarket activity is conducted by London's banks and a dozen internationally linked brokers, complemented by the new London International Financial Futures Exchange, which offers currency futures, three-month Eurodollar deposit contracts, and the like.

To further encourage London's role in international finance the Government recently lowered the corporation tax to 35% and orchestrated the Big Bang in the London Stock Exchange. However, UK taxes still are relatively burdensome, as is the general cost (salaries, rent, etc.) of operating in London, especially in the financial district, known as "the city" (the zone within a mile of the Bank of England).

Chronology of Development

1816
UK became the first country to formally adopt the gold standard.

1914
UK suspended the gold standard due to World War I.

1925
UK resumed the gold standard; some currencies pegged to the pound.

1931
UK suspended its gold standard due to effects of global depression, leading to a 29% pound depreciation.

1947
UK adhered to Bretton Woods System.

1949
UK devalued the pound 30.5% ($4.03 to $2.80).

1957
UK prohibited pound financing of "third country trade" and limited pound refinancing of trade credits.

1967
UK devalued the pound 14.3% ($2.80 to $2.40).

1975
North Sea Oil production begins, eventually reaching 2.5 million barrels/day, and lending strong support to the U.K. balance of payments and therefore, the spot pound.

1979

UK terminated foreign exchange controls on the pound (October), and the Conservative Thatcher government began its privatization program.

1982

In April, the UK government temporarily froze all of Argentina's assets in Britain in response to its seizure of the Falkland Islands, highlighting the "sovereign risk" question.

1986

In October, the Financial Services Bill was implemented (the "Big Bang") to further deregulate the financial markets, including a merging of the stockbroker and jobber *(market maker)* functions (previously separated in *single-capacity trading*), the end of minimum commissions, the enlargement of the primary dealers in UK government bonds from 10 to 27, including the admission of many foreign firms to their rank, and the merger of the stock exchange and the International Securities Regulatory Organization whose 200 members dominate the enormous Eurobond market.

1987

In January, the Bank of England, in conjunction with the American bank regulators, proposed uniform risk-based capital-asset ratio requirements (including on off-balance sheet items) for British and American banks.

PARIS

Paris ranks as the world's fourth leading international banking center, reflecting the might of its great economy (fourth largest in the Free World), its regional (EEC) and global ties, the general centralization of French business activity in the capital, and the consistent policy of the French government toward that end. In 1985, its international banking activity represented 6.7% of the total market, up slightly from 1984 (6.6%), though down from 1983 (7.0%).

In 1985, its Eurocurrency loans to nonresidents totaled $128 billion, while such loans to residents totaled $49 billion. With French franc loans to nonresidents totaling $24 billion, its international banking activity totaled $200 billion.

The success of Paris in international finance reflects the sharp dichotomy of French regulation. While the French franc is highly protected and controlled, activity in other currencies is free of reserve requirements and other regulations.

The volume of international banking in Paris reflects both the scale of operations of France's major banks, as well as the extensive representation of foreign banks there. In particular, there are approximately 100 subsidiaries or branches of foreign banks in Paris, and some 50 representative offices, which puts Paris in third place in Europe for foreign bank representation, well after London and just behind Frankfurt. Also, some 500 international companies have their main European offices in Paris.

The giant French banks headquartered in Paris include the $98-billion Banque Nationale de Paris, the $91-billion Credit Agricole Mutuel, the $89-billion Credit Lyonnais, and the $86-billion Societe Generale. Other major French banks include the $26-billion Banque Indosuez, the $25-billion Banque Paribas, the $18-billion Banque Francaise du Commerce Exterieur, the $17-billion Credit Commercial de France, and the $11-billion Credit Industrial et Commercial.

Among the foreign banks in Paris, representation is especially strong among the American, British, Japanese, and Arab banks (the latter reflecting special governmental attention to links with the Arab world). Spanish and Portuguese banks are also well represented, in part to serve the numerous nationals from those countries working in France.

ZURICH AND GENEVA

Switzerland ranks as the world's fifth leading international banking center, despite the small size of its domestic economy (6.5 million people) and its harsh foreign exchange controls in the 1960s and 1970s to slow the rise of the Swiss franc (due to concerns with export competitiveness). The reason is that the country, politically neutral and with highly developed banking skills, has served for many years as a traditional haven for overseas investors, as well as in recent years for the treasury operations of many multinationals. The availability of secret, numbered bank accounts enhances the attractiveness of Switzerland, reinforced by a 1984 referendum in which voters rejected a proposal that would have opened bank records to authorities investigating domestic and foreign tax evasion. A final factor is Switzerland's structural current account surplus situation which essentially requires it to be a capital exporter. (Incidentally, Switzerland's banking skills were honed by a traditional emphasis on banking; its 432 banks and 5,501 bank offices are both international records relative to its small population.)

In June, 1985, Swiss trustee accounts totaled $115 billion and represented 3.8% of global international banking activity, up from 3.7% and 3.4% in the previous two years. Separately, Swiss nontrustee activity in 1985 represented 2.5% of international banking activity, compared to 2.3% in 1984 and a higher 2.8% in 1983. The 1985 activity included $32 billion in Eurocurrency loans to nonresidents and $8 billion to residents, as well as $34 billion in Swiss franc loans to nonresidents. Total 1985 international banking activity (both trustee and direct banking activity) was $189 billion or 6.3% of such activity globally.

Switzerland's rise as an international banking center owes much to its "big 3" banks, the $50-billion Union Bank of Switzerland, the $46-billion Swiss Banking Corporation, and the $32-billion Credit Suisse. Two smaller banks of importance are the $4-billion Bank Leu and the $3-billion Banca della Svizzera Italiana. Those leading banks not only do a lot of direct international lending, but also represent one third of the fiduciary business. Another third is spread over the private and cantonal banks.

International lending and about a third of the fiduciary businesses is done by foreign banks in Switzerland. However, the growth of foreign banking there has been considerably retarded by restrictive regulation (especially regarding licensing) of the Swiss National Bank (central bank) because of the inherent limitations on controlling such entities. Reflecting the latter orientation, the total number of branches and subsidiaries of foreign banks in Switzerland was unchanged between 1970 and 1980.

Switzerland's growth as an international banking center has not only been moderated by its go-slow attitude on foreign bank branches, but also by the high cost of doing business there. The high cost reflects both an expensive fee structure by the Swiss banks and government stamp taxes. (To avoid the latter, Swiss banks conduct much of their fiduciary activity on the books of their Luxembourg branches, where there are no stamp taxes.)

LUXEMBOURG

The Grand Duchy of Luxembourg has an area of 999 square miles and a population of 365,000. The capital, Luxembourg-Ville has a population of 79,000.

History. The Congress of Vienna in 1815 converted Luxembourg from a French department into a Grand Duchy. It was granted autonomy from The Netherlands in 1848 and a formally neutralized by the London Conference of 1867. The Belgium-Luxembourg Economic Union (BLEU) has existed since 1921 and the Benelux Economic Union since 1948. It is currently ruled by a center-left coalition between the Parti Chretian and the Parti Ouvier Socialiste, with Jacques Santer (the former Minister of Finance) as Prime Minister.

Economy. Luxembourg has traditionally relied upon steel production (90% by Arbed, which is 31% owned by the Luxembourg Government), but with the decline in that industry, Luxembourg has stopped mining iron ore (1981), and the industry's share of GNP has fallen below 20%. Since 1975 the Government has been actively promoting divestification, especially into financial services (banking and insurance), which currently represent over 25% of GNP.

Luxembourg has developed into the leading Euro-Deutschemark center, (in 1985, 36% of Luxembourg's Eurocurrency assets were DM-denominated), with German banks representing half of Luxembourg's banking assets. Also, its banks are very active in the ECU market, including both deposits and bonds. With slowing Euromarket activity over the past few years, Luxembourg is now emphasizing private banking, such as portfolio management, on the basis of being an "economical Switzerland" plus very strict bank secrecy laws.

Advantages as a Banking Center

1. A central location in Europe next to Germany, France and Belgium and near The Netherlands; and particularly useful for Scandinavian institutions.
2. A skilled, multilingual workforce, generally speaking German, French and English.
3. Strong government support of the financial sector since the mid-1960s.
4. Relatively moderate operational costs, aside from high real estate costs.
5. General political and social stability (e.g., no strikes in 60 years),

despite some restiveness over austerity measures, due to the second highest per capita GNP (after Switzerland) among industrialized countries ($15,000).

6. Provides a foothold into the EEC.

7. Serves as a financial center of the EEC, including the presence of the European Investment Bank (EIB) and the European Monetary Cooperation Fund (FECOM).

8. Headquarters of CEDEL (Eurobond clearing); the functionally related Luxembourg Stock Exchange, with its relaxed and cheap listing requirements, lists two-thirds of all Eurobonds (80% of all its quotations are Eurobonds).

9. Moderate regulation by the quasi-central bank, the Institute Monetaire (with a role for the Belgian central bank).

10. A general encouragement of foreign bank branches.

11. No minimum reserve requirements and modest capital: asset ratio requirements of 1:33 (cf. 1:18 in Germany).

12. Low de facto bank taxation due to very generous provisions for potential losses; such provisions totalled Luxfr 452 billion ($9.8 billion) in 1985, the interest from which forms a major portion of banks' income.

13. Strict bank secrecy laws passed in 1981, and providing jail sentences for violators.

14. No withholding taxes on nonresident investment income (i.e., on interest, dividends or capital gains).

15. Moderate bank charges, especially compared to Switzerland.

16. Courteous treatment of middle-class customers, especially compared to Switzerland.

17. Useful for geographic diversification of portfolios.

18. The volatility of interest and exchange rates is prompting more customers to seek professional management, a service currently being emphasized in Luxembourg.

19. Good quality loan portfolios with Eurocurrency lending to industrial countries representing nearly 75% of all lending (9% to Latin America, and some to Eastern Europe).

Unfavorable Factors as a Banking Center

1. Highly selective in granting bank charters to avoid a large supervisory burden.
2. Excluding generous loan loss provisions, bank taxation would be burdensome as the corporation tax rate is a relatively high 40%.
3. Personal income tax rates are among the steepest in Europe.
4. Luxembourg could eventually be forced to comply with EEC rules which might not conform with its role as a financial center.

Chronology of Development

1960
19 banks with liabilities totaling Luxfr. 23 billion.

1970
37 banks with liabilities totaling Luxfr. 236 billion (1,000% deposit growth from 1960).

1971
CEDEL Eurosecurity clearing system inaugurated in Luxembourg.

1974
76 banks; 5,646 employees; assets: Luxfr. 1,067 billion; 28% growth from previous year.

1975
76 banks; 5,846 employees; assets: Luxfr. 1,478 billion; 39% growth.

1976
78 banks; 6,031 employees; assets: Luxfr. 1,709 billion; 16% growth.

1977
90 banks; 6,306 employees; assets: Luxfr. 2,115 billion; 24% growth.

1978
97 banks; (21 German; 13 American; 9 Scandinavian); 6,705 employees; assets: Luxfr. 2,509 billion; 30% growth.

1979
108 banks; 7,091 employees; assets: Luxfr. 3,253 billion; 30% growth.

1980
111 banks; 7,600 employees; assets: Luxfr. 3,917 billion; 20% growth.

1981

Bank secrecy law passed.

113 banks; (29 German; 14 Scandinavian; 12 American); 8,069 employees; assets: Luxfr 5,081 billion; 30% growth.

1982

115 banks; 8,621 employees; assets: Luxfr. 5,997 billion; 18% growth.

Banco Ambrosiano Holdings, S.A., the Luxembourg subsidiary of Italy's llth largest bank, incurs an estimated $400 million loss, causing the failure of the parent.

The value-added tax on sales of gold was eliminated (leading to many German gold purchases in Luxembourg).

The Institute Monetaire replaced the weaker Commissariat au Controle des Banques as Luxembourg's quasi-central bank.

1983

Schroder Munchmyer, Heugst & Co. (Hamburg), Germany's largest private bank requires a DM 420 million rescue package due to high risk transactions involving IBH Holding A.G. (construction machinery group), substantially through its Luxembourg subsidiary to avoid domestic limits on loans to a single customer (SMH gave 8 times its capital to IBH).

1984

115 banks/ 9,382 employees (totalling 6% of the Luxembourg workforce); assets: peaked at Luxfr. 7,790 billion in June.

A dispute with Bundesbank erupted due to its wanting consolidated balance sheets for German banks, as Luxembourg (1:33) and Germany (1:18) have very different capital-asset ratio requirements, while German banks represent about half of the duchy's bank assets.

The ratio of nonbank to interbank deposits was 1:4, reflecting the growth of private banking (cf. 1:8 in 1979).

A law was passed to regulate the status of fiduciary deposits; e.g., to clarify the responsibilities of banks handling such deposits and thus facilitate such operations as back-to-back deals and make it possible for small banks to handle large deposits, with part of the funds being placed with other institutions.

Citicorp reestablished its private banking subsidiary after a short-lived presence in the early 1970s.

The number of investment funds rose to 132, with a value totalling Luxfr. 398 billion ($8.6 billion).

1985
120 banks; Germany implements (but more gradually than expected) its new consolidated gearing ratio (1:18).

Principal Banks in Luxembourg

Badische Kommunale Landesbank International SA: 9 blvd Roosevelt, BP 626, 2450 Luxembourg-Ville; tel. 47-59-91-1; telex 1791.

Bank of America International SA: 35 blvd Royal, 2449 Luxembourg-Ville; tel. 208-41; telex 2290.

Bank of Credit and Commerce International Group: 39 blvd Royal, 2449 Luxembourg-Ville; tel. 47-03-91; telex 1240.

Bank Oppenheim Pierson International SA: 123 ave de la Faincerie, BP 239, 1511 Luxembourg-Ville; tel. 47-68-67-1; telex 1220.

Banque Generale de Luxembourg SA: 27 ave Monterey, 2163 Luxembourg-Ville.

Banque Internationale à Luxembourg SA: 2 blvd Royal, BP 2205, 2953 Luxembourg-Ville; tel. 4-79-11; telex 3626.

Banque de Luxembourg SA: 80 place de la Gare, BP 2221, 1022 Luxembourg-Ville; tel. 49-924; telex 3425.

Banque Nationale de Paris (Luxembourg) SA: 24 blvd Royal, 2449 Luxembourg-Ville; tel. 47-641; telex 1426.

Banque Paribas (Luxembourg) SA: 10A blvd Royal, 2449 Luxembourg-Ville; tel. 40-830; telex 2332.

Bayerische Landesbank International SA: 25 blvd Royal, BP 602, 2449 Luxembourg-Ville; tel. 47-59-11-1; telex 1248.

Bayerische Vereinsbank International SA: 38-40 ave Monterey, BP 481, 2449 Luxembourg-Ville; tel. 42-86-11; telex 2654.

Berliner Bank International SA: 60 Grand'rue, BP 71, 2010 Luxembourg-Ville; tel. 47781; telex 1801.

BfG Luxembourg SA: 17 rue de Fosse, BP 1123, 1011 Luxembourg-Ville; tel. 47-71-01-1; telex 1415.

BHF-Bank International: 88 Grand'rue, 1660 Luxembourg-Ville; tel. 28-521; telex 2661.

Caisse d'Epargne de l'Etat du Grand-Duche de Luxembourg-Banque de l'Etat: 1 place de Metz, BP 2105, 2954 Luxembourg-Ville; tel. 2-98-51; telex 3417.

Christiania Bank Luxembourg SA: BP 544, 2015 Luxembourg-Ville; tel. 47-15-15; telex 2843.

Citicorp Investment Bank (Luxembourg) SA: 43 blvd Prince-Henri, 1724 Luxembourg-Ville; tel. 477-957-1; telex 3798.

Commerzbank International SA: 11 rue Notre Dame, 2240 Luxembourg-Ville; tel. 47-79-11-1; telex 1292.

Compagnie Luxembiurgeoise de la Dresdner Bank AG/Dresdner Bank International: 26 rue de Marche-aux-Herbes, BP 355, 2013 Luxembourg-Ville; tel. 47-601; telex 2558.

Copenhagen Handelsbank International SA: 12 rue Goethe, BP 406, 1637 Luxembourg-Ville; tel. 27-022; telex 2457.

Credit Suisse (Luxembourg) SA: 23 ave Monterey, 2163 Luxembourg-Ville; tel. 20265; telex 1356.

Den Danske Bank International: 18 ave Marie-Terese, BP 570, 2015 Luxembourg-Ville; tel. 40-401; telex 1665.

Den norske Creditbank (Luxembourg) SA: 21 blvd Prince-Henri, BP 297, 1724 Luxembourg-Ville; tel. 21101; telex 1776.

Deutsche Bank Compagnie Financiere Luxembourg: 25 blvd Royal, 2449 Luxembourg-Ville; tel. 46-44-11; telex 2748.

Deutsche Girozentrale International SA: 16 blvd Royal, BP 19, 2449 Luxembourg-Ville; tel. 42471; telex 2841.

DG Bank International SA: 3 blvd Joseph II, BP 661, 2016 Luxembourg-Ville; tel. 44-90-31; telex 1878.

East West United Bank SA: 10 blvd Joseph II, BP 34, Luxembourg-Ville; tel. 47-57-71; telex 1373.

Helaba Luxembourg/Hessische Landesbank International SA: 4 place de Paris, BP 1702, 1017 Luxembourg-Ville.

Hypobank International SA: 37 blvd Prince-Henri, BP 453, 1724 Luxembourg-Ville; tel. 44751; telex 2628.

International Bankers Inc.: 41 blvd Prince-Hentri, 1724 Luxembourg-Ville; tel. (352) 47-28-55; telex 2931.

International Trade & Investment Bank SA: 22-24 blvd Royal, BP 320, 2449 Luxembourg-Ville.

Kreditbank SA Luxembourgeoise: 42 blvd Royal, 2449 Luxembourg-Ville; tel. 47-97-1; telex 3418.

Landesbank Rheinland-Pfalz und Saar International SA: 6 rue de l'Ancien Athene, BP 84, 114 Luxembourg-Ville; tel. 47-59-21; telex 1835.

Landesbank Schleswig-Holstein International SA: 18 blvd Royal, BP 612, 2016 Luxembourg-Ville; tel. 46-842-1; telex 1806.

Manufacturers Hanover Bank Luxembourg SA: 26 route d'Arlon, BP 121, 1140 Luxembourg-Ville; tel. 47-23-91-1; telex 2485.

NORD/LB-Norddeutsche Landesbank Luxembourg SA: 26 route d'Arlon, BP 121, 1140 Luxembourg-Ville; tel. 47-23-91-1; telex 2485.

PKbanken International SA: 47 blvd Royal, 2449 Luxembourg-Ville.

Privatbanken International (Denmark) SA: 16 blvd Royal, 2449 Luxembourg-Ville.

Provinsbanken International (Luxembourg) SA: 25A blvd Royal, BP 173, 2449 Luxembourg-Ville; tel. 4-62-75; telex 1891.

Skandinaviska Enskilda Banken (Luxembourg) SA: 16 Blvd. Royal, BP 621, 2449 Luxembourg-Ville; tel. 47-79-81-1; telex 3751.

Societe de Banque Suisse (Luxembourg) SA: 26 route d'Arlon, BP 2, 1140 Luxembourg-Ville; tel. 47-25-411; telex 1481.

Svenska Handelsbanken SA: 27 ave Monterey, BP 678, 2163 Luxembourg-Ville; tel. 47-59-61; telex 2404.

The Taiyo Bank (Luxembourg) SA: 33 blvd Prince-Henri, 1724 Luxembourg-Ville.

Trade Development Bank (Luxembourg) SA: 34 avedela Porte-Neuve, 2227 Luxembourg-Ville.

Trinkhaus & Burkhardt (International) SA: 14 blvd EmmanuelServais, 2535 Luxemboug-Ville.

UBAE Arab German Bank SA: 22-24 blvd Royal, BP 115, Luxembourg-Ville; tel. 2-44-81.

Union Bank of Finland International SA: 189 ave de la Faiencerie, BP 569, 2015 Luxembourg-Ville; tel. (352) 4776111; telex 1575.

Union de Banques Suisses (Luxembourg) SA: 36-38 Grand'rue, Luxembourg-Ville; tel. 47-38-51; telex 1280.

Vereins-und Westbank Internationale SA: 3 ave Pasteur, 2311 Luxembourg-Ville; tel. 47-76-50; telex 2668.

West LB International SA: 32-34 blvd Grand-Duchesse Charlotte, BP 420, 1330 Luxembourg-Ville; tel. 44-74-11.

Banking Association

Association des Banques et Banquiers Luxembourg: BP 13, 2010 Luxembourg-Ville; tel. 29-501; telex 1701.

BRUSSELS

Brussels ranks as the world's seventh leading international banking center, reflecting its relatively large, export-oriented economy, its regional (EEC) and global ties, epitomized by the location of the EEC Commission there, its use as a regional center by American and other multinationals (some 500 international companies have their main European offices there), its related receptivity to the use of the English language, and the concentration of Euro-French franc and ECU trading there. In 1985, its international banking activity represented 3.8% of the market, up from 3.3% in the two previous years.

In 1985, its Eurocurrency loans to nonresidents totaled $83 billion, while such lending to residents totaled $27 billion. With Belgian franc lending to nonresidents totaling $4 billion, its international banking activity totalled $113 billion.

The volume of international lending in Brussels reflects both the scale of operations of Belgium's major banks, as well as the extensive representation of foreign banks there. The "Big 3" domestic banks include the $27 billion Société Generale de Banque, the $21 billion Banque Bruxelles Lambert and the $19 billion Kredietbank International Group. French banks figure prominently among the foreign banks in Brussels. Finally, Euroclear (Eurobond clearing system) is located in Brussels as is S.W.I.F.T. (just outside in La Hulpe).

AMSTERDAM

Amsterdam ranks as the ninth leading international banking center, reflecting the Netherlands' strong, export-oriented economy (world's second largest agricultural exporter), its regional (EEC) and global ties (via its multinationals such as Shell, Philips, and Unilever), its exemplary transportation facilities and significant trading there in Euro-Swiss francs and Euro-Italian lira. In 1985, its international banking activity represented 2.6% of the global market, a steady share for 1984-1986.

In 1985, Eurocurrency lending to nonresidents totaled $52 billion, while such loans to residents totaled $9 billion. With guilder lending to nonresidents totaling $16 billion, its international banking activity totalled $77 billion.

The volume of international lending in Amsterdam reflects the scale of operations of the Netherlands' large banks as well as the extensive representation of foreign banks there. Major Dutch banks include the $41-billion Algemene Bank Nederland, the $37-billion Rabobank Nederland, and the $35-billion Amsterdam Rotterdam Bank. Exemplifying the stature of foreign banks in the Netherlands, Credit Lyonnais Bank Nederland has $4 billion in assets, placing it among the country's largest banks.

CHANNEL ISLANDS (JERSEY, GUERNSEY)

Jersey. With 45 square miles, Jersey is the largest of the Channel Islands. Its population totals 76,000. Although the Crown appoints the Lieutenant Governor, it has a distinct legal/tax system from the United Kingdom. Nevertheless, it draws heavily on the Bank of England in the regulation of its banking industry, while also belonging to the Basle Committee Bank Supervisors Grouping.

Complementing tourism and agriculture (hothouse tomatoes and its celebrated dairy cows), financial services (deposits, booking international loans, investment management) is the fastest growing industry. Reflecting this, the "bank profits tax" now accounts for nearly a fifth of total tax revenues. Activity is centered in the capital of St. Helier, which has 52 banks, including the principal European and American ones and some from the Far East.

Jersey's attractiveness as a financial center is due to its: (1) proximity to Europe's financial capitals, (2) political stability, (3) low taxation, (4) selectivity in granting bank licenses (only banks of international standing are considered, with special consideration being given to those offering new types of services or broadening the geographical representation). Conversely, constraining Jersey's growth is its (1) limited housing and restrictive immigration rules, and (2) shortage of qualified workers (partially offset by growing computerization).

Chronology of Development

1981
Bank deposits totaled $20.7 billion, while bank profits totaled $72 million.

1982

Bank deposits rose 10% to $22.7 billion, while bank profits rose 10% to $79 million.

1983

Bank deposits rose to 13% to $25.7 billion among 46 banks; bank profits rose 4% to $82 million.

1985

As of 30 June, bank deposits totaled $30.7 billion among 52 banks.

Guernsey. Guernsey, with 24 square miles, is the second largest of the Channel Islands; its population totals 53,000 and its capital is St. Peter Port. Its chronology of development, in brief, is that in 1983 bank deposits totaled approximately $6 billion, rising to $8.3 billion among 48 banks by 30 June, 1985.

BANKS IN JERSEY

British Clearing Banks

Barclays Bank PLC: POB 8, 13 Library Place, St. Helier: tel. (0534) 78511; telex 419152.

Lloyds Bank PLC: 9 Broad St. St. Helier; tel. (0534) 73551; telex 4192071.

Midland Bank PLC: POB 14, 8 Library Place, St Helier; tel (0534) 73696; telex 4192122.

National Westminister Bank PLC: POB 20, 23-25 Broad St, St Helier; tel (0534) 78865.

Royal Bank of Scotland PLC: 6 Mulcaster St; St Helier; tel (0534) 27351; telex 4192369.

Other Banks

Algemene Bank Nederland (Jersey) Ltd: 8 Hill St, St Helier; tel (0534) 73631.

Allied Irish Banks (CI) Ltd: Eagle House, Don Rd. St Helier; tel (0534) 78567; telex 4192394.

Bank of America (Jersey) Ltd: POB 193, 11 The Esplanade, St Helier; tel (0534) 75471.

The Bank of India: 35-37 New St, St Helier; tel (0534) 73788; telex 4192107.

Bank of Ireland (Jersey) Ltd: POB 416, Union House, Union St, St Helier; tel (0534) 23451; telex 4192428.

Bank of Nova Scotia (CI) Ltd: Queen's House, 13/15 Don Rd, St Helier.

Banque Nationale de Paris, SA: POB 158, Templar House, Don Rd, St Helier; tel (0534) 76011; telex 4192352.

Barclays Bank Finance Co (Jersey) Ltd: POB 191, 2 Halkett Place, St Helier; tel (0534) 77990; telex 4192037.

Barclaytrust International Ltd: POB 82, Barclaytrust House, 39-41 Broad St, St Helier; tel (0534) 73741; telex 4192066.

Brown Shipley (Jersey) Ltd: POB 583, Channel House, Green St, St Helier; tel (0534) 74777; telex 4192105.

Charterhouse Japhet (Jersey) Ltd: POB 348, 22 Hill St, St Helier; tel (0534) 79437; telex 4192136.

Chase Bank & Trust Co (CI) Ltd: Hilgrove House, 10 Hilgrove St, St Helier; tel (0534) 25561; telex 4192209.

Citibank (Channel Islands) Ltd: POB 561, Green St, St Helier; tel (0534) 70707; telex 4192313.

Commercial Bank of Wales (Jersey) Ltd: 31 Broad St, St Helier; tel (0534) 73364; telex 4192101.

Grindlays Bank (Jersey) Ltd: POB 80, West House, Wests Centre, St Helier; tel (0534) 74248; telex 4192062.

Hambros Bank (Jersey) Ltd: POB 78, 13 Broad St, St Helier; tel (0534) 78577; telex 4192241.

Hill Samuel & Co (Jersey) Ltd: POB 63, 7 Broad St, St Helier; tel (0534) 73244.

Hongkong & Shanghai Banking Copn (CI) Ltd: POB 315, Hongkong Bank Bldg, Grenville St, St Helier; tel (0534) 71460; telex 4192254.

Kleinwort, Benson (Channel Islands) Ltd: POB 76, Wests Centre, St Helier; tel (0534) 35521; telex 4192284.

Lazard Brothers & Co, (Jersey) Ltd: POB 108, 2-6 Church St, St Helier; tel (0534) 37361; telex 4192154.

Lloyds Bank Finance (Jersey) Ltd: POB 10, Broad St, St Helier; tel (0534) 77588.

Midland Bank Trust Corpn (Jersey) Ltd: 28-34 Hill St, St Helier; tel (0534) 72156; telex 4192098.

Samuel Montagu & Co (Jersey) Ltd: POB 335, Queen's House, 13-15 Don Rd, St Helier; tel (0534) 79004; telex 4192267.

Morgan Grenfell (Jersey) Ltd: 12 Dumaresq St, St Helier; tel (0534) 71390; telex 4192007.

National Westminster Bank Finance (CI) Ltd: POB 20, 23- 25 Broad St, St Helier.

The New Guarantee Trust Of Jersey Ltd: 27 Hill St, St Helier; tel. (0534) 36341; telex 4192288.

Royal Bank of Scotland (Jersey) Ltd: 44 Esplanade, St Helier.

Royal Bank of Scotland PLC: 22 High St, St Peter Port; tel. (0481) 23074; telex 4191607.

Royal Trust Bank (Jersey) Ltd: Royal Trust House, Colomerie, St Helier; tel. (0534) 27441; telex 4192351.

Standard Chartered Bank (CI) Ltd: POB 89, Conway St, St Helier; tel. (0534) 74001; telex 4192013.

S.G. Warburg & Co (Jersey) Ltd: 39-41 Broad St, St Helier; tel. (0534) 74715; telex 4192041.

Westpac Banking Corpn (Jersey) Ltd: Charles House, Charles St, St Helier; tel. (0534) 79500; telex 4192190.

Other Banks

Aitken Hume (Guernsey) Ltd: Berthelot House, Berthelot St, St Peter Port; tel. (0481) 26618.

Allied Bank International (Guernsey) Ltd: Suite B, St John's House, Union St, St Peter Port; tel. (0481) 23986.

Ansbacher (CI) Ltd: POB 79, La Plaiderie, St Peter Port; tel. (0481) 26421; telex 4191524.

Australia and New Zealand Banking Group (Channel Islands) Ltd: St Julian's Court, St Julian's Ave. St Peter Port; tel. (0481) 26771.

Bank of Bermuda (Guernsey) Ltd: POB 208, Bermuda House, St Julian's Ave, St Petere Port; tel. (0481) 26268; telex 4191502.

Banque Belge: Suite 5a, Albert House, South Esplanade, St Peter Port; tel. (0481) 26614.

Barclays Finance Co (Guernsey) Ltd: POB 269, Cambria House, New St, St Peter Port.

Barclaytrust Channel Islands Ltd: POB 184, Valley House, Hirzel St, St Peter Port; tel. (0481) 24706; telex 419679.

Barfield Bank & Trust Co. Ltd: POB 71, Barfield House, St Julian's Ave, St Peter Port; tel. (0481) 26541.

Brown Shipley (Guernsey) Ltd: Challel House, Forest Lane, St Peter Port; tel. (0481) 23069.

Canadian Imperial Bank of Commerce (CI) Ltd: Suite 4, Albert House, South Esplanade, St Peter Port; tel. (0481) 710151.

Carolina Bank (Guernsey) Ltd: 4 North Quay, St Peter Port; tel. (0481) 28321; tel. 4191198.

Chemical Bank & Howard de Walden Ltd: St Julian's Court, St Julian's Ave, St Peter Port; tel. (0481) 23478.

First National Bank of Boston (Guernsey) Ltd: Valley House, Hirzel St, St Peter Port; tel. (0481) 23721; telex 4191540.

First National Bank of Chicago (CI) Ltd: Union St, St Peter Port; tel. (0481) 23561.

Guinnes Mahon (Guernsey) Ltd: POB 188, La Vieille Cour, St Peter Port; tel. (0481) 23506

Hambros Bank (Guernsey) Ltd: POB 6, Hambro House, St Julian's Ave, St Peter Port; tel. (0481) 26521; telex 4191110.

Hanson Guernsey Ltd: POB 252, Hirzel Court, Hirzel St, St Peter Port; tel. (0481) 23055; telex 4191426.

Italian International Bank (Channel Islands) Ltd: St Julian's Court, St Julian's Ave, St Peter Port; tel (0481) 23776; telex 4191529

Leopold Joseph & Sons (Guernsey) Ltd: Albert House, South Esplanade, St Peter Port; tel. (0481) 26648; telex 4191505.

Kleinwort, Benson (Guernsey) Ltd: POB 44, The Grange, St Peter Port; tel. (0481) 2711; telex 4191316.

Lazard Bros & Co (Guernsey) Ltd: POB 275, 16 Glategny Esplanade, St Peter Port; tel (0481) 213670.

Lloyds Bank International (Guernsey) Ltd: POB 136, Sarnia House, Le Truchot, St Peter Port; tel. (0481) 26761; telex 4191514.

Lombard Banking (Jersey) Ltd: POB 119, Common House, Les Banques, St Peter Port; tel. (0481) 24561; telex 4191667.

Manufacturers Hanover Bank (Guernsey) Ltd: Manufacturers Hanover House, Le Truchot, St Peter Port; tel. (0481) 23961.

Midland Bank Trust Corpn (Guernsey) Ltd: 22 Smith St, St Peter Port; tel. (0481) 23765; telex 4191586.

Morgan Grenfall (Guernsey) Ltd: POB 96, Morgan Grenfall House, Lefebvre St, St Peter Port; tel. (0481) 26383; telex 4191609.

National Westminster Bank Finance (CI) Ltd: POB 272, Manor Place, St Peter Port; tel (0481) 26486.

National Westminster Guernsey Trust Co Ltd: POB 16, 35 High St, St Peter Port; tel. (0481) 26101; telex 4191608.

Orion Bank (Guernsey) Ltd: POB 48, Royal Bank House, St Julian's Ave, St Peter Port; tel. (0481) 26124; telex 4191527.

Pierson Heldring & Pierson (CI) Ltd: POB 253, Sydney Vane House, Rue de Commerce, St Peter Port; tel. (0481) 28921.

Rea Bros (Guernsey) Ltd: POB 116, Commerce House, Les Banques, St Peter Port; tel. (0481) 26014; telex 4191388.

BANKS IN GUERNSEY

British Clearing Banks

Barclays Bank PLC: POB 41, 6-8 High St., St Peter Port; tel. (0481) 23176; telex 4191671.

Lloyds Bank PLCPB: Smith St, St Peter Port; tel. (0481) 25131; telex 4191454.

Midland Bank PLC: 13 High St, St Peter Port; tel. (0481) 24201; telex 4191617.

National Westminster Bank PLC: 35 High St, St Peter Port; tel. (0481) 26851.

Republic National Bank of New York (Guernsey) Ltd: Sarnia House, Le Truchot, St Peter Port; tel. (0481) 710901.

N.M. Rothschild & Sons (CI) Ltd: POB 48, St Julian's Ave, St Peter Port; tel. (0481) 23021; telex 4191527.

Royal Bank of Scotland (Guernsey) Ltd: POB 62, 22 High St, St Peter Port; tel. (0481) 23074; telex 4191607.

Standard Chartered Bank (CI) Ltd: Valley House, Hospital Lane, St Peter Port; tel. (0481) 26944; telex 4191546.

Eurocurrency Market Centers

WESTERN HEMISPHERE

- New York-Miami-Los Angeles-San Francisco
- Toronto
- Nassau
- Cayman
- Panama
- Netherland Antilles
- Bermuda
- Barbados
- Antigua

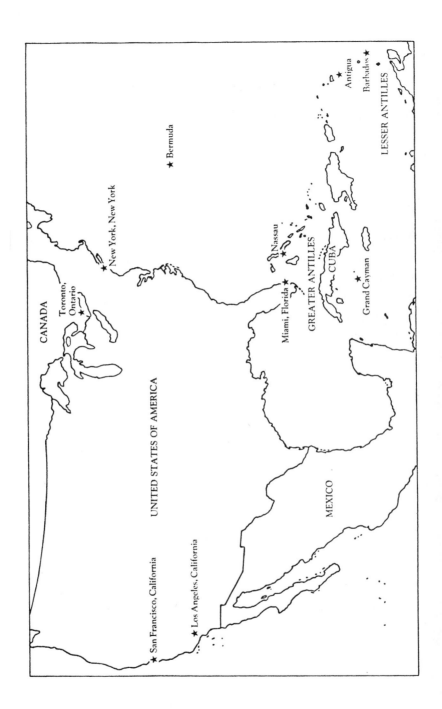

NEW YORK-MIAMI-LOS ANGELES-SAN FRANCISCO:
INTERNATIONAL BANKING FACILITIES (IBFs)

General Overview. Any U.S. depository institution can set up an IBF, which essentially is a separate set of books on which *eligible* assets and liabilities are recorded. Depository institutions include commercial banks, agencies and banks of foreign banks, Edge Act and agreement corporations, savings and loan associations, savings banks and credit unions. In practice, agencies and branches of foreign banks account for 57.4% of the IBFs, commercial banks (and savings and loan associations) for 30.2% and Edge Acts for the remaining 12.4%.

Since their authorization as of December 3, 1981, IBFs have enabled New York and other U.S. banking centers (Miami, Los Angeles, San Francisco, Chicago, Atlanta, and Houston) to expand their international banking activity, previously limited to dollar loans to nonresidents, into Eurobanking. The IBFs are unique *onshore/offshore* Eurobanking units of authorized depositories (almost entirely commercial banks and their Edge Act corporations) that are exempt from reserve requirements (Regulation D), FDIC insurance fees, state and local taxation (at the option of those authorities), and until their demise on March 31, 1986, interest rate controls (Regulation Q). They remain subject to federal corporate income taxation and prudential regulations. In short, while geographically onshore, legally they are largely offshore.

The procedure of setting up an IBF involves simply sending a letter of intention to one of the twelve regional Reserve Banks, or twenty-five Bank branches (such as Seattle for Washington State) two weeks in advance of the start date, and then keeping the appropriate books. IBFs in practice vary from a 10–20 person department at a giant money center bank to a part-time function at a small institution.

IBF balance sheets have grown to $320 billion, to represent a considerable sector of the American banking industry, and even a relatively larger portion for money center banks and active agencies and branches of foreign banks. In particular, note should be taken that many big banks have multiple IBFs, parented by the parent bank, its many Edges around the country, and its Delaware subsidiary. Chemical Bank, for example, has seven IBFs.

Exhibit 3-2
IBF LIABILITIES: 1981-1986
(in millions of U.S. dollars)

Date[a]	Total	Weekly Reporting Banks		Agencies/Branches of Foreign Banks		All Other[b] Entities	
1981	55,597	n.a.	(n.a.)[c]	n.a.	(n.a.)	n.a.	(n.a)
1982	152,694	64,395	(781)	80,958	(1,556)	7,340	(23)
1983	189,319	83,200	(2,484)	98,640	(1,574)	7,625	(186)
1984	172,373	60,428	(1,423)	108,823	(3,771)	5,267	(216)
1985	260,542	90,440	(2,211)	199,696	(10,396)	10,217	(609)
1986.1	257,059	86,168	(8,805)	168,263	(15,588)	9,034	(581)
1986.2	265,564	83,790	(2,136)	178,074	(16,181)	8,998	(478)
1986.3	285,326	81,898	(2,720)	195,664	(19,441)	8,515	(761)
1986.4	301,131	76,131	(2,065)	216,479	(21,111)	8,522	(511)

n.a. = not available

[a]End of period.

[b]Non-weekly reporting banks, other U.S. depository institutions, and U.S. offices of Edge and agreement corporations.

[c]Numbers in parentheses refer to foreign currency deposits. Minor descrepancies in the totals result from distinction made between U.S. offices of the establishing entity and all other parties with which the IBFs deal.

Source: Federal Reserve Board, Form G.14(416).A (monthly report).

Historical Development of IBFs. IBFs were first proposed in the late 1960s in response to the foreign lending restraints imposed on American banks as a consequence of the Voluntary Foreign Credit Restraint Program. That balance of payment control, which was mandatory in practice, prevented American banks from increasing their lending to industrialized countries. IBFs involving solely foreign funding were viewed as ways for American banks to continue to increase their lending to developed nations, without any resulting balance of payments outflow, and in fact with some services (administrative costs and profits) inflows. However, the Fed maintained its adamant opposition because it feared that such IBFs would interfere with the implementation of domestic monetary policy.

Shortly later in the 1969-1970 period, a Fed governor suggested the authorization of IBFs as an alternative to Nassau-Cayman *shell* (brass plaque) branches, which simply served to record deals largely done in New York. That suggestion fell through as did a similar one by the President's Council of Economic Advisors staff in 1974 that was predicated on the desirability of attracting petrodollars spawned by the previous year's oil price shock.

Momentum supporting the IBF concept was gathering in New York (especially promoted by the New York Clearing House Association) and in other American money centers, despite the adamant opposition of the Fed and some regional bankers, who saw a loss of relative competitiveness should the idea be approved only for the big banking cities. The New York State legislature, which saw IBFs as a way of repatriating Nassau-Cayman business to New York City (as well as some of London's business) with all the beneficial employment and income effects, enacted a state/local tax exemption statute for the proposed IBFs, subject to the Fed's providing the corresponding exemptions to its Regulations D (reserve requirements) and Q (interest rate ceilings).

By 1981, the Fed was under rapidly growing pressure from the big banks, and from state and local authorities where the major banks were located, to authorize IBFs. While the Fed was quite capable of resisting such pressures if it felt that its monetary policy apprehensions warranted doing so, it was growing increasingly concerned about its only very limited influence in international meetings dealing with Euromarkets supervision due to the absence of such a market in the United States.

To enhance its role in such discussions, as well as no doubt influenced by growing lobbying in support of IBFs, it authorized such entities in June for a start date of December 3, 1981 (the half-year lag was to give local authorities adequate time to pass the corresponding legislation for state-city income tax exemptions and so on). With only a two-week advance notice required to create such entities, it was quickly deluged with applications from American banks wanting to shift their Nassau-Cayman business to New York IBFs (which would paradoxically reduce their taxation because New York State and local authorities tax Nassau-Cayman business when it was effectively done in New York) and from agencies and branches of foreign banks, especially Japanese and Italian ones as they had generally not set up branches in Nassau-Cayman.

The initial burst of IBF activity was so spectacular that within four weeks of their start date, IBFs had already recorded over $53 billion in deposits, making the IBF sector one of the fastest growing financial markets in history. Rapid momentum was maintained in 1982, when the market jumped to $120 billion. However, it slowed down to a 21% growth rate in 1983, reflecting a certain market maturity as well as the consequence of widespread economic weakness and the global debt crisis. Further slowing to a 13% growth rate occurred in 1984 for much the same reasons. In 1985 the even further slowing to an 11% growth rate can be attributed as well to the declining spot dollar, in which an overwhelming percentage of IBF activity is done. Yet further slowing to a 6% annualized growth rate in the first half of 1986 can be explained likewise, but accelerated growth in the second half led to a 16% growth rate being posted for the year as a whole.

Location of IBFs. The approximately 540 IBFs are to be found in twenty-four states and the District of Columbia, but chiefly in New York State (44%) and California (18%), reflecting the presence in New York City, Los Angeles, and San Francisco of the big U.S. money center banks and most of the agencies and branches of foreign banks. Florida (16%), Illinois (6%), and Texas (3%), reflecting IBF activity in Miami, Chicago, Houston, and Dallas, are also important, while the other nineteen states and Washington D.C. account for the 13% balance.

Advantages of IBFs. IBF deposits have grown to $290 billion because of the many advantages they offer. As already mentioned, they are free of reserve requirements (which currently are 12% for transaction accounts and 3% for nonpersonal time deposits less than 1.5 years) and FDIC insurance (per the IBF Deposit Insurance Act of December

26, 1981, IBF deposits are not insurable), with the latter exemption reducing the cost of taking a deposit by 8.5 basis points (FDIC insurance premiums are one-twelfth of 1% of total deposits).

As IBF deposits are typically million-dollar multiples (with undesirable rates given on deposits of less than $1 million, or even less than $5 million at the larger banks), the $100,000 insured account ceiling renders such insurance largely irrelevant anyway in the Euromarket aside from the closer supervisory scrutiny involved in such insurance programs.

Conversely, one could argue that historically, the FDIC has fully protected all deposits regardless of size in nearly all bank failures (Penn Square of Oklahoma was an exception because many large depositors were corruptly involved in the affairs of the bank), an observation borne out in the Continental Illinois case. One could thus deduce that, at least, deposits in major banks are safe because the government would not allow such a devastating failure. Finally, as mentioned, IBFs were exempt from Regulation Q, but that exemption is no longer relevant as Regulation Q was largely phased out on March 31, 1986.

Another advantage is that IBFs are exempt from state and local taxation, a significant factor in a city like New York that has marginal state and city corporate income tax rates of 9% (since January 1, 1985) for each jurisdiction, or 18% in total. (Previously, the marginal corporate income tax rate for New York State and New York City together was as high as 25.8%.) Moreover, it should be noted that New York imposes state and city corporate income tax on Nassau and Cayman activity that is actually transacted in New York. However, the significance of the exemption depends not only on the various states' and cities' total marginal tax rates, but also on what degree there is a "clean" (as opposed to "dirty") tax statute. Most IBF states like Florida have a "clean" tax statute, whereas the New York one is "dirty."

Specifically, in the case of banks or foreign branches functioning in New York before December 3, 1981, they enjoy the exemption for the first nine years *only* on the degree of "new business" (that is, relevant activity above that of the 1975-1977 base period) generated plus a percentage of the 1975-77 "floor". That percentage is zero for the first five years, 20% in the sixth year, 40% in the seventh year, 60% in the eighth year and 80% in the ninth year. Concurrently, all IBFs enjoy the tax exemption only to the degree that they are funded from abroad, not locally, as from the parent.

A further tax issue is to what degree indirect overhead expenses can be attributed to the IBF, such as the proportional cost of senior bank management and the bank's economists. It is an adversary situation in which the banks wish to minimize the lightly taxed IBFs' expenses, while maximizing general expenses at the much more highly taxed parent bank. Government tax authorities have proposed an attribution based simply on the volume of IBF deposits relative to the parent bank's deposits, but that is resisted by the banks, which justifiably claim that IBF expenses are relatively modest. For example, one New York City bank's $10-billion IBF is administered by ten employees, while it takes the 19,000 other employees to take care of the remaining $47 billion of the bank.

A couple of further exemptions have reinforced the attractiveness of IBFs. First, interest income on IBF deposits is exempt from the traditional 30% withholding tax on nonresident interest income (an exemption extended to bond interest by 1984 tax legislation). Also, IBFs are exempt from the Fed's *policy* of prohibiting U.S. depositories (commercial banks) from taking nondollar deposits. Historically, however, due to a strong spot dollar, nondollar deposits have accounted for only about 3% of total IBF deposits due to time zone and other problems. But they have been increasing in the wake of the spot dollar's decline, especially at agencies and branches of foreign banks, and now have reached 9% of overall deposits.

Another IBF advantage is that they offer superior safety of principal, as U.S. *sovereign risk* historically provides unimpeded access to funds (unless you happened to be an Iranian during the 1979 hostage crisis, or a belligerent in the Suez War of 1956). IBF managers felt they could get away with offering lower deposit rates than Nassau or other centers because of the sovereign risk question, but corporate treasurers and the like have resisted more than marginally lower rates, a major disappointment for the wide-eyed IBF optimists of 1981.

A final IBF advantage is that the availability of Eurobanking in the U.S. offers opportunities for further geographical diversification to international investment managers. Swiss fiduciaries have used IBFs to temporarily park funds while they were looking for long-term investment opportunities in U.S. real estate and other long-term American investments.

Limitations of IBFs. Offsetting their many advantages, IBFs suffer from many limitations that prevent them from equally competing in the Euromarket. The absence of a "level playing field" explains, in part, the failure of the IBF market to approach, let alone surpass, the London Euromarket.

The most severe handicap of IBFs is that they are not permitted to accept deposits from or extend credit to U.S. residents, apart from the parent and other IBFs. Should the parent borrow funds from its IBF, it is required to pay the standard 3% reserve requirement on Eurocurrency borrowing. The resultant *Chinese Wall* between the U.S. banking system and the IBF sector is to prevent IBF operations from interfering with the implementation of Fed monetary policy.

The ban on business with U.S. residents is reinforced by the further provision that IBFs are permitted to accept only deposits related to operations *outside* the U.S. (for example, GM-Germany can deposit in an IBF, but not if it is simply a conduit for funds from GM-United States), and extend credit only to finance operations outside the U.S. (that is, again, no conduit operations permitted).

Moreover, an IBF must notify all of its nonbank customers of the regulation, and obtain written acknowledgment of receipt of such notice from nonbank customers that are foreign affiliates of U.S. corporations. For other customers, no receipt is required.

The effect of the ban on U.S. resident activity in the IBF market is to cut off from that market the world's largest economy. Moreover, corporations of that economy are active users of the Euromarket, conducting substantial operations, including overnight Eurodollars with Eurocenters such as Nassau, Cayman, and London, the IBF market's principal competitors. Thus, the U.S. resident restriction is an especially limiting one.

Another significant limitation is that IBFs are prohibited from issuing any negotiable instruments, such as negotiable CDs, as such instruments could be bought by U.S. residents in the secondary market (that is, penetrate the Chinese Wall). That prohibition hurts the market because corporate treasurers, when making a deposit of a month or more, invariably want to buy a negotiable CD as opposed to a higher-yielding but non-negotiable time deposit. From experience, they know that unexpected cash needs often arise. Their preference for negotiable CDs, as well as that of others, has resulted in a global Eurodollar CD market (in London, Singapore, Luxembourg, and Nassau) of around $115 billion (described in the section on Eurocurrency market instruments). Thus the prohibition on negotiable instruments puts the IBFs at quite a competitive disadvantage with other major banking centers.

A related limitation on the market is that deposits by nonbanks are subject to a two-day minimum maturity, although overnight deposits are permitted for foreign banks, foreign central banks and other official institutions, other IBFs and an IBF's U.S. parent institution. Like the negotiable CD restriction, it hurts the market because treasurers of multinational corporations make a substantial amount of overnight deposits, which are readily available at other Eurocenters.

A related prohibition is that IBFs are not permitted to offer transaction accounts, such as demand deposits, but that is not particularly regarded as a limitation. Another limitation that is not considered as significant is that deposits and withdrawals by nonbanks must be a *minimum* of $100,000 (except to close an account or withdraw accumulated interest). The insignificance of that restriction is reflected in the fact that large bank IBFs are disinclined to accept deposits of less than $1 million.

Another handicap of IBFs is that, while being exempt from state and local taxes (with the qualifications already noted), they are subject to Federal income tax with its current marginal corporate income tax rate of 34%. Conversely, some Eurocenters as Nassau and Cayman have no corporate income tax and several others have quite low corporate income taxes on Euro-operations, such as ACUs in Singapore. However, IBFs benefited from the substantial reduction in America's marginal corporate income tax rate in the Tax Reform Act of 1986.

A final handicap that IBFs face is that, as American financial institutions, they are subject to U.S. court subpoena, as opposed to the bank secrecy regulations in Switzerland, Luxembourg, Nassau, Cayman, and other international money centers. However, such regulations are of lessening significance given the growing inclination of banks and regulators to cooperate in criminal investigations (such as, the Bank of Nova Scotia case discussed in the "Nassau" section).

The IBF Market in Late 1986

As of November 26, 1986, the IBF market as shown in Exhibit 3-3, totaled $281 billion, and remained dominated, as always, by the U.S. "agencies and branches" of foreign banks, which with $194 billion in liabilities, represented 69% of the market. Next were the "weekly reporting banks," based mainly in New York, which with liabilities of $81 billion, represented 28% of the market. Finally, were "all other enti-

Exhibit 3-3

ASSETS AND LIABILITIES OF INTERNATIONAL BANKING FACILITIES[1]
FOR NOVEMBER 26, 1986 FOR ALL STATES
(In millions of U.S. dollars)

Assets

	Total For All Entities[2]	Weekly Reporting Banks[3]	Agencies & Branches[4]	All Other Entities[5]
Offices of Establishing Entity				
1. Gross Claims on non-U.S.	66,393	16,292	49,496	606
(1) Denominated in $US	57,404	15,342	41,456	606
(2) Denominated in Other Currencies	8,990	949	8,040	0
2. Loans and Balances Due From Other IBFs	49,624	3,356	42,901	3,368
3. Gross Due From:				
a. Banks in Foreign Countries	40,083	8,594	30,174	1,315
b. Foreign Governments and Official Institutions	1,128	1,045	78	5
4. Securities of non-U.S. Addressees	7,075	155	6,814	105
5. Loans to non-U.S. Addressees				
a. Commercial and Industrial Loans	34,249	18,065	15,806	378
b. Banks in Foreign Countries	34,929	12,320	21,851	758
c. Foreign Governments and Official Institutions	27,893	17,109	10,325	459
d. Other Loans	1,022	696	308	18
6. All Other Assets in IBF Accounts	3,439	1,343	2,007	89
7. Total Assets Other Than Claims on U.S. and Non-U.S. Offices of Establishing Entity (Sum of Items 2. through 6.)	215,000	64,736	143,454	6,810
(1) Denominated in $US	199,442	62,684	130,263	6,495
(2) Denominated In Other Currencies	15,559	2,053	13,191	315

Exhibit 3-3

	Total For All Entities [2]	Weekly Reporting Banks [3]	Agencies & Branches [4]	All Other Entities [5]
Assets				
8. Total Assets Other Than Claims on U.S. Offices of Establishing Entity (Sum of Items 1. and 7.)	281,394	81,028	192,950	7,416
(1) Denominated in $US	256,845	78,026	171,719	7,101
(2) Denominated in Other Currencies	24,548	3,002	21,231	315
Liabilities				
9. Gross Liabilities Due to Non-U.S. Offices of Establishing Entity	99,972	40,460	58,796	716
(1) Denominated in $US	87,399	39,812	46,871	716
(2) Denominated in Other Currencies	12,573	647	11,925	0
10. Liabilities Due To:				
a. Other IBFS	53,618	6,329	46,275	1,014
(1) Overnight Maturity/Notice	3,896	739	3,143	14
b. Banks in Foreign Countries	70,647	8,609	60,296	1,742
(1) Overnight Maturity Notice	6,044	1,792	4,057	196
(2) 2-6 Days Maturity/Notice	1,898	366	1,460	71
(3) 7 Days or Over Maturity/Notice	62,705	6,451	54,779	1,475
c. Foreign Government and Official Institutions	15,152	10,680	4,184	288
(1) Overnight Maturity/Notice	5,920	4,684	1,130	105
(2) 2-6 Days Maturity/Notice	2,492	2,097	394	1
(3) 7 Days or Over Maturity/Notice	6,740	3,899	2,659	182

d. Other Non-U.S. Addressees				
(1) 2-6 Days Maturity/Notice	21,119	6,017	11,864	3,238
(2) 7 Days or Over Maturity/Notice	1,643	603	808	232
e. All Other Liabilities in IBF Accounts	19,476	5,414	11,056	3,006
	4,047	1,857	2,087	103
f. Total Liabilities Other Than Due To U.S. and Non-U.S. Offices of Establishing Entity	177,101	34,989	135,162	6,949
(1) Denominated In $US (Sum of Items 10.a through 10.e)	164,582	33,492	124,705	6,385
(2) Denominated in Other Currencies	12,519	1,497	10,457	564
11. Total Liabilities Other Than Due To U.S. Offices of Establishing Entity (Sum of Items 9. and 10.f)	277,073	75,449	193,958	7,666
(1) Denominated in $US	251,981	73,304	171,576	7,102
(2) Denominated in Other Currencies	25,091	2,145	22,383	564

Residual

12. Net Due From (+) / Net Due To (−) U.S. Offices of Establishing Entity (Item 11. Minus item 8.)	−4,321	−5,580	1,008	250
(1) Denominated in $US	−4,864	−4,722	−143	1
(2) Denominated in Other Currencies	543	−857	1,151	249

Memoranda

1. Amount Included in Item 10.d for Liabilities Due To Non-U.S. Addressees with Maturity/Notice of 2 Days Only	398	98	296	4
2. Net Due From (+) / Net Due To (−) Non-U.S. Offices of Establishing Entity (Item 1. Minus Item 9.)	−33,579	−24,168	−9,300	−111

Number of Reporters	171	34	122	15

[1]Unless otherwise noted, figures include only amounts denominated in U.S. dollars.

[2]This report contains data only for those entities whose IBF assets or liabilities are at least $300 million, that is, for those entities that file a monthly report of IBF accounts on form FR 2072.

[3]"Weekly Reporting Banks" refers to large U.S.-chartered banks that file a weekly report of condition (FR 2416). Assets and liabilities of these banks are published in the Federal Reserve statistical release H.4.2.(504).

[4]"Agencies and Branches" refers to U.S. agencies and branches of foreign banks.

[5]"All Other Entities" includes non-weekly reporting banks (see note 3 above), other U.S. depository institutions and U.S. offices of Edge and Agreement corporations.

Source: *Federal Reserve Board, G14 (416)A,* monthly.

tites", including non-weekly reporting banks, other U.S. depository institutions, and U.S. offices of Edge and Agreement Corporations, which, with $8 billion in liabilities, represented 3% of the total market.

In terms of asset profiles, agency-and-branch IBFs emphasized their "gross claims on non-U.S. offices of (their) establishing entity," (26%); "loans and balances due from other IBFs"—the inter-IBF market is largely among Japanese IBFs, (22%); and gross, due from banks in foreign countries, (16%). Weekly reporting bank IBFs have a different asset profile which emphasized "commercial and industrial loans" to foreign companies, (22%); loans to "foreign governments and official institutions," (21%); and gross claims on non-U.S. offices of the establishing entity," (20%).

Reflecting the spot dollar's substantial depreciation against the major Europe currencies and the yen since February 1985 — a decline of around 35% — as well as the outlook for some further depreciation to rectify the enormous U.S. current account deficit, assets denominated in foreign currencies represented 9% of the total IBF assets. Among IBFs of "agencies and branches" it was a significantly higher 11%.

In terms of liability profiles, agency-and-branch IBFs emphasized liabilities to "banks in foreign countries" (31%); and liabilities to "non-U.S. offices of the establishing entity," or more specifically, to their global branch network outside the United States, (30%); and liabilities to other "IBFs" (24%). The American weekly-reporting banks have a somewhat different liability profile, emphasizing "gross liabilities due to the non-U.S. offices of the establishing entity," or more specifically, the global foreign network of the parent (53%), deposits of foreign governments and official institutions (15%), deposits of "banks in foreign countries" (11%).

As with the assets, the depreciating spot dollar has left a rising percentage of foreign-currency-denominated deposits in its wake. Overall, foreign currency deposits were 8.9% of the total IBF liabilities. Among IBFs of "agencies and branches," they were significantly higher at 12%.

Exhibit 3-4
TABLE OF INTERNATIONAL BANKING FACILITIES
(For March 26, 1986)

Table of States by Entity

State	Banks & S & Ls	Agencies/ Branches	Edge Corps	Total
Arkansas	0	0	1	1
California	21	67	10	98
Colorado	1	0	0	1
Connecticut	2	0	0	2
Delaware	2	0	0	2
District of Columbia	7	3	1	11
Florida	30	30	25	85
Georgia	4	2	2	8
Hawaii	2	0	0	2
Illinois	7	19	6	32
Kentucky	2	0	0	2
Louisiana	1	0	0	1
Massachusetts	4	1	0	5
Michigan	2	0	0	2
New Jersey	4	0	0	4
New York	40	181	17	238
North Carolina	2	0	0	2
Ohio	6	0	0	6
Pennsylvania	6	2	1	9
Rhode Island	1	0	0	1
South Carolina	1	0	0	1
Texas	13	0	3	16
Virginia	2	0	0	2
Washington	3	5	0	8
Wisconsin	0	0	1	1
Total	163	310	67	540

Source: Federal Reserve Board

Exhibit 3-5
POTENTIAL OF IBFs STILL A DISTANT VISION
by Eugene Sarver

Corporations, governments and official institutions represent approximately half of the $2 trillion global Eurocurrency market. Their strong interest in that market stems from the high interest rates it offers for their deposits and the favorable lending rates it charges on loans. The market's capacity to operate on a narrow spread stems from its being the market for currencies outside their country of origin (either geographically or legally) and, hence, free from domestic regulatory controls and related costs. While traditional Eurocenters as London, Paris, Luxembourg, Singapore and Nassau dominate the nonbank side of the Eurocurrency market, Eurocenters of growing corporate and governmental interest have been the International Banking Facilities (IBFs) in the United States, which are now entering their third year of operation as a $167 billion market.

The IBFs are unique onshore, offshore "Eurobanks" that operate in dollars and other currencies, with extensive exemption from central bank regulation and local taxation. In practice, they are simply a separate set of books in which financial institutions with IBFs record eligible assets and liabilities. These U.S. entries into the global Eurocurrency market competition—concentrated in New York, California and Florida—offer solid business advantages, which have enabled them to grow to their current impressive size in just two years.

While the initial rapid growth of IBFs was largely due to interbank activity, corporations, governments and official institutions, with a growing awareness of the market's advantages, are increasing their participation at a faster rate than banks. Nevertheless, their role remains secondary to interbank activity due to the restrictions that hamper the

market, still slow recognition by government financial boards of the market's usefulness, and the global economic slowdown and related Latin American debt crisis.

On the deposit side, corporations now account for $17.0 billion or 9% of the market, up from $12.8 billion a year ago and $2.6 billion in February 1982. Concurrently, foreign governments and official institutions have placed $10.5 billion in IFBs, or 7% of the market, up from $6.2 billion a year ago and $3.4 billion in February 1982.

While the asset side simply reflects the banks' choices of where it is most profitable and convenient to book a loan, it is nevertheless useful to note that currently $36.0 billion of "commercial and industrial loans" and $22.5 billion of loans to "foreign governments and official institutions" are booked by IBFs; they represent 22% and 14% of IBF assets, respectively.

There are currently 477 IBFs in operation. Institutions qualified to establish IBFs include any U.S. depository institution (primarily commercial banks), Edge Act corporations (federally incorporated organizations engaged solely in international banking activities) and agencies and branches of foreign banks.

U.S. banks have fathered 144 (30% of total) of the IBFs, while the corresponding numbers for foreign agency/branches and Edge Act corporations are 264 (55%) and 69 (15%). New York's 208 IBFs, 44% of the total is far ahead of the No. 2 state, California, with 84 (18%). Florida is third with 79 (17%); Illinois fourth with 30 (6%); and finally, Texas, fifth with 20 (4%). New York's preeminent role results from its having 58% of foreign agency/branch IBFs as well as 26% of the domestic bank IBFs. However, its 16 (23%) Edge Act corporation IBFs were well behind Florida's 27 (39%), though ahead of California with 11 (16%).

The IBFs can be established by simply sending a letter two weeks in advance to the appropriate regional Federal Reserve Bank. They have proven quite popular with the banking community because of the special privileges accorded them by the Federal Reserve Board and by the 18 localities (17 states and the District of Columbia) in which they are located.

Concurrently, the banking community feels hampered by the many restrictions on the IBFs, as well as by the tax uncertainty surrounding the New York ones, so that the full potential of the market remains a distant vision. In fact, the IBFs represent only 8% of the $2,055 billion global Eurocurrency market and less than half the size of the London market.

The relatively modest size of the American Euromarket reflects its history. While the Eurocurrency market dates to the early 1950s when Chinese (Peking), Soviet and East European banks moved their dollar deposits from New York to the Soviet-owned Banque Commerciale pour l'Europe du Nord in Paris (telex code: Eurobank:hence, Eurodollars) and the Moscow Narodny Bank in London, the Fed, despite New York's and San Francisco's preeminent role in international banking (accepting foreign deposits and making foreign loans) delayed the U.S. entry into the Euromarket for over 30 years. Its deep concern over the potentially disruptive effects of Eurobanking in America on its monetary control maintained its resolve despite the increasing support the idea generated, starting in the late 1960s.

While the Fed did ultimately approve the IBF concept on June 18, 1981 (with a December 3, 1981 starting date to give the state legislatures time to pass corresponding tax exemption legisla-

tion), it was not motivated so much by the prospect of a new industry a la Singapore, but rather by the strengthening effect of having a domestic Euromarket on the Fed's bargaining position in international banking regulation. The restrained enthusiasm of the Fed, some would say ambivalence, explains both the concessions the Fed made and the limitations it imposed. The latter have had an especially moderating effect on the corporate side of the market.

The Fed made two major concessions to give viability to the IBFs—exemptions from Regulation D (reserve requirements) and Regulation Q (interest rate ceilings). Moreover, it convinced Congress to pass on December 26, 1981, the IBF Deposit Insurance (Exemption) Act—the 8.5 basis points, or .085 percent of cost represented by the insurance premium would undermine the interbank placement market characterized by multimillion dollar deposits against which $100,000 protection is almost meaningless.

Also, the Fed did extend one special privilege to the IBFs, denied to domestic banks—acceptance of foreign currency deposits. The potential of the privilege was great since currently 20% (28% was the peak in the weak dollar year of 1979) of the Eurocurrency market or the equivalent of $410 billion is nondollar—about half of the latter is Deutschemarks, a quarter Swiss francs and the rest yen, sterling, French francs and other currencies.

Concurrently, states/cities that sought IBF business granted tax exemptions to the IBFs (which are still subject to federal corporate income tax). In states such as Florida and Delaware, the tax exemption is a "clean statute," while in New York it is muddled by concepts such as the "floor amount" (only asset growth above the 1975-1977 base is exempted subject to a 10-year phaseout) and "ineligible funding" (assets funded domestically via deposits of the parent, are not eligible for tax exemption). Moreover, the apportionment of indirect expenses (such as, the management fee paid by the IBF to the parent institution), that affects the tax liability of the parent is another complication.

On the basis of the Fed and state concessions, the IBFs are able to offer corporate and governmental depositors, etc. Eurodollar time deposit rates comparable to those of Nassau and London, with the added advantage of U.S. sovereign risk. (At times, IBF rates are one-sixteenth to one-eighth percent lower reflecting the lower sovereign risk, but, in general, the treasurers of multinational corporations have been averse to sacrificing yield for the added security). This has proven attractive to multinationals around the world, and especially to companies in Latin America that share the New York/Miami time zone.

Discussions with American, European and Japanese bankers indicate that a major factor in nonbank deposits in IBFs is the sovereign risk question, including the absence of capital controls and the availability of a lender of last re-

sort via the parent's access to the Fed window. ("Virtually *no* country risk" was how one banker phrased it.) Generally, such depositors are "geographically sensitive" and have a queasy feeling of dealing with "shell branches" in the Caribbean. Moreover, the IBFs represent added geographical diversification for fiduciary monies (especially important to the big Swiss banks). Compared with the alternative of depositing in a U.S. domestic bank, such customers enjoy a 40-basis-point advantage (essentially the impact of the absence of reserve requirements and the FDIC assessment).

Another factor in nonbank deposits, mentioned particularly by Swiss and French bankers, is the convenient utilization of IBF deposits to "shelve money" while a suitable final U.S. investment objective (e.g. real estate or equities) is being identified. A final point is that only the Japanese IBFs have focused on overseas subsidiaries of their country's major companies (such as Mitsubishi-Panama), while for other foreign agency/branch IBFs the customer base has been multinationals in general.

*Reprinted with permission of *The Journal of Commerce—International Edition* (New York, Monday, March 5, 1984).

Exhibit 3-6
A GUIDE TO THE CORPORATE USE OF IBFs

- Deposits can only be made by non-U.S. residents (i.e. foreign corporations, foreign subsidiaries of U.S. corporations using foreign-generated funds).

- All deposits must be time deposits (no demand deposits or negotiable CDs are permitted).

- Deposits must be for a minimum of two days (there is no maximum term, but the average term is two months and the outer limit is generally five years).

- Deposits must be at least $100,000 (large IBFs often have discretionary $1,000,000 minimums, while their average deposit is $10,000,000; small IBFs have an average size deposit of $1,000,000 and accept deposits as low as the statutory minimum).

- Deposit rates continuously fluctuate, but are usually somewhat *below* the bid side of LIBOR.

- Interest paid on IBF deposits is exempt from U.S. withholding tax.

- To make a deposit into an IBF, the standard procedure is for the corporate treasurer to make the arrangements with (a) a bank account officer; (b) a bank trading room salesperson, or (c) directly with the IBF staff (the funds are then wired in from the company's clearing bank or transferred from the company's DDA—demand deposit account—at the IBF's parent institution).

TORONTO

Toronto ranks as the world's tenth leading international banking center, reflecting the active international role of Canada's large banks, in the context of a well developed financial infrastructure, including well qualified staff, no capital or foreign exchange controls, political stability, good communication and transportation facilities, a relatively moderate effective tax rate on banks despite a 52% marginal corporate rate because of liberal deductions for loan loss reserves, etc., heavy external borrowing to finance economic development, and very close financial ties with the United States, enhanced by a shared time zone with New York. In 1985, Canadian international banking activity represented 2.4% of the global market, down marginally from 2.6% in the two previous years.

In 1985, Canada's Eurocurrency loans to nonresidents totaled $41 billion, while such lending to residents totaled $25 billion. With Canadian dollar lending to nonresidents totaling $3 billion, its international banking activity totaled $70 billion.

Conversely, with respect to Eurocurrency funding (liabilities are approximately 95% Euro-dollars, with the balance mostly Euro-pounds, Euro-marks, and Euro-yen, reflecting Canada's business ties to those countries), statistics for end-March 1986 (shown in Exhibit 3-7) include a total of C$104 billion (equivalent) of such liabilities, with such liabilities to the United States being C$44 billion, to the UK C$11 billion, to "other EEC" being C$4 billion, to "other OECD" being C$6 billion, to "other countries" being C$25 billion, and to "Canadian residents" being C$14 billion.

Toronto, with a population of 600,000 (2.9 million in the metropolitan area), is the largest city in Canada, and the capital of Ontario province. It is Canada's leading commercial and industrial center (6,000 manufacturing establishments), while its stock exchange is the

Exhibit 3-7

CHARTERED BANKS: TOTAL FOREIGN CURRENCY LIABILITIES BOOKED IN CANADA

(millions of Canadian dollars)

Country of residence and type of bank customer

Year[a]	United States			United Kingdom			Other EEC Countries			Other OECD Countries		
	Banks	Other	Total	Banks	Other	Total	Banks	Other	Total	Banks	Other	Total[c]
1979	3,919	8,454	12,373	4,417	80	4,497	2,581	269	2,851	1,234	763	1,996
1980	6,965	9,775	16,740	6,813	69	6,881	2,950	291	3,241	2,103	425	2,528
1981	10,708	15,242	25,950	14,868	370	15,238	2,961	514	3,475	1,756	790	2,546
1982	14,474	12,317	26,791	15,281	267	15,548	3,285	521	3,807	1,879	819	2,698
1983	16,682	15,526	32,208	11,435	327	11,762	1,898	589	2,487	2,148	1,086	3,234
1984	18,111	15,535	33,634	10,334	678	11,013	2,663	683	3,346	2,977	1,297	4,274
1985	19,730	19,828	39,557	10,655	664	11,319	2,624	749	3,373	3,467	1,590	5,057
1986[b]	20,552	23,502	44,054	9,932	1,123	11,055	2,939	955	3,894	4,331	1,747	6,078

[a] End of period.
[b] End of March.
[c] Balance of foreign currency liabilities are to non-OECD and Canadian customers.
Source: Bank of Canada Review (June 1986).

largest in Canada and the third largest in North America. Moreover, to enhance Toronto's role in international finance, the Ontario Provincial Government announced in December 1986 that it would introduce sweeping legislative changes in its securities industry. The two major changes allow foreign firms to own 100% of a Canadian securities firm by the middle of 1988, (currently the limit is 10%) and allow Canadian banks, and trust companies, to buy up to a 100% stake in Canadian securities firms by the middle of 1987.

Complementing the Toronto Stock Exchange, Toronto has the head offices of 25 trust companies, and 22 federally chartered banks, including 19 foreign bank subsidiaries. The large Canadian banks include the $64-billion Royal Bank of Canada, the $55-billion Bank of Montreal, the $49-billion Canadian Imperial Bank of Commerce, the $43-billion Bank of Nova Scotia, and the $35-billion Toronto Dominion Bank. Most of the large banks are headquartered in Toronto and even those headquartered in Montreal (Royal, Bank of Montreal) do most of their Eurocurrency dealing out of their Toronto branches.

One factor that has retarded the growth of Eurobanking in Canada has been the restrictions of foreign banks there. Until 1980, they could not even obtain a banking license, although about 15 foreign banks established near-bank subsidiaries carrying on business (such as leasing) and consumer finance activities. In the 1980 Bank Act (revised every ten years), foreign banks were allowed to operate through a bank subsidiary (not branch) in Canada if two conditions were met.

1. The potential to make a contribution to competitive banking in Canada.
2. Reciprocity in the legislation of the home country.

Moreover, foreign bank assets in total in the 1980 Act could not exceed 8% of the entire banking system, a ceiling reached by the 58 foreign bank subsidiaries in 1984; it was subsequently raised to 16%. Other than size limitations, Schedule B foreign banks subsidiaries have all the powers allocated to Schedule A Canadian-chartered banks. Capital requirements on foreign bank subsidiaries are a minimum of $5 million in authorized capital, of which at least half must be paid up, and such subsidiaries have a de facto asset: capital limitation of 20 times a bank's paid-in capital and reserves.

While Toronto is the leading international banking center in

Canada, the corresponding roles of Montreal and Vancouver will be significantly upgraded if a plan recently unveiled by Finance Minister Michael Wilson is realized. Specifically, he has proposed that the metropolitan areas of the leading Quebec and British Columbia cities be designated as International Banking Centers (IBCs) and exempt from taxation with respect to *eligible* international banking activities.

Wilson believes that the measure would strengthen the international competitiveness of Canadian financial institutions, especially vis-à-vis American (cf. IBFs), British, Japanese, and Swiss ones, and in so doing would generate new, incremental business and corresponding jobs. In particular, the IBCs are seen as leading to the repatriation of much of the C$60 billion of Canadian bank loans that are booked abroad (e.g., in the Bahamas and Barbados) in favorable tax locations.

Operationally, the IBCs would be allowed to accept deposits from and make loans to nonresidents. Care would have to be taken that such loan monies would not be onlent to Canadian residents. Various certification forms would be filed with the Minister of National Revenue.

While Minister Wilson feels that significant activity could be diverted to Canada from such favorable tax locations as Panama and the Channel Islands, a report he commissioned (the Rasminsky-Lawson report) is not so optimistic. The report, prepared in May 1985 by a former governor of the Bank of Canada and the present vice governor, saw little in the way of either costs or benefits from creating IBCs.

While awaiting the federal initiative, the province of Quebec has already moved ahead to establish Montreal as an International Finance Center. Its strategy is to give large corporate and personal tax breaks to lure international banking business from foreign locations. The tax breaks include exemption from its corporate tax rate of 5.9%, its payroll levy of 3.22% for health services, and the annual tax on capital of 0.48%; moreover, employees will benefit from temporary income-tax reductions or holidays.

The outlook for Wilson's proposed IBCs is uncertain, given the strong objection of Toronto to preferential status for its rivals, Montreal and Vancouver. Ontario views the Wilson initiative as a ploy to gain support for the faltering Mulroney government, and has promised to respond "dollar for dollar" with tax breaks of its own. Supporting Toronto's position is a study commissioned by its mayor, Art Eggleton, and prepared by the management consulting firm of Woods Gordon. It showed that if Toronto is not included in the IBC legislation, it will lose at least 350 banking jobs and suffer long-term damage to its competitive position.

NASSAU (BAHAMAS)

Nassau, located on the 83-square-mile island of New Providence, is the capital of The Bahamas. The latter is composed of an 800 mile long chain of 700 Caribbean islands, 30 inhabited, comprising 5,382 square miles. Nassau's metropolitan population is 139,000, while that of The Bahamas is 226,000.

History. British settlement began in 1647 and the islands became a British Crown Colony in 1717. They were granted internal self-government in 1964 and full independence, within the Commonwealth, on July 10, 1973.

Economy. The major industries, in addition to international banking, include tourism (1.5 million tourists anually), oil refining, transshipment and agriculture. The Bahamas' major trading partners include the U.S., U.K., Nigeria and Canada.

Advantages as a Banking Center

Nassau's advantages as an international finance center include:

1. The absence of income taxes, withholding taxes, corporation taxes, capital gains taxes, death taxes and gift taxes.
2. The presence of many major international banks and wide recognition of Nassau as a major Eurocurrency trading center.
3. The existence of bank secrecy (though limited by the Bank of Nova Scotia case).
4. The flexibility possible under the law.
5. The political stability resulting from an uninterrupted 257 year history of parliamentary democracy.
6. The highly favorable quality of life, including ample first class office space, hotels and restaurants.
7. Ralative proximity to and direct air links with principal North American business centers, including daily flights to Miami and New York.
8. A shared time zone with New York, Miami and Toronto.
9. Excellent telephone and telex services, including direct-distance dialing to the United States and Canada.
10. Maturity gained by long years of experience as an offshore center.
11. A highly qualified financial community to administer the affairs of absentee investors and "shell" banks.

Exhibit 3-8
EXTERNAL LIABILITIES OF BANKS IN THE BAHAMAS
(billions of U.S. Dollars)

Year[a]	Interbank Deposits	Nonbank Deposits	Commercial Banks	U.S. Bank Branches	Other Offshore	Tota
1971	n.a.	n.a.	4.3	8.1	1.7[c]	14.1
1972	n.a.	n.a.	5.1	12.5	2.6[c]	20.2
1973	n.a.	n.a.	5.7	20.3	4.3[c]	30.3
1974	n.a.	n.a.	12.3	26.7	5.6[c]	44.6
1975	n.a.	n.a.	16.9	37.3	7.8[c]	62.0
1976	n.a.	n.a.	23.9	53.9	11.3[c]	89.1
1977	n.a.	n.a.	27.0	61.5	12.9[c]	101.4
1978	n.a.	n.a.	32.0	71.9	15.1[c]	119.0
1979	n.a.	n.a.	30.2	80.2	16.8[c]	127.2
1980	n.a.	n.a.	33.6	92.0	19.3[c]	144.9
1981	n.a.	n.a.	43.4	105.3	22.1[c]	170.8
1982	n.a.	n.a.	34.8	98.2	20.6[c]	153.6
1983	101.4	55.1	32.0	105.2	22.0	156.5
1984	92.7	56.0	32.1	96.5	20.1	148.7
1985	83.3	58.1	29.5	93.2	18.7	141.4
1986[b]	104.2	51.3	28.2	91.8	35.5	155.5

n.a. = not available   [b] end of June
[a] end of period   [c] estimated by author

Source: International Monetary Fund, *International Financial Statistics Yearbook, 1986; Internation Financial Statistics,* November 1986.

Unfavorable Factors as a Banking Center

1. A disadvantage of Nassau is that New York State and New York City tax Nassau activity *actually* transacted in New York City as if it were standard New York City taxable activity; hence, much of such activity has been shifted to state-city tax-exempt IBFs in the United States
2. Some political inquietude resulting from the alleged involvement of some government officials in narcotics trafficking.

Chronology of Development

Early 1950's
Tax haven status prompts inflow of foreign companies.

1965
Banks and Trust Companies Regulation Act passed, under pressure from U.S./U.K. governments.

1981
241 banks and trust companies operating. Foreign assets of deposit banks peak at $150.3 billion.

1982
At end-1982, 335 active bank and trust companies: Authorized Dealers and Authorized Agents under Exchange Control Regulations: 3; Authorized Dealers under Exchange Central Regulations: 7; Authorized Agents under Exchange Control Regulations: 8; Other banks: 232; Restricted Bank and Trust Companies and Nominee Trust Companies: 84; non-active bank and trust companies: 11. Euro-deposits decline due to the impact of new IBF competition.

1983
A Florida grand jury investigating income tax evasion and drug smuggling obtained by subpoena records from the Bank of Nova Scotia Nassau branch (related to a $1,825,000 fine, 73 days at $25,000/day on its Miami branch), forcing de facto relaxation of the Euro-center's secrecy laws.

GRAND CAYMAN (GEORGE TOWN)

George Town, capital of the Cayman Islands, a British Crown Colony, has emerged as a major Eurocurrency center. The Cayman Islands themselves are composed of three Caribbean islands, Grand Cayman (76 square miles), Cayman Brac (14 square miles) and Little Cayman (10 square miles), that are located 475 miles southeast of Miami and 180 miles northwest of Jamaica. The population of 20,300 (including 3,000 expatriates) is 20% European, 15% African and 65% mixed. George Town has a population of 8,900 among the 18,000 on Grand Cayman.

History. The islands were dependencies of Jamaica until 1959, when they became a unit territory within the Federation of the West Indies. In 1962, upon the dissolution of the Federation, the Cayman Islands became a British Crown Colony, with the British government appointing the Governor, but largely self-governing. Due to the *country risk* advantages of being a Crown Colony, there is no desire whatever for independence.

Economy. The major industries, in addition to international banking, include tourism (350,000 tourists anually), and the standard tax haven/offshore businesses. The latter include 400 insurance companies and 16,000 international corporations. There is also local construction, some agriculture and the Cayman Turtle Farm (45,000 tortoises are raised for their meat, shells, skin and fat).

Advantages as a Banking Center

The advantages of Grand Cayman, the "Switzerland of the Caribbean," as an international banking center include:

1. Low country risk as a Crown Colony.
2. The absence of income taxes, withholding taxes, corporation taxes, capital gains taxes, death taxes and gift taxes (government revenue is derived from import duties, usually 20%, and stamp duty).
3. The British legal system.
4. The existence of bank secrecy (though limited by the Bank of Nova Scotia case).

Exhibit 3-9
CAYMAN ISLANDS—
ALL BANKS - EXTERNAL ASSETS AND LIABILITIES
(Millions of U.S. dollars)

Year	Total Assets	% Growth	Total Liabilities	% Growth
1976	21,997	**	22,064	**
1977	31,487	43.1	31,133	41.1
1978	49,033	55.7	48,585	56.1
1979	61,811	26.1	64,648	33.1
1980	84,527	36.8	83,401	29.0
1981	109,572	29.6	107,919	29.4
1982	125,958	15.0	120,069	11.3
1983	131,281	4.2	130,448	8.6
1984	150,626	14.7	149,418	14.5
1985	175,592	16.6	172,593	15.5

Source: *Inspector of Banks & Trust Companies*, Cayman Islands Government

5. Political stability resulting in part from the highest standard of living in the Caribbean.
6. The highly favorable quality of life, including ample first class office space, hotels and restaurants.
7. Relative proximity and direct air links with principal North American business centers, including daily flights to Miami.
8. Excellent telephone and telex services, including the highest telex line density in the world (1/200 people).
9. Maturity gained by long years of experience as an offshore center.
10. Shared time zone with New York, Toronto, and Miami
11. A stable currency, the Cayman dollar, worth U.S.$ 1.20.
12. Acceptance of "shell" banking.
13. A highly qualified financial community to administer the affairs of absentee investors and "shell" banks.

Unfavorable Factors as a Banking Center

(1) A disadvantage of Cayman is that New York State and New York City tax Cayman activity *actually* transacted in New York City as if it were standard New York City taxable activity; hence, much of such activity has been shifted to state-city tax exempt IBFs in the United States; (2) less international recognition than Nassau despite less country risk.

Chronology of Development

1966
Passage of the Banks and Trust Companies Regulations Law, creating "Class A" licenses (onshore and offshore transactions) and "Class B" licenses (offshore transactions).

1975
Over 150 banks and trust companies in operations (mostly B licenses); over 6,000 companies incorporated and hundreds of private trusts.

1979
Bank external liabilities total $64.4 billion; Law 28 of 1979 sets the "A" license fee at $20,000 and the "B" license fee at $7,000; over 200 international bank and trust companies, plus about 5,000 companies and 600 exempt trusts.

1980
Bank external liabilities total $83.4 billion; foreign assets of U.S. bank branches total $33.0 billion.

1981
Bank external liabilities total $107.9 billion; 350 international bank and trust companies.

Foreign assets of U.S. bank branches rise 28% to $42.1 billion.

1982
Bank external liabilities total $120.1 billion; at end-1982, 428 international bank and trust companies licensed: 33 with "A" license and 395 with "B" license; license fees: "A" C$20,000; "B" unrestricted— C$7,000; "B" restricted— C$5,000.

Foreign assets of U.S. bank branches rise 11% to $4.67 billion

1983
Bank external liabilities total $130.4 billion; Law 32 of 1983 raises the "A" license fee 37.5% to $27,500 and the "B" license fee 21.4% to $8,500. A Florida grand jury, investigating tax evasion and drug smuggling, obtained, by subpoena, records from Bank of Nova Scotia's Cayman branch, related to a $1,825,000 fine (73 days at $25,000/day on its Miami branch), forcing de facto relaxation of the Eurocenter's secrecy laws.

Foreign assets of U.S. bank branches rise 5% to $49.0 billion.

1984
Bank external liabilities total $149.4 billion.

Exhibit 3-10
DEPOSITS AT CAYMAN BRANCHES OF U.S. BANKS

Year[a]	Deposits
1980	$31.8 billion
1981	$42.1 billion
1982	$47.0 billion
1983	$50.0 billion
1984	$50.3 billion
1985	$48.8 billion
1986[b]	$47.1 billion

[a]End of period
[b]End of June
Source: Federal Reserve Bank of New York (unpublished)

1985
Bank external liabilities total $172.6 billion

1986
At end-November, there were 30 banks with category "A" licenses and 465 banks with category "B" licenses.

PANAMA

Panama has an area of 29,306 square miles (785,650 km^2 plus 1,430 km^2 in the Canal Zone) and a population of 2,000,000. Its principal cities are Panama City (440,000) and Colon (85,000). Principal industries include oil refining, shipping, regional warehousing and international banking, with its main trading partners including the U.S., the Canal Zone, Ecuador, Venezuela, and West Germany.

Panama developed as a major deposit-loan center for Latin America, boosted by the region's rapid growth. However, the Latin American debt crisis from 1982 on, accentuated by the collapse of a Panamanian Eurobank, Banco de Ultramar, have constrained the center's prospects.

Advantages as a Banking Center

1. A strong mercantile tradition dating back to Spanish colonial days.
2. A strategic central location between the two Americas, enhanced by the Panama Canal.
3. The modernizing and economically stimulating effects of the U.S. military and civil presence (especially from the Canal Zone).
4. The bilingualism (Spanish-English) of the business communities of Panama City and Colon.
5. The availability of qualified indigenous personnel.
6. The availability of excellent international sea/air transport facilities (the international airport, 15 miles from Panama City, is served by 14 foreign and 4 Panamanian airlines).
7. The availability of excellent international mail/telex/telephone communications—the best in Latin America, exemplified by the installation of a telephone satellite system in 1968.
8. The use of the U.S. dollar as the country's unit of exchange, with free circulation and no monetary or exchange controls of any kind.

Exhibit 3-11
REPUBLIC OF PANAMA
ANALYSIS OF THE DEPOSITS OF THE BANKING SYSTEM[1]
31 December 1985
(in thousands of Balboas[3])

Banks	Total Deposits		
	Total	Domestic	Foreign
TOTAL	24,485,377	3,998,754	20,486,623
Offical Banks - SUB TOTAL	992,174	941,559	50,615
1. Banco Nacional de Panama	713,363	662,748	50,615
2. Caja de Ahorros	278,811	278,811	
Private Banks - SUB TOTAL	**23,493,203**	**3,057,195**	**20,436,008**
1. Citibank, N.A.	664,690	204,341	460,349
2. The Chase Manhattan Bank, N.A.	489,599	316,972	172,627
3. Banco Fiduciario de Panama, S.A.	361,704	71,057	290,647
4. Banco General, S.A.	238,482	198,782	39,700
5. Banco de Credito Internacional, S.A. (2)	—	—	—
6. Primer Banco de Ahorros	228,052	185,557	42,495
7. Banco de Colombia	399,091	93,078	306,013
8. Bank of America, N.T. & S.A.	258,252	96,386	161,866
9. Lloyds Bank International (Bahamas)	330,065	24,631	305,434
10. Banco Sudameris Internacional, S.A.	432,314	77,645	354,669
11. Banco Cafetero, S.A.	377,996	306,085	71,911
12. Banco Exterior, S.A.	266,717	134,495	132,222
13. Banco del Comercio, S.A.	54,882	9,102	45,780
14. Banco de Santander y Panama, S.A.	429,923	85,288	344,644
15. Banco de Bogota, S.A.	94,034	16,121	77,913
16. Republic National Bank, Inc.	33,227	2,788	30,439
17. The First National Bank of Chicago	3,439,165	5,911	3,433,254
18. Banco Interoceanico de Panama, S.A.	76,901	13,966	62,935
19. Marine Midland Bank, N.A.	105,111	77,561	27,550
20. Korea Exchange Bank	69,185	10,162	59,023
21. Tower International Bank Inc.	42,874	10,769	32,105
22. Algemene Bank Nederland N.Y.	46,071	2,604	43,467
23. Deutsch Sudamerikanische Bank, A.G.	1,343,565	152,424	1,191,141
24. Swiss Bank Corporation (Overseas), S.A.	864,130	29,703	834,427
25. Banco Continental de Panama, S.A.	95,948	52,333	43,615
26. Banque Anval, S.A.	75,174	4,356	70,818
27. Banco Industrial Colombiano de Panama, S.A.	136,466	2,430	134,036
28. The Bank of Tokyo, Ltd. *	1,106,393	46,592	1,059,801
29. Banco Internacional de Panama, S.A.	79,117	52,488	26,629
30. American Express Bank (Panama), S.A.	2,247,124	1,947	2,245,177

Exhibit 3-11

Banks   Total Deposits

	Total	Domestic	Foreign
31. Banco Comercial Antioqueno, S.A.	86,351	2,290	84,061
32. The First National Bank of Boston	92,064	44,795	47,269
33. Banco do Brasil, S.A.	620,800	14,978	605,822
34. Banco Sudamericano de Desarrollo, S.A.	69,975	11,966	58,009
35. The International Commercial Bank of China	89,580	7,141	82,439
36. The Bank of Nova Scotia *	34,967	10,114	24,853
37. Banco Union	158,195	27,075	131,120
38. Banco Real, S.A.	224,999	2,822	222,177
39. Union Bank of Switzerland (Panama) Inc.	542,951	56,457	486,494
40. Bankers Trust Company Inc.	22,495	17,755	4,740
41. The Royal Bank of Canada *	179,504	11,160	168,344
42. Banco de Iberoamerica, S.A.	372,881	28,377	344,504
43. Banco Internacional de Costa Rica	147,649	3,389	144,260
44. Merril Lynch International Bank	650,614	25,000	625,614
45. Banco Latinoamericano de Exp., S.A. (BLADEX)	401,451	131,083	270,368
46. Banco Rio de la Plata (Panama),S.A. *	194,850	5,985	188,865
47. The Sanwa Bank, Ltd. *	1,161,781	30,015	1,131,766
48. Banco Agro Ind. y Com. de Panama,S.A. *	24,127	5,460	18,667
49. The Dai-Ichi Kangyo Bank, Ltd. *	956,016	41,030	914,986
50. Banco Trasatlantico, S.A.	26,993	18,223	8,770
51. Banco Cormercial de Panama, S.A.	95,779	83,455	12,324
52. The State Bank of India	72,382	13,826	58,556
53. Bank Leumi Le Israel, B.M.	40,017	16,622	23,395
54. Bank of Credit & Commerce Internal (Overseas), Ltd.	277,638	34,210	243,428
55. Banco Consolidado (Panama),S.A.	77,699	1,871	75,828
56. Banco Ganadero, S.A.	68,180	3,607	64,573
57. Banco do Estado de Sao Paulo, S.A.	328,261	11,576	316,685
58. The Sumitomo Bank, Ltd., *	1,220,986	15,889	1,205,097
59. Thi Mitsui Bank, Ltd. *	351,842	5,300	346,542
60. Banco Panameno de la Vivienda	20,108	19,142	966
61. Credit Suisse	240,512	872	239,640
62. Banco Central, S.A.	64,334	23,908	40,426
63. Banco de Latinoamerica, S.A.	16,313	6,049	10,264
64. Banco de Bilbao (Panama), S.A.	43,453	3,686	39,767
65. Banque Indosuez	64,955	6,402	58,553
66. Banco Agro Ganadero de Prod. y Des	11,355	11,224	131
67. Banco del Istmo, S.A.	54,885	18,867	36,018

* The statement period does not correspond to December 31.

[1] Refers to banks with a general licence, according to their date of establishment.

[2] It is reorganizing and is not conducting business.

[3] A balboa equals a U.S. dollar.

Source: *Balance de Situacion* (published)

The official monetary unit, the *balboa,* exists only for accounting purposes, and in coinage, but not in banknotes.

9. Total income tax exemption of offshore business.

10. The total absence of taxes on bank deposit interest, both domestic and offshore.

11. The relative ease of bank registration, including a modest $500 fee if the bank is established under Panamanian law and $1,000 if the bank is established abroad. A type "A" license allows both domestic and offshore business, and requires $1 million in paid-up capital (which may be reached over 10 years, with the initial minimum only $250,000). A type "B" license, allowing only offshore business, requires $250,000 in paid-up capital. A "representation license" is also available.

12. A dynamic international business environment that includes: the Colon Free Trade Zone (bonded warehousing and manufacturing, which handles more than $500 million of shipments annually); ship registration fostered by a very low registration tax of $1/net ton, annual tax of 10¢/ton, and specific exemption of international shipping income from Panama's income tax; and reinsurance business, all in addition to international banking.

13. Good availability of locally and internationally trained lawyers, who provide fast and competent service.

14. Local availability of most of the large international auditing firms.

15. Local availability of many management companies offering specialized services, such as administrative and consulting services.

Chronology of Development

1903
Panama became independent from Colombia, which it had joined in 1821.

1904
Citibank established the first U.S. banking office in Panama .

1914
Panama Canal opened by United States.

1927
Favorable company legislation initiated (based on Delaware corporation law), which led to 50,000 company registrations by 1981.

1948
Creation of Colon Free Trade Zone, with over 1,000 companies by 1980.

1957
Investment Incentives Act promoted development of Colon Free Trade Zone.

1960s
A series of financial scandals, frequently involving "paper" or "pirate" banks damaged Panama's reputation as a financial center.

1970
Cabinet Decree No. 238 (the Banking Reform Law) eliminated "paper" or "pirate banks" and established a National Banking Commission, in lieu of a central bank, to supervise and license banking activities. Registered banks reduced to 20 from 247. Assets of the banking system totalled $857 million.

1974
Law No. 93 created a three category bank license system: "general," "international," and "representative" statuses. Class 1 registrations, 30; Class 2 registrations, 13; Class 3, 3.

1975
Assets of the banking system totalled $10.3 billion, 1,200% growth from 1970.

1976
Reinsurance (Companies) Law No. 72 stimulated significant reinsurance business activity. Volume totalled $20 million in first year.

1979
U.S. began gradual restoration of the Canal Zone to Panama.

1980
Assets of the banking system totalled $23.1 billion (125% growth from 1975), with external liabilities of $18.7 billion.

1981
114 banks registered: U.S., 17; Panama, 12; Colombia, 8; Japan, 7; Venezuela, 7; international, 5. By category, 60 with "General Licenses," 43 with "International Licenses," and 11 with "Representation Licenses."

1982
The Latin American debt crisis which largely began with Mexico in August and thereafter broadened to South America, reversed the growth of international banking in Panama.

1983

124 foreign banks registered; at end-June assets were $46.3 billion and deposits $38.3 billion; banking sector 9% of GNP, directly employing 8,000 people. Collapse of Banco Ultramar, a private Venezuelan bank (assets of $86.4 million at end-June 1982), causing large losses to foreign and Panamian depositers. Libra Bank and Toronto Dominion withdrew from Panama.

BANKS IN PANAMA

Principal Foreign Banks with General Licence

Banco de Bogota, SA (Colombia): Calle 36, No 7-47, Apdo 8653, Panama 5; tel. 64-6000; telex 3140; f. 1967.

Banco do Brasil: Edif. Interesco, planta baja, Calle Elvira Mendez 10, Apdo 9696, Panama 4; tel. 63-6566; telex 3223; f. 1973.

Banco Cafetero, SA (Colombia): Avda Manual Maria Icaza No 18, Campo Alegre, Apdo 384, Panama 9a; tel. 64-6777; f. 1966.

Banco de Colombia, SA: Edif. San Martin, Calle 30A, No 6-38, Apdo 6836, Panama 1; tel. 27-3633; f. 1964.

Banco del Comercio, SA (Colombia): Calle 13 No 8-52, Apdo 4599, Panama 5; tel. 63-5655; f. 1967.

Banco Exterior, SA (spain): Edif. Banco Exterior, Avda Balboa y Calles 42 y 43, Apdo 8673, Panama 5; tel. 27-1122; telex 3126; f. 1967.

Banco Fiduciaro de Panama, SA (France): Via Espana 200, Apdo 1774, Panama 1; tel. 63-6600; f. 1048.

Banco de Iberoamerica, SA (Multinational): Edif. Banco de Iberameica, Calles 50 y 53, Apdo 6553, Panama 5; tel. 63-5366; telex 2972; f. 1975.

Banco Latinamericano de Exportaciones, SA (BLADEX) (Multinational): Apdo 6-1497, El Dorado, Panama City; tel. 63-6766; telex 2356; f. 1979.

Banco de Santander y Panama, SA (Spain): Via Espana y Calle 55, Apdo 484, Panama 9A; tel. 63-6262; f. 1967.

Banco Sudameris Internacional, SA: Avda Balboa y Calle 41, Apdo 1846, Panama 9A; tel. 27-2777; telex 2289; f. 1966.

Banco Union, CA (Vanezuela): Torre Banco Union, Calle Samuel Lewis, Apdo 'A', Panama 5; tel. 64-9133; telex 2761; f. 1974.

Bank of America National Trust and Savings Association (USA): Calle 50 esq. con Calle 53; Apdo 7882, Panama 5; tel. 63-5500; f. 1964.

The Bank of Tokyo Ltd (Japan): Via Espana y Calle Aquilino de la Guardia, Apdo 1313, Panama 1; tel. 63-6777; telex 2779; f. 1973.

Bankers' Trust Co (USA): Avda Manuel Maria Icaza No 7a, Campo Alegre, Apdo 6360, Panama 5; tel. 64-8666; telex 2471; f. 1975.

The Chase Manhattan Bank, NA (USA): Via Espana 120, Apda 9A-76, Panama 9A; tel. 63-5800; telex 2067; f. 1915.

Citibank NA (USA): Via Espana 124, Apdo 555, Panama 9A; tel. 64-4044; telex 2129; f. 1904.

Credit Suisse (Switzerland): Apdo 6-4396, Estafeta El Dorado, Panama City; tel. 63-7333; telex 3612; f. 1982.

The Dai Ichi Kangyo Bank Ltd (Japan): Edif. Plaza Internacional, Via Espana, Apdo 2637, Panama 9A; tel. 69-6111; telex 2030; f. 1979.

Deutsch-Suderamerikanische Bank AG (Fed. Repub. of Germany): Torre Banco Germanico, Calle 50 y Calle 55 Este, Apdo 5400, Panama 5; tel. 63-5055; telex 2420; f. 1971.

The First National Bank of Boston (USA): Via Espana No 122, Apdo 5368, Panama 5; tel. 64-2244; telex 3232; f. 1973.

First National Bank of Chicago (USA): Edif. La Rotonda, Via Espana y Calle Venezuela, Apdo 8051, Panama 7; tel. 64-3533; f. 1970.

Lloyds Bank International Ltd (Bahamas): Avda Manuel Maria Icaza 8, Campo Alegre, Apdo 8522, Panama 5; tel. 63-6277; telex 2696; f. 1966.

Marine Midland Bank, NA (USA): Ava Balboa y Calle 39, Apdo 5322, Panama 5; tel. 27-1933; telex 3172; f. 1973.

Merrill Lynch International Bank Inc (USA): Calle Aquilino de la Guardia 18 y Calle 52, Apdo 5000, Panama 5; tel. 63-5066; telex 2167; f. 1977.

The Mitsui Bank Ltd (Japan): Avda Ricardo Arango y Calle 53 Este, Urb. Obarrio, Apdo 8-028, Panama 8; tel. 23-9903; telex 3322; f. 1980.

The Sanwa Bank Ltd (Japan): Edif. Vallarino, planta baja, Calle Elvira Mendez y Calle 52, Apdo 6-2494, Panama City; tel. 64-6633; telex 2503; f. 1980.

The Sumitomo Bank Ltd (Japan): Edif. Plaza Internacional, planta baja, Via Espana, Apdo 8-029, Panama City; tel. 69-3344; telex 2027; f. 1980.

Swiss Bank Corpn (Overseas), SA: Calle Elvira Mendez Nos 6 y 10, Apdo 3370, Panama 4; tel. 63-7181; f. 1971.

Union Bank of Switzerland (Panama) Inc.: Edif. UBS, Calles 50 y 56, Urb. Obarrio, Apdo 6792, Panama 5; tel. 63-9766; f. 1975.

Principal Foreign Banks with International License

American Express International Banking Corp (USA): Calle Manuel Maria Icaza No 14, Apdo 10709, Panama 4; tel. 63-5522; telex 2776; f. 1971.

Banco de la Nacion Argentina: Avda Federico Boyd y Calle 51, Apdo 6-3298, El Dorado, Panama City; tel. 69-4666; telex 3440; f. 1977.

The Bank of Tokyo (Panama) SA (Japan): Via Espana y Calle Aquilino de la Guardia, Apdo 1313, Panama 1; tel. 63-6777; telex 2779.

Banque Nationale de Paris (France): Edif. Omanco 4, Via Espana 200, Apdo 201, Panama 1; tel. 64-8555; telex 328-2266; f. 1973.

Credit Lyonnais (France): Edif. Interseco 7, Calle Elvira Mendez No 10, Apdo 1778, Panama 9A; tel. 63-6522; telex 2231; f. 1978.

Interamerican Bank Corpn, SA (Bahamas): Edif. Embajador, Calle 50 y Elvira Mendez, Apdo 8625, Panama 5; tel. 64-7003; f. 1974.

Mitsubishi Trust and Banking Corpn (Japan): Edif. Banco Nacional, Torre B, mezzanine, Apdo 3651, Balboa Panama City; tel. 64-1400; telex 2507; f. 1981.

Financiers and Finaglers

Emerging Eurocurrency centers attract finaglers as well as financiers, well exemplified in the case of Panama by a young, aggressive German banker. Noting that any company name in Panama could be registered as a Panamanian citizen's private property as long as it did not contain the word "bank" or "trust", he saw an entrepreneurial opportunity. (Probably because he had heard of a similar scam that took place previously in Monaco.)

Using a Panamanian woman as his front, who happened to

work for the Panamanian branch of a large French bank, he registered as "her" property the names of many of the leading banks and brokerage houses in the world that did not contain the word "bank" or "trust"; e.g., Credito Italiano or Societe Generale. When those banks decided to set up a branch in Panama, they found that they first had to buy back their name for a rather stiff price.

When the manager of one French bank tried to register its name and found it already registered as the property of the employee of another French bank, he was furious. Wasting no time, he called up his fellow manager at the French bank where the woman was employed and demanded that she be dismissed.

However, she was pregnant at the time and about the worst violation of Panamanian labor laws is to fire a pregnant woman. So the saga went on, involving a generous severance package, etc., and ultimately, the entrepreneurial German banker was pressured by the governmental authorities to return the "names", his hopes of easy money dashed by the commitment of the Panamanian authorities to receptiveness for foreign banks.

NETHERLANDS ANTILLES (CURACAO)

Constitutionally on a level of equality with the Netherlands homeland, the Netherlands Antilles consists of two groups of islands: (1) Curacao, Aruba, and Bonaire, are near the South American coast; while (2) St. Eustatius, Saba, and the southern part of St. Maarten are southeast of Puerto Rico. The total area is 385 square miles, with Curacao, whose capital is Willemstad, accounting for 171 square miles; population is 250,000. Major industries are refining Venezuelan crude, tourism, electronics, shipbuilding, and financial services.

American companies have for some time tapped the Eurobond market via finance subsidiaries set up in the Antilles (U.S. corporate Eurobond issuance totalled $6 billion in 1983). Such subsidiaries have created 4,000 jobs and generate $157 million in annual tax revenues.

Also, a considerable offshore deposit market has developed which peaked in 1982 at $8.10 billion. Using the offshore banking unit vehicle, Curacao benefits from tax exemptions and proximity to South America.

Chronology of Development

1955
The U.S.-Netherlands tax treaty, signed in 1948 and providing for zero withholding taxation of interest payments to each other's residents, was extended to the Netherlands Antilles, providing the legal infrastructure for the development of a Eurobond market there.

1982
OBU liabilities peak at $8.10 billion.

1984
The Netherlands Antilles began negotiating a new tax treaty with the United States.

The repeal of the 30% U.S. withholding tax levied on interest paid to foreign investors in U.S. debt securities threatens Antilles role as Eurobond center.

The U.S. Internal Revenue Service promulgated two revenue rulings, reducing the Netherlands Antilles' role in the Eurobond market, henceforth considering interest payments to an Antilles *conduit* to be a direct payment to the ultimate beneficiary country, making applicable the tax treaty status of that country, but *grandfathering* existing Eurobonds.

1986
The new U.S.-Antilles tax treaty was signed on August 8, preventing treaty benefits to third-country persons (that is, *treaty shopping*). Expected to go to the U.S. Senate for ratification in 1987.

BERMUDA (HAMILTON)

The Bermudas are a group of about 150 coral islands, of which 20 are inhabited, primarily Bermuda Island with the capital, Hamilton. They lie 600 miles east of North Carolina, and are just one-hour's flying time (773 miles) from New York. Their area totals 21 square miles and the population is 56,000, including 1,600 in Hamilton and 1,650 in St. George's.

History. Bermuda was discovered by Juan de Bermudez in 1543, and has been inhabited (by the British) since 1609. It became a self-governing British colony in 1620, and thus the oldest such colony. A

Exhibit 3-12
NETHERLANDS ANTILLES OBU* LIABILITIES 1976-85
(billions of U.S. dollars)

Year	OBU Liabilities
1976	1.15
1977	1.71
1978	2.10
1979	3.36
1980	4.50
1981	7.21
1982	8.10
1983	7.44
1984	5.33
1985	4.92

*Offshore Banking Unit
Source: International Monetary Fund, *International Financial Statistics Yearbook, 1986.*

British Crown Colony since 1684, Bermuda was granted internal self-government in 1968. The late 1960s and early 1970s were marred by racial rioting (61% of the population is black) and the murders of several officials, including the Governor, which required the use of air-lifted British troops. However, calm has been completely restored, with the moderate United Bermuda Party (UBP), in the wake of the October 1985 election, firmly in control (31 Assembly seats versus 7 for the radical Progressive Labour Party (PLP), 2 for the radical Progressive Labour Party or (PLP), and 2 for the centrist National Liberal Party (NLP)).

Economy. The economy is largely based on tourism (30% of GDP), with close to 600,000 visitors (80% from the U.S.) each year. Next in importance is international business (20% of GDP), including registration of overseas companies (6,000), 1,200 insurance companies (which will be reduced by the U.S. Tax Reform Act of 1986, which is leading to the repatriation of American insurance companies), ship registration (flag of convenience for UK/Commonwealth ships—over 900,000 tons/176 vessels registered for global sixth place) and international banking. The three banks, with assets totaling $5.2 billion at end-1985, are the $2.7 billion Bank of Bermuda (1,120 employees, including 127 abroad), the $2.2 billion N.T. Butterfield & Son Ltd (the oldest bank, with 761 employees), and the $300 million Bermuda Commercial Bank (32.4% owned by Barclays), with 95 employees. American military facilities (including a listening post for Soviet submarines), in return for which the US runs the civilian airport, also contribute to the economy.

Advantages as a Banking Center

1. A government strategy committed to international financial services, (in part, to offset a structural merchandise trade deficit of nearly $400 million annually), but with a policy of only encouraging operations by reputable, offshore corporations.

2. Political and social stability fostered by a moderate governing party, political status as a Crown Colony, and an $18,000 per capita GDP.

3. A favorable location, close to the United States, and sharing the New York-Miami time zone; complemented by a year-round temperate climate.

4. Ample availability of first-class office space, hotels, and related facilities.

5. Exemplary transportation and communication facilities, including frequent flights to North America and London. (Service by American Airlines, British Airways, Eastern Airlines, Pan Am, Air Florida and Delta.)

6. An especially well developed infrastructure of legal, accounting and related services; supplemented by various financial activities, including the world's first computer-based futures exchange (Futex), with *gold* and *ocean freight* contracts. (Middle management and senior office personnel can be brought in if not obtainable locally.)

7. Favorable taxation and financial regulation, including the absence income taxes, withholding taxes, corporate taxes, taxes on profits and most other forms of direct taxation. (Import duties, averaging 22%, are the major revenue source.)

8. Competent financial administration by the Bermuda Monetary Authority, established in 1969.

9. More aggressive strategies and increased emphasis on innovation in new and existing services to counter intensified banking competition from Cayman, Bahamas and Barbados.

Unfavorable Factors as a Banking Center

1. A high cost of living.
2. Burdensome indirect taxes.
3. A prohibition on the granting of additional bank charters.
4. Some political dissidence, centered in the PLP, and focused on movement toward independence (opposed by most Bermudians because of the tangible advantages of the UK link), "Bermudianization" of the economy and more equitable wealth sharing.

Chronology of Development

1968
Bermuda granted internal self-government.

1973
The Governor (Sir Richard Sharples) was assassinated.

1977
Serious rioting in the wake of the execution of two blacks for a series of murders, including Governor Sharples; British troops restore order.

1978
Deposits of BIS reporting commercial banks in Bermuda total $1.6 billion at end-June.

1979
Deposits of BIS reporting commercial banks total $2.0 billion at end-June.

1980
Deposits of BIS reporting commercial banks total $2.3 billion at end-June.

1982
At end-year, Eurocurrency deposits at Bermuda's three banks totaled approximately $3.9 billion, largely U.S. dollars.

1983
At end-year, Eurocurrency deposits totaled approximately $4.2 billion.

1984
At end-year, Eurocurrency deposits totaled approximately $4.6 billion.

1985
At end-year, Eurocurrency deposits totaled approximately $4.7 billion.

BARBADOS (BRIDGETOWN)

Barbados is the most easterly of the Caribbean islands and has an area of 166 square miles. The population totals 253,000, while its capital of Bridgetown has a population of 8,000.

History. Barbados was discovered by the British in 1627 and was a British colony until 30 November 1966 when it became independent within the Commonwealth. Political power has alternated between the Barbados Labour Party (BLP), led by such leaders as Sir Grantley Adams, his son Tom Adams, and Bernard St. John, and the Democratic Labour Party (DLP) led by Errol Barrow, the current Prime Minister.

Economy. The Barbados economy is largely based on light manufacturing (electronic components), tourism (368,000 visitors in 1984) and agriculture (especially sugar, but low sugar prices have reduced its role to 2.8% of GDP).

Complementing those activities, offshore banking and insurance, and company and ship registration are growing. Reinforcing offshore banking is a long international banking tradition with a Barclays presence since 1837 and a Royal Bank of Canada presence since 1911. Moreover, Barbados is the location of the Caribbean Development Bank, an associate institution of CARICOM, in which the UK, Canada, Venezuela, Colombia and Caribbean countries have an equity interest.

Advantages for Offshore Banking

1. A strong government commitment fostered by a structural merchandise trade deficit and high unemployment (around 18%).
2. A well-educated (97% literacy), English-speaking labor force, reflecting numerous educational institutions, including a campus of the University of the West Indies.
3. Higher social stability resulted from a highly Anglicized culture (whence its sobriquet, "Little England"), a relatively high $4,240 per capita GNP, and economic assistance via the Lomé Convention (of the EEC), and the Caribbean Basin Initiative (CBI) of the United States.

4. High political stability, with its vigorous two-party system based on the Westminister model, functioning within the context of representative government since 1639, (including the second oldest Parliament outside England), and full internal self-government since 1961 (preceded by local ministerial government in 1954).

5. A judicial system based on British law with final appeal with the Judicial Committee of the Privy Council, in London.

6. A well developed infrastructure, including energy, air and seaport facilities, and outstanding international telecommunications. There are daily direct flights to North America and Europe, fully automatic telephone service with direct dialing to most of the world and all of North America, automatic telex and facsimile transfer links worldwide, and reliable telecommunications links providing high-speed electronic data transmission.

7. A moderate structural current account deficit due to a large structural *services* surplus and a small structural *unilateral transfers* surplus offsetting most of the structural *merchandise trade* deficit. The latter is narrowed by domestic oil production of over 700,000 barrels per year, which fulfills half of local consumption.

8. A stable local currency (the Barbados dollar, pegged since 1975 at BDS$2.00 = US$1.00), and a highly regarded central bank (established in 1972).

9. The local availability of a half-dozen major international accounting firms including Coopers & Lybrand, Deloitte Haskins & Sells, Pannell Kerr Forster, Peat Marwick Mitchell & Co., Price Waterhouse, and Touche Ross International; also, the availability of internationally-oriented law firms.

10. Ample first class hotels, restaurants and office space in a highly appealing environment.

11. A moderate annual offshore banking fee of $12,500.

12. A moderate, *regressive* tax rate of only 2.5% on the first $5 million of net income ranging downward in half percent steps to just 1% on net income over $15 million.

13. A moderate paid-up capital requirement of $125,000 for a resident bank and $500,000 for a non-resident bank.

14. Moderate required additions to an offshore bank's paid-up capital,

being 25% of its profits to a reserve account annually until the reserve is equal to the paid-up capital.

15. Bank confidentiality has been provided for in that no statement, return, or information is required by the Central Bank of Barbados with respect to the affairs of any particular customer of a licensee (other than the names of any Barbadian resident customers).

16. Interest paid to non-residents is exempt from withholding tax, as are dividends on shares or securities of non-residents that are held by offshore banks.

17. Offshore banks are exempt from interest rate regulation under the Rate of Interest Act.

18. Dividends, royalties, interest, foreign securities, funds, gains, and assets generated or managed by an offshore bank are automatically exempt from the provisions of the Exchange Control Act.

19. Up to 35% of the remuneration of specially qualified foreign employees relocated to Barbados in connection with an offshore bank's activities may be paid free of Barbadian income tax and in any foreign currency (i.e., only 65% is subject to income tax).

Disadvantages for Offshore Banking

1. A general lack of international recognition, which largely focuses on Nassau and Cayman.

2. A relatively remote location, offset by proximity (300 miles) to northern South America (Venezuela) and a similar time zone to New York and Miami (an hour later in winter).

3. Stamp duty at a flat rate of $5 is chargeable on a variety of documents executed by offshore banks in the course of carrying on their business.

Profile of Eurobanking in Barbados

Pursuant to Barbados' extensive legislation promoting Eurobanking, four institutions have obtained offshore banking licenses. They include the Royal Bank Trust Company Barbados Ltd. (1981), Barclays Bank International (1981), Barbados Bank and Trust (1981), owned by R.S. Kirby, a local firm of chartered (certified) accountants, and Intel (1985), a large California computer firm that formerly had a Barbados factory employing 1,000 people.

However, it is estimated that over 90% of the Eurodeposits are in

Royal Bank, and these deposits are wholly from Royal Bank branches elsewhere rather than the market. Royal Bank would accept "outside deposits," but the combination of a $1 million deposit minimum and unaggressive rates has thus far precluded "outside deposits." In particular, Royal Bank books its Latin American loans in Barbados and then funds them from the Royal branch network, with the choice of Barbados reflecting the tax advantages of the Canada-Barbados double-taxation treaty.

Barclays with a far lower $25,000 deposit minimum and more competitive rates does receive Eurodeposits from the market. However, a policy of being quite selective about its customers (requiring references and refusing cash deposits), reflecting central bank policy, has moderated its Eurodeposit growth.

The other offshore banks are very limited in size, reflecting in one case, an accomodation for an accounting firm's customers and, in the other, a convenience for a multinational corporation. However, the other foreign banks operating domestially in Barbados are potential candidates for offshore licenses, including the Bank of Nova Scotia, the Canadian Imperial Bank of Commerce, the Caribbean Commerce Bank and the Bank of Credit and Commercial International.

ANTIGUA (ST. JOHN'S)

The nation of Antigua comprises the islands of Antigua (108 square miles, 75,000 population) and Barbuda (68 square miles, 1,200 population), with the capital at St. John's (35,000 population). A weak economy, based largely on tourism, with a structural merchandise trade deficit, has spurred the Antiguan Government to develop exportable services. Its special advantages in doing so include a central Caribbean location (New York time zone in summer and one hour later in winter), an English-speaking population, the privileges accorded Antigua by the Lome Convention (EEC assistance to the former colonies of its member nations) and the Caribbean Basin Initiative (CBI—U.S. assistance program to co-operating Caribbean nations), and the presence of four foreign banks conducting domestic banking (Swiss American Banking Corporation, Barclays, Royal Bank of Canada, and the Bank of Nova Scotia).

Reflecting its emphasis on exportable services, Antigua has for many years registered offshore corporations; currently, over 400 companies are so registered. Moreover, it recently passed its Maritime Law for ship registration, (that is "flags of convenience") in the style of

Panama and Liberia. Eurobanking naturally complements such offshore activities.

Just as Bank of America served as the catalytic force in the establishment of the Asia Dollar Market in Singapore, the Swiss American Banking Corporation played the same role in Antigua. In fact, its Miami lawyers helped draft the enabling legislation, the International Banking Center Act (IBCA).

To create a viable Eurocenter, the IBCA exempted Eurodeposits from domestic reserve requirements, exempted Eurobanks from the domestic 40% corporation tax (there is no individual income tax), exempted depositors in such banks from the tax on nonresident interest income, and made the banks subject only to an annual $5,000 license fee, a $10 million capital requirement (the latter relatively stiff requirement was to keep out "fly-by-nighters," and, at any rate, was reduced to $1 million in 1984), and the submission of a short annual statement to the Inspector-General of Banks.

The four banks with offshore licenses include the Swiss American Bank (a wholly owned subsidiary of the Inter-Maritime Bank of Geneva, which bought out the previous American share of troubled Home State Financial Services, led by the recently convicted William C. Warner, a key figure in the ESM Government Securities scandal), another foreign bank already in Antigua and two completely offshore banks(the goverment regards the identity of the licensees as a confidential matter). Current Eurocurrency deposits at Swiss American, the leading Eurobank, total the equivalent of $13 million, and include U.S. dollars (75%), pounds (reflecting the "colonial links" and customers in the UK and Channel Islands), Swiss francs (reflecting the parent company and the customer deposits it generates), Deutschemarks, yen, and guilders. Deposit growth projections of the bank call for $250 million in deposits by 1991.

Despite the optimistic forecasts of Swiss American Bank, the growth of Antiguan Eurobanking is restrained by several factors. These include investor aversion to small Eurocenters and lack of recognition of Antigua as an international banking center. The latter reflects, in part, the low profile approach of the government, which does not want a "media blitz" until memories of a recent "banking" scandal there are largely forgotten. The latter involved individuals who registered their Antiguan offshore companies' names as banks (such as Bank of the Caribbean), even though they were *not* banks (which until a few years ago was legal) and then sought to fraudulently obtain deposits abroad in Miami, Tokyo, and Hawaii.

Eurocurrency Market Centers

ASIA

- Tokyo
- Singapore
- Hong Kong
- Manila
- Taipei
- Vanuatu
- Bahrain

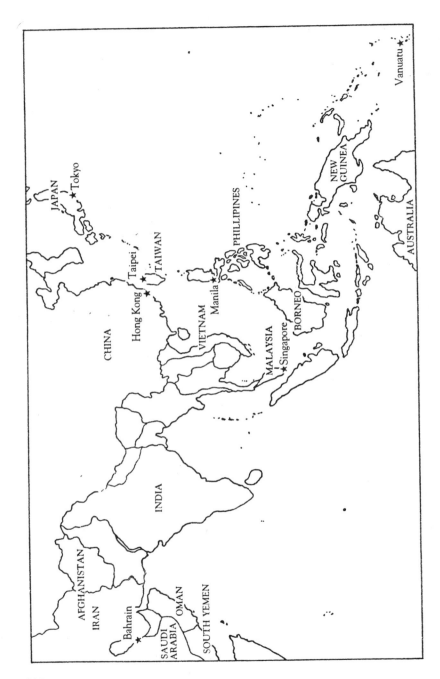

TOKYO

Tokyo, despite the inconvenience of its time zone and its traditionally conservative financial regulation, ranks as the world's third leading international banking center, reflecting the might of its economy (second largest GNP in the Free World), its international commercial ties substantially through its trading companies, and the global dominance of its big banks. In 1985, its international banking activity represented 10.4% of the market, well up from 8.6% in 1983 and 9.1% in 1984.

In 1985, Eurocurrency loans to nonresidents totalled $109 billion, while such loans to residents totalled $147 billion. With yen denominated loans to nonresidents totalling $57 billion, its international banking activity totalled $313 billion.

Tokyo's rapidly ascending international finance role reflects the enormous size of its banking institutions and their need for foreign customers (owing to Japan's massive current account surpluses—$87 billion in 1986—and sluggish domestic economy), as well as the substantial ongoing deregulation of the Japanese financial markets. While traditionally tight administrative control was exercised by the Bank of Japan and the Ministry of Finance, especially to minimize the internationalization of the yen(which would strengthen the yen, and thereby reduce Japan's export competitiveness), since 1978 there has been intensifying deregulation of the Japanese markets. The latter accelerated in 1985 due to foreign pressure (especially from the United States) to appreciate the yen in order to moderate Japan's mammoth and expanding merchandise trade surpluses.

The enormity of Japan's banks is reflected in the fact that the world's biggest banking company is Japanese, as are four of the top five. The biggest is the $207 billion Dai-Ichi Kangyo (which means "number one" bank, a reference to its being the oldest Japanese bank) while the world's third through fifth banking companies are Fuji Bank ($143 billion), Sumitomo Bank ($136 billion), and Mitsubishi Bank ($133 billion). Moreover, 13 of the largest 25 banking concerns are Japanese, including the $99-billion Sanwa Bank, the $83-billion Norinchukin Bank, the $81-billion Industrial Bank of Japan, the $76-billion Tokai Bank, the $73-billion Mitsui Bank Ltd., the $66-billion Bank of Tokyo Ltd., and the $65-billion Long-Term Credit Bank of Japan Ltd. In particular, Japan's banks have become the world's largest international lenders. In 1985, they had $650 billion in such loans outstanding, compared with $600 billion for American institutions.

Complementing the Japanese banks, foreign banks are well represented in the Tokyo market. Ongoing deregulation has expanded the scope of their activities, including even underwriting.

The Tokyo Offshore Market

The most recent development was the 1 December 1986 inauguration of offshore banking in Tokyo, known as the *Japan offshore market* or JOM. It represents the culmination of detailed work by a bankers committee headed by Mr. Yusuke Kashiwagi, chairman of the Bank of Tokyo and formerly a top bureaucrat. As of opening day, 181 banks had the necessary authorization and outstanding assets totaled $52.2 billion—although $45.4 billion represented amounts passed along from other accounts, leaving a net for new assets of $6.8 billion. One month later, on December 31st, total assets stood at $93.7 billion, slightly ahead of Ministry of Finance (MOF) forcasts. A level of over $110 billion was estimated for January 31st.

Through the creation of the offshore market, Japanese financial officials hope to spur around-the-clock trading, promote growth of Tokyo as an international financial center, and increase the use of the yen as an international currency. The particular incentives of the market are that participating Japanese banks are allowed to make loans to foreigners and take deposits from them without many of the taxes and other regulations that apply to domestic banking. However, the government will apply local taxes, corporate taxes and stamp taxes, making the tax rate for the Tokyo offshore market considerably higher than applied to similar markets elsewhere (e.g., IBFs).

Moreover, there are stricter regulations in a number of areas to prevent leakages of offshore activity into the domestic markets, with the concomitant high paperwork expense, etc. For example, offshore entities must pay reserves on the receipt of domestic funds, which is not required of the American IBFs. Also, they are not permitted to deal in securities or certificates of deposit.

SINGAPORE: THE ASIA DOLLAR MARKET

Singapore, the "Zurich of Asia," is composed of a major island off the tip of Malayan Peninsula and forty adjacent islets, 85 miles north of the equator at the southern tip of the peninsular Malaysia. It comprises

226 square miles and has a population of 2,310,000 (Chinese, 76%; Malay, 15%; Indian, 7%). Founded in 1819 by Sir Stamford Raffles (British East India Company), it formed part of the Straits Settlements, and assumed full internal government in 1959. It joined the Federation of Malaysia in 1963, but withdrew in 1965, and proclaimed itself a republic. Major industries include oil refining, shipping (world's second largest port), shipbuilding, electronics, textiles, truck farming, fishing, tourism, and financial services. Moreover, Singapore's "financial supermarket" was significantly englarged in September 1984, with the opening of the Singapore International Monetary Exchange (SIMEX), which has a mutual offset link with the International Monetary Market (IMM) of the Chicago Mercantile Exchange. Its stock exchange, the third largest in Asia after Tokyo and Hong Kong, has 317 listed companies with a market capitalization of $35.3 billion.

Advantages as a Banking Center

1. A strategic location in the fast growing Asia region.

2. A strong, well established banking center (1860, first UK bank; 1902, Citibank), with substantial foreign exchange volume.

3. A skilled, multilingual, low-cost labor force.

4. Traditional regional entrepôt, reflected in Singapore being the world's second largest port.

5. Political stability under Prime Minister Lee (Kuan Yew) and the People's Action Party.

6. A rapidly growing (10%/year) economy (current GNP: $12.5 billion) with a structural merchandise trade deficit (currently around $6 billion) that made mandatory the development of the *services* sector.

7. A natural time advantage involving overlaps with Sydney (3 hours ahead), Tokyo (1.5 hours ahead), Hong Kong (0.5 hours ahead), London (6.5 hours behind, opening at 3:30 p.m. Singapore time).

8. Good international communications and transport.

9. A strong local currency (U.S. $1:S$2.16) and ample foreign exchange reserves.

10. The historical antipathy of Hong Kong to providing the necessary tax environment and of Japan (Tokyo) to providing the necessary regulatory environment (liberalized foreign exchange controls).

11. A legal system based on the British judicial system.
12. Pleasant living conditions for executives.

The *Asia dollar market* might more appropriately be called the "Asia currency market" since officially fourteen currencies are traded, importantly the Deutschemark and the yen, but dollar transactions represent more than 90% of the market. Funds are received from the central banks, other government agencies, local corporations, multinational corporations, and wealthy individuals. They are traded interbank via seven local, internationally linked brokers, and ultimately lent out in the form of internationally syndicated, medium-term credits to borrowers in the Asia-Pacific region. Singapore interest rates (SIBOR) are generally fractionally higher (⅛%) than LIBOR, though harmonized after the London opening — with the relative thinness of the market, Asia-based loan demand, and consortium rollovers affecting rates.

Negative factors include a high income tax rate applicable to the offshore banking center (40%) and conservative guidance by the Monetary Authority of Singapore; also the $37,500 annual license fee is above that of other nearby centers.

Chronology of Development

1968
Advised by J.D. van Oenen of Bank of America (Singapore branch), whose bank saw an opportunity for dollar deposit gathering in Asia as a consequence of the dollars generated by the U.S. presence in Viet Nam, the Monetary Authority of Singapore (MAS) in August removed the 40% *withholding tax on nonresident interest earnings*. In October, the Bank of America (a relative newcomer to Singapore in the 1950s) became the first Asian currency unit (ACU), inaugurating the Asian dollar market. ACU deposits grew to $30 million by end-1968, with the market being a net *depositor* into the Euro-dollar market.

1969
ACU deposits quadrupled to $170 million by end-1969.

1970
ACU licenses grew to twelve, while ACU deposits doubled to $390 million by end-1970; an Asia dollar CD market was attempted, but the absence of a viable secondary market doomed it to failure.

1971

ACU deposits grew 172% to $1.06 billion by end-1971; the rapid expansion of Asian lending (Indonesia, Thailand, etc.) resulted in the market being transformed into a net *borrower* from the London Euro-dollar market. Several London-based Eurocurrency brokers established offices in Singapore. The Asian dollar bond market was initiated with a $10 million issue for Development Bank of Singapore (government guarantee).

1972

ACU deposits tripled to $2.98 billion by end-1972, with 25 ACUs in the market; the MAS abolished the 20% *minimum liquidity ratio* for ACUs, while also relaxing regulations to enable local corporations/individuals to borrow from ACUs and maintain accounts in external currencies. Also, the *stamp duty* of 10% on negotiable CDs was abolished. Two Asia dollar bond issues totalled $51 million.

1973

ACU deposits doubled to $6.28 billion by end 1973. The corporate tax on offshore loan income was reduced to 10% from 40%. The 40% withholding tax on nonresident bond interest was cancelled. Stamp duties on offshore loan agreements were waived. Three Asia dollar bond issues totalled $70 million.

1974

ACU deposits doubled to $12.6 billion by end-1974 among sixty ACUs. No issuance of Asia dollar bonds due to high inflation weakening the capital sector. Foreign exchange daily turnover of $350 million/day.

1975

ACU deposits remained at $12.6 billion as of end-1975, but ACUs increased by 6 to 66. Three Asia dollar bond issues totalled $47 million.

1976

ACU deposit grew 50% to $17.35 billion by end-1976. Exemption from *estate duty* was provided for nonresident ACU deposits. Asia dollar bond market showed maturity with ten issues aggregating $280 million, including a $60-million Development Bank of Singapore issue.

1977

ACU deposits grew 15% to $19.7 billion by end-1977 among 69 ACUs. A concessionary income tax rate of 10% was hereinafter applied to all offshore income derived from Asia dollar operations (excluding foreign exchange profits/transactions with domestic banking units). Over $340 million equivalent in Asia bonds issued, including four *convertibles,* three *floating rate notes,* and two *depository receipts.*

1978
ACU deposits grew 37% to $27.0 billion by end-1978, among the 80 ACUs. MAS reauthorized the initiation of a CD market involving three instruments (standard one-month to one-year maturity; fixed rate, medium term of five years; floating rate medium term; with $50,000 minimum). First Boston (Asia) and Merrill Lynch International (Asia) provided the initial secondary market. CD volume grew to $850 million by end-year. Exchange controls were completely lifted. The Gold Exchange of Singapore, was established (November 22), with futures contracts in 100-ounce and kilobar lots. In the Asia dollar bond market, there were 12 issues totalling $403 million.

1979
ACU deposits grew 41% to $38.2 billion by end-1979, with the number of ACUs increasing by seven to 108 as of March 1980. While the net size of the market increased by 38% to $32.2 billion (approximately 5% of the Eurocurrency market), Asia dollar CD volume, due to Japanese bank issuance, totalled $1.89 billion at end 1979, with 45% being fixed rate issues and 55% being floating rate issues. In the Asia dollar bond market, there were 8 issues totalling $358 million.

1980
ACU deposits grew 43% to $54.4 billion (4% of Europool) by end-1980 among 115 ACUs at end-1980; CD volume was $2.35 billion ($1.58 billion in floating rate CDs). Foreign exchange turnover was $4.7 billion/day. Use of ACUs by Singapore banks to swap out of Singapore dollars to avoid the 26% reserve requirement drew MAS criticism. The outstanding value of Euro-dollar CDs stood at $2.5 billion, an increase of $600 million. Lack of liquidity hampered growth of the Asia dollar bond market, with 18 issues amounting to $659 million.

1981
ACU deposits grew 58% to $85.8 billion by end 1981, with the number of ACUs increasing by 17 to 137 during the financial year ending March 1982 (new countries represented included Denmark, New Zealand, and Saudi Arabia). The *net* size of the market, calculated by deducting inter-ACU transactions, grew similarly by 58% to reach $70.3 billion (about 6% of the Eurocurrency market). The outstanding value of Euro-

dollar CDs stood at $3 billion, an increase of $700 million over the year. In the Asia dollar bond market, there were 22 issues valued at a record $1.2 billion.

1982

ACU deposits grew 20% to $103.3 billion by end-1982, while the net size of the market grew a like 20% to $84 billion. The outstanding value of the Euro-dollar CDs was unchanged at $3.1 billion; in the Asia dollar bond market there were 16 issues valued at $1.0 billion.

1983

ACU deposits rose 8.4% to $112.0 billion by end-1983, a moderate rate but one that exceeded overall Eurocurrency market growth (5%). Negotiable CD issuance slowed slightly; in the Asian dollar bond market there were 16 issues valued at $1.1 billion.

1984

The Singapore International Monetary Exchange (SIMEX), linked to the Chicago IMM (a "mutual offset arrangement"), was created on September 7 by issuing a new charter to the Gold Exchange. Initial futures contracts, identical to IMM ones, included the three-month Euro-dollar time deposit, the Japanese yen, the Deutschemark, and gold.
ACU deposits grew 15% to $128 billion by end-1984. In the Asian dollar bond market, there were 8 issues valued at $804 million. In December, ACUs were authorized to issue negotiable CDs denominated in Japanese yen.

1985

In 1985.1, ACU deposits grew at a slightly faster rate of 16%; while by the end of the year, they totalled $155 billion, among 180 ACUs (124 of which are operated by commercial banks, 54 by merchant banks, one by Elders PICA (PTE) Ltd., a private investment company, and one by ASEAN Finance Corporation, Ltd., a multibank-owned financial institution).
All of the financial markets were hurt in December by the collapse in December of blue-chip Pan-Electric Industries, a refrigerator maker and ship salvager, that went bankrupt owing more than $200 million. The result was a three-day closure of the Singapore and Kuala Lampur Exchanges, which are closely linked with about 60% of share issues mutually traded. Additionally, nearly half of Singapore's 25 brokerages were caught up in the crisis and five went bankrupt.

FOREIGN BANKS IN SINGAPORE

Full Commercial Banks

Algemene Bank Nederland NV (Netherlands): 18 Church St, Singapore 0104; tel. 915511; telex 24396.

Ban Hin Lee Bank Bhd (Malaysia): 15 Phillip St, 01-00 to 03-00, Singapore 0104; tel. 5337022; telex 24191.

Bangkok Bank Ltd (Thailand): Bangkok Bank Bldg, 180 Cecil Street, Singapore 0106; tel. 2219400; telex 21359.

Bank of America NT & SA (USA): Clifford Centre, 24 Raffles Place, Singapore 0104; tel. 91322; telex 24570.

Bank of Canton Ltd (Hong Kong): 6 Raffles Quay, 01-01 Denmark House, Singapore 0104; tel. 2243363; telex 23832.

Bank of China (People's Republic of China): 4 Battery Rd, 01-00 Bank of China Bldg, Singapore 0104; tel. 2242411; telex 23046.

Bank of East Asia Ltd (Hong Kong): 137 Market St, 01-00 Bank of East Asia Bldg, Singapore 0104; tel. 2241334; telex 21049.

Bank of India: 108 Robinson Rd, GMG Bldg, Singapore 0106; tel. 222011; telex 21482.

Bank Negara Indonesia 1946: 3 Malacca St, Singapore 0104; tel. 5334375; telex 21749.

Bank of Tokyo Ltd (Japan): 16 Raffles Quay, 01-06 Hong Leong Bldg, Singapore 0104; tel. 2208111; telex 25363.

Banque Indosuez (France): 3 Shenton Way, 01-05 Shenton House, Singapore 0106; tel. 2207111; telex 24435.

Chase Manhattan Bank NA (USA): 50 Raffles Place, 01-01 Shell Tower, Singapore 0104; tel. 224288; telex 21370.

Citibank NA (USA): 5 Shenton Way, 06-00 UIC Bldg, Singapore 0104; tel. 224611; telex 24584.

First National Bank of Chicago (USA): 76 Shenton Way, 01-02 Ong Bldg, Singapore 0207; tel. 2239933; telex 24530.

Hongkong and Shanghai Banking Corpn (Hong Kong): 10 Collyer Quay, 01-01 Ocean Bldg, Singapore 0104; tel. 2243377; telex 21259.

Indian Bank: 59 Robinson Rd, 00-01 Public Insurance Bldg, Singapore 0106; tel. 2229433; telex 34885.

Indian Overseas Bank: 5 Shenton Way, 01-01 UIC Bldg, Singapore 0106; tel. 2251100; telex 23098.

Kwangtung (Guandong) Provincial Bank (People's Republic of China): 60 Cecil St, 01-00 KPB Bldg, Singapore 0104; tel. 2239622; telex 26166.

Malayan Banking Bhd: 2 Battery Rd, 01-00 Malayan Bank Chambers, Singapore 0104; tel. 224466; telex 21036.

Malayan United Bank Bhd: 133 Cecil St, 01-01 and 02-01 Keck Seng Tower, Singapore 0106; tel. 2251366; telex 25416.

The Mitsui Bank Ltd (Japan): 16 Raffles Quay, 01-04 Hong Leong Bldg, Singapore 0104; tel. 2209761; telex 21319.

Standard Chartered Bank PLC (UK): 6 Battery Rd, Chartered Bank Bldg, Singapore 0104; tel. 2258888; telex 24290.

United Commercial Bank (India): 140-142 Robinson Rd, 01-00 Chow House, Singapore 0106; tel. 2239722; telex 21682.

United Malayan Banking Corpn Bhd: UMBC Bldg, 22 Malacca St, Singapore 0104; tel. 915122; telex 21769.

Restricted Banks

American Express International Banking Corpn (USA): 4 Shenton Way, 01-04/05 Shing Kwan House, Singapore 0106; tel. 2202311; telex 21172.

Banca Commerciale Italiana (Italy): 36 Robinson Rd, 03-01 and 04-01 City House, Singapore 0106; tel. 2201333; telex 24545.

Bank of Communications Co Ltd (Taiwan): 4 Shenton Way, 08-01 Sing Kwan House, Singapore 0106; tel. 2239197; telex 22662.

Banque Nationale de Paris (France): 20 Collyer Quay, 01-01 Tung Centre, Singapore 0104; tel. 2240211; telex 24315.

Bayerische Landesbank Gironzentrale (Federal Republic of Germany): 30 Robinson Rd, 05-00 to 07-00 Tuan Sing Towers, Singapore 0104; tel. 2226925; telex 21445.

Credit Suisse (Switzerland): 6 Battery Rd, 27-01/02 Standard Chartered Bank Bldg, Singapore 0104; tel. 2203233; telex 24650.

Dresdner Bank AG (Federal Republic of Germany): 20 Collyer Quay, 22-00 Tung Centre, Singapore 0104; tel. 2202122; telex 29366.

European Asian Bank (Federal Republic of Germany): 50 Raffles Place, Shell Tower, Singapore 0104; tel. 2244677; telex 21189.

First Commercial Bank (Taiwan): 5 Shenton Way, 01-02 UIC Bldg, Singapore 0106; tel. 2215755; telex 24693.

Habib Bank Ltd (Pakistan): 141 Market St, 01/02-00 Harapan Bldg, Singapore 0104; tel. 2230388; telex 21679.

Korea Exchange Bank (Republic of Korea): 2 Finlayson Green, 01-00 Asia Insurance Bldg, Singapore 0104; tel. 2241633; telex 21956.

Mitsubishi Bank Ltd (Japan): 20 Collyer Quay, 01-02 Tung Centre, Singapore 0104; tel. 2205666; telex 21913.

Moscow Norodny Bank Ltd (UK): 50 Robinson Rd, MNB Bldg, Singapore 0106; tel. 2209422; telex 21726.

The Sumitomo Bank Ltd (Japan): 6 Shenton Way, 01-09 DBS Bldg, Singapore 0106; tel. 2201611; telex 21656.

Principal Offshore Banks

Amsterdam-Rotterdam Bank NV (Netherlands): 65 Chulia St, 36-01 OCBC Centre, Singapore 0104; tel. 5336101; telex 26778.

Australia and New Zealand Banking Group Ltd (Australia): 10 Collyer Quay, 08-01 Ocean Bldg, Singapore 0104; tel. 918355; telex 23336.

Banco do Brasil SA: 65 Chulia St, 38-01 OCBC Centre, Singapore 0104; tel. 911177; telex 25668.

Banco Urquijo Union SA (Spain): 65 Chulia St, 28-01 OCBC Centre, Singapore 0104; tel. 916244; telex 33308.

Bank Bumiputra Malaysia Bhd (Malaysia): 150 Cecil St, 03-01/02 Wing On Life Bldg, Singapore 0106; tel. 2222133; telex 34837.

Bank of Montreal (Canada): 5 Shenton Way, 28-01 UIC Bldg, Singapore 0106; tel. 2201688; telex 20660.

The Bank of New York (USA): 10 Collyer Quay, 24-02 Ocean Bldg, Singapore 0104; tel. 914522; telex 23055.

Bank of New Zealand: 65 Chulia St, 31-05 OCBC Centre, Singapore 0104; tel. 915744; telex 22149.

Bank of Nova Scotia (Canada): 10 Collyer Quay, 27-01/03 Ocean Bldg, Singapore 0104; tel. 918688; telex 22177.

Bankers Trust Co. (USA): 50 Raffles Place, 26-01/06 Shell Tower, Singapore 0104; tel. 2229191; telex 28626.

Banque Paribas (France): 16 Raffles Quay, 39-01 Hong Leong Bldg, Singapore 0104; tel. 2226144; telex 20414.

Barclays Bank PLC (UK): 50 Raffles Place, 23-01 Shell Tower, Singapore 0104; tel. 2248555; telex 26877.

Canadian Imperial Bank of Commerce: 105 Cecil St, 09-02/04 The Octagon, Singapore 0104; tel. 2208228; telex 24005.

Chemical Bank (USA): 50 Raffles Place, 32-01 Shell Tower, Singapore 0104; tel. 2204944; telex 23022.

The Commercial Bank of Korea Ltd (Republic of Korea): 5 Shenton Way, 17-03 UIC Bldg, Singapore 0106; tel. 2235855; telex 20465.

Continental Illinois National Bank and Trust Co of Chicago (USA): 65 Chulia St, 21-01 OCBC Centre, Singapore 0104; tel. 916466; telex 22030.

Credit Lyonnais (France): 65 Chulia St, 37-01 OCBC Centre, Singapore 0104; tel. 919477; telex 27225.

The Dai-Ichi Kangyo Bank Ltd (Japan): 16 Raffles Place, 01-02 Hong Leong Bldg, Singapore 0104; tel. 2206355; telex 21622.

Den Danske Bank af 1871 A/S (Denmark): 50 Raffles Place, 24-01 Shell Tower, Singapore 01014; tel. 2241277;telex 28030.

Deutsche Genossenschaftsbank (Federal Republic of Germany): 30 Robinson Rd, 12-01 Tuan Sing Towers, Singapore 0104; tel. 2239711; telex 34559.

First City National Bank of Houston (USA): 10 Collyer Quay, 25-07 Ocean Bldg, Singapore 0104; tel. 2256088; telex 23689.

Fuji Bank Ltd (Japan): 6 Shenton Way, 07-01 DBS Bldg, Singapore 0106; tel. 2202033; telex 24610.

Grindleys Bank PLC (UK): 6 Shenton Way, 23-01 DBS Bldg, Singapore 0106; tel. 2208177; telex 21796.

The Gulf Bank KSC (Kuwait): 21 Collyer Quay, 17-01 Hongkong Bank Bldg, Singapore 0104; tel. 2243722; telex 22437.

Gulf International Bank BSC (Bahrain): 50 Raffles Place, 01-01/06 Shell Tower, Singapore 0104; tel. 224877; telex 28096.

The Industrial Bank of Japan Ltd: 6 Shenton Way, 14-01 DBS Bldg, Singapore 0106; tel. 2200133; telex 21880.

InterFirst Bank Dallas, NA (USA): 5 Shenton Way, 11-01 UIC Bldg, Singapore 0106; tel. 2205755; telex 21961.

Irving Trust Co (USA): 10 Collyer Quay, 14-01 Ocean Bldg, Singapore 0104; tel. 919188; telex 23213.

Kuwait Asia Bank EC (Bahrain): 10 Collyer Quay, 27-04 Ocean Bldg, Singapore 0104; tel. 2237477; telex 28451.

Lloyds Bank International Ltd (UK): 50 Raffles Place, 18-01 Shell Tower, Singapore 0104; tel. 2203222; telex 23023.

The Long-Term Credit Bank of Japan Ltd: 65 Chulia St, 32-01 OCBC Centre, Singapore 0104; tel. 919633; telex 23813.

Manufacturers Hanover Trust Co (USA): 50 Raffles Place, 33-00 Shell Tower, Singapore 0104; tel. 2245500; telex 25805.

Marine Midland Bank, NA (USA): 4 Shenton Way, 16-01/12 Shing Kwan House, Singapore 0106; tel. 2205444; telex 24480.

Midland Bank PLC (UK): 65 Chulia St, 48-01 OCBC Centre, Singapore 0104; tel. 916188; telex 20035.

The Mitsui Trust & Banking Co Ltd (Japan): 6 Shenton Way, 16-03 DBS Bldg, Singapore 0106; tel. 2208553; telex 23796.

Morgan Guaranty Trust Co of New York (USA): 6 Shenton Way, 30-01 DBS Bldg, Singapore 0106; tel. 2208144; telex 24460.

National Westminster Bank PLC (UK): 50 Raffles Place, 05-01/06 Shell Tower, Singapore 0104; tel. 2204144; telex 28491.

Den Norske Creditbank (Norway): 1 Shenton Way, 22-01 Robina House, Singapore 0106; tel. 2206144; telex 21737.

Philippine National Bank: 180 Cecil St, 10-01/02 Bangkok Bank Bldg, Singapore 0106; tel. 2228261; telex 21792.

Rainier National Bank (USA): 79 Robinson Rd, 21-03 CPF Bldg, Singapore 0106; tel. 2220877; telex 23669.

Republic Bank Dallas, NA (USA): 3 Shenton Way; 14-08 Shenton House, Singapore 0106; tel. 2238222; telex 20681.

The Royal Bank of Canada (Asia) Ltd: 140 Cecil St, 16-01 PIL Bldg, Singapore 0104; tel. 2245711; telex 26935.

Saitama Bank Ltd (Japan) Raffles Quay, 38-01 Hong Leong Bldg. Singapore 0104; tel. 2207075; telex 20371.

Sanwa Bank Ltd (Japan): 50 Raffles Place, 25-01 Shell Tower, Singapore 0104; tel. 2249822; telex 28573.

Security Pacific Bank (USA): 6 Raffles Quay, 08-00 Denmark House, Singapore 0104; tel. 2257022; telex 33731.

Societe Generale (France): 30 Robinson Rd, 01-01 Tuan Sing Towers, Singapore 0104; tel. 2227122; telex 27213.

State Bank of India: 6 Shenton Way, 10-01 DBS Bldg, Singapore 0106; tel. 2222033; telex 23184.

The Sumitomo Trust & Banking Co Ltd (Japan): 5 Shenton Way, 02-16 UIC Bldg, Singapore 0106; tel. 2249055; telex 20717.

Swiss Bank Corpn: 10 Collyer Quay, 15-03 Ocean Bldg, Singapore 0104; tel. 5337904; telex 24140.

The Taiyo Kobe Bank Ltd (Japan): 50 Raffles Place, 24-02 Shell Tower, Singapore 0104; tel. 2227871; telex 23058.

The Tokai Bank Ltd (Japan): 24 Raffles Place, 22-01/06 Clifford Centre, Singapore 0104; tel. 918222; telex 21848.

The Toronto-Dominion Bank (Canada): 65 Chulia St, 24-01 OCBC Centre, Singapore 0104; tel. 2205322; telex 24020.

Union Bank of Switzerland: 50 Raffles Place, 38-01 Shell Tower, Singapore 0104; tel. 2203622; telex 21549.

Westpac Banking Corpn (Australia): 65 Chulia St, 42-01 OCBC Centre, Singapore 0104; tel. 5338673; telex 21763.

HONG KONG

The 403-square mile British colony is on the southern coast of China, about 80 miles southeast of Canton and surrounded by the Chinese province of Guandong. It includes Hong Kong proper, an island of about 30 square miles, many other islands, and Kowloon and the New Territories on the mainland. The New Territories (370 square miles, including a number of small islands) are held under a 99-year lease from China, which expires in 1997.

The population totals five million, with the capital city of Victoria on the island of Hong Kong having 1.2 million people. Government administration is by a Crown-appointed governor, advised by executive and legislative councils.

Hong Kong is a major center for shipping, commerce, and industry, situated as it is at a crossroad of world trade. Light industries, particularly machinery, textiles, and clothing, are important. Tourism is important and growing. Agriculture and fishing are intensively practiced, but much food must be imported, mostly from China. Finally, of course, banking is especially important in the world's self-proclaimed "third largest international financial center."

Exhibit 3-13
NUMBER OF SYNDICATED LOANS TO ASIAN COUNTRIES ARRANGED BY FINANCIAL INSTITUTIONS IN HONG KONG, SINGAPORE, AND OTHER MARKETS

Year	Hong Kong	Singapore	Total (including others)
1974	7	1	43
1975	18	0	51
1976	24	4	60
1977	28	5	60
1978	36	15	61
1979	53	10	106

Source: Bank of Japan, *Development of International Markets in Hong Kong and Singapore.*

During the past 15 years, Hong Kong developed as a major Eurocurrency *placement* center, complementing Singapore's role as a *deposit-taker* (reflecting the division of labor, at end-1981, Hong Kong's liabilities to Singapore of $43 billion greatly exceeded its claims of $28 billion). Its evolution into a major Eurocurrency center has been due to general geographical, historical, and infrastructural factors, as well as special incentives resulting from specific regulatory/tax changes. With the removal in 1983 of the 15% withholding tax on interest from foreign currency deposits, it is now positioned to compete vigorously with Singapore as a deposit- taker as well. Exemplifying Hong Kong's "placement power," its leading bank, the Hong Kong and Shanghai Banking Corporation ranked sixth in the world during January-June 1983 as a lead manager of syndicated loans (39 loans totalling $797 million, 2.3% of the global total).

Favorable Factors as a Banking Center

1. Hong Kong's long-established role as a trade center, with trade volume growing at an average rate of 21% for the past ten years.

2. Hong Kong's role as an intermediator of trade and finance with China.

3. The Government's strongly advocated "no intervention" policy; that is, a laissez-faire business climate.

4. Low tax rates with no hidden taxes and actual tax rates not exceeding nominal ones; for example, a graduated tax on foreign residents with only a 25% maximum rate (40% in Singapore), and an overall corporate tax rate of 16.5% (40% in Singapore, aside from ACUs, which are taxed at only 10%).

5. A well-developed, mature financial market infrastructure, including professional backup services such as law and accounting firms; in particular, superior legal resources for loan syndication endeavors.

6. Good understanding of English among many of the local banking employees.

7. Slight time difference between Hong Kong and Japan, China, and Korea (in addition, it is possible to make same-day transactions with London and Bahrain).

8. The relative social stability of the society.

9. Proximity to the fast growing countries of northern Asia (Korea, Taiwan, and Hong Kong itself), facilitating transactions and information gathering on conditions and creditworthiness.

10. Excellent air transport (including its own airline, Cathay Air Pacific) and communications facilities.

11. The absence of *capital adequacy ratio requirements* which has been particularly important for Japanese banks in Hong kong.

Special Incentives. The incentives resulting from specific regulatory/tax changes include:

1. The abolition of foreign exchange controls, so that the offshore and domestic markets have in effect merged and funds flow freely between them.

2. The removal of the 15% withholding tax on interest from foreign currency deposits.

Negative Factors

1. A negative factor is the future of the status of Hong Kong when the English lease from China for the New Territories expires in 1997, and the entire area reverts to Chinese control. However, China has

indicated that for a period of 50 years (until 2047), Hong Kong's capitalist economy and much of its day-to-day administration will be preserved after China regains overall sovereignty.

2. A series of banking scandals in recent years.

Chronology of Development

1973
Termination of foreign exchange controls, effectively merging the domestic and offshore markets.

1980
The Hong Kong Commodities Exchange added "gold futures" trading.

The Australian-owned, Cayman-based Nugan Hand Bank failed, leading to DTC (deposit taking company) reforms.

1981
The offshore market was estimated at $40 billion.

1982
The banking sector included 125 banks and 367 deposit-taking companies.

Removal of the 15% withholding tax on nonresident interest earnings from *foreign currency* deposits.

The real estate market "collapsed" early in the year, followed by the sharp simultaneous deterioration of the Hong Kong stock market, and the Hong Kong dollar in October 1982, in the wake of Prime Minister Thatcher's unsuccessful trip to China.

The HK$650-million (U.S. $97-million) DTC Dollar Credit failed, hurting Hong Kong's financial reputation as well as that of the Banking Commissioner's Office.

Formal negotiations commenced between the United Kingdom and the People's Republic of China with respect to Hong Kong's future.

1983
The Hong Kong dollar was pegged to the U.S. dollar at 7.8/$ in mid-October.

The 10% withholding tax on interest derived from *Hong Kong dollar deposits* was abolished in mid-October.

The offshore market was estimated at $72 billion.

The Hang Lung Bank, a DTC has to be rescued by the government — it was involved with Dollar Credit and Financing in a US$21-billion check-kiting scheme.

The colony's most venerable company, Jardine, Matheson & Co., announced it would relocate to Bermuda.

1984

The able Robert Fell, formerly chief executive of the London Stock Exchange, was appointed by Financial Secretary Sir John Bremridge to replace the limited Colin Martin as Banking Commissioner.

1985

A new, unified Hong Kong Stock Exchange opened, replacing the Kam Ngan, Far East, and Hong Kong-Kowloon Exchanges.

The Overseas Trust Bank and its subsidiary Hong Kong Industrial and Commercial Bank collapsed; Wing On Bank foundered and was rescued by Hang Seng Bank; the foundering HK $5.5 billion Ka Wah Bank was set to be taken over by CITIC.

1986

Hong Kong had 143 fully licensed commercial banks, with 1,547 branches (1/3,370 inhabitants), 35 licensed deposit-taking companies or DTCs equivalent to merchant banks) and a further 280 that are registered. Fianancial Secretary Bremridge hopes to get legislative agreement on a wide set of financial reforms such as capital adequacy ratio requirements.

1997

The British 99-year lease on the New Territories expires and Hong Kong reverts to the People's Republic of China.

2047

China's guarantee of the capitalist structure of the Hong Kong economy expires.

MANILA

The Philippines consists of 7,000 islands, but the two largest, Luzon in the north and Mindanao in the south, account for 66% of the country's area. Manila, on the island of Luzon, has a population of 1.7 million out of a total national population of 55 million.

Exhibit 3-14
**OFFSHORE BANKING UNITS IN THE PHILIPPINES
FINANCIAL HIGHLIGHTS—1985 GROSS REVENUE**
(in millions of U.S. dollars)

	Rank	Amount
American Express Intl. Banking Corp.	11	11.2
Bankers Trust	13	10.9
Bank of Boston	21	3.6
Bank of California	15	10.45
Bank of Credit & Commerce Intl (Overseas) Ltd.	18	9.05
Bank of Nova Scotia	1	34.15
Bank of Tokyo	5	24.8
Banque Indosuez	14	10.85
Bank Nationale de Paris	6	23.85
Barclays Bank	2	30.6
Chase Manhattan Bank	3	29.15
Chemical Bank	4	29.5
Credit Lyonnais	7	22.05
European Asian Bank	20	4.65
First Interstate Bank of California	9	14.05
First National Bank of Chicago	10	13.6
International Bank of Singapore	N.A	N.A.
Korea Exchange Bank	17	8.85
Manufacturers Hanover Trust Bank	N.A	N.A.
Midland Bank	16	9.2
Rainier National Bank	19	5.4
Security Pacific National Bank	12	10.9
Societe Generale	8	12.45
TOTAL		329.25

N.A. = Not available.
Source: SEC Business Day publication of the Top 1000 Corporations in the Philippines in 1985.

	1985 NEAT* (in millions of U.S. dollars)		1985 Total Assets (in millions of U.S. dollars)	
Rank	Amount		Rank	Amount
11	1.0		14	116.5
19	(8.4)		15	110.45
15	0.45		18	62.15
10	1.05		19	79.75
7	1.6		16	106.95
6	1.9		3	299.55
3	2.7		4	251.35
13	0.8		17	98.6
4	2.2		5	233.6
1	4.75		6	212.95
18	(7.55)		1	336.55
2	2.95		2	305.9
5	1.9		7	212.75
21	Neg.		21	52.8
17	(2.2)		9	156.2
8	1.15		10	155.7
N.A.	N.A.		N.A.	N.A.
20	Neg.		11	132.1
N.A.	N.A.		N.A.	N.A.
14	0.7		12	127.25
12	0.85		20	54.6
9	1.1		13	126.35
16	(0.75)		8	199.75
	6.2			3,431.8

() = Losses
Neg. = Negative
*NEAT = Net Earnings After Taxes

History. The Philippines were a Spanish colony from the 16th century until the Spanish-American War of 1898, when it became an American possession. On 4 July, 1946 it became independent. Ferdinand Marcos, elected in 1965 and 1969, ruled by decree from 1972 to 1986, when he was forced from office by the election of Corazon "Cory" Acquino, wife of the assassinated opposition leader.

Economy. The Philippine economy is largely based on agriculture (coconuts, sugar, timber), minerals (copper, gold, nickel) and light manufacturing. Tourism is important (nearly 1 million visitors annually), as are U.S. military payments (related to the Clark Air Base and the Subic Bay Naval Station), and the remittances of Filipinos working abroad (Middle East, USA). The government promotes the growth of the financial services industry.

Advantages as a Banking Center

1. A strategic location in the fast growing Asia region.
2. A government committed to promoting international financial services due, in part, to a large structural merchandise trade deficit, a poor price outlook for the commodities on which the Philippines traditionally depends, high unemployment and a surging birth rate (2.5% per year).
3. Ample office space and hotel facilities.
4. A good transportation and communications infrastructure.
5. The availability of an educated, English-speaking, low-cost labor force.
6. Favorable taxation and regulation of the "offshore banking units" (OBUs).
7. Moderate *offshore banking* requirements including: (a) an annual fee to the central bank of $20,000; (b) the holding, at all times, of at least $1 million of net office funds either in deposits with the central bank or investments in primary issue of foreign currency-denominated securities of the Philippine Government; (c) minimum deposits that are the equivalent of $50,000; (d) no Philippine peso deposits; (e) residents as well as non-residents may be clients.

Unfavorable Factors as a Banking Center

1. Recurrent balance of payments problems, and therefore the threat of foreign exchange controls, due to the merchandise trade deficit, the $26 billion external debt and capital flight. (In 1983, foreign currency deposits at bank branches, but *not* OBUs, were frozen, tarnishing Manila's image as a banking center. Moreover, Citibank-Manila's freezing of international bank deposits in fulfillment of the government order led Wells Fargo to sue it to recover its $2 million in deposits (two $1-million deposits with Citibank in June 1983, with maturities December 9th and 12th of the same year). The suit has dragged on, with Citibank arguing that deposit freezing at Citibank-Manila involved an "act of state" which under U.S. law would exempt Citibank-New York from legel responsibility, while Wells Fargo argues that frozen deposits at Citibank-Manila can and should be paid from other Citibank branches. Weakening Wells Fargo's case is the fact that Citibank-Manila paid a premium of 75 basis points for Manila deposits, indicating a possibility of risk.

2. Political and social unrest caused by widespread poverty and corruption, and exemplified by the Communist (the New People's Army) and Muslim (Moro National Liberation Front) insurrections, the opposition activities of Marcos loyalists and the uncertain role of the military (especially the "reformist" officers).

Chronology of Development

1976
Legislation authorizing offshore banking units took effect in September.
1982
As of mid-year, 25 OBUs were functioning.
1983
In October, the government due to balance of payments problems, imposed foreign exchange controls. Citibank responded by freezing $600 million is deposits placed in its local branch by international banks. OBU deposits were *not* affected. Subsequently, Philippine authorities unfroze almost half of the funds. Wells Fargo sued Citibank to recover its $2 million in matured deposits.

1985

Four foreign banks (notably Citibank), the only ones so permitted, were operating full service branches, while over 30 OBUs (notably from the US, UK, France and Japan) were functioning.

As of December, OBU assets totaled $3.432 billion, with the largest being the Chase OBU ($336 million) and the Chemical OBU ($306 million).

1986

As of December, Wells Fargo's suit against Citibank was still continuing.

FOREIGN AND OFFSHORE BANKS IN THE PHILIPPINES

Foreign Banks

Bank of America NT & SA (USA): Donna Narcissa Bldg, 8747 Paseo de Roxas, Makati, Metro Manila; tel. (02) 8157000; telex 45445.

Hongkong and Shanghai Banking Corpn. (Hong Kong): Cibeles Bldg, 6780 ayala Ave, Makati, Metro Manila; tel. (02) 877031; telex 22361.

Standard Chartered Bank (UK): 7901 Makati, Metro Manila; tel. (02) 855091; telex 22434.

Major Offshore Banks

American Express International Banking Corpn (USA): 3rd Floor, Corinthian Plaza, Paseo de Roxas, Makati, Metro Manila; tel. (02) 8186731; telex 45340.

The Bank of California, NA (USA): 2nd Floor, Corinthian Plaza, Paseo de Roxas, Makait, Metro Manila; tel. (02) 863056; telex 5556.

Bank of Credit and Commerce International (Overseas) Ltd (Cayman Islands): Pioneer House, 108 Paseo de Roxas, Makati, Metro Manila; tel. (02) 8170031; telex 66096.

Bank of Hawaii (USA): 19th Floor, Corinthian Plaza, Lepanto Bldg, Makati Manila; tel. (02) 8185374.

Bank of Nova Scotia (Canada): 3rd Floor, Corinthian Plaza, Paseo de Roxas, Makati, Metro Manila; tel. (02) 881931.

Bankers Trust Co (USA): 3rd Floor, Corinthian Plaza, Paseo de Roxas, Makati, Metro Manila; tel. (02) 881931.

Banque Indosuez (France): Ground Floor, Corinthian Plaza, Paseo de Roxas, Makati, Metro Manila; tel. (02) 889341.

Banque Nationale de Paris (France): 7th Floor, Citibank Center, 8741 Paseo de Roxas, Makati, Metro Manila; tel. (02) 8158821; telex 63707.

Barclays Bank PLC (UK): 4th Floor, Dolmar Gold Tower Bldg, 107 Alvarado St, Legaspi Village, Makati, Metro Manila; tel. (02) 8159291; telex 63768.

The Chase Manhattan Bank, NA (USA): 18th Floor, Filinvest Financial Centre Bldg, Paseo de Roxas, Makati, Metro Manila; tel. (02) 8189851.

Chemical Bank (USA): 19th Floor, Filinvest Financial Centre Bldg, 8753 Paseo de Roxas, Makati, Metro Manila; tel. (02) 8181011.

Credit Lyonnais (France): 14th Floor, China Bank Bldg, Paseo de Roxas, Makati, Metro Manila; tel. 8171616; telex 63896.

Crocker National Bank (USA): 9th Floor, Metrobank Plaza Bldg, Den. Gil J. Puyat Ave Ext., Makati, Metro Manila; tel. (02) 8188391.

European Asian Bank (Federal Republic of Germany): 17th Floor, Filinvest Financial Center Bldg, 8753 Paseo de Roxas, Makati, POB 2286, Metro Manila; tel. (02) 8173961; telex 63625.

First Interstate Bank of California (USA): 12th Floor, Metrobank Plaza, Sen. Gil J. Puyat Ave Ext., Makati, Metro Manila; tel. (02) 865966.

First National Bank of Boston (USA): 8th Floor, SOLIDBANK Bldg, 777 Paseo de Roxas, Makati, Metro Manila; tel. (02) 8170458.

First National Bank of Chicago (USA): 17th Floor, SOLIDBANK Bldg, 777 Paseo de Roxas, Makati, Metro Manila; tel. (02) 8183511.

International Bank of Singapore: Ground Floor, Bancom II Bldg, cnr Rada and Legaspi Sts, Legaspi Village, Makati, Metro Manilla; tel. (02) 8179951.

Korea Exchange Bank (Republic of Korea): 19th Floor, Metrobank Plaza, Sen. Gil J. Puyat Ave Ext., Makati, Metro Manila; tel. (02) 8172178.

Manufacturers Hanover Trust Co. (USA): 4th Floor, Corinthian Plaza, Paseo de Roxas, Makati, Metro Manila; tel. (02) 8159901. ,

Philadelphia National Bank (USA): Rm 807, Pacific Bank Bldg, 6776
Ayala Ave, Makati, Metro Manila; tel. (02) 817458.

Rainier National Bank (USA): llth Floor, Metrobank Plaza, Sen. Gil J.
Puyat Ave Ext., Makati, Metro Manila; tel. (02) 853891.

Societe Generale (France): Ground Floor, Corinthian Plaza, Paseo de
Roxas, Makati, Metro Manila; tel. (02) 856061; telex 404.

Wells Fargo Bank, NA (USA): 3rd Floor, GF & Partners Bldg, 139 H.
de la Costa St, Salcedo Village, Makati, Metro Manila; tel. (02)
8173228.

TAIPEI

Taipei, with 2.3 million people, is the largest city of Taiwan, also
referred to as the Republic of China (ROC),Nationalist China, and
Formosa ("beautiful" in Portuguese). Taiwan itself, including the 14 islands of the Taiwan group and 63 in the Peughu group (Pescadores), as
well as Quemoy and Matsu, composes 13,971 square miles (244 miles x
89 miles) and has 18 million people.

Controlled successively by the Dutch (1641-1662), the Ming
(1662-1683) and Manchu dynasties (1683-1895), it became a Japanese
colony in 1895 as a consequence of the Sino-Japanese War, until 1945.
In 1949, the Chiang-Kai-shek forces made it the seat of Nationalist
China. In 1971, it lost general diplomatic recognition in the wake of
the PRC replacing the ROC in the UN, while in 1979 U.S. recognition
was withdrawn and in 1980, it lost its membership in the IMF and
World Bank.

The government is dominated by the Kuomintang or Nationalist
Party. Generalissimo Chaing Kai-Shek, elected to five presidential
terms, died in 1975 at 87. His elder son, Chiang Ching-Kuo, is the current president.

Taiwan's impressive economic performance, based on a 30% savings rate, is characterized by high growth (1985: + 8.8%), low inflation (1985: + 0.2%), large trade (1985: + $10.6 billion), and cur-
rent account surpluses (1985: + $12.6 billion) and by equitable and
improving distribution of income. Its total 1982 trade of $39.7 billion
almost equalled the PRC's $40.1 billion. International reserves total a
mammoth $50 billion.

Taiwan has 25 domestic banks (14 government-controlled) and 29
foreign banks from the U.S., Canada, the UK, France, Germany,

Netherlands, Japan, Singapore, Thailand, and the Philippines. The initial three foreign banks were Dai-Ichi Kangyo (1959), Citibank, and Bank of America (both 1965).

In 1983, the Taiwan government, promulgated the *Offshore Banking Act* to: (1) stimulate the sluggish domestic banking sector; (2) improve funding of domestic companies; (3) encourage increased foreign corporate investment; (4) promote more sophisticated money markets, and foreign exchange and cash management systems; (5) promote more effective trade services through large branch networks; (6) enhance international recognition of the Republic of China. OBU licensing began in June 1984.

Taiwan gives significant privileges to "offshore banking units" (OBUs) including:

1. Exemption from deposit reserve requirements.
2. Exemption of deposits and loans from all interest rate controls.
3. Exemption of OBU income from the business income tax (aside from interest earnings on loans to ROC borrowers).
4. Exemption of OBUs from business tax on their gross business receipts (otherwise 5.4%).
5. Exemption of OBU instruments from stamp duties.
6. Exemption of OBUs from withholding tax requirements on interest paid on their deposits.
7. Exemption from "loan loss reserve requirements" (aside from home country regulations).
8. Exemption from the obligation to disclose any information to third parties (aside from court orders/law).
9. Telecommunications equipment and information systems may be imported upon application on a case-by-case basis.
10. Exemption of the OBUs from the bank requirement of newspaper publication of their balance sheet.

Advantages as a Banking Center

1. Strategic location in the fast growing Pacific Basin.
2. A strong domestic economy generating repeated balance of payments surpluses (cf. Singapore and Hong Kong's large trade deficits).

3. Political and social stability fostered by fast growing incomes amidst narrowing differences, the accelerating Taiwanization of the ruling KMT Party, including the Taiwenese vice president who is the heir apparent to President Chiang, and growing tolerance and support for the political opposition which did quite well in the December 1986 elections.

4. A skilled workforce.

5. Low-cost environment.

6. The extensive domestic and foreign banking presence (45 banks in total).

7. The strong support of the government.

8. An income tax rate applicable to taxable aspects of the OBUs of only 15% (Hong Kong, 18.5%; Singapore, 40%).

9. An annual license fee of only U.S. $20,000 (Hong Kong, $28,777; Singapore, $37,500).

Unfavorable Factors as a Banking Center

1. Aversion to Taiwan provoked by the two-China question, given the disparate size of the two claimants.

2. The growing aversion to the smaller Eurocenters due to the increasing preceptions of deposit risk provoked by the global debt crisis.

3. Overregulation of domestic banks due to a spate of frauds a few years ago.

4. Poor local accounting practices which makes it difficult to assess domestic risks.

5. Tight foreign exchange controls.

6. Inadequate hotel and office space.

7. Some restrictions on international information flows.

Exhibit 3-15
TAIWAN ENCOURAGES GROWTH OF EUROBANKING
by Eugene Sarver

Taiwan's strong, export-oriented economy has received yet another boost with the initiation this past summer of Eurobanking in Taipei.

Building upon an international financial atmosphere fostered by the presence of 31 major foreign banks, Taipei's domestic and foreign banks can now set

Exhibit 3-15 (con't)

up special units to engage in Eurobanking free of almost all business taxes, reserve requirements, withholding taxes, stamp duties, interest rate controls and even loan loss reserve requirements.

Taiwan laid the basis for joining the $2.3 trillion Eurocurrency market when its Parliament passed the "Offshore Banking Act" on December 12, 1983, and the government promulgated the related rules on April 20, 1984.

The Eurobanking entities, labeled "Offshore Banking Units," were authorized from May 21, with the initial $20,000¹ annual license taken by the International Commercial Bank of China on June 5th. Soon thereafter, it was joined by the First Commercial Bank and three other major Taiwan banks.

The Ministry of Finance and the central bank are promoting Eurobanking in Taipei for a variety of reasons including stimulating the sluggish domestic banking sector, improved funding of domestic companies and encouraging increased foreign corporate investment in Taiwan.

Also, the government expects the OBU sector to promote more sophisticated money markets and foreign exchange and cash management systems, and lead to more efficient trade services through large branch networks.

Finally, the government hopes an active Euromarket in Taipei will enhance international recognition of Taiwan, which has been eroding since it lost its U.N. seat to the People's Republic in 1971, exacerbated by the termination of U.S. recognition in 1979 and IMF/World Bank membership in 1980.

Taipei enjoys many key advantages conducive to Euromarket growth, but also suffers some significant handicaps.

Favorable factors include a strategic location in the fast growing Pacific Basin, a strong domestic economy generating repeated balance of payments surpluses, political and social stability fostered by fast growing incomes and narrowing differences, and a skilled workforce. Additional positive factors include Taipei's low-cost environment, the extensive domestic and foreign banking presence (45 banks in total) and the strong support of the government.

Offsetting the favorable factors are a variety of negatives, including the aversion to Taiwan provoked by the two-China question, given the disparate size of the two claimants. Of late, the PRC has been making significant overtures to Taiwan to become an autonomous PRC region à la Hong Kong (and even keep its armed forces), but such invitations continue to be rejected.

Of greater significance is the growing aversion to the smaller Eurocenters due to the increasing perceptions of deposit risk provoked by the global debt crisis. Centers such as Bahrain and Panama have been losing deposits, as Eurodepositors increasingly prefer New York and London, despite the lower yield such secure centers offer.

Finally, additional burdens weighing on the young Eurocurrency center include overregulation of domestic banks due to a spate of frauds a few years ago, poor local accounting practices that makes it difficult to assess domestic risks, tight foreign exchange controls, inadequate hotel and office space and some restrictions on international information flows.

Taiwan's late entry into Eurobanking is not completely bad timing. Coming soon after the freezing of local foreign currency deposits in Manila, tarnishing that competitor Eurobanking center, and the beginning of capital flight from a Hong Kong destined to revert to the PRC in 1997, is definitely a plus for the new Taipei center.

Also, compared to the other two

Exhibit 3-15 (con't)

"little dragons of Asia" involved in Eurobanking, Singapore and Hong Kong, Taiwan has several competitive advantages. It is the only "dragon" with a trade surplus, and its $50 billion GNP is twice that of Hong Kong and four times that of Singapore.

Also, its income tax rate applicable to the taxable aspects of the OBUs is 15 percent compared to 18.5 percent in Hong Kong and 40 percent in Singapore. Moreover, its US$20,000 annual license fee is below that of Hong Kong ($28,777) and Singapore ($37,500).

However, Taiwan has a lot of catching up to do as the Asia dollar market in Singapore totals $112 billion, while the offshore market in Hong Kong is approximately $72 billion.

Looking ahead, Taipei has definitely committed itself to Eurobanking. It has not only created an optimal regulatory structure for Eurobanking, but it has insured the availability of trained personnel by arranging extensive training programs in New York for its bankers and Ministry of Finance officials.

The Chemical Bank and Bank of America programs have helped convert Taipei's stodgy domestic bankers into Eurobankers prepared to offer facilities matching those of Singapore, New York, and London.

"Made in Taiwan" is soon an imprint to be found on loan syndications as well as cameras.

Source: *The Journal of Commerce,* 13, February 1985; reprinted with permission.

Chronology of Development

1983
The Cabinet approved in February a joint Ministry of Finance-Central Bank proposal to create OBUs with many significant regulatory exemptions.

1983
The Legislative Yuan passed and the government promulgated the Offshore Banking Act (December 12).

1984
The Government promulgated the Rules for Implementing the Offshore Banking Act (April 20).

Beginning May 21, OBU licenses were authorized. Five banks received licenses to create OBUs, led by the International Commercial Bank of China on June 5 and followed by the First Commercial Bank of Taiwan, the Chang-Hwa Bank, and the Hua-Nan Commercial Bank.

1985
Citibank and Bank of America were granted OBU licenses.

VANUATU (PORT VILA)

Vanuatu, composed of 83 islands, is located in the South Pacific, some 1,500 miles northeast of Sydney, Australia, between Fiji (500 miles west) and New Caledonia. Its land mass totals 4,700 square miles within territorial waters of over 300,000 square miles. The population totals 136,000, with the population of the capital of Port Villa on the island of Efate being 15,000.

History. During the 19th century the New Hebrides (now Vanuatu) were settled by both the British and French, who in 1887 established a Joint Naval Commission for the islands. Subsequently, a joint civil administration was agreed upon, and in 1906 the territory became the Anglo-French Condominium of the New Hebrides (Nouvelle Hebrides). Under this arrangement, there were three elements in the structure of administration: the British National Service, the French National Service and the Condominium (Joint) Departments. Each power was responsible for its own citizens and other non-New Hebrideans who chose to be "ressortissants" of either power.

After World War II local political activity grew, fostered by the fact that more than 36% of the New Hebrides was owned by foreigners (e.g., U.S. tourism interests). Activity intensified in the 1970s and in 1978, a measure of self-government was introduced. In 1979, a constitution was adopted and elections were held. Then on 30 July 1980, the New Hebrides became independent within the Commonwealth under the name Vanuatu. Father Walter Hadye Lini (leader of the Vanuaaku Party or VP) led the new government. Also in 1980, there was a secessionist movement in the second most important island, Espiritu Santo, led by Jimmy Stevens and financially supported by the local French planters and right-wing U.S. organizations (Phoenix Foundation/John Birch Society). But with the imprisonment of Mr. Stevens, following his defeat by soldiers brought in from Papua-New Guinea, the movement died out. With the VP having taken 24 of the 39 seats in the unicameral Parliament in the November 1983 general election, Father Lini has retained his position.

Economy. Complementing widespread subsistence gardening, Vanuatu exports copra, fish and beef. Tourism is strongly promoted, with the Land Leasing Act of April 1983 providing for secure leases of view of the abolition of foreign-owned freehold title upon the country's independence in 1980. In 1985, there were approximately 25,000 visitors to Vanuatu, as well as 76,000 cruise ship passenger arrivals. A huricane with devastating 100 mph winds did over $150 million damage in February 1987, leading to substantial aid from Australia, New Zealand and France.

Additionally, there has been significant development of Vanuatu as a tax haven-offshore center, including offshore banking and company and ship registration. Several foreign banks and over 500 overseas companies are located there, while ship registrations ("flags of convenience" à la Liberia) total over 135.

Advantages as a Banking Center

1. A strong government commitment reinforced by a private Finance Center Association and fostered by a structural merchandise trade deficit.

2. An English-speaking population, with English along with French and the native Bislama being official languages.

3. Social stability reinforced by the historic commitments of Britain and France to the nation.

4. General political stability under the dominant VP, which has 62% of the seats in the Parliament.

5. An internationally-oriented judicial system involving judges from other Pacific countries and Papua New Guinea Supreme Court judges(Vanuatu is ethnically linked to Papua New Guinea).

6. A modern international airport with direct flights to Australia, Fiji, New Caledonia and the Soloman Islands; also, two deep seaports served by several cargo lines.

7. Comprehensive 24 hour international telecommunications in the form of telephone, facsimile, telex and telegraph services by satellite to the rest of the world.

8. A convenient time zone for Asia, being 1 hour ahead of Sydney and 3 hours ahead of Hong Kong.

9. Excellent living accommodations and other personal amenities, including Rotary, Kiwanis and Lions Clubs, a golf and country club and a drive-in movie theatre.

10. There are 6 international firms of chartered accountants including Price Waterhouse and Coopers and Lybrand.
11. There are 6 firms of solicitors.
12. There are 9 trust companies.
13. A *complete* absence of company income, personal income, withholding and capital gains taxes; also no estate or gift duties; no tax treaties.
14. A complete absence of exchange controls.
15. Bank secrecy is required.

Disadvantages as a Banking Center

1. A general lack of international recognition, which in Asia is focused on Singapore, Hong Kong, and Tokyo.
2. A somewhat unstable local currency (currently tied to the SDR at SDR 1 = VT 122) due to the need to avoid appreciation versus the depreciating Australian dollar, as most tourists come from Australia.
3. Some political unrest due to the conflict of the VP with the principal opposition group, the Union of Moderate Parties.

Chronology of Development

1969
The initial trust company was registered.

1971
The companies Regulations Act passed for tax haven-oriented registration of companies (modeled on the UK Companies Act of 1948); other legislation provided for special banking, trust company, insurance and companies law, including special provision for exempted (offshore) companies.

1978
Deposits of BIS-reporting commercial banks totaled $152 million at end-June.

1979
Deposits of BIS-reporting commercial banks totaled $452 million at end-June.

1980

Deposits of BIS-reporting commercial banks totaled $479 million at end-June.

1981

Eurocurrency deposits totaled $148 million.

Laws and Regulations were passed establishing the Vanuatu Ship Registry (based on those of Liberia).

The Vatu was devalued to SDR 1 = Vt 106.2 in September.

1982

Eurocurrency deposits totaled $144 million.

Initiation of Vanuatu's first Five-year Development Plan (1982–86), with a budget of Vatu 11,000m., aimed at self-sufficiency for the economy within 10–15 years.

1983

Eurocurrency deposits totaled $114 million.

1984

Eurocurrency deposits totaled $127 million.

The Vatu was revalued by 5.3% to SDR 1 = Vt 100.6 in March.

1985

Eurocurrency deposits totaled $227 million.

The Vatu was devalued by 9.3% against the SDR in April to SDR 1 = Vt110.0.

There were 107 licensed banks/financial institutions at end-year.

1986

Eurocurrency deposits totaled $249 million at end-June.

The Vatu was devalued by a further 9.8% in March to SDR 1 = Vt122, and 14.1% in October to SDR 1 = Vt142 due to the depreciation of the Australian, New Zealand and U.S. dollars against the SDR.

The Vanuatu Companies Act passed expanding previous company legislation.

Four international banks were operating in Vanuatu.

Foreign Banks

Australia and New Zealand Banking Group Ltd (Australia): Kumul Highway, POB 123, Port Vila; tel. 2536; telex 1012.

Banque Indosuez Vanuatu: Kumul Highway, POB 29, Port Vila; tel. 2412; telex 1020 INDOSU NM.

The Hongkong and Shanghai Banking Corpn: POB 169, Port Vila; tel. 2714; telex NH 1017.

Westpac Banking Corporation (Australia): rue Higginson, Port Vila; tel. 2084; telex 1018.

BAHRAIN (MANAMA)

Bahrain is a nation comprised of 35 islands, notably Bahrain Island, situated 15 miles east of the Saudi Arabian coast in the Persian (Arabian) Gulf. Its area totals 264 square miles and its population totals 351,000, including 239,000 Bahraini citizens and 112,000 foreign workers and their families. Among Bahrainis, 59% are Shi'ites and 41% are Sunnis. Manama, the capital, has a population of 122,000, while

---

Exhibit 3-16
EUROHOSPITALITY

Hospitality to foreigners is one of the vital qualities of an international banking center. It has been an important factor in the impressive growth of Bahrain. But, as everywhere, *not* everybody seems to have gotten the word...

A couple of years ago a vice president of an American bank arrived at Bahrain's airport on his way to serve as an instructor at a financial training conference there. Coming on short notice, he didn't have time to receive his "NOC" ("No Objection Certificate", Bahrain's visa nomenclature) before he left. Thus, it was delivered to him at the airport by a messenger from his bank.

Unbeknownst to him, several of the other conference participants also received their NOCs at the airport as opposed to arriving with them, which was proving increasingly infuriating to the rather rigid immigration officer. The hapless vice president was the "straw that broke the camel's back", as the churlish immigration officer, in viola-tion of his superior's instructions for the conference participants, refused to admit him to Bahrain.

"Where should I go?" asked the shocked banker. "Where did you come from?" "London." "So go back to London." "But that's nearly eight hours away."

Trying to appear accommodating, the immigration officer confided to the banker, "Just hop a flight to one of the nearby Emirates or Qatar. And you can immediately return, without even getting off the plane. Then, since you would have *arrived* with your NOC, I could immediately admit you." Unswayed by the officer's logic and deterred by the expense (a couple of hundred dollars) and senselessness of it all, the banker decided to visit some relatives in Karachi, two hours away. And when he returned the next day, he was readily admitted. And the surly immigration officer was nowhere to be seen ...

Maharraqtown on an adjoining island containing the international airport, has 62,000 people. Among the alien population are over 25,000 Indians and Pakistanis, 13,000 Westerners, largely British, and many Filipinos.

History. Bahrain, a traditional Arab monarchy, became a British Protected State in the 19th century. In 1961, the present ruler, Sheikh Isa bin Salman al-Khalifa, succeeded his deceased father. The January 1968 UK announcement of its intention to withdraw British military forces from the area in 1971, led Bahrain in March 1968 to join the British-protected Qatar and the Trucial States (now the UAE) in a Federation of Arab Emirates. In 1970, Iran, which had territorial claims to Bahrain, accepted a UN report that its inhabitants overwhelmingly favored complete independence. Then in 1971, Bahrain (and Qatar) seceded from the Federation of Arab Emirates and became a separate independent state on 15 August 1971. A National Assembly was elected on 7 December 1973, but dissolved by Amiri decree in 1975 (current rule is by the Amir through an appointed cabinet), with promised subsequent elections yet to materialize. In December 1981, more than 70 people, linked to Iran, were jailed for plotting to overthrow the government, and there were subsequent incidents in 1984 and 1985.

Economy. During the 19th century, Bahrain's economy was dominated by pearl-diving and trade, but in 1932, the discovery of commercial quantities of petroleum transformed the nation. Petroleum refining of Saudi as well as local production has become the major industry, complemented by oil and natural gas production, aluminum smelting and some agriculture and light industry. Tourists numbering over 200,000 annually, three- quarters from other Gulf countries, also contribute to the economy. Finally, of course, international banking is highly important, with OBUs employing 2,539 persons at end-1983, (of which 59% were Bahrainis), with the total employment impact being 12,000-15,000.

Advantages As a Banking Center

1. An ideal location, close to the oil rich countries of Saudi Arabia, Kuwait, Qatar and the United Arab Emirates, and half-way between Singapore and the European banking centers; a three hour

overlap with both Singapore and London based on 8:00 a.m. – 2:00 p.m. banking hours.

2. It shares the (Sunni) Moslem, Arabic culture of its wealthy neighbors and their weekly work schedule (open Saturday and Sunday).

3. It extends considerable receptiveness to foreigners (relatively modest entrance requirements, which are even waived for UK citizens) and provides a liberal social environment, rooted in its history as a trading center (it was the site of the ancient trading civilization of Dilmun), and exemplified by its modern attitudes toward women and liquor.

4. Its role as the Gulf entrepôt prior to the initiation of international banking there.

5. English is widely spoken.

6. A strong political will to be an international banking center in light of its declining petroleum reserves (expected to be exhausted by 1997) and fast growing population (it jumped 245% between 1959 and 1981).

7. Its ample first class office space, hotels and restaurants.

8. Its large international airport, serviced by numerous international airlines.

9. Its ultra-modern satellite-linked communication systems, exemplified by direct-dial service to New York.

10. Political stability, with a progressive welfare-oriented Amir backed up by the like Sunni royal house of Saudi Arabia, exemplified by Saudi assistance to its petroleum refining and banking industries, and by the recent construction of a $1.1 billion, 15 mile causeway connecting the two countries; Bahrain's active participation in the 6 country Gulf Co-operation Council (GCC) also enhances stability.

11. Being open Saturday and Sunday when all other banking centers are closed

12. Favorable legislation with respect to OBU licensing ($25,000 annual fee), regulation and taxation.

13. A well regarded yet unobtrusive banking authority, the Bahrain Monetary Agency

14. An efficient and active brokerage system composed of six interna-

tionally-linked brokers, exemplified by annual brokerage fees totalling over $16 million

15. An active foreign exchange forward market, totaling approximately $29.3 billion and composed (at end-1985) 49.4% of U.S. dollars, 31.0% regional currencies (Saudi riyals, Kuwati dinars, UAE dirhans, Qatar riyals, and Bahraini dinars) and 19.6% of other currencies.

16. The unwillingness of Lebanon (Beirut), a competitive site to Bahrain, to provide a favorable tax and regulatory climate prior to 1975, and its civil war thereafter.

17. Speculative interest in short-sales of forward riyals in Bahrain by Saudi speculators expecting small devaluations of the currency.

18. The unwillingness of the Saudi authorities to permit foreign bank offices in Saudi Arabia.

19. The syndicated loan orientation of Bahrain's two major local banks, the $8 billion Arab Banking Corp. and the $6 billion Gulf International Bank.

Unfavorable Factors as a Banking Center

1. The dwindling oil revenues of the Gulf region due to the decline in export volumes and prices (reversed in late 1986).

2. The related drop in project lending into Saudi Arabia

3. The Iran-Iraq war.

4. The collapse of the al-Manaak Kuwait Stock Exchange in 1982

5. The initiation of a withholding tax on interest paid by Saudi borrowers to foreign lenders.

6. General Saudi misgivings about the offshore riyal market (the internationalization of its currency, largely by foreign contractors selling forward future riyal receipts).

7. Saudi measures to encourage the growth of its own banking industry.

8. The inclination of the Gulf region's central banks and wealthy individuals to bypass Manama and deal directly in Tokyo, London, Zurich or New York, for those centers' investment opportunities and expertise.

9. The growing aversion to non-first tier banking centers in the light of increased perception of bank risk spawned by the global debt crisis

10. Potential unrest in Bahrain related to its Shi'ite majority, possible Iranian intrigues, and resentment of the suspension of the National Assembly.

11. The relatively high total costs of running OBUs.

12. Lack of management quality and depth in many banks.

13. Lack of consistency in bank reporting of loan loss provisions.

Profile of OBUs

The OBUs in Bahrain are all significant on-site banking operations because of the prohibition of Nassau/Cayman type "brass plaque" operations. Reflecting this, there is an annual $25,000 licensing fee, well above that of the Caribbean off-shore centers. The OBUs have been established by banks throughout the world. Reflecting their global character, the 78 OBUs functioning at the end of 1983 included banks from the U.S. (8), Canada (2), U.K. (6), France (8), West Germany (1), Switzerland (3), Luxembourg (1), Spain (1), Netherlands (1), Belgium (1), Turkey (1), Bermuda (1), Brazil (3), Cayman Islands (1), Bahamas (1), Oman (2), Jordan (1), Saudi Arabia (1), UAE (1), Kuwait (1), India (2), Pakistan (2), Malaysia (1), Japan (2), Hong Kong (4), Philippines (1), Korea (1), and Bahrain itself (19). The paramount role of Arab bank OBUs is reflected in the fact that at end-1983, they increased their share of total OBU assets to 50.0% from 46.4% at end-1982. This was mainly at the expense of European bank OBUs.

Profile of OBU Activity at End-1985

At the end of 1985, the *interbank* claims at US$ 38.5 billion constituted 67.7% of the total assets as compared to US$ 41.6 billion or 66.4% a year earlier. The interbank funds amounted to US$ 38.8 billion or 68.2% of the total liabilities as against US$ 43.0 billion or 68.6% at end-1984. Loans to *non-bank* clients stood at 27.9% of the total assets at end-1985, while deposits from this sector were 23.1% of the total liabilities.

Deposits from *Arab* countries fell to US$ 38.4 billion or 67.6% of the total liabilities, while claims on them were US$ 26.3 billion or 46.2% of the total assets. *Western European* countries provided US$ 11.1 billion of deposits or 19.5% of the total, and received US$ 13.3 billion or 23.4% of loans, while deposits from *offshore centers* had been US$ 4.0 billion or 7.0% of total liabilities and claims on them were US$ 6.6 billion or 11.6% of the total assets.

The analysis of currencies shows that assets and liabilities denominated in *US dollars* decreased, respectively, from US$ 48.3 billion to US$ 43.0 billion and from US$ 44.7 billion to US$ 38.9 billion. The market share in US currency fell from 77.1% to 75.8% on the assets side, while on the liabilities side it declined from 71.3% to 68.5% (the decline in the dollar's role reflected the depreciation of the spot dollar from February 1985 onward). Assets denominated in *regional currencies* fell to US$ 9.1 billion from US$ 9.9 billion, while liabilities in those currencies fell to US$ 13.4 billion from US$ 13.7 billion. However, in a smaller market, the market share in regional currencies rose from 15.8% to 16.1% on the assets side, and rose from 21.8% to 23.6% on the liabilities side.

The maturity analysis shows that at the end of 1985 assets with maturities of up to one month constituted 43.6%, over 1 to 6 months 32.5%, and over 6 months 23.9%, compared to the corresponding shares of 40.6%, 35.8% and 23.6% a year earlier. Liabilities with maturities up to one month were 51.9%, over 1 to 6 months 37.7% and over 6 months 10.4% of the aggregates as against 48.7%, 41.8% and 9.5%, respectively a year earlier.

Outlook for the OBUs

As the statistics below indicate, OBU growth, in terms of both the number of OBUs and OBU assets/liabilities has plateaued and even reversed since 1983. Some banks (Continental Illinois, Security Pacific, Banco Comercio e Industria de São Paolo) have left, and several others have closed their dealing rooms (Barclays, Midland). The Bahrain Monetary Agency (BMA) explains the general business contraction on the basis of such factors as the global debt crisis and recession, the dramatic drop in Middle East oil revenues, its becoming more selective in granting fresh licenses, and the expectation of those in search of business in Bahrain of stiff competition from banks already established there.

Other factors are the 7 year-old Iran-Iraq War and additional factors cited in the section on "Unfavorable Factors as a Banking Center". The outlook is for the present plateaued situation to continue, as most of the factors that spawned it are still with us, if to varying degrees.

To offset the relative decline of its offshore banking activities, the BMA has adopted the "Luxembourg strategy" of actively developing complementary financial activities to the customary lending and correspondent banking. Two such activities are investment banking business, including arranging mergers, and portfolio management.

Chronology of Development

1964
Citibank moves its Middle East Center to Bahrain.

1973
The Bahrain Monetary Agency is founded.

1975
The Bahrain Monetary Agency initiates operations. The outbreak of the Lebanese civil war leads many banks and other international firms to begin transfering their Middle East headquarters from Beirut to Bahrain.

The Bahrain Monetary Agency (BMA) hires Alan Moore (British banker) to advise on its initiation of "offshore banking units" (OBUs), involving minimal regulations, but a significant operational level.

Initial OBUs licensed; OBU assets at end-year total $1.7 billion.

1976
OBU assets total $6.2 billion at end-year; growing foreign exchange volume totals $500 million.

1977
OBU assets total $15.7 billion at end-year; foreign exchange volume is $2.5 billion.

Bahrain chosen as headquarters of the new Gulf International Bank, equally owned by Saudi Arabia, Kuwait, Iraq, Bahrain, Oman, and the United Arab Emirates (recipient of substantial SAMA/Saudi Arabia Monetary Authority deposits).

1978
36 OBUs in operation, with 4 in process; 22 representative offices; 19 regular banks (including Chase and Citibank); 4 brokers (3 with London affiliates); OBU assets total $23.4 billion at end-year.

1979
OBU assets total $27.8 billion at end-year; Iran-Iraq war begins.

1980
OBU assets total $37.5 billion at end-year.

1981
65 OBUs in operation (9 Far East/Subcontinent; 9 Bahrain incorporation; 8 UK; 8 USA; 8 Gulf states; 6 France); OBU assets total $50.7 billion at end-year.

1982
72 OBUs, 18 commercial banks and 58 bank representative offices; OBU assets hit record $61.1 billion (August) but drop to $59.0 billion by end-year.

Collapse of the Souk al-Manakh Kuwait Stock Exchange in August (involving a cumulative default on post-dated checks worth $94 billion).

1983
Kleinwort, Benson withdraws from Kuwait. OBU assets hit record of $62.7 billion at end-year, boosted by window dressing (drop to $59.0 billion in January, 1984).

1984
OBU assets rise to $62.7 billion by end-year.

Arab Asian Bank fails at end-1984 and is taken over by the Bin Mahfouz family of Saudi Arabia.

1985
OBU assets total $56.8 billion among 74 OBUs as of end-year.

OFFSHORE BANKING UNITS (OBUs) IN BAHRAIN

Al Bahrain Arab African Bank EC (Albaab): POB 20488; tel. 230491; telex 9380.

Al Saudi Banque (Paris): POB 5820; tel. 257319; telex 8969.

Algemene Bank Nederland: POB 350; tel. 255420; telex 8356.

Allied Banking Corporation: POB 20493; tel. 26141; telex 9349.

Al-UBAF Arab International Bank EC: POB 529; tel. 276344; telex 9671.

American Express International: POB 93; tel. 231383; telex 8536.

Arab Bank Ltd: POB 813; tel. 256398; telex 8647.

Arab Banking Corporation: POB 5698; tel. 232235; telex 9384.

Arab International Bank: POB 1114; tel. 261611; telex 9489.

Arab Investment Company SAA (TAIC): POB 5559; tel. 271126; telex 8334.

Arab Malaysian Development Bank: POB 5619; tel. 257059; telex 9393.

Arab Solidarity Bank: POB 20491; tel. 230145; telex 9373.

Arlabank International EC: POB 5070; tel. 232124; telex 9345.

Bahrain International Bank: POB 5016; tel. 274545; telex 9832.

Bahrain Middle East Bank: POB 797; tel. 275345; telex 9706.

BAII (Middle East) Inc.: POB 5333; tel. 258258; telex 8542.

Banco de Vizcaya: POB 5307; tel. 253340; telex 9060.

Banco do Brasil SA: POB 5489; tel. 250113; telex 8718.

Banco do Estado de Sao Paulo (BANESPA) SA: POB 26615; tel. 232241; telex 9347.

Bank Bumiputra Malaysia Berhad: POB 20392; tel. 231073; telex 8884.

Bank Negara Indonesia 1946: POB 20715; tel. 277562; telex 8208.

Bank of America NT SA: POB 5280; tel. 245000; telex 8616.

Bank of Bahrain and Kuwait: POB 597; tel. 253388; telex 8919.

Bank of Baroda: POB 1915; tel. 253681; telex 9449.

Bank of Credit and Commerce International SA: POB 569; tel. 245520; telex 8346.

Bank of Nova Scotia: POB 5260; tel. 255522; telex 8582.

Bank of Oman Ltd: POB 20654; tel. 232882; telex 9566.

Bank of Tokyo Ltd: POB 5850; tel. 246518; telex 9066.

Bank Saderat Iran: POB 825; tel. 255977; telex 8688.

Bankers' Trust Co of New York: POB 5905; tel. 259841; telex 9510.

Banque Indosuez: POB 5410; tel. 257019; telex 8976.

Banque National de Paris: POB 5253; tel. 250852; telex 8595.

Banque Paribas: POB 5993; tel. 259275; telex 9078.

Barclays Bank International Ltd: POB 5120; tel. 242024; telex 8747.

British Bank of the Middle East: POB 57; tel. 255933; telex 8230.

Canadian Imperial Bank of Commerce: POB 774; tel. 250551; telex 8593.

Chase Manhattan Bank NA: POB 368; tel. 250799; telex 8286.

Chemical Bank: POB 5492; tel. 252619; telex 8562.

Citibank NA: POB 548; tel. 257124; telex 8225.

Commercial Bank of Australia: POB 5467; tel. 254792; telex 8687.

Credit Commercial de France: POB 26514; tel. 231150; telex 9422.

Credit Suisse: POB 5100; tel. 232123; telex 8418.

European Arab Bank (Middle East) EC: POB 5888; tel. 250600; telex 8940.

FRAB-Bank (Middle East) EC: POB 5290; tel. 259862; telex 9024.

Grindlays Bahrain Bank: POB 5793; tel. 258610; telex 8723.

Grindlays International Ltd: POB 20324; tel. 254023; telex 9254.

Gulf International Bank BSC: POB 1017; tel. 256245; telex 8802.

Gulf Riyad Bank EC: POB 20220; tel. 232030; telex 9088.

Habib Bank Ltd: POB 566; tel. 271811; telex 9448.

Hanil Bank of South Korea: POB 1151; tel. 256624; telex 7048.

Hongkong & Shanghai Banking Corporation: POB 5497; tel. 255828; telex 8707.

Korea Exchange Bank: POB 5767; tel. 255418; telex 8846.

Kredietbank NV: POB 5456; tel. 254284; telex 8633.

Kuwait Asia Bank EC: POB 20501; tel. 243645; telex 9611.

Lloyds Bank International Ltd: POB 5500; tel. 245050; telex 8641.

Manufacturers Hanover Trust Co: POB 5471; tel. 254375; telex 8556.

Massraf FayBsal Al-Islami Bank of Bahrain: POB 20492; tel. 275040; telex 9270.

Midland Bank PLC: POB 5675; tel. 257100; telex 8719.

National Bank of Abu Dhabi: POB 5886; tel. 255776; telex 8982.

National Bank of Bahrain: POB 106; tel. 258800; telex 8242.

National Bank of Pakistan: POB 775; tel. 244191; telex 9221.

National Westminster Bank PLC: POB 820; tel. 255412; telex 8559.

Overseas Trust Bank: POB 5628; tel. 245145; telex 9238.

Saudi European Bank SA: POB 26380; tel. 232884; telex 8732.

Saudi National Commercial Bank: POB 20363; tel. 231182; telex 9298.

Scandinavian Bank Ltd: POB 5345; tel. 253341; telex 8530.

Societe Generale: POB 5275; tel. 242002; telex 8568.

Standard Chartered Bank PLC: POB 29; tel. 266946; telex 8385.

State Bank of India: POB 5466; tel. 253640; telex 8804.

Swiss Bank Corporation: POB 5560; tel. 257221; telex 8814.

Union de Banques Arabes et Francaises (UBAF): POB 5595; tel. 257393; telex 8840.

United Bank of Kuwait Ltd: POB 5494; tel. 256774; telex 8649.

United Gulf Bank: POB 5964; tel. 233789; telex 9556.

Yamaichi International (Middle East) EC: POB 26894; tel. 253922; telex 9468.

Yapi Ve Kredi Bankasi AS: POB 1104; tel. 270089; telex 9931.

4

Principal Nondollar
Eurocurrency Markets

The creation of the Euro-dollar market in the early 1950s was followed by the proliferation of Euromarkets in other major currencies, especially after the termination of most European foreign exchange controls in 1958. While most of the nondollar Eurodeposit market is composed of Deutschemarks and Swiss francs, there are rapidly growing Euro-yen and ECU markets, as well as a significant market in Euro-sterling. Moreover, Euromarkets in French francs, Dutch guilders, Belgian francs, Italian lira, Canadian dollars, and Australian dollars are active.

While the Euromarkets are similar in function, they have many disparate characteristics, both of a general nature and in terms of their interest rate features. Distinguishing characteristics of the markets include their age and their size, varying from older and larger in the case of Deutschemarks to younger and quite small in the case of Italian lira. Also, the markets have different rates of growth and outlooks for growth, which largely reflect the outlook for the underlying spot currency, as the market is largely "investor-driven," reflecting their preference for appreciating or hard currencies.

While London is the major center for most Eurocurrencies, especially the major markets in dollars and Swiss francs, Paris is the leading Euro-sterling market (which obviously could not be London), Brussels is the major center for Euro-French francs, and Luxemburg is the leading marketplace for Euro-Deutschemarks and Euro-Belgian francs. Moreover, there are some differences in the case of the related secondary centers.

Different banks tend to dominate the trading in the individual Euromarkets, with offshore branches of banks from the "home country" of the Eurocurrency generally taking the leading role. Thus, the Big 3 German and Swiss banks dominate the Euro- mark and Euro-Swiss markets, respectively, but different large American, British, German, Swiss, and French banks are seen playing leading roles in the several Euromarkets.

Another distinguising trait of the Euromarkets is the size of a typical deposit. Typical Euro-dollar transactions are $10 million and typical Euro-Deutschemark deposits are a smaller DM 12 million, while typical Euro-French franc transactions are a still smaller FFr 25 million.

A final but most important general distinction between the Euromarkets is the "height" of the barriers separating the *domestic* from the corresponding *Euromarket.* Euro-dollars and Euro-French francs exemplify well the potential difference in such barriers.

In the case of Euro-dollars, the barrier is quite low, being principally the 3% reserve requirement on domestic U.S. banks borrowing Euro-dollars. Minor factors include the 8.5 basis point equivalent FDIC premium and the perception of greater risk in the Euro-dollar market due to different examination and "lender of last resort" situations, as well as differential information and transaction costs.

Finally, the unwillingness of many banks to arbitrage small rate differences between the domestic and Euro-dollar markets that do not reach threshold ROE (return on equity) and ROA (return on assets) requirements, especially in light of the present or potential weakness of many energy and Latin America loan-oriented banks and stiffened capital:asset requirements, constitutes a further separation of the markets. Collectively, these barrier elements are of minor importance, as is reflected in identical, or nearly so, domestic and Eurodeposit rates across the maturity spectrum.

Conversely, the barriers between the domestic and Euro-French franc markets are very formidable and the characteristically higher Eurorates balloon out to as much as 5,000% overnight (which corresponds to an unrealistically high devaluation of nearly 14%) in front of expected French franc devaluations. The dominant barrier is that French *residents* (banks, corporations) are not permitted to lend French francs to *nonresidents* (banks, corporations), a regulation that is strictly enforced. Hence, the natural principal supplier of French francs to the Euromarket is not available, with the resultant scarce supply explaining the higher Eurorates.

A similar but reverse situation prevailed in the late 1970s in the case of the Euro-Deutschemark and Euro-Swiss markets. In those situations, residents were permitted to deposit into, but *not* borrow from the corresponding Euromarkets, resulting in higher rates in the domestic markets, which had less relative supply.

Besides disparate general characteristics, the various Euromarkets have distinct interest rate features. The most obvious are the large differences in general interest rate levels, which substantially reflect different inflation situations, although business cycle and monetary policy factors are also influential.

Eurocurrencies can be loosely grouped into low-, medium-, and high-interest-rate groups. The low groups (three-month deposit rates ranging from 4.5–6% in mid-1986) would include the yen, the mark, Swissy, and the guilder. Composing the middle group (6.875–8.5%) is the U.S. dollar, French franc, Belgian franc, and Canadian dollar. Finally, the high group (9.75–11.375%) includes sterling, lira, and the Australian dollar. These groups are relatively stable through time (except that French and Belgian rates are often in the high group), although the interest rate levels themselves fluctuate due to changing world growth and inflation cycles (related to oil price shocks and the like).

Another distinction between the Eurocurrencies is the shape of their yield curves for *money market* deposits (from one month to one year), which helps determine forward exchange as well as funding strategies. Positive, negative, flat, and frequently mixed yield curves are all evident among the Eurocurrencies.

A generally positive yield curve is seen in the case of Euro-dollars, and closely related Euro-Canadian dollars, with the latter rates somewhat higher to promote northward flows, as well as to compensate for higher inflation. Concurrently, low inflation and inflationary expectations give a relatively flat configuration to the yield curve for several Eurocurrencies, including the mark, the yen, the guilder, and Swissy. Finally, short-term money market pressures (e.g., when a devaluation is expected) frequently give the yield curve in sterling, French francs, and ECUs a negative tendency.

Different historical as well as recent interest rate trends are evident among the various Eurocurrencies reflecting the impact of disparate inflation-unemployment tradeoff preferences, different structural balance of payments situations, and dissimilar and changing monetary policy orientations.

Over the past four years, a scrutiny of historical short-term Eurodeposit rate trends indicates that interest rates for yen, marks, guilders and Swissy have been in the low 4–6% range, reflecting current account surpluses, low inflation, and the perception of conservative central bank management. Concurrently, U.S. dollars, Canadian dollars, and ECU rates, reflecting overall economic performances moderately inferior to those of the low rate group, have been in the middling 7–10% range. Finally, significant volatility including high rates is observed in the case of Euro-French franc, Euro-sterling, Euro-Belgian franc, Euro-lira, and Euro-Australian dollar rates, reflecting intermittant balance of payments and/or inflation problems, as well as changing fiscal-monetary policy mixes.

A related interest rate feature is the vulnerability of a Eurocurrency to extreme interest rate movements, which could make the covering of a short position a very expensive proposition. While this is not a problem with respect to most Eurocurrencies, it does endanger the trader in Euro-French francs and lira, and occasionally in sterling. In particular, periodically necessary EMS realignments, fostered by disparate inflation performances, are largely synonymous with Italian lira and French franc devaluations. Short-term expectations of the latter drive up French franc and lira deposit levels to celestial levels. Concurrently, the volatility of the price of oil as well as political uncertainties often focus pressure on sterling, a phenomenon often reinforced by a characteristic Bank of England spot pound support maneuver of *squeezing* the Euro-sterling market.

A final distinction in Euromarket interest rate characteristics is recurrent short-term rate influences. Eurodollar rates are regularly buffetted by U.S. M-1 releases, discount rate changes, and the expected outcomes of FOMC meetings. Similarly in the Euro-Deutschemark market, traders are attentive to the "central bank money stock" announcements, discount/Lombard rate changes, and Central Bank Council meeting decisions. All of the markets are affected by tax dates and the ends of accounting periods, such as end-month (especially Swissy), and even more, end-quarter and end-year. Various markets are associated with more unique pressures, such as pension payments (a monthly phenonemon in the Euro-guilder market), quarterly and semiannual interest/dividend payments (Euro-Canadian dollars), quarterly natural gas/oil payments (guilders and Canadian dollars), and bank reserves reporting day (Euro-sterling).

This section is comprised of descriptions of the major nondollar Eurocurrency markets, including those for Deutschemarks, Swiss francs, yen, ECUs, pounds sterling, French francs, Dutch guilders, Belgian francs, Italian lira, Canadian dollars, and Australian dollars. Following is a summary of the factors creating interest rate differentials between domestic and Euromarkets and a table containing Eurocurrency deposit rates for the nine major Eurocurrencies. The latter is particularly useful for identifying the yield curves characteristics of the various Eurocurrencies.

The Euro-Deutschemark Market

HISTORICAL DEVELOPMENT

The Euro-Deutschemark market has developed into the world's *second* largest Euromarket after that of the Euro-dollar. Its size based on the historical strength of the Deutschemark and its central role in the European Monetary System, reflecting low inflation (1986: –1.1% and 1.5% expected in 1987), as well as Germany's being the world's second largest exporter ($169 billion in 1983), coupled with having the fourth largest GDP in the world ($627 billion in 1983). With respect to the foreign currency liabilities of banks in countries monitored by the Bank for International Settlements (BIS), dollar liabilities at end-1985 totaled $1,287.3 billion, while Deutschemark liabilities were the equivalent of $208.3 billion, almost triple the 1977 level of $69 billion and well ahead of the third major Eurocurrency, the Swiss franc, at $101.5 billion.

The growth rate of the Euro-Deutschemark market, once greater than that of the Euro-dollar (35%/year compared to 25%/year for the Euro-dollar market during 1978–80), slackened in 1984, as central banks and Arab money managers slowed and even reversed their diversification into Deutschemarks. The Deutschemark was relatively weak, while the strength and importance of the dollar increased. Furthermore, the Polish crisis called into question substantial outstanding German loans to Poland, while labor unrest, tax (Flick) and spy scandals, and the aggravated East-West tensions over missile deployment further reduced the attractiveness of the Deutschemark. However, strength in Germany's structural trade (1986: + DM112 billion and DM90 billion expected in 1987) and current account surpluses (DM39 billion in 1985 and DM78 billion in 1986, and DM60 billion expected in 1987, over triple the DM18 billion level of 1984), and continuing low inflation have led to a much stronger mark and increased demand for the Euro-Deutschemark in the 1985-1986 period, accelerating growth of the market.

MARKET PARTICIPANTS

Most of the market volume is handled by the affiliates of the "Big 3" German banks (Deutsche Bank, Dresdner Bank, and Commerzbank) in Luxembourg (where 70% of the Euro-Deutschemark transactions take place to circumvent German reserve requirements) and London, as well as by Bank of America, Barclays Bank International, Credit Lyonnais, Citibank, and Chase. The typical interbank Euro-Deutschemark deal involves DM12 million.

INTEREST RATE FACTORS

Euro-Deutschemark interest rates follow domestic rates closely, as there are few barriers between the markets. One barrier, a supplementary reserve requirement on domestic German banks accepting offshore Deutschemark deposits, was lowered in May 1980 and again in September 1980, until the reserve requirements were the same as those applicable to domestic liabilities by the end of 1980. Eurorates for short dates are usually tied to the domestic market (domestic rates move first), unless heavy spot purchases of the Deutschemark depress rates until domestic Deutschemarks become unavailable. Hence, Euro-Deutschemark traders are attentive to domestic German financial developments, such as the policy outcomes of Central Bank Council meetings (every other Thursday), discount rate/Lombard rate changes, the targeted monetary aggregate of *Central Bank Money* (currency plus minimum required reserves on domestic bank liabilities using the reserve ratio existing in January 1974), German tax dates (usually the 10th and 15th of every month, with the most important being the tenth of December), pension payments (end-quarter), and end-month, end-quarter, and end-year accounting periods. Banks are required to report their foreign currency positions on a *monthly* basis (as a consequence of the failure of Bankhaus Herstatt in 1974).

INTEREST RATE MOVEMENTS: 1976-1987

Euro-Deutschemark rates, as exemplified by three-month Euro-Deutschemarks, remained low from 1976 (4.7%) through the end of 1978 (3.3%). However, in 1979 and 1980, three-month Euro-Deutschemarks traded in the 8% to 9% range. The rates are known to parallel Euro-dollar deposit rates, with inflationary pressures on both being reflected in the upward movement and sharp fluctuations of the rates. In 1981, the three-month Euro-Deutschemark rose to 12.50%, although by year-end, it had eased to 10.75%. Subsequently, it fell further to 6.25% by the end of 1982, and troughed at 4.88% in April 1983, gradually rising to 6.25% by December. In 1984, the three-month Euro-DM traded in a narrow range of 5.50% (end-March and end-December) to 6.13% (mid-April). The relatively low rates reflected the Bundesbank's decision to have the spot DM bear the brunt of U.S. dollar strength. Given the government priority to lowering domestic interest rates to stimulate the German economy, Euro-Deutschemark rates were expected to fall, especially when a declining spot dollar and interest rates reduced pressure on the spot Deutschemark.

That expectation was fulfilled in 1985 when spot dollar weakness, especially in the wake of the September Group of 5 Plaza meeting and somewhat lower dollar interest rates, enabled the three-month Euro-Deutschemark to fall from 5.88% in January to 4.75% at the end of the year (the rate peaked at 6.13% when the spot dollar peaked in February and troughed at 4.38% in late September). During January-July 1986, it hovered around 4.5%, with a range from 4.31%–4.69%, while in the latter half of 1986, it trended somewhat higher at around 4.65%. The outlook for early 1987 is for interest rates to move somewhat lower and then stabilize at that lower level despite above target money expansion (7.8%, as of October 1986, well above the 3.5%–5.5% target) and a firming of repurchase yields from 4.35% to 4.50% in early December. Factors nudging rates downward include low inflation (a 1986 CPI of – 1%, and a slightly higher 1.5% projected for 1987), a strong Deutschemark, a need to stimulate an economy retarded by a strong currency (exemplified by 9% unemployment) and U.S. pressure for cooperative reflation along the lines of the U.S. arrangement with Japan. A rate of 3.95% at the end of 1987.1 reflected the latter factors; a further 25-50 basis point decline in 1987.2 is likely.

The Euro-Swiss Franc Market

HISTORICAL DEVELOPMENT

Based on the strength of the Swiss franc, resulting from Switzerland's political stability, low inflation rate (in 1986, 0.0% year/year), favorable balance of payments based on a structural current account surplus, (SFr 9.6 billion in 1985 and SFr 12.0 billion in 1986) as well as the important role of the Swiss franc in international finance (due to the international credits extended by Swiss banks and the extensive international operations of major Swiss firms, such as Nestle), and its status as the "haven country," the Euro-Swiss franc has developed into the *third* largest Euromarket after the dollar and the Deutschemark. (This despite its small size; its GDP totalled only $96 billion in 1982 and exports $26 billion in 1983). With respect to the external positions of banks in the industrial countries monitored by the Bank for International Settlements (BIS), Swiss franc liabilities at end-1985 totalled the equivalent of $101.5 billion, more than tripling in size from 1978 ($27.9 billion).

Prior to 1980, to prevent excessive appreciation of the Swiss franc against the faltering dollar, with its negative implications for export competitiveness, numerous regulations were put in effect, which later were gradually lifted. For example, prior to May 31, 1979, Swiss banks could lend abroad, but were *not* allowed to borrow Swiss francs from offshore. They were required to balance their foreign currency position daily, and the central bank was authorized to sterilize Swiss franc proceeds of exchange market intervention. Also, until June 8, 1979 there was the requirement that foreign borrowers of Swiss francs convert 50% of the proceeds at the Swiss National Bank ("capital conversion rule"). Furthermore, until more recently (November 1, 1979), 40% negative interest rates were charged on nonresident deposits increased beyond the October 31, 1974 level (the first SFr 100,000 or SFr 250,000 was exempt depending on the circumstances, and the maximum was SFr 5 million free on any account). The 10%-per-quarter negative interest rate requirement was reduced to 2.5% per quarter (10%/year) on November 1, while on December 1, 1979, negative interest rates on Swiss franc deposits of foreigners were suspended, but deposits by foreigners were still not permitted to earn interest. From February 1980, such interest was permitted with some restrictions.

On March 11, 1980, the National Bank lifted all limits on the forward sales of Swiss francs to nonresidents. As of August 31, 1980, the Swiss Federal Council permitted the payment of interest on deposits denominated in Swiss francs to nonresidents without restrictions, which led to an increase of $3.4 billion equivalent in external liabilities over the previous year. Furthermore, as of September 1, 1980, Swiss banks were allowed to participate freely in the granting of loans to nonresidents, although approval is needed for lending abroad more than SFr 10 million for longer than one year, which is generally not granted, and a 30% withholding tax applies on borrowing from abroad. The central bank strongly discourages short-term speculation in Swiss francs.

MARKET PARTICIPANTS

The major activity in the market takes place in London, Paris and Amsterdam by the "Big 3" Swiss banks (Union Bank of Switzerland, Swiss Bank Corporation, and Credit Suisse), Citibank, Bank of America, and other major banks in those cities. Interbank deals range from SFr 250,000 to SFr 100 million, with the typical size deal being SFr 5–10 million.

INTEREST RATE FACTORS

Euro-Swiss franc rates follow domestic rates closely, with the Euro-rate less costly by 0.25%–0.50%. Often the Eurorate will move first due to the inertia of the domestic market. Banks are required to report their positions on a monthly basis, which leads to significant rate tightness at month-end (rates as high as 80–100%). Pressure is correspondingly greater at quarter- and year-end. However, the Swiss National Bank (the central bank) provides the market with liquidity by making short-term swap arrangements with commercial banks to mitigate, although only partially, such pressures. Another factor is the growth of the targeted monetary aggregate, the *Monetary Base* (currency plus clearing accounts of commercial banks at the Swiss National Bank).

INTEREST RATE MOVEMENTS: 1978–1987

Euro-Swiss franc rates, exemplified by three-month Euro-Swiss deposits, were on an upward trend 1978–September 1981, rising from less than 1% to peak near 12%. By end-1981, it had eased to 9.50%, while by October 1982, it troughed at 3.38%, reflecting generally declining inflation, and monetary easing prompted by the objective of stimulating the recessionary economy, as well as to compensate for the undershooting of monetary growth targets. Subsequently, it peaked at 5% in August 1983 and then declined to the low 4% area in the balance of 1983. In 1984, it traded in a range of 3.38% (March) to 5.44% (September), ending the year at 5.19%. In 1985, it peaked at 6.19% in February in tandem with the strong spot dollar, but fell throughout the year, also in tandem with the spot dollar, to 3.94% at end-December. During January-July 1986, it averaged around 4.50%, with a range from 3.69%–5.50%, with the low rate resulting from negligible inflation, the current account surplus, and the related strengthening of the spot SFr. For the balance of 1986, rates moved lower to around 4%. In 1987, Switzerland is expected to match any reductions in German rates in the context of slowing real GDP (to an estimated 2.8% in 1986, after 3.2% in 1985, and a projected even lower 2.3% in 1987), low inflation (an expected flat CPI in 1986, and 1.5% in 1987), and a money supply under control (1.8% growth as of October, below the 2% target). A rate of 3.81% at the end of 1987.1 reflected the latter factors.

The Euro-Yen Market

HISTORICAL DEVELOPMENT

In response to Japan's position as the world's third largest exporter ($145 billion in 1983)—although a high (if declining) percentage of these exports are invoiced in U.S. dollars coupled with having the third largest GDP in the world ($1,727 billion in 1985), the Euro-yen market has developed very rapidly. It is supported as well by Japan's low inflation (1986: –0.3% and an expected 1.0% in 1987), its large trade surplus (1986: $93 billion and an expected $95 billion in 1987), and current account surplus (1986: $86 billion and an expected $90 billion in 1987), and finally the accelerating pace of financial deregulation in the wake of Treasury Secretary Regan's historic 1984 visit. Estimated at $1.6 billion in 1978, the Euro-yen market grew rapidly to $4 billion in 1979, to over $10 billion in 1980, to $17 billion by the end of 1982, to over $21 billion by end-1983, to $31 billion at end-1984, and to a greatly enlarged $97 billion at end-1985. The related Euro-yen bond market jumped 525% in 1985 to the equivalent of $6.89 billion, making it the third most frequent currency of denomination for such bonds. Nevertheless, it remains relatively small (compared to Japan's GNP) due to the Japanese authorities' ambivalence over the internationalization of the yen (which enhances its value and thereby reduces Japan's export competitiveness).

The Bank of Japan (central bank) exercises tight control over the domestic yen market, which imposes obstacles on the Euro-yen market, but some regulations are being liberalized, resulting in rapid Euro-yen growth. The yen is used as a transaction medium (30% of Japanese exports are denominated in yen), a reserve asset (central banks diversifying out of dollars into yen, such that now over 3.7% of the world's official foreign exchange reserves are held in yen as opposed to 64% in dollars and 11% in Deutschemarks) and an intervention vehicle (the Canadian government borrowed yen to support its currency in March 1979). Also, growing arbitrage takes place between Europe and Japan (between the forward and deposit rates). Finally, the Middle East is showing more interest in depositing yen in Europe, reflecting increased market sophistication on the part of Arab investors.

The major hindrance to the development of the Euro-yen market has been heavy regulation of the domestic market by the Bank of Japan. Japanese banks have a limit on yen taken from overseas (that is, Euro-yen since there is a limit on the flow of funds into the Tokyo market). Also, banks in Tokyo have swap limits which determine how much yen they can borrow from abroad if they need to arbitrage against the domestic market.

Foreigners have no limit on deposits made in the Tokyo market (*free yen* accounts), while the Bank of Japan limits the banks on interest rates they can pay to foreigners, which is sometimes lower than Euro-yen rates (the banks pay domestic rates). A 25% reserve requirement on foreign currency and "free yen" deposits was established in June 1977. In November 1977, the central bank imposed reserve requirements of 50% on incremental "free yen" deposits, later raising the reserve requirements from 50% to 100%, while in April 1978 it reduced them from 100% to 50%. Almost a year later, in February 1979, the reserve requirements on "free yen" deposits was reduced from 50% to zero on incremental balances.

In March 1980, the central bank freed the interest rates paid to foreign central banks and other depositors on free yen deposits from the domestic interest rate restrictions. The lifting was a measure to shore up the exchange rate and provided an inflow of $2 billion of yen into the Tokyo market. Also, the Japanese banks were allowed to borrow in the Euro-yen market to a maximum of $4 billion.

In 1983, the wake of President Reagan's visit to Japan, where talks focused on the undervaluation of the yen and the related $20 billion Japanese bilateral trade surplus with the U.S., Japan announced a financial liberalization program, partially focused on the Euro-yen market. Reforms included the deposit, syndicated lending, and bond segments of the market.

On the deposit side, since December 1984, the issuance and trading of Euro-yen CDs with maturities up to six months has been permitted. Concurrently, on the lending side, both Japanese and non-Japanese banks were allowed to make short-term Euro-yen loans from June 1984. However, an important remaining restriction is, with the apparent exception of Euro-yen lending by non-Japanese banks to non-residents, the prohibition of syndicated Euro-yen loans with maturities beyond one year.

MARKET PARTICIPANTS

Centered in London, the major participants in the Euro-yen market are the principal Japanese banks, especially the Bank of Tokyo, Sumitomo, Mitsui Trust and Banking, as well as Citibank and Chemical Bank. Interbank deals generally are 1 billion or the equivalent of $6.5 million.

INTEREST RATE FACTORS

Euro-yen rates are to some degree a function of the foreign exchange swap rates, sometimes below Tokyo domestic market rates, but sometimes above, depending on whether the amount is within the regulations set by the central bank (however, in general the Euroyen rates closely track the gensaki or repo rate). Permission must be granted for Japanese domestic banks to borrow from the Euro-yen market. Also, Euro- yen rates will be higher than the domestic rates when the spot yen comes under selling pressure.

Other factors affecting the Euro-yen include the yields on the bond market. Foreigners can purchase bonds in the Tokyo market; if the yield is greater than the Euro-yen, then foreigners borrow Euro-yen to finance purchases of the bonds. Also, the external borrowing limits put pressure on the rates. For example, if the domestic yen rate is 12.06% in Tokyo and the Euro-yen is 11.50% in Europe, this situation reflects the fact that no Japanese firms can borrow in Europe because of the yen limit imposed by the Bank of Japan, restricting borrowers to go into the Tokyo market. Tight times are at quarter-end, especially the year-end, due to the window dressing associated with accounting periods. Another factor is the targeted monetary aggregate of *M-2 + CDs* (currency plus demand and time deposits plus certificates of deposits).

INTEREST RATE MOVEMENTS: 1977-1987

The Euro-yen rates declined in 1977 through 1978 from 8 or 9% to 3 or 4% with occasional negative interest rates for almost six months when the spot yen was under strong upward pressure and the markets had very long yen balances (very liquid market), due to limits on interest rates and the ceiling on yen in the Tokyo market. During 1979, the rates rose, with the three-month maturity averaging 7.95%, and closing year-end at 8.30%. In 1980.1, it rose rapidly, peaking around 13.5% in March. Due to the economic slowdown, it declined subsequently and was down to 9.5% by year-end. Further declines were registered throughout 1981, with the year-end rate down to 6.65%. That level remained largely unchanged throughout 1982, with the rate fluctuating in a narrow range of 6.25–7.55%, and closing the year at 7.10%.

In 1983, three-month Euro-yen fluctuated in an even narrower range of 6.40–6.90%, with a 6.50% level at end- December. The relatively low rate reflected the low inflation (1983, + 3.0% year/year) and sluggish economy; concurrently, the rate was high in real terms, reflecting the need to maintain the yen's value vis-à-vis the overvalued dollar, as well as the problems of financing the large fiscal deficit. During 1984 the three-month Euro-yen traded in a narrow 50-basis- point range of 6.13% (April) to 6.63% (February), and stood at 6.25% at the end of the year.

The steady yen rates reflected the decision by the Bank of Japan to allow the spot yen to bear the brunt of the surging dollar. In 1985, it traded in a range of 6.19% (mid-June) to 7.88% in early December. The big jump in rates (over 110 basis points) came in late October as the central bank acted to strengthen the spot yen (to weaken protectionist sentiment in the U.S. and Europe) and moderate excessive capital market (bullish) speculation.

During January-July 1986, the rate declined approximately 200 basis points from the 6.5% level to the 4.5% level, due, in part, to three 0.50% cuts in the Japanese discount rate. Cuts were made in January (unilaterally), March (in conjunction with the U.S. and Germany), and April (in conjunction with the U.S.), with the 3.5% resultant rate being a record post-war low. The considerable drop in rates reflected the yen's appreciation, sluggish domestic economic conditions (a 2% AR drop in real GNP in 1986.1), low inflation and a massive current account surplus. For the balance of 1986, further rate drops occurred, highlighted by a 50 basis point cut in the discount rate to 3% on October 31, in the context of a Japan-US agreement of Finance Minister Miyazawa and Treasury Secretary Baker to reflate the Japanese economy with both fiscal and monetary policy, while preventing further appreciation of the yen. The orchestration of lower rates, despite the protests of Japan's savers' lobby reflected governmental concern with sluggish domestic economic conditions (including bankruptcies of companies undermined by the yen's appreciation). In particular, the 3-month rate fell to 4.31% by the end-1986, and further declined to 4.00% by end-1987.1.

The ECU (European Currency Unit) Market

HISTORICAL DEVELOPMENT

The ECU was created in 1979 with a value and composition identical to its predecessor unit, the European Unit of Account (EUA), but, unlike the EUA, with a *revision* clause permitting changes. It serves as the unit of account for European Economic Community activities (budget, loans, agricultural policy), especially the concurrently created European Monetary System (EMS).

Offering stability to borrowers and lenders, the ECU market has grown phenomenally. At the end of 1985, the private ECU deposit market was estimated at ECU 3 billion (making it the fifth most important Eurocurrency), and in both 1984 and 1985, the ECU loan market totalled nearly ECU 3 billion, triple the 1983 level. Moreover, the ECU has become the fourth most important unit of denomination in the Eurobond market with ECU bond issues in 1985 totalling the equivalent of $6.88 billion, a 150% growth rate from 1984. ECU bonds have even been SEC- registered for sale in the United States (such as the ECU 150 million issue by the EEC in 1984). Finally, on the retail level, ECU instruments include checking accounts, savings accounts, a credit card (Visa), and traveler checks.

As of late April 1987, its value was approximately $1.15. Its current composition is as shown in Exhibit 4-1 (the Spanish peseta and Portuguese escudo are expected to be added in 1989 as part of the routine five-year *recomposition* cycle).

Exhibit 4-1
COMPOSITION OF AND RELATIVE WEIGHTS IN
THE EUROPEAN CURRENCY UNIT

Currency	Composition	March 13, 1979 Weight (%)	Sept. 14, 1984 Weight (%)	Sept. 17, 1984* Composition	Weight (%)
M	0.82800	33.0	36.9	0.71900	32.0
Fr	1.15000	19.8	16.7	1.31000	19.0
K£	0.08850	13.3	15.1	0.08780	15.0
T	109.00000	9.5	7.9	140.00000	10.2
Fl	0.28600	10.5	11.3	0.25600	10.1
Fr	3.66000	9.3	8.1	3.71000	8.2
Kr	0.21700	3.1	2.7	.021900	2.7
RA	—	—	—	1.15000	1.3
RL	0.00759	1.2	1.0	0.00871	1.2
Fr	0.14000	0.3	.03	0.14000	0.3
		100.00	100.00		100.00

*Latest revision.

Several hundred European banks (U.S. domestic banks are not so permitted) offer ECU accounts for clients, deal ECUs for their own account, and participate in the ECU clearing system known as MESA (for Mutual ECU Settlement Accounts). A significant difference between the ECU market and other currency markets is that notice must be given on the day before value date instead of on the value date. Soon MESA is expected to be replaced by a BIS-run ECU clearing function. ECU deposits are available from call or sight deposits to time deposits with maturities from one month to a year or longer, with the longer-term deposits being the most common.

Regarding the ECU as a foreign exchange instrument, its dollar price is monitored three times a day and is fixed once a day by the Commission of the European Community as the official value of the ECU. The ECU is traded for spot and five dates through one year in an active interbank market. The quote convention is U.S. dollars per ECU (that is, American or *direct* terms), the same as for the British pound. In addition to the bank market, the ECU is quoted on stock exchanges in Paris, Brussels, Amsterdam, Copenhagen, Rome, and Milan. Reflecting the ECU's growing use, in January 1986, the Chicago Mercantile Exchange began trading ECU futures, involving a trading unit of ECU 125,000 and standard delivery dates of March, June, September, and December.

At the same time, the FINEX Division of the New York Cotton Exchange (which also has a trade-weighted dollar contract) began trading a similar but slightly smaller contract (ECU 100,000). Complementing those contracts, the Philadelphia Stock Exchange in mid-February 1986, began trading a currency options contract with a contract amount of ECU 62,500, one-cent intervals and expiration dates at end-March, June, September, and December, plus two the near-term months.

MAJOR PARTICIPANTS

While over 350 European banks deal in ECUs, 94% of activity is concentrated in France, Italy, the United Kingdom, and Belgium-Luxembourg. The five leading ECU banks are Kredietbank and Generale Bankmaatschappij (Brussels), Lloyds Bank (London), which introduced the ECU certificate of deposit in 1981, Kredietbank SA Luxembourgeoise (Luxembourg), and Credit Lyonnais (Paris). The absence of the German banks is due to a Bundesbank prohibition.

INTEREST RATE FACTORS

The ECU interest rates represent the weighted value of the ECU component currencies' interest rates for the period designated. The three major ECU component currencies, the Deutschemark, the French franc, and the pound, with respective September 1984 recomposition weights (subject to moderate change due to currency fluctuations) of 32%, 19% and 15%, respectively, largely determine ECU interest rates. Hence factors, which in turn, influence their interest rates, are the ECU interest rate factors.

INTEREST RATE MOVEMENTS: 1982-1986

ECU interest rates as exemplified by the three-month deposit rate (prime bank bid) ended 1982 at a lofty 12.31%, particularly reflecting the tight French franc market (24%). By end 1983, amidst the European stagflation, the rate had fallen to 9.19%, rising a bit to 9.38% at end-1984. However, the rate resumed its decline in 1985 to 8.50% in the summer and fall, before rising to 9.63% by year-end.

During 1986, the rate briefly rose by January to 10.63%. Thereafter, it fell to the 9.88/9.50% level during February-March, to 8% in April and to 7.31% in May-June. In August, it fell further to 7.06%. The decline reflected sluggish growth, low inflation, credit easing, and currency appreciation in the EEC countries.

The Euro-Sterling Market

HISTORICAL DEVELOPMENT

Based on the UK's position as the world's fifth largest exporter ($94 billion in 1984) coupled with having the world's seventh largest GDP ($430 billion in 1984), the Euro-sterling market has become the fifth largest Euromarket after the dollar, Deutschemark, Swiss franc, and yen. It is supported as well by the dramatic drop in UK inflation (4.6% in 1984, 5.7% in 1985 and 3.7% in 1986 year/year), its favorable current account surplus (£3.0 billion in 1985 and £1.1 billion in 1986) and the popularity of sterling instruments in the international capital market.

However, the impressive size of the Euro-sterling market, the equivalent of $77.5 billion, is a recent development; previously it was one of the smallest of the Euromarkets due to the UK's extensive foreign exchange regulations (especially the prohibition against UK residents holding or lending sterling externally) as well as a fundamental sterling weakness, resulting from Britain's former structural high inflation and merchandise trade deficit. For example, in 1978 the Euro-sterling market was only the equivalent of $10.32 billion (1977, $6.87 billion,

1976, $3.98 billion, 1975, $3.1 billion). Factors behind the changed status of the Euro-sterling market (that is, the essential integration of the previously segregated domestic and Euro- markets) include the Thatcher government's lifting of foreign exchange restrictions (aside from individual bank limits and capital outflows), the Tory government's austere economic policies and the related substantial slowing of inflation, and the development of North Sea oil, which has given the pound petrocurrency status.

The importance of the latter fell dramatically in the period December 1985-August 1986 as North Sea Brent petroleum dropped to below $10 a barrel, but regained importance at end-August 1986, as North Sea Brent jumped to $15 in the wake of an OPEC agreement to cut production by 4 million barrels per day to 16 million barrels.

Since the abolition of exchange and credit controls in 1979, the Euro-sterling market and the domestic market have moved harmoniously, with the Euro-sterling rates usually slightly more expensive than the domestic rates (only 0.25–0.50% differential, reducing arbitrage opportunities), and following domestic rates. The Euro-sterling rates can affect domestic rates if the pound appreciates (that is, movement into sterling). As a result, the Euro-sterling rates ease and force domestic rates down.

MARKET PARTICIPANTS

Paris is the center of the Euro-sterling market, and the principal banks in it include the major French, Belgian, British, and American (Chase, Citibank, Morgan Guaranty) banks, and Algemene Bank Nederland. A typical interbank Euro-sterling deal is for £8-12 million.

INTEREST RATE FACTORS

Recurrent factors influence domestic rates and thereby put pressure on the Euro-sterling rates. The last day of every month is the Bank of England's *reporting day,* which can cause modest rate jumps. Other factors tightening the market value include end-month VAT (value added tax) payments, and corporate tax payment days (nine months after the end of the corporation's accounting year), the two most important of which are September 30, and December 31. Payments for major share (rights) issues also tighten the market. To offset such tightening, the Bank of England buys Treasury bills and bankers' acceptances from the market.

If there is substantial pressure on the spot pound, the Bank of England will use the Euro-market, forcing interest rates as much as 70–80% higher to deter Euro-sterling borrowings in order to keep the spot pound stable. A final factor is the targeted monetary aggregates of *M0* (notes and coins in circulation and in banks, and banks' operational balances with the Bank of England) and Sterling *M3* (currency plus private sector sterling demand and time deposits).

INTEREST RATE MOVEMENTS: 1976–1987

Exceptional volatility has characterized the Euro-sterling market. The 1976 year-end rate for three-month Euro-sterling was 16%; in 1977, it was 6.65%; and in 1978, it was 12.65%; in 1979, it was 16.75%, and it peaked in 1980.1 at 18.50%. The rates eased later in 1981, dropping to 12% in 1981.2, but by year-end had increased once again to 15.50%. In 1982, rates declined (unevenly) throughout the year falling to 10.90% (above the end-October trough of 9.50%) by year-end due to the recession and related slowing in inflation (to 5.4% year-year in December from 12.0% the previous January). In January 1983, the rate rose to 11.75%, but then declined at a moderate rate throughout the rest of 1983, falling to 9⅜% by December. However, temporary pressure was exerted by the Falkland Islands crisis in early April, with rates rising to 13.75% level. In 1984 , three-month Euro-pounds traded in a range of 8.80% (April) to 12.30% (July), rising sharply in July due to pressure on the spot pound related to labor unrest, as well as central bank efforts to moderate excessive £ M-3 growth.

In 1985, it traded in a range of 11.20% (July) to 14.20% (January-February), ending the year at 11.80%. The peak early 1985 rate resulted from two 2% Bank of England dealing rate hikes in response to severe sterling weakness ($1.0345 on February 27), as well as excessive £ M-3 growth. Moderate tightening in the latter half of 1985 reflected the pound's status as a petrocurrency in an environment of bearish oil price sentiment.

In January 1986, it peaked at 13.40%, well above the end-1985 level, in reaction to bearish oil price pressures on the spot pound as well as ministerial resignations provoked by the Westland Helicopter acquisition controversy. Thereafter, rates fell, especially in the March-

April period, so that by June-July, they were in the 9.75–10.0% range. With an inflation rate of only 2.4% (Retail Price Index), they were the second highest real rates among industrial countries (after Australia). In the balance of 1986, rates rose 125 basis points despite 13.3% unemployment due to the need to shore up the faltering spot pound. In early 1987, rates have some scope for decline, but will remain the foil for pressures on the exchange rate. With the pound strong, the rate fell to 9.70% by end-1987.

The Euro-French Franc Market

HISTORICAL DEVELOPMENT

France's position as the world's fourth largest exporter ($95 billion in 1983), a reflection of its having the fifth largest GDP in the world ($512 billion in 1985), has promoted the growth of the Euro-French franc market. It is also supported by France's dramatic drop in inflation (4.7% in 1985, 4.3% in 1986 and an expected 5.0% in 1987), the great improvement in France's current account, (– FFr 1.5 billion in 1985, + FFr 26 billion in 1986 and a projected + FFr 18 billion in 1987) and the related strengthening in the spot French franc. With respect to the external positions of the European countries monitored by the Bank for International Settlements (BIS), French franc liabilities at end-1984 totalled the equivalent of $13.5 billion, well above the 1978 level of $7.4 billion and over quadruple the 1976 level of $3.2 billion. The Euro-French franc market ranks seventh in size behind the Euro-dollar, Deutschemark, Swiss franc, yen, ECU, and British pound.

The Euro-French franc market has grown and become more liquid due to such factors as two-thirds of all French exports being invoiced in French francs, the increase in Arab French franc deposits (related to purchase of French goods), and the diversification of reserves by central banks, despite the Banque de France not easing its regulations separating the domestic from the Euromarket. The Banque de France prohibits French residents (banks, corporations, etc.) from transferring capital abroad, although nonresident-owned funds may flow freely across the borders. Specifically, residents are not permitted to deposit into the Euro-French franc market. Moreover, forward sales of French francs (that is, forward purchases of foreign currencies) are prohibited unless related to an underlying commercial or financial transaction. In March 1982, severe pressure on the spot French franc despite interest rate hikes led the French authorities to impose even more stringent regulations on currency flows, including shortening the maximum period for repatriation of export earnings (lagging). Subsequently, the period was increased to 3 months.

MARKET PARTICIPANT

The major center for Euro-French franc trading is Brussels, with London and New York as secondary centers. The major participants include the foreign (especially London) branches of the "Big 3" French banks (Credit Lyonnais, Societe Generale, Banque Nationale de Paris), major Belgian banks, Deutsche Bank-Dusseldorf, Morgan Guaranty-Zurich, Credit Suisse, Premium Bank of Switzerland, Citibank-London and New York, and Commerzbank. A typical interbank Euro-French franc deal is for FFr 25 million.

INTEREST RATE FACTORS

In general, Euro-French franc rates are 2–4% higher than domestic rates, with the relatively high rate structure for both reflecting France's above-average inflation (June 1986, 2.3% year/year, while the comparable figure for Germany was − 0.8%). Speculation against the French franc (especially when there is anticipation of a devaluation) pushes up the Euro-French franc rates, while the Banque de France controls domestic rates, keeping them lower to promote the government's macroeconomic objectives. Reserve day reporting on the fifteenth of each month causes rates to jump slightly, and year-end rate tightness can also be observed. A final factor is the targeted monetary aggregate of M3 (currency demand deposits, savings, and all time deposits plus short-term non-negotiable financial instruments).

INTEREST RATE MOVEMENTS: 1978–1987

Great fluctuations in the Euro-French franc rates have been observed over the last few years due to speculation against the franc. Rates in 1978, exemplified by three-month deposits, went as high as 14¾%

before declining in early 1979 to 7–8%. By the end of 1979, however, they had risen again to 14%. Rates eased to 11% by the end of 1980, went down to 10½% in February 1981, before soaring to 28¼% in the beginning of September due to rumors of a French franc EMS devaluation, which occurred October 5 (3%); subsequently, Euro-French franc rates closed the year at 17½%. In 1982, French franc Eurodeposit rates exhibited great volatility amidst rumors of another French franc devaluation (due to a large trade deficit and high inflation related to Mitterand's reflationary policies) within the EMS — in May, the rate peaked at 29%, with the anticipated devaluation occurring in June 14 (5.75%). By December, the rate had declined to 20%, with expectations of yet another French franc devaluation postponed to March 1983. Those expectations led to a rate hike in the weeks in front of the March 21 devaluation (2.5%) to 30-38% for three-month Euro-French francs (80% for the one-month) and reportedly as high as 5,000% for one deal on overnight Euro-French francs (Barclays was the fortunate lender).

Subsequently, the rate declined, if unevenly, falling to the 13% level by December, reflecting the success of Mitterand's austerity plan. In 1984, three-month Euro-French francs traded in a wide range of 10.65% (December) to 17.15% (February). The peak February-March rates reflected expectations of a EMS realignment that did not materialize. The end-December rate of 10.65% was due to inflation slowing to 6.7% amidst only 1.6% real GDP growth, while a strong spot dollar prevented the intra-EMS strains that frequently push up Euro-French franc rates.

In 1985, it traded in a range of 9% (November) to 13% at the end of December. For most of the year, it was in the 10-11% range. In January 1986, it dropped dramatically to 11.75%, reflecting temporary abatement of EMS realignment pressures. However, rates rose to the 15%-16% level in February-March in front of the March 18 national elections, in which the Gaulists defeated the Socialists, leading to Chirac becoming the prime minister. Thereafter, rates fell, with a 500-basis-point drop to 7.50% being recorded in April. In July-September rates fell further to 7.25%, reflecting the strength of the spot French franc, low inflation (2.1%), sluggish growth (2.0% projected in 1986), and the relatively large current account surplus. Rates rose somewhat in the fall in tandem with other European rates, and also impacted somewhat by massive student protests. In 1987, the franc's vulnerability precludes a unilateral drop in French interest rates, but France would tend to follow a cut in German rates. Between end-1986 and end-1987.1, the rate modestly increased from 7.65% to 7.75%.

The Euro-Dutch Guilder Market

HISTORICAL DEVELOPMENT

The Euro-Dutch guilder market has developed into the eighth largest such market, largely due to the strength of the Dutch guilder (DG), related to Holland's large current account surplus (1986, DG18, billion boosted by natural gas exports), low inflation (1986 year/year, –0.1%), well managed economy, and the European Monetary System link of the Dutch guilder to the Deutschemark. (The two are regarded as the two strongest EMS units, exemplified by the guilder revaluations of 5.5% in October 1981, 4.25% in June 1982, 3.5% in March 1983 and 3% in January 1987). An additional factor is Holland's role as a major exporter (1983, $65 billion), coupled with its having the world's ninth largest GDP (1985, $124 billion).

With respect to the external positions of banks in the 19 countries monitored by the Bank for International Settlements (BIS), Dutch guilder liabilities at end-1983 totalled the equivalent of $11.5 billion, triple the $3.53 billion in 1976, with comparable 1977 and 1978 totals being $5.0 billion and $7.4 billion, respectively. For end-1984, the corresponding total was $12.3 billion.

The Euro-Dutch guilder market can be expected to continue to grow, for the guilder is viewed as an attractive hard currency. It has appeal as an energy-based currency, and one that is insulated geopolitically (it is not directly exposed, as is Germany, to the Soviet bloc). Its attractiveness has encouraged diversification of Arab oil money into Dutch government securities (Arabs have purchased approximately 20–30% of the Dutch bonds floated), with corresponding effect on the Euro-Dutch guilder market.

Prior to January 28, 1980, the central bank (Netherlands Bank) had put a limit of DG500,000 on external borrowing by corporations without special permission to prevent capital inflow from abroad and thereby appreciation of the guilder (that is, Dutch banks could not have a net external position greater than DG5 million). Also, the "maximum external liability margin" allowed to any bank was DG20 million. These regulations had led to disparate Euro-Dutch guilder and domestic rates and, therefore, two distinct markets.

However, the restrictions were lifted in January 1980 due to a number of factors including the balance of payments deterioration (that is, balance of payments deficits), the unlikelihood of guilder appreciation, Holland's suffering from high inflationary pressure, and the necessity for credit options to expand (corporate business was given priority by the banks). Since the termination, no barriers exist between the domestic and Euro-Dutch guilder markets. High guilder liquidity is reflected in the market with no restrictions and the same interest rates.

MARKET PARTICIPANTS

Most of the Euro-Dutch guilder volume is handled by the large Dutch banks (especially Algemene, Amsterdam-Rotterdam, Slavenberg, Rabo, and NMB), while other active banks include Barclays, National Westminister, Midland, Lloyds Bank International-London, European American Bank, Morgan Guaranty, Citibank, Chemical Bank, Bank of America-London and New York, and the three major German banks. The major trading center is London, with some activity in New York; the average interbank deal is for DG 10–15 million.

INTEREST RATE FACTORS

The Dutch central bank maintains direct controls on bank asset growth, allowing only a 10% increase per annum; however, given the current slow growth of the Dutch economy, credit demands are limited. If demand were to increase substantially, external rates would rise more slowly than domestic rates. Other factors exist that influence rates on a recurring basis. The Dutch watch the Deutschemark rates closely, since Holland is tightly bound to Germany through trade. (Germany is both Holland's major customers and supplier.) Natural gas payments cause end-of-quarter easing, while pension fund payments bring end-of-month tightness. Tax dates, with the most important one in November, cause increases of 200 basis points, with substantial swings at year-end.

The central bank has enormous influence and makes unpredictable moves to affect rates at times. It offers temporary bank loans in response to market tightness, with a fixed amount available at a fixed rate, but does not announce until two days prior when the offering will be made, only the term-end. The special loans (several billion guilders) influence the money market by as much as 25–50 basis points. The central bank will influence the market on a long-term basis by buying bank debts, with quotas set according to the banks' market shares. An important factor in its decision-making is the targeted monetary aggregate of *M2* (currency plus demand, short-term time, liquid savings and foreign-currency-denominated deposits plus claims on government).

Under the previous restrictions, internal demand was always greater than external demand when companies were prohibited to borrow externally in excess of DG500,000 (unless special permission was obtained). Great discrepancies were common; for example, when domestic rates peaked at 25%, the Euro-Dutch guilder rate was only 16%.

INTEREST RATE MOVEMENTS: 1978–1987

In 1978, the average three-month Euro-Dutch guilder rate was 6.20%, but in 1978.4 it ranged from 8.75% to 11%. The rate in 1979 ranged from 6.90% to 15.25% in December, while by December 1980, the rate had dropped to 9.25%. It rose again in 1981, reaching 12.90% in September, although it eased by year-end to 10.80%. Subsequently, the rate fell throughout 1982, falling to 5.20% by end-December. The rate troughed at end-March 1983 at 4.20%, subsequently rising to 6.20% by December. Downward pressure results from an inflation rate that remains relatively low compared to almost all other European countries and an extremely high level of unemployment (around 17%) that generates reflationary pressures. During 1984, it traded in a narrow range of 5.75% (January) to 6.40% (July), rising in July due to the high dollar interest rates and related strong spot dollar.

During 1985, it traded in a range from 7.15% in February when the spot dollar peaked to a low of 5.70% in October, closing the year at 5.80%. By mid-January 1986, it had declined to 5.75%. During January-July 1986 it averaged 5.5%, while trading in a range of 5.20% (April) to 6% (early July); in early September, the rate stood at 5.15%. The slightly greater-than-normal favorable differential between Dutch and German interest rates (due to central bank support of the guilder by raising deposit rates) is narrowing with the end of election period uncertainties. (Prime Minister Lubbers and his center coalition were returned to office for four more years.) In the balance of 1986, Euro-guilder rates rose more than Euro-Deutschemark rates, widening the differential in favor of guilder rates from 70 to 120 basis points. However, guilder rates declined in early 1987 (though bond rates did not match the fall due to the pressure of a rising fiscal deficit), with the rate dropping from 6.25% at end-1986 to 5.30% at end-1987.1. A slight further decline was expected.

The Euro-Belgian Franc Market

HISTORICAL DEVELOPMENT

Reflecting the relatively modest size of the Belgian economy (its $71 billion GNP produced by its 10 million people, is less than two-thirds the size of Holland's), the Euro-Belgian franc market is the smallest Euromarket aside from Euro-lira and Euro-Canadian dollars. However, in 1984 it grew a significant 20% to the equivalent of $7.2 billion (liabilities), reversing a 5% contraction the previous year.

Stimulating the growth of the Euro-Belgian market is an interest rate level several points above its German and Dutch neighbors, who are Belgian's principal trading partners. However, the beneficial effect of the interest rate differential is undermined by a comparable inflation rate differential, which, in turn, leads to periodic devaluations of the Belgian franc within EMS. For example, the Belgian franc was devalued a relative 2% against the Deutschmark and guilder in the April 1986 EMS realignment (while being revalued 4% against the French franc). However, that devaluation could mark the "end of an era" as Belgium has slowed its inflation rate down to the 1% range (a CPI of only 0.6% year/year in June 1986), while moving into current account surplus (despite a structural merchandise trade deficit). The BFr 45 billion surplus in 1985, which should grow to BFr 70 billion this year, reflects surpluses in banking, insurance, and engineering services. Related to Belgium's economic improvements, as well as to give added credibility to its austerity program, the Belgium franc was revalued 2% against the EMS currencies in January 1987 (aside from the mark and guilder against which it was devalued 1%).

MARKET PARTICIPANTS

About 90% of Euro-Belgian franc activity takes place in Luxemburg, with London accounting for most of the balance. The major participants besides the Banque International du Luxembourg, are the "Big 3" Belgian banks, the $25-billion Sóciete Generale de Banque (now known as Generale Banque), the $19-billion Banque Bruxelles Lambert, and the $17-billion Kredietbank International. German banks are also active in the market.

INTEREST RATE FACTORS

Euro-Belgian franc rates closely follow domestic rates as the prohibition on Belgian residents depositing into the Euromarket is poorly enforced. However, slightly higher yields are generally available in the Euromarket, reflecting its greater competitiveness as opposed to the de facto *cartelization* of the highly concentrated Belgian domestic banking market.

INTEREST RATE MOVEMENTS: 1982–1987

Interest rate movements over the past few years have been relatively moderate. However, some years ago, when the Belgian franc was under speculative attack, the overnight rate at times would jump to a few hundred percent.

Euro-Belgian francs rates as exemplified by the three-month deposit rate, were at 12.25% at year-end 1982, down from the 14.40% in July. In 1983, they traded in a range of 9.00% (July) to 12.30% (January), ending the year 10.95%. Rates rose by February 1984 to 12.45%, but fell to 10.55% by the end of the year. Again rates rose in February 1985 (to 10.81%) as the U.S. dollar peaked, but fell back to 8.45% by early December and closed the year at 9.65%. Subsequently, they rose to 9.80% by mid-January 1986, but fell thereafter to 7.25% by July, and slightly further to 7.15% by September, with pronounced drops in the April-May period. Factors behind the decline included the April realignment of the EMS, a steep drop in Belgian inflation, and the proposal of deep budget cuts by the center-right ruling coalition (an extremely austere two-year budget that would reduce the 1987 deficit by about a third). In the balance of 1986, rates rose 30 basis points, in tandem with rising EMS rates, despite a continued strengthening of the Belgian franc against the dollar, and a reduction of Belgium's fiscal gap. (Currently, government debt is slightly over 100% of GNP, and government borrowing represents over 11% of GNP — 8% is the target for 1987). In 1987, rates are likely to decline only marginally despite plans to cut the budget deficit by about a third, low inflation (expected CPI advances of only 0.7% and 1.5%, for 1986 and 1987), and sluggish growth (expected GNP growth of only 2.1% and 1.3%, for 1986 and 1987).

The Euro-Italian Lira Market

HISTORICAL DEVELOPMENT

Despite the large size of the Italian economy (1985 GDP, $319 billion; 1985 exports, $68 billion) ranking sixth in the world, the Euro-lira market, which totaled the equivalent of $4.8 billion at end-1984, is the smallest (aside from Euro-Canadian and Australian dollars) of the major Euro-currency markets. Restraining its growth is investor lack of confidence in the spot lira due to Italy's perennial inflation, trade and fiscal problems. Exemplifying the latter, Italy's 1985 inflation was 8.5% and in 1986, 4.3% (12.7% in 1983), well above its principal EEC partners, while its 1986 trade deficit was Lit 3.7 trillion, with a larger Lit 7 trillion deficit forecast for 1987. (However, Italy had a Lit 10 trillion current account surplus in 1986 and a   Lit 8 billion surplus is expected in 1987.) Moreover, its 1985 budget deficit State sector borrowing requirement (Lit 100 trillion) was over 15% of GDP; while its 1986 budget, also with an excessive but improved deficit of 14% of GDP or Lit 109.3 trillion, was the subject of heavy lobbying of the Italian Parliament.

Conversely, when there are no strains within the EMS (such as the absence of intra-EMs exchange risk in the extended period of calm following a realignment), investors favor the Eurolira market because it offers the highest deposit rates of the major currency markets. The high deposit rates which induce inflows, combined with the episodic threats of devaluation within an EMS realignment (most recently 8% in July 1985 and 3% in January 1987) which induce outflows, account for much of the lira's volatility and its privileged 12% wide band within the

EMS (the other seven members have 4.5% wide bands). A final special feature of the Eurolira market is that it is one of the few such markets in which liabilities exceed assets (cf. Euro-Deutchemark and Euro-Swiss francs where assets significantly exceed liabilities), reflecting the wariness of denominating assets in the "soft" lira.

While the Eurolira market is small, it has been growing rapidly. In 1983, it grew 5.6% to the equivalent of $3.8 billion, and then amidst the EMS stability induced by a firm U.S. dollar in 1984, it leaped 26% to the equivalent of $4.8 billion. However, with the spot dollar weakening since February 1985, intra-EMS strains grew, as did the related expectation of a significant lira devaluation in the spring of 1985. The expected devaluation, which occurred in August (8%) retarded the growth of the market, as did expectations of additional devaluations. While the lira was devalued on a relative basis in January 1987, it has fundamentally strengthened as indicated by it non-recourse to the wider 12% band of fluctuation (i.e., it has remained within the 4.5% wide band).

MARKET PARTICIPANTS

London is the center of the Eurolira market, accounting for 90% of activity. Luxembourg, Amsterdam and New York represent the balance of the market. The principal participating banks are the major Italian ones, including Banca Italiana Commerciale (BCI), Istituto San Paulo di Torino, Banca di Roma, Credito Italiano and Italian International Bank. Dutch and Belgian banks are also active, especially Amsterdam-Rotterdam Bank (AMRO), and Kreditbank-Brussels. A typical interbank Euro-lira deal is Lit 10 billion ($6 million).

INTEREST RATE FACTORS

Euro-lira rates largely reflect domestic lira rates but are generally 1% to 2.5% higher. An important factor causing the latter margin is that Italian residents are prohibited by the Bank of Italy from depositing in the Euro-lira market. High domestic lira themselves rates reflect structural inflation resulting from the need to finance a budget deficit equivalent to 14% of GDP (government debt exceeds total GDP). Another interest rate factor is the targeted monetary aggregate of private sector credit (bank and special credit institution loans plus bonds issued by local authorities, public and private companies—net of loans consolidating debt of local authorities—less state sector borrowing requirements).

INTEREST RATE MOVEMENTS: 1982–1987

Eurolira rates as exemplified by three-month deposits jumped to 26.40% by the end of 1982, well above the 19.75% September level. During 1983, rates traded in a range of 16.90% (May) to 21.75% (February). A narrower range prevailed in the quiet year of 1984 when the spread was only from 14.25% (August) to 17.50% (February). Conversely, 1985 proved a much more volatile year, especially the beginning of December. While rates were as low as 11.50% in July, they jumped 300 basis points to over 17% in early December. Provoking the big uptick were three factors. These included a liquidity shortage in short dates which put compensating pressure on longer dates, an increase in central bank reserve requirements, and some fears of a lira EMS devaluation at the end of December.

Rates peaked in late January 1986 at 19.15% and then declined (especially in April) to 11.25% by end-May, at which rate they stabilized through the end of July, while falling further to 11% by early September. In the balance of 1986, rates rose 50 basis points to 11.50% in tandem with rising EMS rates, despite falling CPI inflation (only 4.3% year/year in 1986). In 1987, officials are trying to guide interest rates lower as reflected in a 10.15% rate at end-1987.1, and the scope for a further basis point drop, but growing pressure on the currency (including the likelihood of another lira devaluation in late-1987) will force an eventual reversal in interest rates. Prompting the devaluation will be the cumulative inflation differential with Germany, as CPI inflation is expected to be 5.0% in 1987, up from 4.3% in 1986.

The Euro-Canadian Dollar Market

HISTORICAL DEVELOPMENT

The Euro-Canadian dollar market is the smallest of all the Euromarkets despite Canada's relatively large GDP (1985, $320 billion) and exports (1986, $90 billion), due to restrictions imposed by the Canadian government, lack of international recognition, and small demand for Canadian dollars. Its total size is estimated at around C$5 billion (U.S. $3.5 billion).

However, it has grown very rapidly since the December 1, 1980 proclamation of the Banks and Banking Law Revision Act. (It was initiated in the early 1970s by institutions such as the Province of Quebec and Hydro-Quebec.) A key provision of the Act was that Canadian banks no longer have to pay reserves on nonresident Canadian dollar deposits booked abroad. Also, related withholding taxes were nullified. As a consequence, such deposits jumped from around C$650 million in the period preceding the Act to C$2.325 billion mid-1983.

Additionally, Canadian dollar deposit growth benefited from currency diversification strategies of central banks and other institutional investors. While the Canadian dollar had a soft tone against the U.S. dollar, on a trade-weighted basis it performed well, given its appreciation against the European currencies and the yen. Moreover, the forward Canadian dollar from June 1983 till June 1984 was at a premium against the U.S. dollar in the entire maturity span out to a year, encouraging funds flows on a covered basis.

A final important factor in the Euro-Canadian dollar market's rapid growth was the corresponding rapid growth of the related Euro-Canadian dollar bond market, now estimated at C$4.2 billion, well above the C$750 million level a few years ago. The relationship is based on prospective purchasers of Euro-Canadian dollar bond issues building up funds in the form of Euro-Canadian dollar deposits; and upon maturity of the bonds, temporarily placing their redemption monies in the Euro-Canadian dollar deposit market. The Euro-Canadian dollar bond market has grown significantly due to a rate advantage over Euro-dollar bonds. A favorable factor for both the Eurodeposit and bond markets is that the forward market in Canadian dollars is a very large one. Hedging up to five years can be done.

Nevertheless, the Euro-Canadian dollar market remains relatively small due significantly to the fact that frequently there is avoidance of the Canadian dollar market by Canadian entities. Typical borrowing is done by borrowing foreign currency and converting it into Canadian dollars. Other borrowings are done in the foreign currency used for transaction purposes in another country and are repaid in the same currency. For example, to avoid a double exposure risk, a Quebec power company that provides energy to the U.S. will raise funds in U.S. dollars, receive payments in U.S. dollars, and repay the loan in U.S. dollars. If the company had borrowed domestic Canadian dollars, or Euro-Canadian dollars, it would have had to convert its U.S. dollar receivables into Canadian dollars to repay the loan. To avoid such exposure risks, most exported raw materials are quoted in U.S. dollars and resource companies are very U.S.-dollar-oriented. Furthermore, interest rates are usually higher in Canada than in the U.S. in order to attract capital into Canada to finance its structural current account deficit (the current account surplus in 1983-1984 was aberrational), projected at C$7.0 billion in 1987, after C$8.8 billion in 1986.

Moreover, companies have had little need to go outside of Canada to raise funds since domestic banks usually have sufficient funds to meet their needs. Additionally, major Canadian corporations do not generally have investments outside the Western Hemisphere. Hence, the Canadian dollar outside North America is not especially acceptable.

Finally, investors in Canadian dollars will buy Canadian dollar spot and invest in domestic money market instruments like Canadian Treasury bills rather than place funds in the Euro- Canadian dollar market, for the domestic rates have been frequently more favorable than the Euro-rates (such as in December 1985 by 25 basis points).

MARKET PARTICIPANTS

The major trading centers are London, Nassau, and Toronto (interbank deposits are not reservable), and the major banks participating include Chase, Citibank, Bank of America-London, Royal Bank of Canada, Bank of Montreal, Bank of Nova Scotia, Toronto Dominion Bank, the Canadian Imperial Bank of Commerce, Barclays, and the "Big 3" Swiss and German banks (the latter two groups if the demand is great). A typical interbank deal size is C$5-20 million.

INTEREST RATE FACTORS

Euro-Canadian interest rates closely follow domestic interest rates with few barriers between the markets. Domestic interest rates, in turn, reflect monetary policy, inflation and the cyclical demand for funds, but also the recurring need to shore up the spot Canadian dollar via northward financial inflows by offering a favorable differential to Canadian dollar investors. (U.S. rates, of course, exert a major influence, with some analysts speaking of Canada as the "thirteenth Federal Reserve district.") For example, during the period January 1962–August 1983, 90-day paper was on average 73 basis points higher in Canada than in the U.S. (155 basis points during 1976-1977 due to pronounced Canadian dollar weakness). However, in the latter half of 1983, Canadian dollar rates were stable, while U.S. dollar rates rose through them, with the acquiescence of the authorities due to a favorable current account, increased foreign equity flows due to a less adverse atmosphere, and concern over unemployment in excess of 11%. A slight distortion in short-term domestic rates may result from the fact that required reserves are calculated on the basis of *Wednesday deposits* as opposed to daily accounting. The setting of the bank rate on Thursdays and oil payments between the 15th and 20th of every month also affect the market.

INTEREST RATE MOVEMENTS: 1978–1987

In 1978, the three-month Euro-Canadian dollar deposit rate increased gradually from 7.20% to 10.65%. It continued to rise throughout 1979, reaching a December average of 13.63%. The three-month rate in line with U.S. dollar deposit rates, peaked again at the end of 1980, and reached a high of 21.75% in August 1981, before easing to 15.25% by the year's end. Subsequently, the 1982 peak was 17.50% at end-June reflecting the weakness of the spot Canadian dollar, and the related inflation rate of 13%. While the Canadian rates are generally kept higher than U.S. rates, to promote financial inflows and strengthen the Canadian dollar, the severe Canadian recession was a limiting factor on the favorable interest rate margin. By October, the recession-induced large drop in U.S. rates allowed the Bank of Canada to ease, with the three-month rate falling to 11.40%, 1.65% above the comparable Euro-dollar rate; by year-end 1982, the rate fell further to 10.40%.

Throughout 1983, the three-month Euro-rate slid unevenly with the 9.5% December rate above the 9% September trough. Of particular note in early June, the Canadian dollar deposit rates fell below comparable U.S. rates and remained so the rest of 1983. During January-June 1984, the three month Canadian dollar rate rose in tandem with the three-month U.S. dollar rate, but remained generally 20–30 basis points below it. However, in mid-June, spot Canadian dollar weaknesses pushed the Canadian dollar deposit rate above the corresponding dollar rate, with a widening differential that reached 100 basis points by end-July and 175 basis points by the end of the year (10.30% vs. 8.55%). In 1985, it varied in a range from 8.30% (October) to 11% (February- March), the latter being the period of peak U.S. dollar strength and Euro-dollar deposit rates. At year-end, it was 9.00%, but had jumped to 9.90% by mid-January 1986 reflecting weakness of the spot Canadian dollar related to declining energy prices and a weak assessment of the Mulroony government. Thereafter, rates declined steadily through end-May to 8.15%, but in June-July rose to 8.75%, before dropping to 8.15% by year-end.

Rates declined further in 1987.1 to 6.90% by the end of the quarter. However, some upward pressures on rates are projected in the balance of 1987 due to higher U.S. rates, and as the Canadian dollar begins to ease moderately against the U.S. dollar. Factors behind the renewed weakness will include the uncertain duration of firm oil prices, persistent inflation in the 4% range (due to increases in indirect taxes, depreciation of the exchange rate, and high price controls on agricultural and energy products), a current account deficit of C$ 7.0 billion expected in 1987 (after C$8.8 billion in 1986), and export losses caused by trade conflicts with the U.S. (such as lumber products). Also, depressing the Canadian dollar will be narrowing in its favorable interest rate differential with the U.S. dollar (only 32 basis points at end-March 1987, compared with 244 basis points at end-October 1986), as U.S. rates rise amidst economic acceleration and spot dollar weakness, but a tandem increase in Canadian rates is moderated by the need to reduce 9.4% unemployment (November) and an expected narrowing of the current account deficit in 1987 to C$7.0 billion.

The Euro-Australian Dollar Market

HISTORICAL DEVELOPMENT

The Euro-Australian dollar market was initiated by the London branches of Australia's largest banks in the late 1970s. Market volume considerably expanded in the mid-1980s due to two factors. First, a considerable U.S. dollar/Australian dollar swap market has developed as a cheaper way to borrow U.S. dollars, a strategy facilitated by the wide 50-basis-point bid-offer spread in Australian dollar deposit rates (cf., 12.5-basis-point spread on U.S. dollar deposits). Those swaps have been a major force behind the phenomenal growth of Australian dollar trading, which has become, for example, one of the most active currencies in the U.S. market.

Second, in 1986 and 1987, there have been several Australian dollar bond issues in the U.S. which have focused increased attention on the Australian dollar markets. Both fixed and floating rate bonds of three- to five-year maturities have been issued by such major firms as Borg Warner, the Bank of Boston, Security Pacific, and SLMA, the U.S. Government sponsored Student Loan Marketing Association (which swapped the proceeds into U.S. dollars, deriving a dollar funding cost slightly below the issuance of a "plain vanilla" dollar straight bond). The generous 13–14% yields on the securities have proven particularly attractive to pension funds and high net worth individuals who feel the 7% differential over comparable maturity U.S. yields gives them adequate protection from potential depreciation of the spot Australian dollar. (However, the securities are illiquid as reflected in wide bid-offer spreads; greater liquidity is available from Australian government paper, although it involves a 10% withholding tax.)

The weakness of the Australian dollar has been a restraint on the growth of the Euro-Australian dollar market. During 1981–1986, it has slid in terms of end-year rates from $1.128 to $0.981 to $0.902 to $0.825 to $0.680 to $0.659. However, it rose in 1987.1, to $0.687 in March. Factors depressing the unit have included a structural current account deficit averaging $9 billion, relatively high inflation (a December/December 9.8% CPI in 1986 and 7.5% expected in 1987) and substandard growth. Weak growth (1.5% in 1986, and a like performance expected in 1987) is caused by an excessive dependence on commodities (foods, coal, and metals) in a deflationary global environment, overpriced manufactured goods fostered by high wages (also excessive holidays and strikes) and protected by high tariffs, and tight monetary policy (the highest real interest rates among industrialized countries) to prevent a precipitous fall of the spot Australian dollar.

MARKET PARTICIPANTS

London is the major center of the Euro-Australian dollar market, followed by Hong Kong, Singapore, and New York (restricted to IBFs because of the Fed policy regarding foreign currency deposits and the 3% reserve requirement on borrowing Eurocurrencies). Active participants in the market include the offshore branches of the "Big 3" Australian banks, including the $30-billion Westpac Banking Corporation of Sydney (formed in 1982 by the merger of the Bank of New South Wales and the Commercial Bank of Australia), the $27-billion Australia and New Zealand Banking Group Ltd. of Melbourne, and the $19-billion National Australia Bank Ltd., also of Melbourne, as well as National Westminister Bank and several American banks including Citibank, Chase, Chemical, and Bankers Trust. New York brokers involved in the *Euro-Aussie* market include Lasser, Noonan, Prebon, Tullet, and Harlow.

INTEREST RATE FACTORS

Euro-Australia dollar rates are nearly identical to domestic rates reflecting arbitrage trading unhindered by significant barriers. However, a couple of factors differentiating the markets are the use of a 360-day interest rate basis in the Euromarket as opposed to 365-day basis in the domestic market, and a 10% withholding tax on nonresident interest earnings in the domestic market.

Euro-Australian rates trade off the domestic rates which are largely determined by the prevailing bank bill rates; i.e., those for negotiable paper sold for standard maturities (30, 60, 90, 120, 150, 180, 360 days) by the twenty officially licensed banks. Recurrent factors tightening Australian dollar rates include the April-May provisional tax time (advance payment of taxes), the corporate tax date at the end of June which marks the end of the fiscal year, and regularly scheduled auctions of Australian government securities.

INTEREST RATE MOVEMENTS 1984–1987

Euro-Australian dollar rates, as exemplified by the three-month deposit rate, were in the 10-13% range in 1984 and in a much higher 13-19% range in 1985. They began 1986 in the 18-19% range, but fell to the 15% level by April. Expectations of further monetary easing in the spring and summer, with a Labor government led by Prime Minister Bob Hawke confronting high unemployment, sent the spot Australian dollar into a steep fall, provoking, in response, some monetary tightening. Subsequently, however, rates fell, with the three-month deposit rate sliding to 13.81% by mid-July. Further drops occurred in the fall, reflecting a slowing economy, a tighter budget, and improved inflation prospects (such as a CPI of 5% in 1987). Rates rose in 1987.1 (from 13.63% at end-December) due to balance-of-payments problems exemplified by expected current account deficits of A$12 billion in 1987 after A$13.8 billion in 1986. Inflation of 9.8% in 1986, and an expected 7.5% in 1987 is also a factor. Nevertheless, some moderate downward adjustment of rates is expected in the balance of 1987.

Exhibit 4-2
FACTORS CREATING INTEREST RATE DIFFERENTIALS
BETWEEN DOMESTIC AND EURO-MARKETS

1. Interest rate ceilings on domestic deposits (such as *Regulation Q* in the U.S.).

2. Reserve requirements on domestic deposits (such as *Regulation D* in the U.S.).

3. Insurance premiums on domestic deposits (such as FDIC in the U.S.).

4. Marginal reserve requirements on accepting deposits from abroad (such as Germany and Switzerland in the late 1960s/early 1970s; *Regulation M* in the U.S.).

5. Intervention of the central bank exclusively in the domestic market as opposed to the Euromarket (like the Banque de France).

6. Perception of greater risk in the Euromarket (due to less rigorous bank examinations; no lender of last resort, subject to the BIS Concordat of 1975, revised in 1983; no reserve requirements; substantial third world credits, global debt crisis, and so on).

7. Quicker response to environmental change (volatility) in the Euromarket due to its *laissez-faire* character (such as no central bank to counter disorderly conditions; more immediate impact from forward foreign exchange market changes).

8. Capital controls: restrictions (to the point of complete prohibition) on residents lending to the Euromarket/nonresidents (such as French regulations).

9. Differentials in transaction costs including communications and brokerage fees (like Fed funds/CD brokers vs. Eurodollar brokers).

10. Differential impact of window dressing and the like at end of accounting periods (such as end-month, end-quarter, and especially end-year).

11. Differences in domestic and foreign credit conditions.

12. Forward exchange rates and exchange rate expectations.

13. Differences in scale of operations, with Eurodeals generally much larger.

14. Disinclination of banks to arbitrage small rate differences due to their policy of not ballooning their balance sheet for small profit, as such reduces ROA (return on assets) and ROE (return on equity); reinforcing the disinclination is the perception of higher risk than previously in interbank depositing due to the global debt crisis, the near failure of Continental Illinois, and similar factors.

Eurocurrency Deposit Rates

Eurocurrency deposit rates, depicted in Exhibit 4-3, have generally declined during the 1982-1986 period. Their descent reflects the comparable drop in global inflation and inflationary expectations amidst economic sluggishness, the related excess supply of key commodities, such as petroleum and copper, and austerity programs in debt-afflicted third world nations, especially in Latin America.

Among the nine leading Eurocurrencies, Euro-sterling generally exhibited the highest interest rates, reflecting monetary tightness, despite high unemployment, to protect a pound threatened by declining oil prices, political problems and a traditional, if provisionally resolved, inflation problem. The French franc also exhibited high rates, reflecting high inflation and fear of devaluations during EMS realignments.

Conversely, low rates are exhibited by the Deutschemark, Swiss franc, Dutch guilder, and Japanese yen, reflecting low inflation, reinforced by favorable balance of payments.

The disparate yield curves among the different currencies, and for a single currency in different time periods, should also be noted. While normal (positively sloped), inverted (negatively sloped), flat and mixed (normal and/or inverted and/or flat at different points along the yield curve), yield curves are all apparent, which has significance for both funding strategies and forward foreign exchange rates, individual currency patterns do assert themselves. For example, the U.S. dollar and Canadian dollar yield curves are generally positively sloped, those for sterling and the French franc are often inverted, and those for the mark, guilder, Swiss franc, and yen are relatively flat. Different inflationary expectations, and short-term money market pressures provoked by currency weakness, explain the difference in yield curves.

Exhibit 4-3
EUROCURRENCY DEPOSIT RATES, 1982–1986
(Prime Banks' Bid Rate, At or Near End of Month)

	1982 Dec	1983 Dec	1984 Dec	1985 Dec	1986 Jan	Feb	Mar	Apr	May	June
Eurodollar										
Overnight	9.25	9.50	8.63	12.25	7.88	7.81	7.63	6.88	6.81	8.25
One month	9.13	9.69	8.38	8.00	7.94	7.81	7.38	6.81	7.00	6.88
Three months	9.19	9.81	8.63	7.88	7.94	7.75	7.31	6.75	7.00	6.75
Six months	9.50	10.06	9.13	7.88	8.00	7.69	7.25	6.75	7.06	6.75
Twelve months	9.63	10.38	9.81	7.94	8.13	7.75	7.25	6.81	7.25	6.81
Euro-Canadian dollar										
One month	10.00	9.13	9.88	9.00	10.69	12.88	10.75	8.38	8.38	8.06
Three months	10.00	9.50	10.81	9.00	10.69	11.69	10.44	8.69	8.44	8.38
Six months	10.13	9.75	10.06	9.00	10.44	10.94	9.88	8.69	8.50	8.56
Twelve months	10.25	10.00	10.44	9.00	10.31	10.31	9.75	8.69	8.75	8.75
Euro-French franc										
One month	23.00	12.13	10.69	12.50	15.00	14.50	15.00	7.75	7.31	7.25
Three months	24.00	12.19	10.69	13.00	16.25	14.00	12.25	7.50	7.31	7.31
Six months	22.00	12.31	11.00	13.13	13.75	12.50	11.00	7.50	7.31	7.31
Twelve months	19.75	12.63	11.38	12.25	12.75	10.75	10.00	7.38	7.50	7.38
Euromark										
One month	5.88	5.25	5.50	4.75	4.56	4.56	4.44	4.56	4.56	4.44
Three months	5.88	5.88	5.50	4.75	4.57	4.44	4.44	4.50	4.56	4.50
Six months	5.94	6.13	5.56	4.75	4.57	4.38	4.44	4.44	4.63	4.56
Twelve months	6.00	6.38	5.56	4.81	4.63	4.38	4.44	4.44	4.75	4.63

Exhibit 4-3

	1982 Dec	1983 Dec	1984 Dec	1985 Dec	Jan	Feb	Mar	Apr	May	June
Euro-Dutch guilder										
One month	5.13	5.81	5.69	5.75	5.69	5.81	5.50	5.75	6.13	6.25
Three months	5.19	6.00	5.75	5.75	5.69	5.81	5.44	5.50	5.81	6.06
Six months	5.38	6.25	5.81	5.81	5.69	5.75	5.44	5.38	5.63	5.81
Twelve months	5.63	6.38	5.94	5.88	5.75	5.75	5.44	5.31	5.63	5.75
Euro-Swiss franc										
One month	2.81	3.38	4.44	3.88	4.06	3.75	4.00	4.13	4.88	5.00
Three months	3.25	3.75	4.56	4.00	4.06	3.75	3.94	4.13	4.69	5.06
Six months	3.44	3.94	4.63	4.00	4.06	3.75	3.81	4.06	4.56	4.88
Twelve months	3.44	3.94	4.69	4.06	4.13	3.81	3.75	3.94	4.44	4.75
Eurosterling										
One month	10.56	9.13	9.50	11.69	12.75	12.56	11.75	10.81	10.00	10.06
Three months	10.44	9.31	9.88	11.81	12.81	12.31	11.31	10.38	9.81	9.81
Six months	10.31	9.50	10.00	11.81	12.75	12.00	10.56	9.81	9.69	9.69
Twelve months	10.31	9.81	10.19	11.69	12.63	11.69	10.25	9.50	9.44	9.63
Euroyen										
One month	6.75	6.25	6.19	7.13	6.38	6.50	5.56	4.94	4.75	4.69
Three months	6.75	6.31	6.19	6.58	6.13	5.88	5.25	4.81	4.75	4.88
Six months	7.10	6.38	6.13	6.50	6.06	6.56	5.13	4.69	4.81	4.63
Twelve months	6.81	6.44	6.13	6.38	6.00	6.56	5.06	4.69	4.88	4.63
European currency unit										
One month	12.44	8.81	9.25	9.63	10.63	9.94	10.06	7.94	7.31	7.38
Three months	12.31	9.19	9.38	9.63	10.13	9.88	9.50	7.56	7.31	7.31
Six months	12.00	9.44	9.50	9.63	9.75	9.44	8.50	7.38	7.31	7.25
Twelve months	11.19	9.63	9.63	9.63	9.13	9.06	8.06	7.19	7.13	7.25

1986

5

Interbank Eurocurrency Trading

Interbank Eurocurrency trading represents a substantial part of total Eurocurrency market activity. Understanding its diverse aspects is thus essential to a comprehension of the dynamics of the market.

The initial section of this unit details the systemic functions of interbank trading both *within* and *among* Eurocurrency centers. Then the immediate business purposes in dealing are clarified. Thereafter, the organization of the trading room, the decision-making process, the chronology of a deal, and the special features of Eurodollar trading are detailed. Finally, the relationships of the Euro-dollar market to the other markets, and the latest developments in Euro-dollar trading (such as futures and options) are discussed.

Interbank Eurodollar transactions are cleared via CHIPS, the Clearing House Interbank Payments System in New York. A description of CHIPS provides a sense of the mechanics of the back office operations in Eurotrading. Also, a description of the S.W.I.F.T. (Society for Worldwide Interbank Financial Telecommunications) system is included as many of CHIPS payments originate as S.W.I.F.T messages.

Complementing the section on interbank trading is a description of the critical role of the international Eurocurrency brokerage system, which links the banks together. An overview of such brokers, in New York and globally is followed by a description of the historical development of Garvin Guy Butler, which has emerged as the leading such firm in New York.

Following are the various dimensions of a Eurocurrency broker, such as his role, qualifications, and responsibilities, as well as the advantages of using a broker, and an identification of the brokers' customers. Completing the section are a description of brokerage house facilities and operations, including a "typical broking day," as well as the houses' revenue-expense "equation," their current problems, and the future of the Eurocurrency brokerage system.

ᕽ The unit concludes with a description of the mathematical relationship between the Eurocurrency and the forward foreign exchange market. Essentially, the interest rate differential between the Euro-dollar rate and the appropriate Eurocurrency rate for the maturity selected determines the forward foreign exchange rate. Any deviation between the two is quickly corrected by alert profit-seeking arbitrageurs.

Interbank Trading in the Eurocurrency Market

FUNCTIONS OF INTERBANK TRADING

Interbank Eurocurrency trading is conducted both *within* a Eurocurrency center and *between* Eurocurrency centers. Trading within a center fulfills the functions of liquidity smoothing, liquidity transfer, and currency transfer, while trading between centers fulfills the function of global liquidity distribution.

Liquidity smoothing involves the bank managing at the margin the structure of its assets and liabilities; it reduces intermediaries' transaction cost by economizing on the volume of precautionary balances that the bank has to hold. *Liquidity transfer* involves intra-marginal transfers of liquidity from one bank to another, reflecting the fact that not all banks are equally able to attract funds from primary depositors or from other banks outside the Eurocurrency center (factors of name, size, nationality, credit standing). Finally, *currency transfer* is the process by which banks match the currency composition of their assets and liabilities through interbank trading (avoiding foreign exchange exposure).

Global liquidity distribution results from the concurrency of four factors:

1. There are large excess demands and supplies of funds in individual local markets.

2. Transaction costs between nonbanks are very high (otherwise non-banks would contract directly).

3. Transaction costs between *nonbanks* and *banks* vary widely, being lower between parties in the same area (if this were not so, each bank would balance its own nonbank business).

4. Transaction costs between peripheral banks in different countries are higher than between peripheral banks and the Eurocurrency center (otherwise funds would flow *directly* between peripheral banks and not *through* a Eurocurrency center).

Banks deal in the interbank market to accomplish four primary purposes:

1. To fund the bank's loan book in Eurocurrencies (for example, where the home base is narrow or it is a lesser known bank).

2. To provide a service to depositing customers (such as Swiss banks).

3. To make profits from deliberate position taking (long-funding or short-funding), based on a forecast of interest rates.

4. To insure that the bank is seen in the marketplace both as a *taker* and a *placer* of funds, so that its name is kept in the market and is favorably received.

ORGANIZATION OF THE TRADING ROOM

The banks' trading rooms feature traders sitting around circular or rectangular "desks," with large phone consoles (direct lines to brokers, outside lines for domestic/international phone calls and intra-bank lines to deal with the corporate officers and others) and Reuters/Tele-rate screens in front of them. Speaker phones, large calculators, and, increasingly, personal computers, round out the traders' equipment. Finally, there are the stacks of numbered loan/deposit tickets to be completed upon consummation of the deals.

Complementing the traders are the back office personnel who send out and receive the confirmations and payments. Separating the two functions enhances the integrity of the operation.

Finally, in New York trading rooms and elsewhere in the U.S., there are frequently special desks for Nassau/Cayman and the IBF. In New York, there is generally a preference to use the IBF as opposed to Nassau/Cayman because the former is tax-exempt, while Nassau/

Cayman deals actually *transacted* in New York are subject to New York State/City taxes.

THE DECISION-MAKING PROCESS

Traders determine the position they want to hold for various maturities by using a variety of information sources. These include newspapers such as *The New York Times* and *The Wall Street Journal*, electronic screens (Reuters, Telerate, Dow), the banks' management and economics department, external consultants (DRI, Wharton, Chase Econometrics, Evans Economics), technical models (charting, momentum oscillators), fellow traders, and the brokers.

They structure their bank's position subject to *external constraints,* such as reserve costs, balance sheet requirements, and tax implications, and *internal constraints,* such as the balance sheet size and mix, and credit and rate limitations. An important consideration is gap management, a situation that arises when assets exceed liabilities for a particular maturity (i.e., LRBA, liabilities repriced before assets), or liabilities exceed assets for a particular maturity (i.e., ARBL, assets repriced before liabilities).

SPECIAL FEATURES OF EUROCURRENCY TRADING

There is an active overnight and short dates market. The latter includes "tomorrow/next" (tom/next), which is settled (delivered) tomorrow and returned the following day, as well as "spot/next" (beginning two business days later), "spot week" (beginning on spot for one week), and "spot fortnight" (beggining on spot for two weeks). Complementing those markets is the term market. Such deals, done for a fixed number of months (generally one, two, three, six, nine or twelve months), begin normally on the spot date (two business days later) and mature on the same day of the month some number of months later. However, if that date is a weekend or bank holiday in the country of origin of the currency deposit (whose banks make the necessary transfers), then the convention is to go *forward* until a business day appears, except that if one thereby would move into the next month, then the convention is to go *backwards* until a business day appears. Traders are attentive to bank holidays to avoid bungled deals, using such resources as Morgan Guaranty's "holiday book annual" (*World Holiday and Time Guide*).

RELATIONSHIP OF THE EUROCURRENCY MARKET
TO OTHER MARKETS

The Eurocurrency markets are intimately linked to the various foreign exchange markets via the swap rates, which determine the outright forward rates. Moreover, the Eurocurrency markets are linked to their corresponding domestic markets. Traders seeking arbitrage opportunities are attentive to both sets of linkages.

DEVELOPMENTS IN THE EUROCURRENCY MARKET

The hotly competitive Eurocurrency market continuously spawns new products and techniques. A good example is Eurodollar futures, available at the CME, LIFFE, SIMEX, and the SFE as well as options on such futures, available at the CME and LIFFE. New techniques of technical analysis include growing use of momentum analysis, to complement the more traditional charting, as an interest rate forecasting tool.

CHIPS:

The Clearing House Interbank Payments System

CHIPS is the international private clearing system for Eurodollar market transactions. Daily transactions average over 125,000/day with average transaction size of $4 million, for a typical day volume of over $500 billion (often more).

CHIPS has a 140 participants including NYC banks, agencies, and branches of foreign banks, and U.S. money center banks outside New York. It includes 21 *settling participants* (the New York Clearing House Association Banks, excluding U.S. Trust and Republic, plus the NYC Edge Act Corporations of the major non-New York banks). CHIPS closes daily at 4:30 p.m. with the *non-settling participants* settling for a net surplus (credit to their account) or net debit position (necessitating a deposit into their account) with their respective settling participants by 6:00 p.m. Thereafter, the settling participants settle among each other, utilizing their accounts at the Federal Reserve Bank of New York for the final settlement.

CHIPS operates by utilizing a $12-million Burroughs 7900 (changing to AIS) computer (with substantial excess capacity and backed up by the New York Clearing House ACH computer) located in an old warehouse at 450 West 33rd Street (at Ninth Avenue). Participants are charged a moderate $.29 per transaction and there is a $50,000 initiation fee for new participants. Instructions are often received via S.W.I.F.T., the Society for Worldwide Interbank Financial Telecommunications.

A current issue is *intraday* overdrafts. Due to the use of the Federal Reserve Bank of New York for the final settlement, CHIPS is subject (since March 27, 1986) to the Fed's new *cross-system net sender debit caps* based on the banks' adjusted primary capital and operational level (also applies to the Fedwire and the 31 automated clearing houses or ACHs). The regulation is implemented using an on-line realtime computer system.

S.W.I.F.T.: Society for Worldwide Interbank Financial Telecommunications

Many Euromarket transactions are effected using S.W.I.F.T., such as many of the instructions messages to CHIPS. S.W.I.F.T. was founded in 1973, as a cooperative nonprofit organization to cope with the vast increase in international payments. It is owned by the banks it serves, with share ownership allocated in proportion to traffic volumes, and any country or group of countries accounting for over 1.5% of total system traffic being entitled to nominate a board member. Much of the impetus came from American banks in Europe, which wished to offer very fast international transfer systems.

Headquartered in La Hulpe (20 kilometers from the original headquarters in Brussels) since 1984, its original membership was 239 banks in 15 countries. Operations started May 1977 with 15 banks in Belgium, France, and Great Britain, transmitting 30,000 messages per day. By September 1980, the total had risen to 740 banks in 20 countries transmitting 200,000 messages per day. Today, 55 countries are members, and there are a further 20 country applications. Some 1,326 banks in 47 active countries, including Czechoslovakia and the People's Republic of China, transmit over 800,000 messages per day. Message switching centers operate in Zoeterwonde, Netherlands, and Culpeper, Virginia (site of the Federal Reserve System's switching center), the latter due to the presence of ATT long lines there. The centers are linked to autonomous regional processing centers located in each member country or main concentration area. Banks physically connect to S.W.I.F.T. by means of computer-based terminals called *interfaces* installed within their own premises — from the smallest microprocessor-driven terminal to the largest computer systems. Regional S.W.I.F.T. offices are to be found in New York, London, Rio de Janeiro, and Hong Kong.

Reflecting the work that has been done on connecting S.W.I.F.T. to CHIPS, in many cases it is possible to provide a complete electronic conversion from S.W.I.F.T. to CHIPS and vice versa (the latter is more complicated). Besides passing payment messages, S.W.I.F.T. also handles foreign exchange confirmation reconciliations (while international mail confirmations take at least five days), foreign collections, documentary credits (letters of credit), securities messages, and statement message (nostro accounts). Message types to be added in the future may include ones for gold and other precious metals, as well as traveler checks.

March 1987 will mark a major network upgrade for S.W.I.F.T. as it is the starting date for the S.W.I.F.T. II system. The current S.W.I.F.T. I system is approaching its capacity of around 1.1 million messages per day, while the successor S.W.I.F.T. II system is *modular* and therefore infinitely expandable. (In the interim period, until all member banks are on S.W.I.F.T. II, *bridge* software, known as S.W.I.F.T. I Emulation will enable S.W.I.F.T. I and S.W.I.F.T. II banks to communicate with each other). Also, it will offer additional capabilities, including on-line transmission, store and forward, bulk data transmission, and off-peak transmissions.

S.W.I.F.T. charges 18 Belgian francs per message unit, unchanged since the initiation of the system. As the standard message is 1.25 message units, the usual bank message cost at current exchange rates is $.48 per message (a fraction of the cost of a similar telex or cable transmission); other costs are a moderate initiation fee and modest annual fees. Besides savings on transmissions, bank members enjoy considerable cost reduction from using S.W.I.F.T.'s standard formats, which cut down costly manual procedures.

Another advantage of S.W.I.F.T. is that because of the highly secure protection measures and devices safeguarding the integrity of information moving through the system (which have never been violated), S.W.I.F.T. assumes full responsibility for the completeness, accuracy, and timely delivery of transaction instructions. A final advantage of S.W.I.F.T. is the ability for a bank to retrieve any message received or sent within a four-month period, and to verify details of the transaction or its transmission.

Reuters, Telerate, et al.

Interbank traders rely heavily on the electronic screens provided by Reuters, Telerate et al. for immediate, comprehensive information on the markets (including financial databases). Reuters screens are dominant in the global Eurocurrency market with 80% market share overall outside the U.S., compared to Telerate's 20% (according to a Dean Witter study). However, Telerate has overall 80% share in the U.S. and 20% overseas.

Officials of the British Reuters claims their service is being accessed by 60,700 users worldwide over teleprinters, terminals, and their Rich, Inc. trading stations. Moreover, Reuters has a presence in 104 countries, receives information from 88 exchanges worldwide, and draws on a staff of 770 journalists, with 14 new bureaus in North America alone; data is also received from 2,280 subscribers. Concurrently, officials of the American Telerate say the company, has 31,300 subscribers — 20,000 domestic and 10,300 based overseas. Information is generated by distilling the Dow Jones Capital Market Report and from over a thousand information providers. Both services provide real-time trading information 22.5 hours a day worldwide on U.S. Treasury and money instruments and 24 hours a day in foreign exchange. Other information vendors who offer instant on-line access to financial data include Security Pacific Market Information (SPMI) and Knight-Ridder Financial Information Services, both of New York.

The scope of information on Reuters and Telerate is staggering. For example, Telerate has 15,000 pages or screens of financial information, and the capacity to go to 30,000 pages. Markets covered include Eurodollars, foreign exchange, financial futures, mortgage-based securities and energy futures. Telerate's "hot pages" are page Eight, where U.S. Treasury coupon rates are provided by the number four broker's (primary dealers') broker, Cantor Fitzgerald, and the page Five U.S. money market composite page.

Concurrently, the older Reuters (since 1851) stresses its unparalleled coverage of the foreign exchange market (especially the exotic or "mutt" currencies), its on-line service which permits two traders to negotiate a transaction at the terminal using digital code while a high speed telex prints a record of their conversation at either end, and is competing with Telerate in the Treasuries market through a composite page MMKT and alliances with Nucom Securities and MKI Securities Corp., two small broker's brokers a la Cantor Fitzgerald. (Knight Ridder competes by offering MoneyCenter, which puts up prices from a primary dealer that has access to Garban Ltd., are of the three larger brokers, along with Fundamental Brokers Inc. and RMJ Securities Corp; SPMI gets its government bond rates through a primary dealer, Prudential-Bache.)

Fees for the four services are comparable. For prices, financial news and third party databases, Telerate charges $450 and an optional $285 per month to receive the full blown Dow Jones Capital Markets Report (Dow Jones & Company of South Brunswick, NJ and its partner, Oklahoma Publishing Corp., Oklahoma City own 52% of Telerate since July 1985). SPMI, which utilizes a two-foot satellite dish installed on customers' roofs, charges $450. Knight Ridder's MoneyCenter, which involves the use of an intelligent workstation (through a leased AT&T 6300 personal computer or the customer can use his own PC, such as an IBM XT at a $75 per month savings) charges $675 per month.

Looking ahead, Neil Hirsch's Telerate is negotiating to offer its full service on Citicorp's Quotron, and has been approached by the Merrill Lynch/IBM venture IMNET to appear on its networks; also Bunker Ramo, the second largest stock quotation vendor, an ADP subsidiary, has expressed interest in carrying Telerate's database. Meanwhile, Reuters is moving to dominate global trading in stocks through an off-floor trading system in international equities traded by 30 market-makers in six foreign countries. Also, it plans an international equity service for the U.S. with Rich (Reuters in 1985 purchased the Chicago-based manufacturer of trading keystations and switching systems, whose equipment gives traders — especially those at Merrill Lynch and Paine Webber — access to 77 information providers, including Reuters and Telerate) and Instinet (Reuters owns 7% of the automated block trading network for U.S. securities) as *the* trading link for large institutions.

The "Coke" and "Pepsi" of information services can be expected to coexist for a long time. This is because the monthly expense of both services is quite incidental to the potential profits that traders can make.

THE INTERNATIONAL NETWORK

Eurocurrency brokers, while concentrated in London and New York, are to be found in all the major Eurobanking centers. Many are branches of international networks, which are generally headquartered in London; others are individual brokers who operate internationally on a *correspondent* basis. Besides the London and New York brokerage centers, a high level of such brokerage activity is conducted in Paris, Frankfurt, Bahrain, Singapore, Toronto, and San Francisco.

Exhibit 5-1
THE EUROCURRENCY BROKERS IN LONDON, NEW YORK, AND SINGAPORE

The Eurocurrency Brokers in London*

1. Astley and Pearce (Exco)
2. Guy Butler (International) Ltd. (MAI)
3. Currency Brokers International Ltd. (Mayflower Holdings)
4. Fulton Prebon UK Ltd.
5. Godsell & Co. Ltd. (Exco)
6. Kirkland-Whittaker (Currency Deposit Brokers Ltd.)
7. Marshall Woellworth & Co. Ltd. (Mercantile House)
8. R.P. Martin Plc.
9. Shortloan International Ltd.
10. Tradition (London Brokers) Ltd.
11. Tullet and Tokyo Forex International Ltd.

*Holding company in parentheses

The Eurocurrency Brokers in New York*

1. Garvin Guy Butler (75)
2. Mabon Godsell (70)
3. Eurobrokers (50)
4. Tullet-Tokyo (50)
5. Lasser-Marshall (50)
6. Noonan-Astley Pearce (50)
7. Dominion Securities (50)
8. Bierbaum-R.P. Martin (50)
9. MKI (25)

*Approximate number of Eurocurrency brokers in parentheses

The Eurocurrency Brokers in Singapore

1. Astley & Pearce (Pte Ltd.)
2. Charles Fulton (Singapore) 1982 Ltd.
3. Harlow Sassoon (Singapore Pte Ltd.)
4. KTD Forex Pte Ltd.
5. Marshalls (Singapore) Pte Ltd.
6. Tan Swee Hee-Butler Pte Ltd.

Exhibit 5-2

THE HOLDING COMPANIES OF THE MAJOR EUROCURRENCY BROKERS
1986 FINANCIAL RESULTS
(in millions of pounds sterling)

Company	Group Turnover	Money/Securities Broking Turnover	Group Pre-Tax Profits	Money/Securities Broking Profits
Mercantile House Holding plc	385.0	175.6	75.4	29.6
Mills & Allan International plc	222.1	151.5	40.0	28.8
Exco International Ltd*	202.9	75.9	87.4	21.6
Tullett & Tokyo Forex International Ltd.	138.0		15.0	
International City Holdings	62.1	45.5	13.0	10.9
RP Martin plc*	39.3	37.2	8.7	9.3

* 1985 results

Source: *Euromoney*, February 1987.

HISTORICAL DEVELOPMENT OF
A TYPICAL EUROCURRENCY BROKERAGE FIRM

Garvin Butler's development is reasonably typical of the New York industry as a whole. It was formed in 1977 by the merger of two complementary firms, Garvin-Bantel (a leading Fed funds broker, founded in 1929) and Guy Butler-London, a leading Eurocurrency broker with an international business strategy. Five years later in 1982, it was acquired by the UK financial conglomerate Mills and Allan.

THE EUROCURRENCY BROKER

The Eurocurrency broker functions by bringing together two banks, one that has a Eurocurrency deposit of a particular maturity to offer and another that needs it. His success depends on his being able to get them to agree on a common rate (normally 12.5 basis points separates the bid and offer), and on the depositing bank having a *line* with "excess capacity" available to the bidding bank.

Banks use the brokers, despite the commission costs involved, due to four trading advantages offered by the brokers. First, the broker always quotes the optimum market — the highest bid and the lowest offer. Second, the broker, through his international branch and correspondent relationships, offers the bank trader access to worldwide markets. Third, use of the broker saves the banks the considerable time and financial costs of having its traders call up several banks to find an appropriate counterparty. Finally, the broker offers the preservation of anonymity to an offering or bidding bank, since a publically known offer or bid by a major bank like Citibank is quite likely to turn the market against it.

The qualifications of a Eurocurrency broker especially involve the capacity to be consistently attentive to clients' needs, to be energetic without being aggravating. This includes remembering all bids/offers and their cancellations, being in good psychological rapport with the customers, and having a sense of where the market is going. The responsibilities of a broker include accurate maintenance of all outstanding bids and offers, including the time involved for *implicit* cancellations (especially if the market has moved), timely provision of information on the market and global economy (obviously starting with the highest-volume clients), and the circumspect handling of big bids/offers so as not to significantly move the market against the client. Finally, the broker should be generally aware of who has lines to whom and not reveal the counterparty involved to the bidder until the depositing bank confirms the availability of an adequate remaining line to the bidding bank. In short, the three major responsibilities of the broker are good *execution,* the provision of timely and significant *information,* and *protection* of the bank clients.

Traditionally, all the customers of a broker were commercial banks. However, that was viewed by the U.S. Justice Department as a monopolist situation in violation of the Sherman and Clayton antitrust acts. Thus, the brokers must offer their services to *any* firm that does interbank-sized deals (that is, million-dollar multiples). In practice, nonbank firms involved in the *brokers' market* include big metal (such as Engelhard), oil (such as Exxon), grain (such as Continental Grain), insurance (like Aetna), industrial (such as Volkswagon, IBM), and investment banking companies (Salomon, Merrill Lynch).

While the presence of such firms expands the market, it also slows it down to the annoyance of the brokers as the offers of such firms are frequently short-term, small, and with many restrictions on counterparties. Also, the presence of such firms in the *brokers' market* upsets the banks who regard corporations as "their customers," *not* their counterparties. (In practice, American banks will not do business with their current customers through the brokers, but are willing to do business with "new clients" through the brokers to initiate a relationship. However, Canadian banks remain highly adverse to doing business through the brokers with any corporations.)

BROKERAGE HOUSE FACILITIES

To conduct their dynamic, high-speed business, the brokerage houses invest heavily in communications and electronics. At their own expense, they provide direct phone lines to the active banks, while providing their brokers with elaborate phone consoles (a client is called by simply pushing one button), multiple speaker phones for constant communication with the best clients (placed on different levels by using soda cans, to differentiate them) and possibly an *open line* (using a speaker phone) to the London office if it has one. To keep the brokers abreast of the changing market, a large slate *rate board* with all the bids and offers by maturities is continuously updated, and Reuters, Telerate, and Dow Jones screens are amply available.

BROKERAGE HOUSE OPERATIONS

Eurocurrency brokerage houses intermediate a variety of transactions. Immediate-term deposits include *overnight deposits, tom/next* (t/n), meaning tomorrow against the following day, and *spot/next* (s/n), meaning the second business day against the following day. *Short dates* include deposits beyond the spot day to just short of one month (generally 1, 2, 3 weeks). *Term deposits* include one month to a year (generally 1, 2, 3, 6, or 12 months). Finally, *medium-term deposits* from two to five years are brokered. Complementing the standard time deposits, Euro-dollar CDs and *forwards* (which are deposits starting on a future date beyond the spot date and maturing on a further date) are brokered as well.

TYPICAL BROKING DAY

Since the Eurocurrency market is a 24-hour global market, which functions in Europe prior to the New York opening, the New York brokers' day starts early. The first brokers arrive some time before 5:00 a.m. and speak with London to get a *rundown* on LIBOR deposits by maturity to fill in the rate board. Then the brokers are busy obtaining orders from 5:00 a.m. (early arrivals are banks with near-term short positions wanting to get good European rates, plus many bank traders like to be called early at home) till 4:30 p.m., the CHIPS deadline for Euro-dollar transactions. Deals are made between U.S. banks, and frequently with European ones as well utilizing a *link desk*, which generally has an open line to London for transactions with English and Continental banks (utilizing branches or correspondents there). Brokers stay busy completing orders, writing tickets, calculating commissions, and, monthly, sending out bills.

BROKERAGE HOUSE REVENUES AND EXPENSES

Revenues are wholly derived from commissions, which are theoretically negotiated by each house with its bank clients in order to avoid the monopolistic implications of standardized pricing. Nevertheless, there is a standard commission in New York, which use to be 2.25 basis points (.000225) or $.625 per $1 million per side per day, but which is currently 2 basis points (.0002) or $.55 per $1 million per side per day (the calculation is $1 million times .0002 divided by 360 days), the same as in London. Banks that do considerable volume, of course, negotiate significant discounts from the standard "bro."

Five categories of expenses comprise the expense side of the ledger. First, *salaries* are a major expense as top brokers earn between $50,000-$100,000 and their managers even more. Second, the state of the art *communication* (such as direct lines, and open lines to London) and information facilities (like Reuters) are costly as well. Moreover, as brokers are usually centrally located in the financial district, *rent* is another major expense. The fourth type of expense is *client relations*, which involves pricey luncheons and dinners, tickets to sports contests, and the like. Completing the expense side is *error adjustment*. When a broker makes an error (like forgetting that a bid was cancelled) and the client loses money (for example the market rates having dropped while a replacement bid is sought), the damaged party is entitled to a *difference check*. (In market vernacular, it is known as "getting stuffed".)

CURRENT PROBLEMS OF BROKERAGE HOUSES

Eurocurrency brokerage houses face four major problems. First is the problem of *declining volume* due to the growing bank preferences for direct dealing (using their own sales force) to reduce commission expenses, and for off-balance sheet instruments (futures market as opposed to the cash market) due to capital limitations. A second problem is the unrelenting bank *pressures to lower commissions*. As already indicated, rates have fallen in line with London. Third are *communications problems* due to misunderstandings and payment errors, which result in costly difference checks. However, the problem is much smaller now due to greatly increased use of tape recording (although, of course, the equipment, tapes, and operational/maintenance personnel have become a significant expense). Finally, there are the ever present *staffing problems*, especially in light of the strong demand for top brokers.

THE FUTURE OF THE EUROCURRENCY BROKERAGE SYSTEM

The future of the Eurocurrency brokerage system is uncertain, but it will definitely be different from the traditional structure as that competitive industry responds to the pressures on it. In particular, declining revenues, due both to drops in volumes and standard commissions, are spurring the quest for new business lines (such as broking swaps, currency options, floors, and caps on loans).

One promising area is diversification into the futures and options markets via subsidiaries, although that would entail significantly enhanced capital. A variety of other changes seems more likely, including increased market share for the large brokers, squeezing out the smaller ones. Other trends reflect increased corporate participation, and a changed market character due to a narrowing of spreads (such as 1/32 as opposed to ⅛). Finally, computerized matching of bids and offers is also dawning, but is intrinsically handicapped by the difficulties of factoring in bank lines, perceptions of bank quality, and similar factors, since operationally, diverse bank views produce a distinctively *nonhomogeneous* market.

The Relationship Between the Eurocurrency and Forward Foreign Exchange Markets

Substantial inter-bank dealing activity results from the linkage between the Eurocurrency and forward foreign exchange market exchange market (e.g., borrowing a foreign currency, and immediately swapping it into the domestic currency, while covering by buying the foreign currency forward). In particular, the forward exchange market rates (*outright forward, swaps*) essentially reflect the *net accessible interest rate differential* between a currency deposit and the U.S. dollar deposit for a particular maturity. *Net* means free of any withholding taxes, etc. and *accessible* means available to all market participants, as many domestic money markets (such as France's) are off-limits to nonresidents. In practical terms, the "net accessible interest rate differential" means the differential between the Eurodollar rate and the appropriate Eurocurrency rate for a particular maturity. *Arbitrage* rapidly corrects any deviations between a forward foreign exchange rate and the interest rate differentials.

If the currency has a higher interest rate than that of the dollar then the currency is at a *discount* in the forward market (that is, a lower value than in the spot market). Conversely, if the currency has a relatively lower interest rate, then it is at a *premium* in the forward market.

By way of example, assume the spot French franc is 8.50, the nine-month Eurodollar deposit rate is 10% and the corresponding nine-month Euro-French franc deposit rate is 14%. The interest rate diffe-rential is 4% (annualized rate). The general formula then to be used to determine the swap rate is as follows:

$$\text{Swap rate} = \frac{\text{Spot rate} \times \text{Interest rate differential}}{100} \times \text{effective time fraction}$$

In terms of our example, it is:

$$\text{Swap rate} = \frac{8.5000 \times 4}{100} \times \frac{9}{12} = .2550$$

Since the Euro-French franc interest rate is *higher* than the Eurodollar rate, the nine-month forward French franc is at a *discount*. Thus, the .2550 swap points are *added* to the spot French franc (*European terms*): 8.500 + .2550 = 8.7550. In *U.S. terms*, spot French is $.1180 and the nine-month forward outright is $.1140.

6

Eurocurrency
Market Instruments

While all the Eurocurrency markets offer time deposits, the Euro-dollar market has developed a wide array of instruments. They include fixed and floating rate negotiable certificates of deposit (CDs), three-month $1-million Euro-dollar deposit futures traded on the Chicago Mercantile Exchange (CME) the London International Financial Futures Exchange (LIFFE), the Singapore International and Monetary Exchange (SIMEX) and the Sydney Futures Exchange (SFE), options on those futures traded on the CME and LIFFE, Eurocommercial paper, Euronotes, and interest rate swaps involving LIBOR-based loans.

The Euro-dollar CD market which globally totals about $110 billion, is dominated by the *London dollar CD market,* which represents over 90% of it. Concurrently, the Euro-dollar futures market, 90% at the CME, had an open interest in early 1987 totaling 194,000 contracts worth $194 billion. The related options market, 97% at the CME, totaled in early 1987 110,577 puts and calls, of which 54% are calls.

The Eurocommercial paper, which was initiated in 1970 but died as a consequence of the termination of U.S. balance of payment controls at the beginning of 1974, was reborn in the 1980s, and now totals over $6 billion in terms of facilities and more than $1 billion in terms of issuance. Concurrently, the related but *underwritten* Euronote market totals over $60 billion in terms of facilities and more than $10 billion in terms of issuance. Finally, LIBOR-based loans form a very substantial part of the fast rising $200 billion global interest rate swap market.

This section includes a description of the global Eurodollar CD market, including the Nassau variant (the negotiable receipt of deposit or NRD), as well as descriptions of the Eurodollar futures and options markets. Complementing those instruments, current descriptions of the dynamic Eurocommercial paper and Euronote markets are provided. Finally, a description of the interest rate (and currency) swap market follows, and an example of an interest rate swap involving a LIBOR-based loan is given to show the symbiotic nature of such swaps.

The International Eurodollar CD Market: London, Singapore, Luxembourg, Nassau

Euro-dollar CDs are negotiable time deposits, denominated in dollars, that are issued by the London, Singapore, Luxembourg, and Nassau branches of major U.S., Canadian, European, and Japanese commercial banks, as well as (in London) the international subsidiaries of U.K. clearing banks. They are issued in bearer form, ranging in maturity from one month to five years. Most Euro-dollar CDs are in million-dollar multiples and are issued with fixed rates and maturities up to a year, with banks generally quoting three-, six-, and twelve-month maturities, corresponding to their loan rollover requirements, rather than for all maturities as in the United States.

American purchasers of Euro-dollar CDs include commercial bank portfolios and trust departments, corporations, money market funds (seeking a higher yield than domestic CDs offer), insurance companies, and other institutions. Investors generally give up between ⅛% and ¼% percent in yield versus a non-negotiable Eurodollar time deposit. Euro-dollar CDs are exempt from withholding taxes, and proceeds to the investor are freely transferable to other money centers. Standard settlement is on the second business day following trade date, with delivery made to the investor's custodian bank in London, Singapore, or Luxembourg, versus payment in New York. However, in Nassau the procedure is generally for negotiable receipts of deposits to be delivered in New York against CDs issued in the Bahamas.

In 1977 the Bank of England approved the issuance of floating rate Eurodollar CDs. Typically issued with maturities of one and a half to three years (although maturities to five years are permitted), they differ from conventional fixed-rate medium-term Eurodollar CDs in that:

Exhibit 6-1
EURODOLLAR CDs: VOLUMES OUTSTANDING 1970-1986
(In billions of U.S. dollars)

	1970	1971	1972	1973	1974	1975
London	4.0	4.8	8.1	10.4	11.1	13.0

	1976	1977	1978	1979	1980	1981
London	16.5	23.0	28.8	43.6	49.0	77.7
Singapore			0.9	1.9	2.6	3.3
Luxembourg					0.7	n.a.
Nassau					n.a.	n.a.

	1982	1983	1984	1985	1986*
London	92.3	100.2	95.8	91.1	105.1
Singapore	3.4	3.8	n.a.	n.a.	n.a.
Luxembourg	n.a.	n.a.	n.a.	n.a.	n.a.
Nassau	n.a.	1.0e	0.6	0.6	0.9e

n.a. = not available.
e = estimate.
* = end-June.
Sources: Bank of England; Monetary Authority of Singapore; Commissariat au Controle des Banques (Luxembourg).

1. The interest rate is reset periodically, based on prevailing Eurodollar deposit (LIBOR) rates instead of remaining constant.

2. Interest is payable quarterly or semiannually, depending on the frequency with which the interest rate changes.

3. They are traded on the basis of *price* rather than *yield,* since the variable interest rate prevents the calculation of a yield to maturity (aside from their final period, when they trade as fixed rate instruments).

Normally, the issuing bank appoints an *agent bank* and several *reference banks,* which are responsible for establishing the interest rate for each period. At 11:00 a.m. London time, two business days prior to the issue date and each subsequent coupon date, the agent bank obtains the appropriate LIBOR quotation from each reference bank, takes an average of these rates (rounding upward to the nearest 1/16% if necessary) and adds the agreed-upon *spread*.

Eurodollar CDs involve *both* credit and sovereign risk. Regarding *credit risk*, the CDs are general obligations of the issuing bank, not just the branch. *Sovereign risk* covers action by either the government of the bank's head office or the U.K./Singapore/Luxembourg/Nassau government. (That is, the imposition of currency controls, interest rate limitations, declaration of a moratorium, etc. due to balance of payments problems, or other unlikely occurrences.)

In the London dollar CD market, as shown in Exhibit 6-2, the most important trends have been the paramount but declining role of American banks and the fast rising role of Japanese banks. While Japanese banks were not given permission by their Ministry of Finance to issue London dollar CDs until September 1972, by the end of 1978, they already claimed 17% of the market (versus 56% for the American banks). By end-1984, their share rose to 35% nearly parallel with the

Exhibit 6-2
EURO-DOLLAR CDS OUTSTANDING AT LONDON OFFICES OF COMMERCIAL BANKS
(in billions of U.S. dollars)

Type of Bank

Date[a]	Total	U.S.	Japanese	Other
1978	27.9	15.5	4.8	7.6
1979	43.3	26.0	7.7	9.6
1980	49.0	26.9	8.9	13.2
1981	77.7	44.7	12.1	20.9
1982	92.3	50.2	18.9	23.2
1983	100.2	46.1	29.3	24.8
1984	95.8	34.2	33.7	27.9
1985	91.1	31.7	28.6	30.8
1986[b]	105.1	31.2	34.5	39.4

[a]End of period.
[b]End of June.
Source: Bank of England (unpublished).

American share, which had fallen to 36%. However, at end-1985, their share declined to 31% versus 35% for the American banks. Nevertheless, by mid-1986, Japanese banks with a 33% share surpassed the American banks 30% share, but both were eclipsed by "other banks" whose share had jumped to 37% admidst rapid market growth to $105 billion.

Exhibit 6-3
DEVELOPMENT OF THE
INTERNATIONAL EURO-DOLLAR CD MARKET

1961
Citibank introduced negotiable CDs in U.S. money market.

1966
Citibank introduced the first London dollar CD with White Weld & Co. (now Credit Suisse First Boston), simultaneously establishing a secondary market.

1968
The International CD Market Association was founded by White Weld & Co., Allen Harvey & Ross, and Nesbitt, Thomson, to oversee the market.

1969
Aggressive issuance by London banks, especially branches of U.S. banks, related to tight U.S. money market conditions, accelerated growth of market.

1970
A Eurodollar CD market was initiated in Singapore, but failed due to the lack of an active secondary market.

1972
In September, Japanese banks were finally given permission by the Japanese Ministry of Finance to issue London dollar CDs. They began issuing *tranche CDs,* involving a small denomination and a wide retail distribution, attracting money that would have normally gone to the Eurobond market.

1974
The U.K. "secondary banking crisis" of 1984 led to a multitiered rate structure for Eurodollar CDs, etc. (prime American, followed by European, U.K., and Japanese names).

1977

In January, the Monetary Authority of Singapore approved once again the issue of negotiable CDs by the Singapore branches of 25-30 major international banks (ACUs); simultanously, First Boston (Asia) and Merrill Lynch International (Asia) created an active secondary market.

1980

Luxembourg banks began to issue Eurodollar CDs. Nassau banks began to issue negotiable receipts of deposit (for Eurodollar CDs).

1986

Japanese banks surpassed U.S. banks as the major country issuer in the London dollar CD market.

The Nassau Negotiable CD Market
(Negotiable Receipts of Deposit/
Negotiable Certificates of Ownership)

HISTORY AND MARKET SIZE

The Nassau Eurodollar CD market was initiated by the Morgan Guaranty Trust Company in May 1980. The following month, Citibank began issuing such CDs, and in October 1982, Chemical entered the market. Finally, Union Bank of Los Angeles began such issuance in December 1983.

At the end of 1983 such CDs were estimated to total around $1.0 billion, with Citibank accounting for $550 million. Federal Reserve Board statistics covering the market begin at end-June 1984 (before then, liabilities on negotiable CDs were included in liabilities to the United States or liabilities to foreigners, according to the address of the initial purchaser), with the Nassau CD volume at end-1984 being $615 million. At end-1985, it fell slightly to $610 million, but jumped to $1.076 billion at end-January 1986, and peaked at $1.237 billion at end-February. Subsequently, the market declined to $565 million by end-July. Factors behind the market's contraction included the high liquidity of banks in the face of soft business loan demand, and the banks' disinclination to pay the 10 basis point premium required in that market.

Exhibit 6-4
INTERNATIONAL CD MARKET ASSOCIATION

Alexanders Discount Co., Ltd.
1 St. Swithin's Lane
London EC4

Allen Harvey & Ross Ltd.
45 Cornhill
London EC3

Bankers Trust International Ltd.
56-60 New Broad Street
London, EC2

A.G. Becker International Ltd.
10-11 Lincoln's Inn Fields
London WC2

Carter Ryder & Co., Ltd.
1 King William Street
London, EC4

Clive Discount Co., Ltd.
1 Royal Exchange Avenue
London, EC3

Credit Suisse First Boston Ltd.
22 Bishopsgate
London, EC2

Gerrard & National Discount Co., Ltd.
32 Lombard Street
London, EC3

Goldman Sachs International Ltd.
162 Queen Victoria Street
London, EC4

Hungarian International Bank, Ltd.
Princes House
92 Gresham Street
London EC2

Jessel Toynbee & Co., Ltd
30 Cornhill
London, EC3

King & Shaxson Ltd.
52 Cornhill
London, EC3

Kuhn Loeb Lehman Brothers
International Ltd.
99 Bishopsgate
London, EC2

Lombard Wall International Ltd.
50 Gresham Street
London, EC2

Manufacturers Hanover Ltd.
8 Princes Street
London EC2

Nesbitt Thompson Ltd.
1 Union Court
Old Broad Street
London, EC2

Smith St. Aubyn & Co., Ltd.
White Lion Court
Cornhill
London, EC3

Wood Gundy Ltd.
30 Finsbury Square
London, EC2

MARKET PROCEDURE

The traditional market procedure is for *negotiable receipts of deposit* (NRDs, pronounced "nerds"), as Morgan Guaranty and Chemical call them, or *negotiable certificates of ownership* (NCOs) as Citibank

Exhibit 6-5
INSTITUTIONS REPORTING LONDON DOLLAR CD FIGURES
TO THE BANK OF ENGLAND

Alexanders Discount Co.*	Goldman Sachs
Allan Harvey and Ross	Hungarian International Bank
A.G. Becker International	Jessel, Toynbee*
Cater Ryder*	King and Shaxson*
Citibank NA Eurodealer	Nesbitt Thomson*
Civic Discount*	Salomon Brothers
Credit Suisse White Weld*	Smith St. Aubymn*
First Boston Corporation	Union Discount*
Gerrard and National	SG Warburg
Gillet Brothers Discount*	Wood Gundy*

*Members of the International CD Market Association.

calls them, to be delivered in New York against CDs issued in the Bahamas. The reason for the unusual procedure is that the Bahamian government has been concerned over the legal issue of "holder in due course," involved with negotiable instruments, if, for example, they are stolen. However, in December 1983, the Union Bank of Los Angeles (a $9 billion wholly-owned subsidiary of Standard Chartered Bank) began allowing purchasers through its New York agent, Morgan Guaranty Trust, to take possession of its Nassau CDs (in a $200 million issue largely sold through Merrill Lynch on a best efforts basis), and Citibank began doing likewise in 1984.

MARKET FEATURES

For American banks, Nassau CDs are advantageous because they can be issued free of reserve requirements and FDIC assessment, and they can generally be issued, as *negotiable* instruments, 2-3 basis points below comparable inter-bank deposit rates. Such is useful for funding Nassau assets (a 3% Eurocurrency reserve requirement must be paid if the funds are transferred to the U.S. parent bank). Moreover, Nassau shares the New York time zone, and for American banks lacking a London branch, Nassau provides a Eurodollar CD issuance opportunity for *liability diversification* and enhanced international recognition. However, New York banks normally prefer to use their IBFs, because Nassau income is subject to New York State and New York City taxes, from which the IBFs are exempt.

Normally, Nassau CDs tend to yield 5-10 basis points more than CDs issued in London, largely reflecting the *illiquidity* of the secondary market. Often they can only be sold back to the issuing banks, which have 25 basis point bid-ask spreads, as opposed to the 5-10 basis point spreads standard in the London dollar CD market. However, Merrill Lynch maintains a 5 basis point spread secondary market in Citibank and Morgan Nassau CDs. Also enhancing Nassau CD yields is somewhat greater *country risk.* This was of concern to Latin American companies during the 1982 Falklands War because of the traditional Bahamas-U.K. link. Separately, regarding the potential problems presented by Bahamian law, Merrill Lynch's legal counsel is "of the opinion that it is unlikely that Bahamas law offers any defenses which are appreciably different from those afforded at bank under the New York law."

The purchaser profile for the CDs is similar to London dollar CD purchasers, with money market funds, insurance companies and multinational corporations being especially important. Such purchasers are motivated by the somewhat higher yield of Nassau CDs, and the recognition that such CDs represent obligations of the parent bank, and are not deterred by the illiquid secondary market because they plan to hold them until maturity. In the case of money market funds, their fiduciary responsibility dictates buying liquid instruments as opposed to making somewhat higher yielding time deposits; the choice of Nassau CDs reflects their slightly higher yields than London and domestic negotiable CDs.

Exhibit 6-6
THE THREE-MONTH EURODOLLAR FUTURE
(Time Deposit Contract)

Historical Development

The three-month Eurodollar Time Deposit contract was initiated by the International Monetary Market (IMM) of the Chicago Mercantile Exchange in December 1981. Nine months later, in September 1982, a similar contract was offered by the London International Financial Fu-

Exhibit 6-6 (con't)

tures Exchange (LIFFE). Subsequently, SIMEX (the Singapore International Monetary Exchange) offered a contract identical to the IMM contract, and the Sidney Futures Exchange offered a contract fungible with the one at LIFFE.

Market Volume

The IMM Eurodollar contract has become the most actively traded *money market* future in the world; and after the Treasury bond contract at the Chicago Board of Trade (CBT), the second most active future in the world. In the first week of December 1986, daily volume in the IMM Eurodollar contract averaged 59,000 and the *open interest* (outstanding contracts) totalled 231,000. (Comparable numbers for the related contract in Treasury Bills was 7,500/38,000, and Bank CDs with 5,000/25,000). Concurrently, in LIFFE, the daily volume averaged 4,500 contracts and open interest averaged 24,000.

Contract Specifications(IMM)

Commodity Specification: Each futures contract is for a $1,000,000 Eurodollar time deposit with a three-month maturity.

Yield: Add-on.

Hours: 7:30 AM – 2:00 PM Chicago time (LIFFE hours are 8:30 AM – 3:00 PM London time).

Months Traded: March, June, September, December, and spot month.

(LIFFE: March, June, September, December.)

Quotations: Bids and offers are quoted in terms of the IMM Index, 100.00 minus the yield on an annual basis for a 360-day year (for example, a deposit rate of 9.80% is quoted as 90.20).

Minimum Fluctuations: .01 (1 basis point), so that for each .01 increase in the IMM Index, the Clearing House shall credit $25/contract to those Clearing Members holding open *long* positions and vice versa.

Daily Limits: Daily limits were *eliminated* in February 1986 because their absence in the cash market reduced the competitiveness of the competing futures market. (Previously, no trading was permitted at a level more than 1.00 (100 basis points) IMM index points above or below the preceding day's settlement index (closing), except as provided by Rule 3906 (Expanded Daily Limits) and except that there was *no limit* *in the spot month* and in the succeeding contract month beginning on the last day of trading of the spot month).

Expanded Daily Limits: Expaned daily limits were obviously eliminated as well. (Previously, whenever on two successive days any contract month closed at the normal daily limit in the same direction (not necessarily the same contract month on both days), an expanded daily limit schedule went into effect as follows: (1) the third day's daily limit in all contract months was *150%* of the normal daily limit; (2) if any contract month closes at its expanded daily limit on the third day in the same direction, then the fourth day's expanded daily limit, and each successive day thereafter, shall be *200%* of the normal daily limit, so long as *any* contract month closed at its expanded daily limit.)

Termination of Trading: It shall terminate at 3:30 P.M. (London time) on the *second* London bank business day immediately preceding the *third* Wednesday of the contract month (delivery is two business days later). In the event the third Wednesday of the contract month is a bank holiday in New York City or Chicago, trading shall terminate on the *first* London bank business day preceding the third Wednesday of the contract month. If the termination of trading date determined by the preceding two sentences is an *exchange holiday,* futures trading shall terminate on the next preceding business day common to London banks and the Exchange. (LIFFE terminates two business days common to both London and New York prior to the *second* Wednesday, unless it is not a business day in London and New York, in which case delivery is effected on the next business day common to both London and New York.)

Delivery: Delivery is by *cash settlement;* (LIFFE provides the option of a cash settlement or a three-month Eurodollar deposit facility at one of a list of banks in London designated by LIFFE as deliverable names). The *final settlement price* shall be determined by the Clearing House as follows: On the last day of trading the Clearing House shall determine the London Interbank Offered Rate (LIBOR) for three-month Euro-dollar Time Deposit funds both at *the time of termination of trading* and at a *randomly selected time within the last 90 minutes of trading.* The final settlement price shall be 100 minus the *arithmetic mean,* rounded to the nearest 1/100th of a percentage point, of the LIBOR at these two times. To determine the LIBOR at either time, the Clearing House shall select at random *12 reference banks* from a *list of no less than 20* participating banks that are major banks in the London Eurodollar market. Each reference bank shall quote by telex to the Clearing House its *perception* of the rate at which three-month Eurodollar Time Deposit funds are currently offered by the market to *prime* banks. *The two highest and the two low-*

Exhibit 6-6 (con't)

est quotes shall be eliminated. The arithmetic mean of the remaining
eight quotes shall be the LIBOR at that time. If for any reason there is difficulty in obtaining a quote within a reasonable time interval from one of
the banks in the sample, that bank shall be dropped from the sample, and
another shall be randomly selected to replace it. (LIFFE's "delivery settlement price" is based on an average of the offer rates estimated by a *random sample of designated banks* taken between 10:00 and 11:30 A.M.
on the last trading day, with the settlement rate 0.25% *less* than the average thus obtained; differences between the settlement rate and the actual rate on the deposit facility delivered by the seller are made good by a
cash settlement.)

Typical Strategies Involving
the Eurodollar Future

A variety of strategies are used by participants in the Eurodollar future market. Standard ones include the *long hedge,* the *short hedge,* the
TED spread, the *simulated Eurocurrency hedge* and *gold futures spread*
opportunities. In situations that are charted, such as the TED spread,
trading decisions are often based upon technicals such as *topping out action, channels, head and shoulder formations, and long term support
lines.*
Long Hedge: Fixing the interest rate on the later, *uncovered* part of a
long-funded position (liability maturity exceeds the asset maturity) by
buying a futures contract, so that a *potential loss* if interest rates fall
would be *offset* by the profit derived from *reversing out (selling)* the futures contract.

The Four Euromarket Futures/Options Exchanges

Virtually 24 hour global trading is now possible with Eurodollar
futures/options exchanges in North America, Asia and Europe. Such
trading is facilitated by the CME-SIMEX and LIFFE- SFE linkages.

CHICAGO MERCANTILE EXCHANGE
INTERNATIONAL MONETARY MARKET

The world's leading Eurodollar futures/options exchange is the Chicago Mercantile Exchange (CME), which offers Eurodollar futures and options in its International Monetary Market (IMM) Division. The CME itself has the world's largest facility for futures and options trading, and has a membership of 2,725 traders. It is second only to the Chicago Board of Trade in trading volume with 56 million contracts exchanged in 1985. Its Eurodollar futures contract is *fungible* with that offered by SIMEX. Trading hours at the IMM are 8:00 a.m. – 2:00 p.m. Presiding over the exchange is its chairman, John F. Sander, its president, William J. Brodsky, and its chairman, executive committee and special counsel, the famed Leo Melamed (the initial developer of financial futures). Regulation of the CME is provided by the Commodity Futures Trading Commission.

THE SINGAPORE INTERNATIONAL MONETARY
EXCHANGE LTD. (SIMEX)

SIMEX was the first financial futures exchange in Asia and the first exchange involved in a mutual offset trading arrangement with another exchange, the CME. In particular, it offers Eurodollar futures contracts that are offsettable with the CME contracts. It expects to offer options on Eurodollar futures contracts in 1987. It was created in 1984 by reconstituting and expanding the Gold Exchange of Singapore (GES), which itself had been established in 1978. Trading hours at SIMEX are 9:00 a.m. – 3:00 p.m. (10:00 p.m. – 4:00 a.m. Chicago time). Presiding over the exchange are its chairman, Ng Kok Song and its general manager, Ang Swee Tian.

THE LONDON INTERNATIONAL FINANCIAL FUTURES
EXCHANGE LTD. (LIFFE)

LIFFE opened in September 1982 and is now the largest futures exchange *outside* the United States. It was established to provide a market within the European time zone (between the Far East and North

American markets) for financial futures, and more recently, financial options. Its 373 members (end-1985) include the leading organizations that participate in London's international monetary and commodity markets, including major U.S. banks and brokers. It offers both Eurodollar futures contract and options on those futures. Trading hours are 8:30 a.m. – 4:00 p.m. Trades are cleared through LIFFE General Clearing Members and ICCH in London. Quotes on the LIFFE futures and options are available on Reuters, Telerate, IDM, ADP COM-TREND, QUOTRON, TOPIC, FUTREND, UNICOM, ICU CITISERVE, CMS (MANIFEST MKI) and DATASTREAM. Regulation of LIFFE is provided by the Bank of England and the Board of the Exchange, especially its Market Supervision Department. Presiding over the exchange are its chairman, R.B. Williamson and its chief executive M.N.H. Jenkins. It is located adjacent to the Bank of England.

SYDNEY FUTURES EXCHANGE LTD. (SFE)

The SFE, established in 1960, is the leading international financial futures exchange in the Asia/Pacific basin. In mid-1986, its daily trading volume exceeded 20,000 contracts. It has 29 Floor members over 300 Associate members, and more than 70 local members. The SFE offers Eurodollar futures contracts that are linked, since 30 October 1986, to the LIFFE contracts. Linked options on the Eurodollars futures contracts were initiated in December. In fact, the SFE has been in the forefront of international developments in financial futures since 1979, when it introduced the world's first cash settlement futures contract in US dollars. Trading hours are 9 a.m. - 6 p.m., with a 1.5 hour break before the beginning of LIFFE Eurodollar trading. SFE trades are cleared through LIFFE General Members and ICCM in London, in exactly the same way as those currently executed on LIFFE. It is presided over by its chief executive, Leslie V. Hosking and its chairman A. John Oliver.

The Option on the Eurodollar Future

Building upon the success of the three-month Eurodollar future, which has become the most widely traded money market future, the IMM in 1985 introduced options on Eurodollar futures in its Index and

Options Market Division. It has become the most important option on a money market future, with total puts and calls outstanding as of mid-December 1986 totalling 163,000. As with the future, the market serves for the orderly transfer of risk from risk averters (hedgers) to risk-takers (speculators).

While going long or short in the Eurodollar futures market leaves one with a financial position, purchasing an option on a financial future only leaves one with the right but *not* the obligation to assume a position in the underlying instrument.

There are two types of options, call options and put options. Call options give the buyer the right to buy a specified quantity of the underlying instrument or commodity at a fixed price, known as the exercise or strike price, until an expiration date. (The latter refers to *American options,* while *European options* are only exercisable on their maturity date.) Conversely, put options give the option buyer the right to sell a specified quantity of the underlying instrument or commodity at a fixed price until an expiration date.

As applied to the option on the Eurodollar future, a holder of a call option who exercises will, as a result, be long one Eurodollar future of a particular maturity date. Conversely, a holder of a put option on the Eurodollar future who exercises will be short one Eurodollar future of a particular maturity date.

A key element in the options market is the premiums charged for particular options of various strike prices. Three factors are especially influential in determining the premiums.

First is the intrinsic value of the option. If the strike price of a call option is lower than the current market price of the underlying commodity or financial instrument, it is said to be "in the money." Thus, if the strike price of an option on a particular Eurodollar future is 93.00 and the underlying future is currently priced at 93.50, that option is said to be "in the money."

If both the strike price and the underlying future are identical, then the option is said to be "at the money." Thus, if the strike price is 93.00 and the underlying future is 93.00, that option is said to be "at the money." Finally, if the strike price of a call option is greater than the current market value of the underlying commodity, or financial instrument, it is said to be "out of the money." Thus, if the strike price of a call option on a particular Eurodollar future is 93.00 and the underlying future itself is currently priced at 92.50, that option is said to be "out of the money."

Of course, the opposite analysis applies to put options. If the strike price of an option on a Eurodollar future is higher than the current market price of the underlying future, that option is said to be "in the money." Thus, if the strike price is 93.00 and the current market price of the future is 92.50, that put option is said to be "in the money."

Conversely, if the *strike price* of a put option is below the current market price of the underlying future, that option is said to be "out of the money." Thus, if the *strike price* is 93.00 and the current market price of the underlying future is 93.50, that option is said to be "out of the money." Of course, with the put options as with the call options, an option with a strike price identical to the market value of the underlying financial instrument or commodity is said to be "at the money."

Besides intrinsic value, a second factor that determines option premiums is time to expiration. The more time there is to expiration of the option, the more possibility there is for the option to be "in the money," or even *more* "in the money" than currently. Essentially, an option is a decaying asset until expiration, when as applied to the option on the Eurodollar future, the futures price and the cash market converge and the *only* value would be intrinsic value. (Conversely, the "time value" of an option is defined as that portion of an option's premium that represents the amount in excess of the intrinsic value.)

The final major factor determining the premiums on options and one which *impacts* the value of the time to expiration, is the volatility of the underlying commodity or financial instrument. Basically, the more volatile the underlying commodity or instrument, the more chance there is for the option to be "in the money" between the present moment and the expiration of the option. Estimations of future volatility are determined by market participants on the basis of historical volatility as well as on "expected" future volatility models.

By the way of example, the Canadian dollar is a very stable currency and thus options on it command but small premiums on the volatility factor. Conversely, the Deutschemark is a quite volatile currency and thus options on it command far higher premiums on the volatility factor.

The risk of buyers of options—whether calls or puts—is limited to the premiums they pay. However, the writers of options face high risk as they are obliged to assume *short* positions should holders of call options they have written choose to exercise; or to assume *long* positions should holders of put options they have written choose to exercise. Hence, exchanges impose margin requirements on *writers* of options, but naturally, not on holders of options.

To limit risk, many writers of options already have the positions they may be required to assume. Such options are called "covered options."

For example, the writer of *covered* call options on Eurodollar futures would already be long the corresponding Eurodollar futures. Conversely, the writer of *covered* put options on Eurodollar futures would already be short the corresponding Eurodollar futures. Writers of covered options are *enhancing* the potential income from their futures position with limited risk by writing options.

A very different situation results from options written where there is no corresponding long or short position in the underlying commodity or instrument. These are termed *"uncovered"* or "naked" options, and are viewed as having extremely high risk. Over time, *writers* of options receive greater rewards than the buyers of options to correspond to their higher risk. However, individual writers, especially writers of naked options can face large losses.

With respect to hedgers' use of either Eurodollar futures *or* options on Eurodollar futures, which hedging strategy is best depends on the goals of the hedger. A futures contract locks in a rate, leaving the holder largely indifferent (depending on the correspondence between the amount, dates and instruments involved) to the way interest rates move. Conversely, the hedger who buys an option receives (in return for his/her premium) compensation if adverse conditions evolve, while still being able to reap the benefits if a favorable situation evolves. Additionally, if the hedger buys an option to deal with a contingent situation (e.g., in the case of options on Eurodollar futures, a *possible* later loan or deposit), but later that situation fails to materialize, then the option can be sold back into the market for at least its time value (as well as any intrinsic value).

Exhibit 6-7
CME EURODOLLAR OPTIONS CONTRACT SPECIFICATIONS

Trading Unit—One Eurodollar time deposit futures contract of the specified contract month.

Strike Prices—Stated in terms of the IMM Index for the Eurodollar futures contract in intervals of .25 (such as 89.50, 89.75, 90.00).

Exhibit 6-7 (con't)

When a new contract month is listed for trading, there will be five put and call strike prices: the nearest strike to the underlying futures price, the next two *higher* and the next two *lower*. For example, if the March Eurodollar futures closed at 90.38 on the previous day, the strikes listed for March puts and calls would be 90.00, 90.25, 90.50, 90.75, and 91.00.

A new strike price will be listed for both puts and calls when the underlying futures price touches within half a strike price interval of either the second highest or second lowest strike prices. As an example, if the March Eurodollar futures price touches 90.63 after the options are listed as in the above example, then a new strike price at 91.25 will be listed for puts and calls the next day. (No new options will be listed, however, with less than 20 calendar days until expiration.)

Premium Quotations—Quoted in IMM Index points where each .01 IMM Index point (1 basis point) represents $25. A quote of 0.35 represents an option price of $875 (35 basis points multiplied by $25).

Months Traded—March, June, September, December.

Ticker Symbols—Calls are CE; Puts are PE.

Minimum Price Fluctuation (Tick Size)—.01 IMM Index point, equal to $25 (same as for Eurodollar futures).

Daily Price Limit—None.

Trading Hours—7:30 a.m. to 2:00 p.m. (same as for Eurodollar futures).

Last Day of Trading—Option trading shall terminate at the same date and time as the underlying futures contract (that is, the second London business day before the third Wednesday of the contract month).

Minimum Margin—No margin is required for put or call option *buyers*, but the full premium must be paid in cash. Brokers require margins on *short* option positions and combination option/futures positions.

Exercise Procedure—Option buyers may exercise on any trading day. Brokerage firms have various exercise procedures. Exercise results in a long futures position for a call buyer or a put seller, and *short* futures position for a put buyer or a call seller. The futures position is effective on the trading day immediately following exercise, and is marked-to-market to the settlement that day.

Expiration—Options expire at 5:00 p.m. on the last trading day. However, brokers may set considerably earlier cutoff times for exercising expiring options. A Eurodollar option that is *in-the-money* and has not been liquidated or exercised prior to the termination of trading shall be exercised automatically (in the absence of contrary instructions delivered to the CME clearing house by 5:00 p.m. on the expiration date).

A Day in the Life of Eurodollar Futures and Options on Futures at the IMM

The Wall Street Journal, like many leading newspapers, provides daily information on the IMM and LIFFE *Eurodollar futures* and *options on Eurodollar futures* prices. With respect to the Eurodollar futures, information is available for eight contract dates extending as far as two years (immediately following the expiration of the nearest contract, when a new contract becomes available).

Information for both the IMM and LIFFE Eurodollar futures by contract date is given for the previous day's open, high, low, settlement (closing price), the change at settlement relative to the previous trading day's close, the yield at settlement, the change of the yield from the previous day's settlement, and the open interest (outstanding contracts) at the previous trading day's close. Also, the total *estimated* volume of trades in all contract dates for the day's trading is given, as is the total open interest for the previous trading day. Prices are given in terms of the IMM Index System, which is 100.00 minus the rate of the contract, such that declines in yields translate into increases in contract prices.

To take an example, the December 1986 contract on December 9, 1986, opened at 93.90 (equivalent to 6.10 percent), went as high as 93.91 (6.09 percent), as low as 93.88 (6.12 percent) and closed at 93.89 (equivalent to 6.11 percent). Its change from the previous day's close was −.01 (or one basis point, equivalent to $25 for each 3-month, $1 million contract). The closing yield was 6.11%, up one basis point from the previous trading day (i.e., from 6.10 percent). Finally, open interest at the close of the previous trading day was 43,579; while generally the nearest contract date has the greatest open interest, the fact that the December contract open interest is below the March 1987 open interest of 95,234 reflects the closing out (i.e., *reversing*) of many contracts given the nearness of the December 15th expiration date.

With regard to the IMM and LIFFE *options on Eurodollar futures,* information is provided for the three expiration dates, which extend as far as nine months out at the expiration of the nearest option date. Premiums for generally a half-dozen (starting with five, one *at the money,* two above, and two below) strike prices—both calls and puts—are listed. Estimated volume for the trading day for puts and calls together is given, as is the previous trading days volume broken down by calls and puts. Finally, the open interest (outstanding options), broken down into calls and puts, is given for the previous trading day.

To take an example, the option on the December 1986 Eurodollar futures contract had settlement or *closing strike prices,* and corresponding *call and put premiums,* respectively, for December 9, 1986 as follows: 9350-0.39-.0004; 9375-0.15-0.01; 9400-0.01- 0.12; 9425-.0004-0.36; 9450-.0004-0.61.

The *most* valuable option was the right to sell the December 1986 contract at .9450 (equivalent to a yield of 5.50%), while the *least* valuable option was the right to buy the December 1986 contract at the same strike price of 9450. Obviously, the market believed it was extremely unlikely for the 3-month Eurodollar deposit rate to decline to 5.50% by December 15th, 1986 (e.g., the latest price for the December future was 93.89, equivalent to a 6.11% yield, or 61 basis points away from the 5.5% yield implied by a .9450 strike price.)

Exhibit 6-8

THE WALL STREET JOURNAL WEDNESDAY, DECEMBER 10, 1986

FUTURES PRICES

Tuesday, December 9, 1986

Open Interest Reflects Previous Trading Day.

EURODOLLAR (IMM) – $1 million; pts of 100%

	Open	High	Low	Settle	Chg	Yield Settle	Chg	Open Interest
Dec	93.90	93.91	93.88	93.89	− .01	6.11 +	.01	43,579
Mr87	94.04	94.06	94.02	94.03	....	5.97	....	95,234
June	94.01	94.04	94.00	94.00	....	6.00	....	36,543
Sept	93.87	93.90	93.86	93.86	....	6.14	....	23,415
Dec	93.67	93.67	93.62	93.62	....	6.38	....	12,345
Mr88	93.38	93.39	93.33	93.34	....	6.66	....	9,780
June	93.08	93.08	93.03	93.03	....	6.97	....	6,456
Sept	92.72	92.77	92.71	92.71	− .01	7.29 +	.01	4,831

Est vol 33,084; vol Mon 56,311; open int 232,183, +1,331.

EURODOLLAR (LIFFE) – $1 million; pts of 100%

	Open	High	Low	Settle	Chg			Open Interest
Dec	93.90	93.91	93.88	93.89		94.39	90.20	7,160
Mr87	93.05	94.06	94.03	94.04	+	.02 94.33	90.80	8,637
June	94.03	94.05	94.02	94.02	+	.03 94.15	90.85	4,798
Sept	93.88	93.91	93.88	93.88	+	.04 93.98	91.65	2,186
Dec	93.67	93.67	93.67	93.66	+	.06 93.73	91.96	848
Mr88	93.37	93.37	93.37	93.36	+	.06 93.42	92.08	498
June	93.05	93.05	93.05	93.04	+	.07 93.15	91.99	395
Sept	92.73	92.73	92.73	92.72	+	.08 92.73	92.37	98

Est vol 3,550; vol Mon 3,019; open int 24,620, +162.

FUTURES OPTIONS

EURODOLLAR (CME) $ million; pts. of 100%

Strike		Calls – Settle			Puts – Settle	
Price	Dec-C	Mar-C	Jun-C	Dec-P	Mar-P	Jun-P
9350	0.39	0.57	0.62	.0004	0.05	0.15
9375	0.15	0.38	0.46	0.01	0.10	0.22
9400	0.01	0.22	0.31	0.12	0.19	0.31
9425	.0004	0.11	0.21	0.36	0.33	0.45
9450	.0004	0.05	0.13	0.61	0.51	....
9475		0.02	0.07	....	0.72	....

Est. vol. 4,781, Mon vol. 2,640 calls, 5,241 puts
Open interest Mon; 69,198 calls, 93,306 puts

EURODOLLAR (LIFFE) $1 million; pts. of 100%

Strike		Calls – Settle			Puts – Settle	
Price	Dec-C	Mar-C	Jun-C	Dec-P	Mar-P	Jun-P
9350	0.00	0.00	0.00	0.00	0.00	0.00
9375	0.00	0.39	0.00	0.01	0.10	0.00
9400	0.01	0.23	0.00	0.12	0.19	0.00
9425	0.00	0.11	0.00	0.36	0.32	0.00
9450	0.00	0.06	0.00	0.00	0.52	0.00
9475	0.00	0.02	....	0.86	0.73	....

Actual Vol. Tuesday, 220 Calls, 100 Puts.
Open Interest Monday; 2,077, Calls, 2,129 Puts.

Euronotes and Eurocommercial Paper

Euronotes are short-term coupon-bearing securities issued on an underwritten basis. The facilities for their issuance are frequently called *note issuance facilities (NIFs)* or *short-term note issuance facilities (SNIFs)*. Notes that are sold *directly* to the market, on a "best efforts" as opposed to an underwritten basis, are called *Eurocommercial paper*. Both reflect typically senior, unsecured indebtedness of corporations or governments. Investors are now mostly nonbanks (corporations, institutions) as opposed to the banks' former predominance. Finally, maturities are generally a standard three months or six months as opposed to the more diverse and generally shorter maturities (22 day average) of the U.S. commercial paper market.

As of December 1985, Euronotes with underwritten facilities totalled $62 billion, while drawdowns were estimated at only $10 billion, reflecting the youth of the market. As the comparable 1984 levels were $30 billion and $5 billion, respectively, the market grew a phenomenal 100% in 1985. Concurrently, at end-1985, the Eurocommercial paper market totalled $6 billion, with drawdowns estimated at only $1 billion.

Euronotes are attractive to issuers because the most creditworthy borrowers can finance *below* LIBOR, the benchmark for other Eurodollar borrowing. Moreover, the Euromarket houses can arrange and distribute deals faster than their U.S. counterparts. Concurrently, Euronotes are attractive to investors because relative to the Eurocurrency bank deposit market, they offer better liquidity (an active secondary market), better credits, and even higher yields. Many investors have been lured away from bank instruments, especially negotiable CDs.

In terms of signed facilities in the Euronote market during the January-September 1985 period, the U.S. led in volume by country with 40 transactions totalling $10.3 billion, followed by Australia (31, $4.8 billion), Sweden (20, $3.8 billion), and the U.K. (9, $2.0 billion). The other major participating countries in order were Spain, Netherlands, Norway, Hong Kong, and Canada.

Concurrently in that period, the principal arrangers in terms of volume and number of transactions were Credit Suisse First Boston ($5.0 billion, 23), BankAmerica Capital Markets Group ($4.6 billion, 22), Salomon Brothers International ($3.1 billion, 8), and Citicorp ($2.8 billion, 17). The next tier of arrangers in order included Chase Manhattan Capital Markets Group, Bankers Trust, Morgan Guaranty,

Bank of Tokyo International, and S.G. Warburg & Co. Their volumes varied from $2.8 billion down to $1.3 billion.

The distribution of Euronotes involves a wide variety of techniques, generally involving facilities that are put in place a long time before they are activated (cf. facilities and drawdowns volumes). The traditional workhorse of Euronotes facilities is the *tender panel*. Essentially it is an auction in which the members (usually all underwriting banks) are invited to bid for notes via telex to the agent, who allocates notes only to those who bid the best prices. While this method can be unwieldy with 30 to 60 members in the panel, and involve a potentially troublesome time gap between a borrower receiving bids and allocating paper, it is a particularly useful technique for large distributions ($500 million upwards).

At the other end of the distribution spectrum is the *sole placing agent*, where a borrower uses a single bank to place its paper at a set price. Such facilities are spoken of as a *revolving underwriting facilities* (RUFs). Variations of the latter are the *dual* and *multiple placing agency*.

Other distribution techniques include *dealership placement, issuer set margin (ISM), the continuous tender panel (CTP), the specialized tender panel, unsolicited tenders, multiple options funding facilities (MOFFs)*, and *global note facilities (also known as borrower's option for notes and underwriter standby or BONUS*, a B of A acronym). The latter, which allow borrowers to tap both Euronote and U.S. commercial paper markets, involve *swinglines* or bridging loans as it may require a week to activiate the Euronote mechanisms.

A unique facility of increasing use is the TRUF or *transferable revolving underwriting facility*, which contains documentation to allow underwriters to transfer their commitment to another bank, providing the borrower is satisfied that the *quality* of its backup does not suffer in the process. Finally, a borrowing option of frequent use in note issuance facilities, complementing Euronotes themselves, is the *short-term multicurrency advance*, which gives borrowers a wider choice of currencies than is available with notes, and are also preferred by some banks as an alternative to holding notes.

Euronote facilities involve a variety of fees for underwriting commitments, management, and other services. The *underwriting of facility fee* (between $\frac{1}{32}$ and $\frac{1}{8}$, depending on the borrower and the structure of the deal) is paid on a semiannual or quarterly basis in arrears, regardless of how much the facility is used. In return for the fee, the underwriters are obliged to buy the paper at a preset price or standby rate, known as the *maximum spread,* if it cannot be placed. (The *commitment fee* is similar, but is charged only on undrawn accounts.) However, should the underwriters be forced to take a large proportion of notes at maximum spread, they receive some protection in the form of an extra fee (generally 5-10 basis points), called the *utilization fee.* Also, a *front-end* or *management fee* is usually paid to the manager on signing for arrangement services and to provide some up-front compensation to the underwriters. It is generally 0-20 basis points and is paid on a sliding scale according to the size of the commitment. It should be noted that the fee structure is flexible; for example, an infrequent borrower can lower his underwriting costs by providing a higher *maximum spread.*

Most Euronotes provide for a two-day settlement period, similar to other Eurodollar transactions, as opposed to same-day settlement in the U.S. commercial paper market. Given the growing arbitrage between the two markets, there is increasing competition among the three Euronote clearing services— *Euroclear* (incorporated and managed under contract by the Brussels branch of Morgan Guaranty Trust Co., of N.Y.), *Cedel*(Centrale de Livraison de Valeurs Mobilieres, Luxembourg), and a unit of *First Chicago*—to provide the quickest service.

First Chicago (FC), which targets shorter-term instruments, offers same-day settlement for deals struck by 5 p.m. London time. This involves: (1) the borrower's contacting the dealers of his intention to draw down; (2) the dealers submitting their quotes; (3) the borrower's informing FC of the trade details of deals struck; (4) FC immediately debiting the dealers' accounts (who would already have credit lines with FC) and crediting them with the securities (previously deposited by the borrower); and (5) finally, FCs paying the borrower before the New York close via CHIPS. Easing same-day settlement is the advent of the *grid system,* which involves a system of book entries at a central register as opposed to physical notes.

The growing secondary market in Euronotes, is dominated by Merrill Lynch Capital Markets and Citicorp Investment Bank. A significant role is also played by CSFB Securities, SBC, and International.

EURO-COMMERCIAL PAPER

Special note should be taken of the Eurocommercial paper market because since the summer of 1985, it has become the fastest growing sector of the Euromarket. Actually, it was initiated in the early 1970s by several major U.S. corporations including Alcoa, but folded in January 1974 when the U.S. rescinded its balance of payment controls. The market reopened in June 1980 with a $100-million IC Industries issue lead managed by Merrill Lynch. In 1985, several major corporations and official entities tapped it, including Chrysler, Volvo, ITT Financial, BP, and the Kingdom of Spain.

All the issues have been U.S.-dollar-denominated, aside from an ECU 50-million issue by Saint Gobain Nederland. Amounts have ranged from $25 million to $500 million for the Export Development Corporation of Canada and the Kingdom of Spain, and a jumbo $800 million for Svenska Handelsbank. Paper maturities are generally 7–180 days, but the range is one day to one year. (A shorter maximum of 270 days prevails in the U.S. commercial paper market, as longer maturity paper must be SEC registered.)

A typical issue's terms and conditions include the interest rate on a discount basis, bearer form, large minimum denominations (such as, $500,000), freedom from withholding taxes (or a compensatory "grossing up" for the impact of such taxes), governance by the laws of the State of New York, and nonregistration under the U.S. Securities Act of 1933 (prohibiting its distribution in the U.S., but not foreign branches of U.S. banks). Also, an issuing and paying agent is appointed and dealers are selected. Dealers for the largest offerings have included Manufacturers Hanover, Merrill Lynch Capital Markets, Credit Suisse First Boston, Salomon Brothers International, Citicorp Investment Bank, and SBCI.

The market's many attractions include a cost advantage over comparable forms of finance such as bank advances, with top-quality companies now issuing paper around LIBID (generally 12.5 basis points below LIBOR). Concurrently, relative to the U.S. commercial paper alternative, rates in Europe have fallen, making the two markets roughly comparable. Moreover, Eurocommercial paper is a completely flexible financing technique, enabling a corporation to borrow the amounts and maturities best suited to its particular cashflow.

An additional advantage is that it enables corporations to diversify away from their "house banks" to the small banks, corporate and big institutional investors of the Eurocommercial paper investment community. Finally, a Eurocommercial paper program can be set up in a few days, as opposed to the several months delay entailed in winning the indispensable S&P/Moody's approval for a U.S. commercial paper program. The latter involves ratings of A-1, A-2, A-3, or P-1, P-2, P-3 (P = prime).

Interest Rate Swaps

Interest rate swaps have grown into a huge global market, totalling well over $200 billion. Their spectacular growth reflects the powerful forces of innovation and globalization, spurred by commercial banks such as Citibank, and investment banks such as Salomon Brothers. Along with related currency swaps, they did not suddenly appear, but represent the culmination of an evolutionary process that includes parallel loans, back-to-backs, and cross-border leases.

The basic theory of swaps is that a corporation should: (1) not necessarily borrow in the market related to its underlying cash flow, but rather where it has the best *comparative* borrowing advantage; (2) think of the capital market in *global* terms (not international vs. domestic); (3) consider the funding decision *separate* from its liability structure.

An interest rate swap involves two entities (often separated by a financial intermediary) who have dissimilar liability positions or financing needs in a single currency (or in the case of a currency swap, in two different currencies). In essence, each party engages in a transaction in which it does *not* wish an obligation, but where it has *comparative* market advantage, and swaps it for the one in which it wishes to have one, but where it has a *lesser* comparative market advantage.

Some common uses of interest rate and currency swaps are: (1) to reduce financing costs; (2) to lock in exchange gains; (3) to lock in or postpone tax effects; (4) to secure fixed-rate funding; (5) to diversify investment portfolios; (6) to actively manage currency denomination or interest rate basis of debt; (7) to create forward cover where markets do not exist; (8) to obtain long-term funding in a currency where markets are thin or closed.

Swaps allow the user to manage separately and optimally the interest or currency *basis* on which to take or invest funds. Swaps variations include: (1) fixed/floating where currency is the same; (2) floating/floating where currency is the same; (3) fixed/fixed where currencies are different; (4) floating/floating where currencies are different; (5) fixed/floating where currencies are different.

Exhibit 6-9
NUMERICAL EXAMPLE OF AN INTEREST RATE SWAP
INVOLVING A LIBOR-BASED LOAN

Borrower	Term	Bond Market	Bank Market
"Triple A" credit	5 years	10.0%	LIBOR
Lesser credit	5 years	12.5%	LIBOR + 1.0%
Rate difference	5 years	2.5%	1.0%

Structure

Original Borrowing

Triple A credit borrows at 10.0% fixed

Lesser credit borrows at LIBOR + 1% floating

Swap

Lesser credit pays 11.75% fixed to Triple A

Triple A now has floating debt at LIBOR − 0.75%

Benefits

To Triple A Credit

Straight floating rate cost	= LIBOR
Floating rate per cost swap	= LIBOR + 1.0% − 1.75%
	= LIBOR − 0.75%
Benefit	= 0.75%

To Lesser Credit

Straight fixed rate cost	= 12.50%
Fixed rate per swap	= 11.75%
Benefit	= 0.75%

Swaps transactions are generally the result of the initiative of swap specialists at commercial or investment banks, or even interbank brokerage houses. The characteristics of an effective financial swap intermediary include: (1) ability to find counterparties; (2) warehousing capabilities; (3) skill in structuring transactions and finding new applications; (4) willingness to absorb counterparty credit risk; (5) flexibility and speed to identify and implement opportunities.

Exhibit 6-9 is an example of an interest rate swap involving a LIBOR-based loan. In the example, the treasurer of the AAA credit, expecting interest rates to fall, wants to take out a floating rate LIBOR loan, while the treasurer of the lesser credit, a risk averse individual, wants to borrow fixed-rate money. By both borrowing in the markets where they have *comparative* advantage, and then swapping their debts, both parties save 75 basis points.

7

Syndicated Eurocurrency Bank Credits

Overview

Syndicated Eurocredits were introduced in the late 1960s—the initial one was organized by Banker's Trust for Austria—to enable the international banking community to extend credits beyond the prudential and *legal lending limits* of individual banks. Such credits, which comprise about half of Eurocurrency bank lending, tend to be relatively long in maturity and go predominantly to the public sector (75%); they represent, in particular, most of the medium-and long-term funds for developing countries and centrally planned (Communist) economies for whom cheaper Eurobond financing is generally not available. (Conversely, lending by *individual* Eurobanks tends to the private sector for trade financing, etc.) Borrowers are generally categorized as: (1) industrialized countries; (2) OPEC; (3) high-income developing countries; (4) low-income developing countries. The spreads are progressively larger as one moves from the first to the fourth category.

The advantage of syndicated loans to borrowers is that only a single negotiation is required, as opposed to the difficulties and uncertainties of multiple negotiations with many individual lenders. Concurrently, the advantages to lenders, besides *diversification,* include increased banking relationships, the greater protection in the case of sovereign defaults resulting from creditor involvement from many countries, and the opportunity to sell participations to smaller banks, while earning sizable management fees.

There are generally three or four levels of banks in a syndicate: the *lead banks,* the *co-managers* (larger credits only), the *managing banks* and the *participating banks.* The syndication is marketed on the basis of a *placement memorandum.* In smaller credits to frequent borrowers, especially in periods of market uncertainty, *club loans* are arranged. In such financings, the lead bank and managers fund the entire loan and no placement memorandum is required.

Syndications take from two to twelve weeks to arrange, but six weeks is the norm. After the loan is arranged, an *agent bank* (generally the lead bank) is appointed to: (1) compute the appropriate interest rate charges; (2) receive service payments; (3) disburse payments to participants; (4) inform participants if any problems develop.

Annual payments generally include: (1) LIBOR + spread × amount of loan drawn; (2) commitment fee × amount of loan undrawn; (3) tax adjustment (if any); (4) annual agent's fee (if any). Concurrently, front-end charges include: (1) participation fee × face amount of loan; (2) management fee × face amount of loan; (3) initial agent's fee (if any).

Eurocurrency bank credits totalled $85.015 billion in 1982, but fell 13% to $74.222 billion in 1983. However, the market jumped 52% in 1984 to $112.605 billion, and then slowed slightly to $110.317 billion in 1985. During January-May 1986, such credits totalled $31.498 billion, slightly below the January-May 1985 total of $33.910 billion. Major lead managers include Bank America Capital Markets Group, Chase Manhattan, and Citicorp. Other American banks, as well as British, Japanese, Canadian, Swiss, and French ones, also are prominent. A recent factor stimulating the market has been the growth of *transferable loans,* involving standardized documentation.

Since 1982 a major preoccupation of the market has been debt restructurings. Previously, there had been a number of problem countries such as Zaire, Turkey, Sudan, Nicaragua, Peru, Bolivia, Poland, and Romania, but the loans extended to them were not so large as to jeopardize the very viability of their bank creditors.

However, in August 1982, Mexico, with an external debt approaching $100 billion, was in danger of defaulting. Soon comparable situations developed in Venezuela, Argentina, the Philippines, and the largest debtor, Brazil. Many observers spoke of a global debt crisis.

To cope with the acute Latin American debt problem, a trilateral arrangement developed, involving the commercial banks, the International Monetary Fund, and the U.S. Treasury (which provided some *bridge financing*), to implement debt restructurings. Four general characteristics have emerged from the many restructurings:

1. While willing to reschedule overdue *principal,* banks have felt it important that the borrower remain current on *interest* payments (allowing the banks to keep their reported earnings up).
2. Most reschedulings have provided for either the restructuring of future maturities or the injection of new money, but not both.
3. Reschedulings generally involve spreads over benchmark interest rates that are usually as high or higher than those on loans being restructured.
4. Banks usually urge sovereign borrowers to arrange an agreement with the IMF during the restructuring, since this should insure that a *stabilization* program is undertaken.

Another consequence of the crisis was the creation of the Institute of International Finance (described at the end of this unit). A strong factor in its creation was the provision of objective and comprehensive information to smaller banks to assure their continued participation in the syndicated loan market (especially the restructurings).

Elements of Syndicated Eurocurrency Loans

Syndicated Eurocurrency loans can vary considerably in form, representing the culmination of complex bargaining between the borrower and the banks. Nevertheless, a substantial number of elements are common to most such loans.

First, the *currency of denomination* for the loan must be chosen. Generally, the borrower selects the currency based on the use of the proceeds (to avoid a foreign exchange exposure). However, it is subject to the judgment of the lenders on the ready availability of the magnitude of funds needed in the currency preferred by the borrower.

In contrast to domestic loans, some Eurocurrency loans have *multicurrency options,* which, in turn, can have two aspects. First, it can

Exhibit 7-1
TYPES OF INTEREST RATES* IN INTERNATIONAL LENDING**

London interbank offered rate (LIBOR)
London interbank offered rate/U.S. prime rate
Fixed rate
U.S. prime rate/London interbank offered rate
U.S. bankers' acceptances
U.S. prime rate
U.S. prime rate/CD adjusted secondary market rate
Guarantee commission
Hong Kong interbank offered rate (HKIBOR)
Japanese long-term prime rate
Canadian prime rate
Sterling Acceptances Commission
CD adjusted secondary market rate
SDR deposit rate
Letter of Credit Commission
Singapore interbank offered rate (SIBOR)
Madrid interbank offered rate (MIBOR)
Bahrain interbank offered rate (BIBOR)
Hong Kong prime rate
London interbank offered rate/Canadian prime rate
U.S. prime rate/bankers' acceptances
Kuwait interbank offered rate (KIBOR)
London interbank offered rate/bankers' acceptances
European Currency Unit interbank rate
London interbank offered rate/CD adjusted
  secondary market rate

*Joint rates refer to borrowers' or lenders' option.
**In order of importance in 1981.

give the borrower the option of electing the currency in which he draws down the loan, regardless of the currency in which it is denominated. Alternatively, at drawdown dates, it can give the borrower the option to convert the loan into a different currency from the one in which it was originally denominated. In both cases, the number of eligible currencies would be highly restricted.

The *amount* of the loan reflects two factors. Foremost, of course, would be the borrower's need. However, that amount might have to be reduced as a consequence of the lead manager's judgment on how the borrower's proposed amount would be perceived by the market. That is, an amount viewed as excessive for the borrower's quality and market conditions would be unlikely to be raised and such a failure would damage the reputation of both the borrower and the lead manager. Conversely, if the reception to the loan is better than expected, the principal of the loan could be raised, or the interested banks could be cut back, or some even cut out entirely.

The next feature would be the *type* of loan; most syndicated loans are term loans (one year plus), or revolving credits (as opposed to trade loans or working capital loans). *Revolvers* permit continuous drawdowns and repayments at the borrower's option. Project lending generally involves revolving loans that are ultimately converted into term loans.

Regardless of the type of loan, it would be subject to a *final maturity*. The date chosen would reflect the borrower's need and the market's perception of its quality, adjusted for market conditions. That is, in a period of easy credit, it could be extended, while in a period of tight credit, it would have to be less.

While a few loans, known as *bullet loans* (common in the construction industry) are repaid in full at maturity, most involve an *amortization schedule* (comparable in some ways to sinking funds for bonds). Thus, an amortization schedule must be agreed upon, as well as a *grace period* (generally a year) before the repayments begin. Interest payments are made on the *rollover dates* (such as, every three or six months), while principal payments are made semi-annually on rollover dates.

Perhaps the most critical decision is the choice of the *interest rate basis*. Chosen by the borrower, it is generally six- month LIBOR plus a spread. (Sometimes, it is three-month LIBOR because of the expectation of falling rates, which would allow a rollover at lower rates; twelve-month LIBOR is occasionally seen. The borrower can also be given the choice of the interest period on *each* of the rollover dates.) Instead of using the London interbank rate, the comparable rate in another Euro-center such as Singapore (SIBOR) could be chosen. Also, it is possible to choose the American prime rate (plus a spread perhaps) as the basis for the loan rate. Finally, the choice of LIBOR or prime could be left to the borrower, with the difference being that the prime rate is a *floating* (if sticky) rate, while a LIBOR-based rate is *fixed* for the rollover period (such as six months) chosen.

Generally, LIBOR is chosen as the interest rate basis. However, as no official LIBOR rate exists, an average taken from three reference banks at 11 a.m., two days before the rollover date (as term LIBOR deals usually commence on the *spot date*), is generally used. Members of large loan syndicates have become increasingly insistent that the reference banks chosen be representative in borrowing strength to the various syndicate members. Also, loan syndicates sometimes try to retain the right to name substitute reference banks if the requisite majority of syndicate members feel that the original reference banks have *lower* borrowing costs than would be representative for the syndicate. The latter raises the concern of the borrowers, especially if the original syndicate members have the right to sell participations to smaller banks with higher Eurobanking costs.

The *spread* selected is presumably the smallest one needed to entice the needed lenders. An excessive spread is not only expensive, but its magnitude reflects badly on the borrower. Conversely, an inadequate spread could result in the failure to raise the required sum, or necessitate an excessive extension of credit from the lead manager (exemplified by a Bank of Montreal credit for Brazil).

Spreads are not always fixed for the duration of the loan. Some loans involve *split spreads,* meaning that the latter part of the loan (such as the second four years) is at a slightly larger spread than the first half. Alternately, some loans involve *variable spreads* based on market conditions on the rollover dates. While the spreads in such loans are decided by the banks, the borrower who objects, can repay the loan without notice.

The advantage of such variable spreads to the borrower is that all the *requotes* are for progressively shorter maturities (which, all things being equal, reduces the spread), as well as the possibility of an improvement in market conditions (such as the confidence level), or the borrower's quality, which narrows spreads, while the advantage to the lenders is that the spread can be widened if the borrower's creditworthiness deteriorates or if there is a general market tightening.

The spreads themselves reflect several factors, the foremost of which is the borrowers' *creditworthiness.* The latter reflects not only an analysis of the borrowers' quality, but also the volume of their outstanding loans. Factors such as their countries' foreign exchange holdings and related balance of payments situation also come into play (in particular, reserves relative to imports).

Besides creditworthiness, *market conditions* significantly impact the spreads. In times of market malaise, the spreads considerably widen (such as in the aftermath of the Franklin and Herstatt collapses), while they considerably narrow when the market regains its confidence.

As already noted, the *final maturity* of the loan impacts the spread.

A shorter maturity that entails less risk, obviously entails a smaller spread, and vice versa.

The *general level of interest rates* also affects the spread, with a high level of nominal interest rates implying a narrower absolute spread. The latter is due to competitive forces maintaining the same rate of return on capital, the need to lower spreads as a higher LIBOR weakens loan demand, and to the increased flow of funds into the Euromarket as the higher interest rates raise the opportunity cost of reserve requirements in the domestic market.

Two final factors affecting spreads are the *variation of interest rates* and *liquidity considerations.* In particular, as banks do not eliminate interest rate risk by perfectly matching asset and liability maturities, they require an additional risk premium when rates are more volatile. Finally, the supply of funds to Eurobanks affects spreads, with the higher the proportionate amount of nonbank deposits (for example, due to a U.S. current account deficit), the lower the spread, and the lower the profitability of domestic lending, the greater the shift of funds into the Euromarket, with lower resultant spreads.

A *cancellation clause* is included to be invoked when the borrower and syndicates fail to agree on a new interest rate on a rollover date. Similarly, revolving credits often have a termination clause involving a fee to be paid by the borrower.

Commitment fees of around 1% are standard in syndicated loans to compensate banks for the nonutilized part of the loan. (Previously they were around 0.5%, but regulatory pressures to increase capital against commitments raised them.) However, a *grace period* is granted before the commitment fee becomes applicable.

Banks make loans based on a fixed assessment of their costs. Should their costs increase during the term of the loan, such as from an unexpected increase in reserve requirements, then a *general increase in costs* clause provides that the borrower will fully compensate the affected bank lender.

Related to the latter is the *tax clause,* which provides that the borrower will compensate the lenders for any new withholding taxes on their interest income for which they may become responsible. However, to insure equity, the clause further provides that the lenders will pass along to the borrower the value of any tax credits they receive as a consequence of the borrower paying their new withholding taxes for them.

Syndicated loans do not allow the borrower to ask for any drawdown amount at any time. Rather, the borrower is obliged to draw down on the rollover dates in fixed multiples (such as $10 million, $20 million, or the like), although special provisons (i.e., larger) may be made for the initial drawdown. In some loans, there are caps on the individual drawdowns.

Most syndicated loans are made to sovereign borrowers or top rated corporations so that a collateral requirement would be an improper request. However, it is usual to ask for a *negative pledge*. While no collateral is asked, the borrower agrees not to give any subsequent creditor collateral either, so that in the event of a default, no creditor would be in a privileged position.

A *pari passu* covenant, like a negative pledge, is a covenant used to ensure that the lending banks will be treated equally with other creditors in the event a borrower becomes insolvent and is subsequently liquidated. Most international loans are unsecured, and *pari passu* provisions prevent the subordination of the lending banks to other *unsecured* creditors. (Negative pledges prevent the subordination of lending banks to *secured* creditors.)

Lower-quality borrowers are often accommodated in the market through the medium of a *guarantee from a governmental entity or corporate parent*. In this way, the borrower obtains the higher credit rating of the *guarantor*, which not only reduces the spread, but in many cases, makes the very borrowing possible.

Prepayment clauses are common features of syndicated loans. As they are usually invoked when refinancing is available at a lower cost, they work against the creditors' interests. Thus, prepayments often trigger a penalty fee unless the bargaining power of the borrower (such as a top-rated multinational) is sufficient to obtain penalty-free prepayments. (Prepayments made on any but a rollover date would always trigger a penalty.)

A statement by the borrower regarding the *use of the proceeds* is generally required. Traditionally, the statement may not have been legally binding, but the lenders want some general assurance that the loan would be used, at least partially, in a way that would create an income stream to amortize the loan. Currently, the *use of the proceeds* is generally treated as a legally binding contract.

Relatedly, a wide array of other covenants is added to syndicated loan agreements by protection-oriented lenders. The borrower is often required initially to provide *representations and warranties* as to facts bearing on the lenders' credit judgments and can be obligated to be able to remake such representations and warranties as of the dates of each loan drawdown to maintain the loan commitments. Typically, the borrower must provide *annual audited and periodic unaudited financial statements.* Also, the borrower normally must agree to obtain and maintain all necessary *governmental authorizations and approvals, maintain all of its rights and privileges, pay taxes, maintain insurance,* and otherwise *take care of administration.* The borrower likewise must usually give *notice of material adverse events.*

Additional covenants are *requirements for maintenance of specified current working capital ratios; limits on other long- term and short-term indebtedness* (in specified amounts, or during periods of higher inflation, in terms of financial ratios), and often *limitations on back door substitutes for indebtedness* such as leasing; limitations on dividends and *limitations on capital expenditures.*

Related to specific covenants, syndicated loan agreements provide for *waivers, consents, or amendments* to respond to changed circumstances. Some require lender unanimity, some a specific majority, and some no lender consents at all.

To facilitate the successful fulfillment of the syndication, the loan agreements generally include *the provision that the borrower refrain from other borrowings until the syndication period is over.* Such attempted simultaneous borrowings would cause market confusion, which would be especially harmful to the syndication's managers.

Also related to the final details of the loan is often the requirement of *a promissory note* as *evidence of indebtedness.* It is especially sought by American banks to be in compliance with U.S. banking regulations.

A variety of provisions are added to the agreements to guard against unlikely but possible risks. These include specifying *where* drawdowns and repayments are to take place, and *funding interruption* clauses should the relevant interbank Euromarket cease to actively function (providing for the termination of the loan or additional compensation to the lenders to maintain their price spreads).

As members of a loan syndicate often want to be able to sell *participations* in their share, that issue is dealt with in the loan agreement. Some Eurolending agreements require borrower consent (which generally would not be given as small creditors have higher borrowing costs, and are less inclined to grant *waivers* due to the lack of a direct relationship with the borrower, moreover, while a proliferation of creditors adds to administrative costs) or the consent of a majority of other lenders for a change in the identity in the lender of record. Alternatively, some agreements permit any lenders of record to sell its participation to one or any number of other lenders, with division and substitution of notes, provided only that any such lender be a bank or other financial institution as defined in the agreement.

Besides provisions dealing with the loan itself, a wide array of default-related clauses have emerged, partially in response to the rising level of default problems. (Historically, loan losses have been less in the Euromarket than in the U.S. domestic market, for example, but a Mexico or Argentina by itself could change that record.)

It should be noted that *events of default* include not only failure to pay principal and interest when due, but also failure to abide by *covenants,* or the occurrence of catastrophic events such as bankruptcy or expropriation. First, several provisions are usually inserted to prevent a *payment default.* Notable among these is the widely used *cross default clause,* which states that a default on any of the borrower's outstanding loans constitutes a default on the loan in question. Such an action, like any other event of default, would give the lenders, or a requisite majority thereof, such rights as the loan being accelerated (due immediately), the cancellation of any undrawn commitments, the imposition of higher default rates of interest, and the institution of collection action.

Less drastic preventive measures include *permitting waiver or amendment of most covenants* by some kind of majority vote rather than by unanimous lender consent; for example, permitting new loans preferential both as to time of payment and as to security, as opposed to renegotiating the terms of payment of the initial loan, which might require unanimity and thus give considerable power to small creditors with their distinct interests.

Where a default has been declared, exercising a *set-off against the borrower's deposits* is the most easily available source of collection, and in the case of governmental entities, perhaps the only practical source. Thus, it is generally provided in the loan agreements that, if a lender succeeds in collecting from the borrower, by set-off or otherwise, it must share its collection pro rata with other lenders. However, such clauses usually also allow a bank to avoid the sharing requirement if it has other defaulted loans to the borrower.

Finally, there are also *intercredit agreements* among different lending syndicates, requiring a requisite majority vote of the lenders of all the syndicates involved before collection action against the borrower is taken, as substantial borrowers generally borrow under more than one lending syndicate, and some banks might be members of two or more such syndicates. The former raises the problem of the potentially catastrophic effects of a race to independent collection by different syndicates, and the latter raises the problem of conflicts of interest. While highly salutary, such agreements are limited by the divergent interests of the various syndicates. For example, only some are covered by political risk and convertibility insurance, some lenders are governmental or international agencies with special political interests, and some banks are caught in a unique situation, such as U.S. banks during the Iranian crisis, and UK banks during the Falklands crisis.

Another customary provision of the loan agreements is a clarification of the relations between the managing or agent bank (normally the managing bank becomes the agent after the signing of the loan agreements) and the syndicate member banks. In particular, the agent bank in the loan agreements explicitly disclaims *fiduciary* or trustee responsibility to the other participants, emphasizing that any credit decisions based on information obtained from the borrower by the agent are the credit decisions of each individual participating bank.

Finally, the loan agreements state which body of law and courts will be used to decide any disputes that develop. *Applicable law* is usually UK law or New York or California law (reflecting the federal system in the U.S.).

Eurocurrency Bank Credits During 1983–1986

Eurocurrency bank credits totalled $74 billion in 1983, well ahead of $49 billion in Eurobond issuance. Country statistics that group Eurobonds, foreign bonds, Eurocurrency bank credits, and foreign bank credits together show the principle loan recipients in that year were the U.S. ($20 billion), Japan ($14 billion), France and Canada ($9 billion), Sweden ($7 billion), Australia ($6 billion), Mexico ($5 billion), Brazil and Korea ($4 billion). African and East European borrowers were led by Nigeria ($2 billion) and Hungary ($0.7 billion).

In 1984, Eurocurrency bank credits jumped 52% as the market stabilized in the aftermath of the Latin American debt crisis of 1982–1983. Such credits totalled $113 billion well ahead of Eurobonds at $79 billion. The two leading loan recipients in that year included the U.S., whose $65 billion in credits reflected a dynamic high growth (6.5%) economy as well as a large current account deficit, followed in the distance by Japan at $18 billion. Other principal borrowers included Canada ($13 billion), France and Sweden ($11 billion), Italy and Brazil ($7 billion) Australia and Korea ($6 billion), Hungary and the Soviet Union ($1 billion).

In 1985, Eurocurrency bank credits declined 2% to $110 billion amidst sluggish world growth. They were surpassed by Eurobonds, the issuance of which totalled $136 billion. The U.S. remained the leading loan recipient, with $69 billion in credits, followed by the United Kingdom ($25 billion), Japan ($21 billion), France ($18 billion), Canada ($17 billion), Australia ($14 billion), Sweden ($10 billion), Korea ($6 billion), and Hungary and the Soviet Union ($1.5 billion).

Finally, in 1986, reflecting growing securitization, Eurobonds surged far ahead of Eurocurrency bank credits with the $188 billion in Eurobonds, over twice the $83 billion in bank credits. The U.S. again was the leading borrower ($57 billion), followed by Japan, ($36 billion), the UK ($24 billion), Canada ($22 billion), Australia and France ($20 billion), Italy ($13 billion), West Germany ($12 billion), New Zealand ($13 billion), Austria, and Denmark ($10 billion). Notable by their absence were the Latin American countries, struggling with debt crises. Their absence facilitated the growing borrowing by the Soviet Union ($1.8 billion, a 20% increase) which suffered a hard currency shortfall as a consequence of the sharp drop in petroleum and natural gas (its principal exports) prices during November 1985-August 1986.

Syndicated Lending and the Global Debt Crisis

During the 1970s and early 1980s syndicated lending expanded rapidly as major banks in the industrialized countries sought to recycle petrodollar and other deposits. The combination of *up-front management fees* plus generous spreads over LIBOR, (and banks were frequently able to raise funds below LIBOR, such as at the bid rate or by issuing CDs) were irresistible to the bankers in their pursuit of growing ROA (return on assets) and ROE (return on equity).

However, in the first half of 1982, Argentina encountered debt problems and the bubble burst in August 1982 when Mexico announced

Exhibit 7-2
INTERNATIONAL BOND ISSUES AND BANK CREDITS: 1983-1986
(Millions of Dollars)

By country of borrower	1983	1984	1985	1986 Mar	Apr	May	Jan-May 1986	Jan-May 1985
Industrial Countries	102,652	177,077	226,711	23,629	30,478	17,095	107,226	82,030
Australia	5,737	5,816	14,407	800	1,369	829	7,708	3,641
Austria	1,290	2,254	2,435	338	195	564	1,863	1,044
Belgium	2,168	1,847	3,269	1,220	526	338	2,642	989
Canada	8,571	13,124	17,184	1,257	2,533	914	7,570	7,480
Denmark	3,941	4,825	3,589	176	930	138	1,543	1,590
Finland	12,711	1,713	1,846	203	188	196	1,164	669
France	8,626	11,298	18,773	1,951	1,574	821	5,768	4,806
Germany	3,197	2,165	3,452	595	1,169	2,127	4,841	766
Greece	1,291	1,551	1,588	67	46	370	483	1,140
Ireland	1,869	1,377	1,881	–	317	502	1,263	631
Italy	4,876	6,933	11,033	684	1,943	1,933	6,108	6,312
Japan	14,428	17,526	21,269	2,908	4,059	2,253	12,024	9,057
Netherlands	1,213	1,973	2,299	491	326	57	1,525	516
New Zealand	802	3,208	2,707	662	1,121	495	2,948	640
Norway	1,969	1,324	3,905	279	537	235	1,411	660
Portugal	1,030	1,796	2,383	52	20	107	777	1,018
South Africa	1,300	1,422	825	–	–	–	–	523
Spain	4,977	4,931	3,913	177	685	298	1,474	2,348
Sweden	7,144	11,256	9,890	2,980	897	46	5,370	5,473
United Kingdom	2,726	8,899	25,424	3,071	2,931	1,019	10,125	8,510
United States	20,276	65,054	69,194	4,980	8,670	3,654	28,497	23,385
*Other**	3,950	6,785	5,447	741	442	200	2,125	833

Exhibit 7-2 (con't)

	1983	1984	1985	1986 Mar	Apr	May	Jan-May 1986	Jan-May 1985
Developing countries	**38,256**	**39,725**	**32,139**	**3,607**	**1,437**	**1,633**	**9,400**	**10,356**
Latin American countries	**15,592**	**17,464**	**8,115**	**222**	**150**	**255**	**916**	**1,033**
Argentina	1,750	4,212	3,700	—	—	—	17	—
Brazil	4,475	6,649	—	—	—	—	—	—
Chile	1,405	784	1,085	—	—	—	—	—
Colombia	552	589	1,052	—	—	50	50	—
Mexico	5,138	3,918	109	—	—	50	50	—
Venezuela	237	—	48	—	—	—	—	—
*Other**	2,035	1,312	2,121	222	150	205	849	1,033
Asian countries	**12,978**	**15,893**	**18,410**	**2,845**	**828**	**668**	**6,392**	**6,336**
India	968	945	818	357	—	9	620	298
Indonesia	2,383	1,924	451	657	27	983	400	—
Korea	4,387	6,201	5,898	629	174	254	1,561	2,258
Malaysia	2,197	2,605	2,220	22	—	—	54	931
Philippines	878	925	925	—	—	—	—	925
Thailand	747	1,221	1,497	600	—	406	1,016	625
Other	1,438	2,072	6,602	580	628	—	2,158	900
Middle Eastern and African Countries	**9,686**	**6,338**	**5,614**	**540**	**459**	**710**	**2,092**	**2,986**
Algeria	1,993	821	1,450	300	—	—	407	1,300
Nigeria	2,343	985	—	—	—	—	—	—
Turkey	1,106	741	1,203	120	459	100	862	579
Other	4,244	3,821	2,960	120	—	610	823	1,108
Eastern European Countries	**1,294**	**3,244**	**5,236**	**250**	**360**	**548**	**1,919**	**1,602**
Hungary	741	1,386	1,578	—	210	—	521	317
Soviet Union	1,051	1,489	250	150	548	1,248	541	—
*Other***	460	807	2,169	—	—	—	150	744

International organizations****	16,201	13,287	20,635	2,075	899	899	1,138	7,720

By type of instrument and currency								
International bond issues	76,329	107,411	167,756	19,632	26,116	14,541	92,441	66,276
Eurobonds	48,501	79,458	136,731	15,326	22,051	13,034	76,097	55,311
U.S. dollar	38,428	63,593	97,782	7,791	12,032	8,607	46,078	42,642
German mark	3,817	4,604	9,491	1,490	1,698	1,990	7,590	2,872
British pound	1,947	3,997	5,766	2,098	2,412	307	5,422	2,232
Japanese yen	212	1,212	6,539	2,069	1,579	961	6,686	1,867
European composite units	2,019	3,032	7,038	650	1,729	375	3,432	2,652
Other	2,078	3,020	10,114	1,230	2,602	794	6,890	3,047
Foreign bonds	27,953	31,025	4,306	4,065	1,507	16,344	10,966	—
U.S. dollar	4,545	5,487	4,655	900	400	—	2,364	1,957
German mark	2,671	2,243	1,741	—	—	—	—	687
British pound	811	1,292	958	109	—	77	186	159
Swiss franc	14,299	12,626	14,954	2,335	3,116	911	9,756	4,798
Japanese yen	3,772	4,628	6,379	811	309	123	2,823	2,650
Other	1,730	1,677	2,339	151	239	396	1,216	715
International bank credits	82,074	125,922	116,964	9,928	7,059	5,874	33,825	36,655
Eurocurrency credits	74,222	112,605	110,317	9,085	6,603	5,466	31,498	33,910
Foreign Credits	7,852	13,317	6,648	843	456	408	2,327	2,745
Total	158,403	233,333	284,720	29,560	33,174	20,415	126,266	102,931

*Includes multinational organizations.
**Includes unallocated.
***Includes COMECON institutions.
****Includes regional development organizations.
Source: *World Financial Markets* (June/July 1986). Reprinted with permission of the Morgan Guaranty Trust Company of New York.

Exhibit 7-3
THE "BAKER PLAN'S" SEVENTEEN HEAVILY INDEBTED COUNTRIES

Country	Debt Outstanding 1985* Total (US$ billion)	Of which Private Source (%)	Debt Service 1985-87† (US$ billion) Total	Of which Interest	Ratio of Debt to Exports (%) 1980	1984
Argentina	50.8	86.8	20.4	12.7	90.9	290.2
Bolivia	4.0	39.3	1.6	0.6	210.4	382.7
Brazil	107.3	84.2	39.7	28.0	171.3	219.8
Chile	21.0	87.2	9.2	5.0	75.5	225.1
Colombia	11.3	57.5	6.4	2.5	69.7	150.1
Costa Rica	4.2	59.7	2.4	0.9	139.5	270.8
Ecuador††	8.5	73.8	3.4	2.1	110.9	223.1
Ivory Coast	8.0	64.1	4.0	1.4	119.4	160.5
Jamaica	3.4	24.0	1.3	0.5	98.2	159.9
Mexico	99.0	89.1	44.4	27.2	136.7	213.5
Morocco	14.0	39.1	6.0	2.4	217.3	337.2
Nigeria	19.3	88.2	9.1	3.1	15.7	95.4
Peru	13.4	60.7	5.2	3.1	127.1	247.0
Philippines	24.8	67.8	9.5	4.9	81.6	139.1
Uruguay	3.6	82.1	1.4	0.8	70.7	184.8
Venezuela††	33.6	99.5	17.8	7.8	48.9	91.4
Yugoslavia‡‡	19.6	64.0	13.6	4.0	33.3	62.6
Total	445.9	80.8	194.9	106.9	106.9	203.1

*Estimated total external liabilities, including the use of IMF credit. † Debt service is based on known long-term debt and terms at end-1984. It does not take into account new loans contracted or debt reschedulings signed after that date. Based on estimated interest actually paid on total external liabilities in 1985.
**Latest year for which data are available. Growth rates are computed from time series in constant prices, using beginning- and end-period values. ††The merchandise trade balance for 1984 is not available; the value shown is for 1983. ‡‡Average annual growth rates are for 1980-83, except for GDP which for 1980-84.
Source: *The Economist*, September 27, 1986, p.24.

its inability to make its scheduled debt payments. Brazil followed in December—the global debt crisis had begun in earnest. The crisis though had been brewing for several years amidst spiraling debt ($750 billion for developing countries plus Eastern Europe) and proliferating structural weaknesses (detailed in the exhibit below, "The Ten Latin America Debt Myths").

| Trade Balance 1984 (US$ billion) | | Average Annual Growth Rates 1980-84**(%) | | | | |
Total	Change from 1980	GDP	Exports	Imports	Investment	Per Capita Consumption
3.9	5.3	−1.6	3.6	−14.7	−16.8	−2.7
0.3	0.1	−4.7	−1.7	−15.8	−22.1	−7.8
13.1	15.9	0.1	10.8	−7.3	−8.6	−1.2
0.3	1.1	−1.4	−0.7	−4.2	−11.6	−2.1
0.3	0.6	1.8	0.8	2.4	2.4	−0.1
−0.1	0.3	−0.4	1.1	−9.1	−9.4	−4.8
1.1	0.8	1.1	2.6	−13.7	−16.9	−2.3
1.3	0.9	−2.3	1.3	−8.8	−19.5	−6.6
−0.3	−0.2	1.3	−2.5	−2.1	9.5	−1.4
12.8	15.6	1.3	10.5	−14.5	−10.1	−1.4
−1.4	−0.1	2.5	4.1	−1.0	−2.7	−0.2
3.0	−8.2	−4.7	−13.3	−12.1	−19.3	−4.3
1.0	0.2	−0.7	−0.6	−10.8	−5.3	−3.7
−0.7	1.3	0.8	3.6	−4.8	−12.4	0.0
0.2	0.8	−3.7	2.2	−11.3	−20.2	−4.7
8.0	−0.2	−1.8	−3.8	−19.3	−15.6	−6.4
−1.2	3.7	0.6	−0.6	−8.1	−2.9	−0.5
41.6	37.8	−0.3	1.8	−9.2	−9.7	−1.8

The proximate course of the crisis was the two year spike in interest rates initiated by Fed Chairman Paul Volker's October 1979 *Saturday massacre*. That was when the Fed, alarmed by inflationary pressures and the weak dollar, shifted its monetary policy priority from stable interest rates (Keynesianism) to control of the monetary aggregates (monetarism).

As U.S. domestic interest rates jumped, so did the LIBOR rates and with the Latin American loans generally based on 6-month LIBOR, the jump in rates quickly translated into ominous hikes in scheduled Latin American debt repayments. To cope with the unexpected jump in interest payments, the Latin American countries fell back on still unused short-term credit commitments. But the increasingly nervous banks reduced the lines and declined to make new commitments. Thus, the *net inflow* of funds into Latin America reversed into a *net outflow* of funds, which soon sharply eroded those countries' international reserves. Widespread debt reschedulings and massive currency devaluations followed thereafter.

In retrospect, the creditor banks overlooked several major factors. In particular, they considered some major structural problems of the countries as just temporary short-term imbalances, and did unrealistic projections of future cash flows according to reasonable export-import performances. Moreover, they did inadequate analyses of the implications of the final destination of the funds (e.g., capital flight), and were insensitive to the implacability of many of LDC problems to standard policy prescriptions. Finally, the banks failed to integrate the implications of major drops in oil prices in developing their credit policies toward such oil-producing countries as Mexico and Venezuela, as well as the implications of their own *short-funding* strategies (short-term deposits funding medium term assets).

The global debt crisis has left many changes in its wake besides the various specific proposals to resolve it. Concern with the crisis and related bank solvency led the Committee on Banking Regulations and Supervisory Practices of the BIS to update its 1975 "Concordat" by a 1983 *reformulation* (both are discussed in the chapter on Euromarket supervision) entitled "Principles for the Supervision of Banks' Foreign Establishments." In particular it should be noted that LDC lending is frequently done out of foreign branches for tax and other reasons. Subsequently, many increasingly doubtful loans of American banks were *shifted* from a LIBOR basis to a prime basis to justify transferring them to the parent U.S. bank, so that probable losses on such loans could be used to reduce state and city, as well as federal taxes.

Also, to deal with the overall crisis the major banks created The Institute of International Finance Inc. (described at the end of this chapter). Two major purposes of the Institute were the improved sharing of information on the weak debtor countries; and encouraging the smaller banks (e.g., U.S. regionals) to stay in the debt syndicates, rather than selling their *participations* to the major banks on the basis of threatening to hold up the debt rescheduling process. In particular, smaller banks felt they were misled by the big banks through the latter's provision of inadequate and overly optimistic credit analysis in order to sell participation in loans on which they had made large up-front management fees (as well as gaining other banking business from their relations with the debtors).

A third general result of the debt crisis was considerable *debt swapping* to improve the quality of bank loan portfolios and facilitate loan administration rendered more difficult by widespread reschedulings. Exemplifying the former, banks swapped Bolivian and Nicaraguan debt for Brazilian and Mexican debt, while exemplifying the latter, European banks swapped Latin American debt to American banks in exchange for East European debt. Also, banks used the swapping mechanism to *diversify* portfolios with excessive concentrations of some countries' debts.

With respect to specific proposals to deal with the debt crisis, several have been advanced. First, there is the case-by-case approach, involving the country accepting an IMF adjustment (austerity) program in return for which the country's bank debt committee offers a favorable rescheduling arrangement. Often such arrangements have involved a Western governmental entity, such as the U.S. Treasury, providing *bridge financing.*

One problem with their approach is that countries often find it politically difficult to accept or implement austerity programs. For example, Venezuela flatly rejected an IMF program and Brazil violated seven successive "letters of intent."

A second problem is that the banks have often charged large management fees for the *reschedulings,* while widening the spread over LIBOR on the rescheduled loans. Such additional expenses leave the countries in worse shape though the banks claim it is expensive to reschedule (e.g., to get cooperation of the over 500 banks involved in the large schedulings entails a lot of time, travel, etc.), while the situation of presumably greater risk is the justification for the widened spread over LIBOR.

A variation of the case-by-case approach is the plan of the U.S.

Treasury Secretary Baker of special assistance to 17 heavily indebted countries (announced at the 1985 Seoul meeting of the IMF/World Bank) in exchange for their undertaking significant structural reforms with a *free market* orientation, and adopting *growth-oriented* policies. Such policies would aid faltering growth and thus domestic stability, while boosting declining U.S. exports to such countries (helping to rectify the massive American trade deficit), many of which traditionally have been important markets for U.S. exports. The 17 countries include 12 countries in Latin America and the Caribbean (Argentina, Bolivia, Brazil, Chile, Colombia, Costa Rica, Ecuador, Jamaica, Mexico, Peru, Uruguay, and Venezuela), three countries in Africa (Ivory Coast, Morocco, and Nigeria), and one country apiece in Asia (the Philippines) and Eastern Europe (Yugoslavia).

A second approach is the *debt discounting* approach involving an existing (e.g. World Bank or IMF) or newly created supranational institution that would absorb the debt owed to the banks and transform it into longer-term, lower interest bonds. While it would involve a yield loss for the banks, it would get a lot of questionable debt off their books.

Related to the latter approach, in March 1987, 28 Japanese banks with government approval, created a Cayman corporation factoring company to buy their third-world debt at a discount. The process cleared questionable debt off their books, generated tax deductions (otherwise unavailable), and freed management time, while any success in collecting it will result in dividends to the bank shareholders.

Some other approaches include *stretchouts of grace periods and maturities, interest rate caps, a limitation of debt repayments to a fixed percentage of exports* (Peru suggests 10%), *and a debtors' cartel repudiating debt.* The latter is advocated but not utilized by Castro's Cuba, which is trying, amidst low sugar prices, to pay off its $3.5 billion of hard currency debt. Peru has acted along that line, and as a result has found itself cut off from the international payments and credit system aside from barter trade with the Soviet bloc. Some very recent additional approaches include *debt-for-commodity swaps* (proposed by First Interstate with Peru), *exit bonds* (offered by Argentina to enable small banks to withdraw from the rescheduling process), *Philippine Investment Notes* or *P.I.N.s* (payment of interest in local currency obligations of the central bank that are expected to be used to purchase local equities), *retiming* (Chile's paying interest annually instead of semi-annually, *early-bird special* (Argentina's agreeing to pay extra interest to banks agreeing early to new loans), the *Bradley plan* for partial debt forgiveness, and the creation of a *Multiteral Investment Guaranty Agency* or MIGA by the World Bank (to encourage equity investment in the LDC's).

A more fruitful approach has been debt for equity swaps, widely used by Chile (the initiator in 1984), Mexico, Brazil and the Philippines. While some banks, such as Bankers Trust, have done direct swaps, it usually involves the purchase of debt at a discount, its conversion into the local currency at or near the face value for the debt, and the use of the local currency for equity investment in the debtor country. In the first half of 1986, both Mexico and Chile (often involving the repatriation of flight capital) each did about $300 million of such deals. Altogether approximately $8 billion of loans was traded in the secondary market in 1986, and that volume is expected to double in 1987. Stimulating the growth of that market are brokers such as the Shearson Lehman Brothers Loan Transaction Group, Citibank, Morgan, the Salomon Brothers High Yield Department, Bankers Trust, Libra, Chase and Manufacturers Hanover.

A sticking point is the discount involved—in the fall of 1986, Brazilian government debt could be bought for about 75% of its face value, with the corresponding numbers for other countries being Mexico-55%, Brazil-74%, Ecuador-63%, Philippines-69%, Argentina-65%, Chile-67%, Peru-22%, Bolivia and Nicaragua-below 10%, Venezuela-76%, Poland-42%, Romania-86% (reflecting Secretary General's Ceausescu's obsession with eliminating the external debt) and Yugoslavia-73%.

The April 20, 1987 discounts are seen in Exhibit 7-4, "Indicative Prices for Less Developed Country Bank Loans". Discounts vary from modest for countries such as Turkey and Algeria to over 90% for Nicaragua, Liberia and the Sudan; the discounts themselves, of course, fluctuate continuously.

The swap index is best explained by using an example: a bank may wish to exchange its Chilean debt for Colombian debt, either because it wishes to diversify or concentrate debt, or because it views Colombian debt as significantly better quality (e.g., Colombia is the only Latin

American country that has not rescheduled, and is even able to sell Euro-securities).

The swap "sell" index number for Chile is 1.34, while the swap "buy" index number for Columbia is 3.14. By dividing 3.14 by 1.34, one derives 2.34, which represents the face amount of Colombian debt that must be placed against a face amount of Chilean debt, with the difference to be paid in cash. Thus, to convert the different discounts on Chilean and Colombian debt into a situation which can accountingwise be considered a par exchange (and thus avoid the bank with lower quality Chilean debt from having to register a loss), the bank holding Chilean debt would give its counterparty 1.00 times X in Chilean debt plus 1.34 times X in cash. Hence, to receive $23.4 million in Colombian debt, it would give up $10 million in cash and $13.4 million in Chilean debt.

With many banks having lent two to three times their capital to Latin America (e.g., the "renamed" "Manuel Hanover," as well as Citibank, Chase, and Bank of America), selling substantial debt at a large discount would imply the erosion of much of their capital. Also it would jeopardize the banks' current practice of valuing such debt at its face value.

The Institute of International Finance, Inc.

PURPOSE OF THE INSTITUTE

Its purpose is to serve as a center for the dissemination of information to its members and a forum in which lending institutions can communicate with borrowing countries, multinational organizations and regulators, in order to improve the process of international lending. According to its articles of incorporation, its primary objectives are "To improve the timeliness and quality of information available on sovereign borrowers, to encourage communication among the major participants involved in the international lending process (governments and multilateral organizations and private lending institutions), and to foster a greater understanding within the financial community of the future of international lending."

HISTORY OF THE INSTITUTE

The idea for an organization such as the Institute emerged at a meeting of the International Financial Group held under the auspices of the National Planning Association at Ditchley Park, England, in May, 1982. In October, 1982, representatives of 30 banks from Europe, Japan and North America formed an organizing committee. Providing the leadership was William S. Ogden, former Vice Chairman of the Chase Manhattan Bank. The Institute was formally established and incorporated as a nonprofit organization at a meeting in Washington, D.C. in January, 1983. In the second half of 1983, the Board of Directors was elected and the Institute management was appointed. The Institute began its operations in January, 1984.

ACTIVITY OF THE INSTITUTE

The Institute's staff, currently totalling 35 and implementing a $5 million budget, has prepared country reports on approximately 40 countries. Most are written after a visit to the country concerned, with the mission team generally including one or two Institute staff accompanied by two or three officers of member banks. These reports are supplemented by "updates" or "summaries" when major policy changes occur or more information is available for inclusion in the database.

The country reports discuss recent economic developments, the economic and social policies followed by the country, and the factors affecting the balance of payments and debt servicing. They also cover structural aspects of the economy, often including industrial policies, banking and financial practices, capital market developments, and policies affecting foreign investment. The reports assess the prospects for borrowing countries against specified assumptions about the development of the world economy including industrial countries' growth, world trade, interest rates, exchange rates and commodity prices.

Exhibit 7-4
INDICATIVE PRICES FOR LESS DEVELOPED COUNTRY BANK LOANS
April 20, 1987

Country	Indicative Cash Prices		Swap Index		Trading Commentary
	Bid	Offer	Sell	Buy	
Algeria	95.50	98.00	9.08	20.44	No trades seen; but two-way interest continues.
Argentina	59.50	61.00	1.01	1.05	Still no evidence of buy side support level.
Bolivia	9.00	12.00	0.45	0.46	No trades seen this period; buyback talk continues.
Brazil	63.00	65.00	1.10	1.17	Some trades agreed, but volume remains unexciting.
Chile	69.50	70.50	1.34	1.39	Market holding steady at these levels.
Colombia	86.00	87.00	2.92	3.14	Buying interest continues, but little trading.
Costa Rica	36.00	37.50	0.64	0.65	A number of small trades seen, while technical problems persist.
Dom. Rep.	45.00	47.00	0.74	0.77	A few tugs on the line.
Ecuador	56.00	61.00	0.93	1.05	Better two-way interest, but prices still on workout basis.
Gabon	75.00	80.00	1.64	2.04	No pricing consensus among market participants.
Guatemala	61.00	64.00	1.05	1.14	Trading continues in a localized market for stabilization bonds.[a]
Honduras	40.00	43.00	0.68	0.72	Weak contrarian interest developing.
Ivory Coast	77.00	80.00	1.78	2.04	More sellers coming out of the woodwork.
Jamaica	45.00	50.00	0.74	0.82	Weak contrarian interest developing.
Liberia	4.00	6.00	0.43	0.43	Weak speculative interest seen.

Madagascar	55.00	63.00	0.91	1.10	Levels untested lately.
Malawi	74.00	77.00	1.57	1.78	Rarely traded due to lack of supply.
Mexico	58.75	59.50	0.99	1.01	Prices beginning to weaken from slower bidding after price peak.
Morocco	69.00	71.00	1.32	1.41	Assignment difficulties reported; trading interest continues.
Nicaragua	4.00	7.00	0.43	0.44	Better trading interest, but no trades.
Nigeria	36.00	38.00	0.64	0.66	Market continues to be dominated by a few players.
Panama	68.00	71.00	1.28	1.41	Some trades closing at these levels.
Peru	17.00	19.00	0.49	0.50	No recent developments.
Philippines	70.00	72.00	1.36	1.46	Better trading away from the D/E program.
Poland	45.00	46.00	0.74	0.76	Prices continues to rise on size buying.
Romania	88.00	90.00	3.41	4.09	No recent developments.
Senegal	64.00	66.00	1.14	1.20	Bidding interest continues.
Sudan	2.00	10.00	0.42	0.45	Tranche B credits[b] continue to attract attention; no trades seen.
Togo	68.00	70.00	1.28	1.36	Low level of trading interest.
Turkey	97.00	99.50	13.63	81.75	Interest in the CTLDs and BCAs continues.[c]
Uruguay	73.50	75.50	1.54	1.64	Recent two-way interest.
Venezuela	73.00	74.50	1.51	1.60	Good two-way trading interest; reasonable volume.
Yugoslavia	78.00	80.00	1.86	2.04	Better two-way interest.
Zaire	25.50	27.50	0.55	0.56	Few closing dinners in Kinshasa.
Zambia	18.00	22.00	0.50	0.52	No recent activity.

[a] Dollar denominated supplier credits
[b] Instruments representing capitalized interest
[c] Convertible Turkish lira deposits and bank credit agreements
Reprinted with permission of Salomon Brothers Inc.

Exhibit 7-5
LATIN AMERICAN DEBT MYTHS
by Eugene Sarver

If we were to believe recent media accounts, the Latin American debt crisis is over.

In fact, the very concept of the debt crisis being over implies a simplicity of causation and solution that is just not the real world.

But while we all share an aversion to complexity, the only way the Latin American crisis is really going to be surmounted is by grappling with the structural mess that underlies it. Perhaps there is no way better to begin than by exploding *10 myths* that shroud it:

MYTH NO. 1: The dominating cause of the crisis was the *spike* in London interbank offered rates concurrent with the drop in commodity prices...

Granted that those factors were the "straw that broke the camel's back," we already had a very sick camel. His disease was a complete structural mess epitomized by bloated, corrupt public sectors, including disastrously mismanaged public sector enterprises (even the Argentine state-owned oil company loses money), and the related exorbitant deficit financing to fuel them (in Mexico it totaled 18 percent of GNP).

Another self-inflicted wound was *overvalued* currencies that rewarded capital flight and encouraged locals to vacation in the United States and Europe—after all, they were cheaper than Cancun or Mar del Plata. In fact, Mexico, a paradise of beaches and hospitable mariachis, actually recorded a tourism *deficit* one month.

Moreover, in the early 1980s, inflation was running amok in the region, but the central banks there were keeping *real* domestic interest rates very low (or negative), further boosting capital flight. Thus, the breaking out of the debt crisis was due largely to indigenous mismanagement, not "force majeure."

MYTH NO. 2: A major cause of the crisis has been the monumental size of the debt ...

Admittedly, Brazil, Mexico and Argentina are "win," "place," and "show," in the international debt race, with external debts, respectively, of $98 billion, $93 billion and $45 billion, and Venezuela and Chile make up the tail end of the World Bank's *dirty dozen* major borrower list (over $15 billion in long-term debt), with external debts of $35 billion and $20 billion, respectively ...

But the problem has been more the *use* of debt for capital flight (Venezuela was essentially a revolving door), importation of consumer goods and investment in non-competitive high-cost *import substitution* industries (as opposed to the Asian *export industries* approach).

MYTH NO. 3: The high LIBOR rates were not foreseeable...

But from 1973 to 1981 there was a secular rise in inflation and interest rates, with the 1973 *oil shock* giving warning of the potential for additional shocks (e.g., the 1979-80 oil shock provoked by the Iran-Iraq war).

MYTH NO. 4: The drop in commodity prices was not foreseeable...

But historically, every rise in commodity prices has prompted market corrections (increased supply/decreased demand) and a downtrend in prices.

Exhibit 7-5 (con't)

Moreover, spikes in commodity prices are inherently deflationary and, therefore, sow of seeds of their own demise.

MYTH NO. 5: The banks are victims of the debt crisis...

But in rescheduling, the banks have earned large fees and often widened spreads, while the government's rescue of Continental-Illinois (necessitated by bad *domestic* energy loans) indicates that other large money-center banks would be similarly rescued.

MYTH NO. 6: The Latin American countries have put their economies in order...

While it is true that Brazil and Mexico achieved impressive balance of payments gains in 1984, enabling their foreign exchange reserves to reach $7.5 billion and $7 billion at end-1984, respectively, the merchandise trade surpluses that underscored the improvement ($13 billion for Brazil; $15 billion for Mexico) were largely due to Draconian restrictions on imports, *not* a dramatic jump in exports.

Another major factor was the jump in U.S. imports and the related massive U.S. trade disequilibrium (a $123 billion deficit); exchanging one major disequilibrium for another is hardly a sound basis for solving the debt crisis.

MYTH NO. 7: The democratization trend in Latin America (e.g., Argentina, Brazil) ameliorates the situation...

But the fragile democratic governments shy away from austerity measures likely to provoke significant unrest, as evidenced by the Argentine government's failing fight against inflation.

MYTH NO. 8: The debt crisis is over...

But Argentina broke its IMF agreement by permitting inflation to re-accelerate (to 25 percent/month in January) and had its IMF credits cut off, while additionally it is $800 million in arrears to

commercial banks with no such payments since Nov. 4.

Concurrently, Brazil has violated seven successive Letters of Intent to the IMF and had its IMF credits cut off.

Elsewhere, Bolivia is experiencing 50,000 percent inflation and has gone out of the debt repayment business, while Peru, Costa Rica and the Dominican Republic are all in arrears as well, and the Venezuelan private sector ($7.5 billion of debt) is in arrears because it is not getting dollars at the *preferential rate* agreed to by the government—having to purchase dollars at the *free market rate* (around 13 bolivares per dollar) would immediately bankrupt a large chunk of it.

Moreover, whatever success the Latin American countries have achieved has been largely due to deflationary policies in the face of the continuing population explosion, a sure recipe for unrest, as evidenced by riots in Sao Paulo, Kingston, and Santo Domingo, severe repression in Chile and Peru, and the disequilibrating popularity of the opposition PAN party in Mexico.

Further contradicting the image of Mexico as the big "success story" is that it still cannot do *voluntary borrowing* and such is not immediately foreseeable.

MYTH NO. 9: The banks are "out of the woods."...

But behind the *facade* of the "end of the debt crisis" is what Congressman Schumer (D–N.Y.) of the House Banking Committee calls "a long series of *Faustian* financial agreements"—bargains in which banks make new loans so that debtor nations have enough cash to continue paying interest on their old loans (effectively *capitalizing* the interest, although for obvious bank statement purposes not reported as such)... an arrangement that "enables the banks to continue reporting fictitious profits

Exhibit 7-5 (con't)

on loan portfolios bulging with questionable assets."

In short, much of the Latin American debt remains problematic, especially Argentina's (which one senior bank country risk analyst values as 50 cents on the dollar), and exceeds the capital of the major U.S. bank *lenders,* such as Manufacturers Hanover (whose cross-border loans to Brazil, Argentina, Mexico, and Venezuela of $6.7 billion total 150 percent of its *primary capital* and 100 percent of its *total capital*).

Investor apprehension of that grim reality can be seen in bank equity prices, while bank apprehension can be seen in the nervousness over reschedulings, even *distant* ones such as the National Commercial Bank of Saudi Arabia holding out in the current Philippines negotiations.

Finally, it should be emphasized that reschedulings do not mean that needed restructuring will be undertaken. And there are limits to its long-term viability as a strategy.

In particular, the regional and European banks want out, and even the money-center banks fret about tying up capital in Latin America at a time when regulatory authorities are stiffening up capital: asset requirements and bright new opportunities are opening up in domestic banking with the breakdown of the old rules against interstate and investment banking.

MYTH NO. 10: The multilateral institutions such as the IMF are available to "save the situation"...

But by the members' own choice, they have not expanded their resources adequately to deal with the crisis. While they have an important psychological role in moving sovereign borrowers (against whom the only real sanction is future unavailability of credit) toward appropriate long-term restructuring, their financial clout is minor league.

Moreover, their concerns are global, not national, so they oppose such palliatives as import restrictions, which hurt other members' exports. And they maintain that they cannot quarterback bank responses to the changing situations, despite accepting the concept of *enhanced monitoring.*

Reprinted from *The Journal of Commerce,* 11 April 1985.

Exhibit 7-6
I.I.F BOARD OF DIRECTORS
(as of September 1986)

Barry F. Sullivan (Chairman)
Chairman of the Board and
Chief Executive Officer
The First National Bank of
Chicago

Hans H. Angermueller
Vice Chairman
Citibank, N.A.

James W. Bergford
Executive Vice President
Chase Manhattan Bank, N.A.

Serge Boutissou
Region Executive Manager
International
Credit Lyonnais

Ibrahim S. Dabdoub
Chief General Manager
National Bank of Kuwait, SAK

Thierry de Broqueville
Director and Member
Executive Committee
Banques Bruxelles Lambert

Exhibit 7-6 (con't)

Andre de Lattre
Managing Director
The Institute of International
Finance, Inc.

William F. Farley
President
First National Bank of
Minneapolis

Guillermo Guemez Garcia
Executive Vice President
Banco Nacional de Mexico, S. A.

Hideo Ishara
Managing Director
Industrial Bank of Japan

Anders Ljungh
Executive Vice President
Svenska Handelsbanken

Paul J. Rizzo
General Manager, International
Australia and New Zealand
Banking Group, Ltd.

John J. Simone
Executive Vice President
Manufacturers Hanover Trust Co.

Roy Takata, Jr.
Managing Director
The Bank of Tokyo, Ltd.

Franz Lutolf
General Manager and
Member of the
Executive Board
Swiss Bank Corporation

Giovanni Malvezzi
Deputy Managing Director
Cassa di Risparmio delle
Provincie Lombarde

William J. McDonough
Executive Vice President
and Chief Financial Officer
First National Bank of
Chicago

Adroaldo Moura da Silva
Vice Chairman and
Head of International Division
Banco do Brasil, S. A.

William S. Ogden
Chairman and Chief
Executive Officer
Continental Illinois
National Bank & Trust Co.

A. Derrick Plummer
Senior International
Executive
National Westminster Bank
Plc

Grant L. Reuber
President and Chief
Operating Officer
Bank of Montreal

Kurt Richolt
Member, Board of Managing
Directors
Commerzbank AG

A complementary activity of the Institute is the IIF Country Database, which was available for 43 countries at the end of 1985. It provides statistical and analytical support for the economic reports. The data comes from a wide variety of international and national sources and is checked in the course of country missions. In addition, the IIF makes its own estimates where necessary to reconcile information from different sources or to provide key indicators of interest to international lenders.

The Database includes:

1. Indicators of the shift of resources between the external and domestic sectors of developing countries' economies, the changes in their competitiveness and the growth of their export markets, with estimates of both trade volumes and prices.

2. Estimates of the main credit and debit flows in the current account of the balance of payments, with independent estimates of debt servicing payments based on a crosscheck on national sources. It also identifies the main external financing flows in the capital account. A unique feature of the Database is that it identifies flows by creditor, which is a vital consideration for international lenders and cannot be derived from conventional sources.

3. Extensive information on the borrowing countries' debt. External liabilities are reconciled with flow information through a detailed model to capture the impact of exchange rate changes on the value of debt stocks. The Database gives a breakdown of total debt by creditor and by domestic borrower. Information is also provided on external assets and the Institute's estimates of a country's potential access to IMF credits.

4. Measures of fiscal and monetary policies. For fiscal policy, the presentation concentrates on identifying the public sector borrowing requirement as well as expenditures and reserves of the general government. For monetary policy, the presentation concentrates on the growth in domestic credit, money supply and price performance.

Complementing the country reports and Database are the reports of a group of special committees. These include the Economic Advisory Committee, composed of senior economists from 35 member banks, and the Working Party of some 50 bankers and economists. The latter addresses issues such as multiyear rescheduling, longer-term amortization and the need for country specific proposals; legal and regulatory questions stemming from new mechanisms such as cofinancing and multiyear reschedulings; the role and potential for currency diversification; and the need for increased official lending, both for trade finance and medium-term lending. Two study groups have been established as well, involving the Study Group on Insurance and Guarantees (addresses possible mechanisms to insure bank loans or portfolios, and spread international risk), and the Task Force on the Regulatory, Accounting and Tax Treatment of Cross-Border Lending (addresses the issues of capital adequacy, provisions and interest).

Information on the Institute's current activities is communicated via a quarterly publication, the **IIF Overview,** edited by Dennis Holden.

LEADERSHIP OF THE INSTITUTE

The research and lobbying activities of the Institute are led by a Managing Director. The post was initially given to Andre de Lattre, a former vice governor of the Banque de France. Upon the completion of his 1984-1986 term, he was succeeded by Horst Schulman, the 53-year-old Deputy Managing Director, who previously served as West German Chancellor Helmut Schmidt's personal representative for economic summits and as a Deputy Director of the World Bank.

Overseeing the work of the administrative executives is a Chairman and a 22-member Board of Directors (a list of its members appears at the end of this section). The initial chairman was Richard Hill, a former retired chairman of the Bank of Boston; at the completion of his three year term in December, 1986, he was succeeded by Barry Sullivan, the 55-year old Chairman and Chief Executive Officer of the First National Bank of Chicago, who formerly was an officer at Chase Manhattan Bank.

Selection of the Institute's leadership is done at the meetings of the full membership, two of which are held each year. One is held in the spring (generally in mid-May) and the other in the early fall, at the time and place of the joint IMF-World Bank meeting.

MEMBERSHIP

As of January, 1986, the Institute's membership totalled 182 banks and financial organizations from 38 countries, both developed and developing, as well as offshore financial centers. The membership represents over 80% of total international banking exposure in the developing world. Concurrently, twelve financial institutions and international corporations were Associate members.

Full Membership in the Institute is open to any lending institution which has, or contemplates having soon, international exposure for its own account. Lending institutions eligible for membership can be either private or government-owned, in whole or in part. However, to be a Full Member, an institution must make loans and commitments for its own account and for the purpose of generating profits.

In the fall of 1984, the Board of Directors agreed to create a category of Associate Membership. Associate Membership is open to financial institutions other than commercial banks such as development banks, development agencies, central banks and export credit agencies. Multinational corporations may also join as Associate Members. Associate Members receive all information available to Full Members, including access to the Institute's database on borrowing countries, but have no voting rights.

The Institute's operations are supported wholly by Full and Associate Member fees and Full Member dues assessed annually. For 1986, the Full Membership fee was US$6,000. In addition to this fee, membership dues are assessed individually on the basis of international exposure, with banks having an exposure of $10 billion or more paying $85,000, while lesser exposures of $2-10 billion, and $0-2 billion require payment of $27,000 and $5,000, respectively. The fee for Associate Membership is $15,000.

Exhibit 7-7
MEMBERS OF THE INSTITUTE OF INTERNATIONAL FINANCE, INC.
(as of January 1986)

Argentina
Banco de Galicia y Buenos Aires
Banco Rio de la Plata, S.A.

Australia
Australia and New Zealand Banking
  Group, Ltd.
Commonwealth Trading Bank of
  Australia
National Australia Bank, Ltd.
Rural & Industries Bank of Western
  Australia
State Bank of New South Wales
State Bank of Victoria
Westpac Banking Corporation

Austria
Creditanstalt-Bankverein
Osterreichische Landerbank A.G.

Bahrain
Arab Banking Corporation, B.S.C.
Gulf International Bank, B.S.C.

Exhibit 7-7 (con't)

Belgium
Banque Bruxelles Lambert, S.A. *
Byblos Bank Belgium, S.A.
Generale de Banque
Kredietbank, N.V. *

Brazil
Banco Brasileiro de Descontos, S.A. *
Banco de Credito Nacional, S.A.
Banco do Brasil, S.A. *
Banco Economica, S.A.
Banco Itau, S.A. *
Banco Nacional, S.A.
Uniao de Bancos Brasileiros

Canada
Bank of Montreal *
Bank of Nova Scotia *
Canadian Imperial Bank of Commerce *
Mercantile Bank of Canada
National Bank of Canada
Royal Bank of Canada *

Colombia
Banco de Bogota Trust Company

Denmark
Copenhagen Handelsbank A/S
Den Danske Bank af 1871 Aktieselskab
Privatbanken A/S

Finland
Kansallis-Osake-Pankki
Union Bank of Finland, Ltd.

France
Al Saudi Banque
Banque Arabe et Internationale
  d'Investissement
Banque Francaise du Commerce
  Exterieur
Banque Indosuez
Banque Internationale pour
  L'Afrique Occidentale
Banque Nationale de Paris *
Banque Worms
Caisse Centrale des Banques
  Populaires
Caisse National de Credit Agricole

Credit Chimique
Credit Commercial de France
Credit du Nord
Credit Industriel et Commercial
Credit Lyonnais *

Germany
Bank fur Gemeinwirtschaft AG
Commerzbank AG *
Dresdner Bank AG *
Hessische Landesbank
Vereins-und Westbank AG
Westdeutsche Landesbank Girozentrale *

Greece
Commercial Bank of Greece

India
Bank of India
State Bank of India

Indonesia
Bank Negara Indonesia 1946

Ireland
Allied Irish Banks, Plc
Bank of Ireland

Israel
Bank Leumi Le-Israel B.M.

Italy
Banca Nazionale del Lavoro *
Banca Nazionale dell'Agricoltura
Banca Popolare de Milano
Banco di Napoli
Banco di Roma *
Banco di Sicilia
Cassa di Risparmio delle
  Provincie Lombarde
Conzorzio de Credito per le Opere
  Pubbliche
Instituto Bancario San Paolo
  di Torino
Monte dei Paschi de Siena

Japan
Bank of Tokyo, Ltd. *
Dai-Ichi Kangyo Bank, Ltd. *
Daiwa Bank, Ltd.

Exhibit 7-7 (con't)

Switzerland
Banca del Gottardo
 (Gotthard Bank)
Banca Unione de Credito
Bank Leu, Ltd.
Credit Suisse*
Internationale Genossenschaftsbank A/G
Swiss Bank Corporation*
Swiss Volksbank
Union Bank of Switzerland*

Taiwan
International Commercial Bank
 of China

Trinidad and Tobago
National Commercial Bank of Trinidad
 & Tobago, Ltd.

Turkey
Turkiye Is Bankasi A.S.

United Kingdom
Bank of Credit & Commerce
 International
Bank of Scotland
Barclays Bank International, Ltd. *
Hungarian International Bank, Ltd.
Lloyds Bank PLC*
Midland Bank PLC*
National Westminster Bank PLC*
Royal Bank of Scotland PLC
Saudi International Bank
Standard Chartered Bank PLC
UBAF Bank, Ltd.

United States
American Security Bank, N.A.
AmSouth Bank, N.A.
Bank of America N.T. & S.A. *
Bank of Boston
Bank of New England, N.A.
Bank of New York
Bank of Virginia
Bankers Trust Company*
Centerre Bank, N.A.
Chase Manhattan Bank, N.A*
Chemical Bank*
Citibank N.A.*

Comerica Bank - Detroit
Commerce Union Bank
Commercial Credit International
 Banking Corporation
Continental Illinois National Bank*
First City National Bank of Houston
First Fidelity Bank N.A., New Jersey
First Interstate Bank
First National Bank of Chicago
First National Bank of Maryland
First National Bank of Minneapolis
First Pennsylvania Bank, N.A.
First Wisconsin National Bank
 of Milwaukee
Fleet National Bank
Irving Trust Company
Manufacturers Hanover Trust Company*
Manufacturers National Bank
 of Detroit
Marine Midland Bank, N.A.
Maryland National Bank
Mellon Bank N.A. *
Mercantile Trust Co., N.A.
Merchants National Bank
 & Trust Company
Morgan Guaranty Trust Company*
Northern Trust Company
Norwest Bank Minneapolis, N.A.
Rainier National Bank
Philadelphia National Bank
RepublicBank Dallas, N.A.
Republic National Bank
 of New York
Riggs National Bank
 of Washington, D.C
Salomon Brothers Inc.
 (Phibro Bank, A.G)
Security Pacific
 National Bank
Shawmut Bank of Boston, N.A.
Sun Banks, Inc.
Texas Commerce Bancshares
Wells Fargo Bank

Venezuela
Banco Latino, C.A.
Banco Mercantil, C.A

Exhibit 7-7 (con't)

Associate Members
Atomic Energy of Canada, Ltd.
  (Canada)
Banco Central do Brasil
  (Brazil)
Broken Hill Proprietary Co., Ltd.
  (Australia)
Compagnie Francaise d'Assurance
  pour le Commerce Exterieur,
  COFACE (France)
Compania Espanola de Seguros
  de Credito a la Exportacion, S.A.,
  CESCE (Spain)
Deutsche Finanzierungsgesellschaft

fur Beteiligungen in
  Entwicklungslandern GmbH, DEG
  (Germany)
Export Credits Guarantee Department,
  ECGD (United Kingdom)
General Electric Company
  (United States)
Kreditanstalt fur Wiederaufbau,
  KfW (Germany)
Occidental Petroleum Corporation
  (United States)
Saint-Gobain (France)
Saudi Fund for Development
  (Saudi Arabia)

*Founding Members

8

Eurocurrency Market Supervision

In the mid-1970s, accelerating proliferation of banks' foreign establishments in conjunction with 25% annual jumps in Eurocurrency market deposits and associated assets generated great concern among central bank governors of the major nations. Moreover, their concern was heightened by the 1974 failures of two active international banks, Franklin (New York) and Herstatt (Cologne), and the specter of even greater bankruptcies prompted by the ongoing global recession and the *mismatched* recycling of petrodollars (in the wake of the 1973-1974 initial oil shock).

Their concern was translated into enunciation of new guidelines in September 1975 for international banking supervision by the Bank for International Settlements' Committee on Banking Regulations and Supervisory Practices (the "Cooke Committee," named after its chairman, a Bank of England official). A spring 1980 meeting at the BIS (the "central bank for central banks") in the wake of the second oil shock (1979-1980) of the central bank governors of the Group of Ten counties and Switzerland led to an elaboration of the 1975 guidelines. Finally, a May 1983 report of the Basle Institution's Committee on Banking Regulations replaced the 1975 *Concordat* in a *reformulation* guided by the principle that banking authorities cannot be fully satisfied about the soundness of individual banks unless they can examine the totality of each bank's business worldwide through the technique of *consolidation*.

Exhibit 8-1
SUPERVISION OF BANKS' FOREIGN ESTABLISHMENTS

The following is a September 1975 report issued by the Bank for International Settlements' Committee on Banking Regulations and Supervisory Practice.

I. INTRODUCTION

The objects of this section are to set out certain guidelines for cooperation between national authorities in the supervision of banks' foreign establishments, and to suggest ways of improving its efficacy.

Three types of foreign banking establishments are distinguished:

1. *Branches,* which are integral parts of a foreign parent bank.

2. *Subsidiaries,* which are legally independent institutions incorporated in the country of operation and controlled by one foreign parent bank.

3. *Joint ventures,* which are legally independent banks incorporated in the country of operation and controlled by two or more parent institutions, most of which are foreign and not all of which are necessarily banks.

In addition, banking supervision is considered in this section from three different aspects: liquidity, solvency, and foreign exchange operations and positions. The Committee recognizes that these different aspects are to some extent overlapping. For instance, liquidity and solvency problems can shade into one another; and both liquidity and solvency considerations are among the reasons why countries supervise their banks' foreign exchange operations.

II. THE NEED FOR COOPERATION

The Committee is agreed that the basic aim of international cooperation in this field should be to ensure that no foreign banking establishment escapes supervision.

It is also agreed that each country has a duty to ensure that foreign banking establishments in its territory are supervised; and that in the case of joint ventures involving parent institutions in more than one country, there is no practicable alternative to supervision by host authorities.

Acceptance that supervisory authorities are responsible for ensuring that foreign banks in their territory are supervised will not, however, necessarily preclude there being gaps in the supervision of such establishments. Thus, owing to differences in definition, a particular foreign establishment may be classified as a bank by its parent, but not by its host, supervisory authority; and in some countries not represented on the Committee, there may be no supervision whatever of foreign banking establishments.

Furthermore, it is desirable not only that all foreign banking establishments are supervised, but that this supervision is adequate, judged by the standards of both host and parent authorities. In that connection, the Committee noted that host authorities are interested in the foreign banks operating in their territories as individual institutions and from the point of view of what happens in their own markets, while parent authorities are interested in them as parts of larger institutions which they are responsible for supervising.

Exhibit 8-1 (con't)

For a variety of reasons, therefore, adequate supervision of foreign banking establishments, without unnecessary overlapping, calls for contact and cooperation between host and parent supervisory authorities. It is one of the Committee's purposes to foster cooperation of that kind among its member countries. In addition, the Committee considers that any guidelines for cooperation it may agree on should be communicated to other countries with a significant role in international banking, in the hope of obtaining their cooperation too. The Committee has already established contacts with the supervisory authorities of a number of such countries and will consider which other countries it might approach.

III. SUPERVISORY RESPONSIBILITIES AND INTERESTS OF HOST AND PARENT AUTHORITIES

Having agreed on the need for contact and cooperation between supervisory authorities, the Committee went on to consider the extent to which the division of responsibilities for supervision could be codified. Their discussions showed that it is not possible to draw up clear-cut rules for determining exactly where the responsibility for supervision can best be placed in any particular situation. Nevertheless, the Committee was able to agree on a number of general guidelines in this field.

Liquidity. In managing their liquidity, foreign banking establishments rely heavily on local practices and comply with local regulations, including those established for monetary policy purposes. Responsibility for supervising their liquidity must therefore rest in the first place with the host authority. Moreover, in practice, only the authority on the spot can carry out the continuous supervision of liquidity which may from time to time be required. For the management of liquidity in foreign currencies, and especially the currency of the parent bank, local practices and regulations may be less important and not all host authorities accept the same degree of responsibility.

In the case of a foreign branch, liquidity cannot be judged in isolation from that of the whole bank to which it belongs. This applies particularly when a branch is free to deposit funds with its parent bank. Furthermore, the parent authority, in controlling the liquidity of the parent bank, must take account of calls that its foreign branches might make on its liquid resources. For these reasons, the liquidity of foreign branches is a matter of concern to parent authorities also.

In the case of foreign subsidiaries or joint ventures, parent authorities may be concerned. For example, such banks may have standby facilities available to them from their parent institutions. In such cases, the parent supervisory authority concerned ought to be informed by the host authorities of the importance they attach to these standby facilities in judging the liquidity of the banks in question. Moreover, though the legal position of foreign subsidiaries and joint ventures is different from that of foreign branches, parent authorities cannot be indifferent to the moral responsibilities of the parent institutions.

Solvency. In the case of solvency controls, there is again some sharing of responsibility for supervision between host and parent authorities, with the emphasis varying according to the type of establishment concerned. For foreign subsidiaries and joint ventures, primary responsibility rests with host authorities; but, in addition, parent authorities must take account of the exposure of their domestic banks' foreign subsidiaries and joint ventures because of those parent banks' moral commit-

Exhibit 8-1 (con't)

ments to those foreign establishments. For foreign branches, solvency is indistinguishable from that of the parent bank as a whole. It is therefore essentially a matter for parent supervisory authorities. The "dotation de capital" imposed by the host authorities in certain countries on foreign branches is above all intended to do two things: (1) to oblige foreign branches that set up in business in those countries to make a certain minimum investment in them; (2) to equalize competitive conditions between foreign branches and domestic banks.

Foreign Exchange Positions. Banks' foreign exchange positions are supervised partly for prudential reasons, partly for balance-of-payments reasons, and partly for the purpose of maintaining orderly market conditions. So far as concerns prudential supervision the considerations set out in the previous paragraphs govern the division of responsibility, while the other matters are by definition the concern of host authorities.

IV. AIDS TO COOPERATION

The Committee considers that, in seeking to improve the supervision of banks' foreign establishments and to implement the guidelines for cooperation set out earlier in this report, efforts should be made to remove, or at any rate reduce, certain restraints which at present hamper such cooperation. In particular, it believes that action could usefully be taken in the following areas:

1. *Direct transfers of information between supervisory authorities.* Parent authorities may wish to obtain copies of reports submitted to host authorities, particularly in cases where host authorities waive certain requirements in respect of foreign banks established in their territory, where their control requirements are less stringent than those of the parent authorities, or where they take into account, for prudential purposes, commitments to such banks by their parent institutions. Normally, they should obtain such reports direct from the banks concerned, provided that host authorities are previously informed. At the same time, it would be desirable that host authorities be permitted to transfer copies of such reports to parent authorities when circumstances so warrant. The Committee is aware that such transfers of information are often impossible because of banking secrecy laws in host countries; but many of its members consider that the operation of these laws should over time be modified so as to permit them. (This same point also applies in the case of the proposals in the next two paragraphs.) The Committee wishes to emphasize that the sole purpose of such transfers would be to facilitate prudential control of banks and that in no circumstances would they be directed to the affairs of individual customers.

2. *Direct inspections by parent authorities of their domestic banks' foreign establishments.* These are likely to be particularly helpful for purposes of solvency control, including control of banks' foreign exchange positions. Such inspections already take place, sometimes on an informal basis and sometimes as a result of formal reciprocal agreements between pairs of countries. Wherever possible, steps should be taken to facilitate such arrangements, if necessary by amendment of legislation.

Exhibit 8-1 (con't)

3. *Indirect inspections of foreign banking establishments by parent authorities through the agency of host authorities.* Host authorities that do not allow direct inspections by parent authorities of their domestic banks' foreign establishments should give favorable consideration to carrying out, at the request of the parent authorities concerned, specific inspections for foreign banks operating in their territory and to reporting their overall findings to them.

The Committee believes that, in seeking to remove restraints on transfers of information between, and foreign inspections by, supervisory authorities, it would be wise to begin with foreign branches, where the problems presented appear less difficult than with subsidiaries and joint ventures.

Both the 1975 Concordat and the 1983 *reformulation* took the view that international banking regulation should focus on the three problem areas of *solvency, liquidity,* and *foreign exchange operations and positions.* Concurrently, the division of labor between the parent authorities and the host authorities was viewed as determined by the nature of the bank foreign establishment; specifically, whether it was a *branch, subsidiary,* or *joint venture* (consortium).

A branch was viewed as an *integral* part of the foreign parent bank, while a subsidiary was characterized as a legally *independent* institution wholly or majority owned by a bank incorporated in a country other than that of the subsidiary. Finally, joint ventures or consortia were viewed as legally *independent* institutions incorporated in the country where their principal operations are conducted and controlled by two or more parent institutions, most of which are usually foreign and none of which is typically a majority shareholder.

Summarizing the 1983 reformulation, the BIS views branch solvency as primarily a parent authority matter, while subsidiary solvency is viewed as joint responsibility of both host and parent authority (the latter viewed as needing to exercise supervision on a consolidated basis). Finally, joint venture solvency is viewed as primarily a host authority responsibility, qualified by parent bank responsibilities due to "comfort letters" and the like.

Regarding branch liquidity, primary responsibility is with the host authority, given the importance of understanding local practices and regulations, and the functioning of domestic money markets. However, parent authorities have a role as well, given the close linkages between parent and branch liquidity. For subsidiaries, the responsibilities are similar, but parent authorities should take account of any standby and other facilities, granted by parent banks. A similar situation applies to joint ventures. In all cases, however, there is a strong parent responsibility on basis of the principle of *consolidated supervision*.

Exhibit 8-2
PRESS COMMUNIQUE ISSUED BY THE BANK
FOR INTERNATIONAL SETTLEMENTS
(April 15, 1980)

1. At their meetings in Basle on March 10 and April 14 the central bank Governors of the Group of Ten countries and Switzerland exchanged views on the evolution during recent years, and the future prospects, of the international banking system in general, and the Eurocurrency market in particular.

2. The Governors recognize the important part played by the banks in recycling the large surpluses that have arisen during the last few years. They noted that international bank lending aggregates have been expanding at an annual rate of some 25 percent. Moreover, the contribution of the international banking system to recycling the large OPEC surpluses that have re-emerged will lead to further substantial growth of these aggregates.

3. In view of the present volume of international bank lending and of its prospective future role, the Governors are agreed on the importance of maintaining the soundness and stability of the international banking system and of seeking to avoid any undesirable effects either worldwide or on the conduct of policy in particular countries.

4. With these considerations in mind, the Governors have decided to strengthen regular and systematic monitoring of international banking developments, with a view to assessing their significance for the world economy, for the economies of individual countries (including particularly the operation of their domestic monetary policies,) and for the soundness of the international banking system as a whole. A standing Committee on Euromarkets will consider the international banking statistics compiled by the BIS and other relevant information and report to the Governors at least twice a year, and more frequently if developments call for it. These arrangements for closer surveillance could provide a framework for intensifying, if appropriate, cooperation on monetary policies between the countries concerned.

5. Recognizing that individual banks, or the international banking system as a whole, could in the future be exposed to greater risks than in the past, the Governors reaffirm the cardinal importance that they attach to the maintenance of sound banking standards; particularly with regard to capital adequacy, liquidity, and concentration of risks.

6. To this end they place high priority on bringing into full effect the initiatives already taken by the Committee on Banking Regulations and Supervisory

Exhibit 8-2 (con't)

Practices with regard to the supervision of banks' international business on a consolidated basis, improved assessment of country risk exposure, and the development of more comprehensive and consistent data for monitoring the extent of banks' maturity transformation.

7. The Governors note that differences in the competitive conditions between domestic and international banking that arise out of official regulations and policies stimulate growth of international bank lending in general; and that transactions channeled through the Eurocurrency market can pose problems for the effectiveness of domestic monetary policy in those countries where such differences are particularly significant. The Governors will continue efforts already being made to reduce the differences of competitive conditions, fully recognizing the difficulties arising from differences in the national structure and traditions of banking systems.

    The report deals exclusively with the responsibilities of banking supervisory authorities for monitoring the prudential conduct and soundness of the business of banks foreign establishments. It does not address itself to lender-of-last-resort aspects of the role of central banks.

As regards the supervision of banks' foreign exchange operations and positions, there is joint parent and host authority responsibility. Host authorities should monitor the foreign exchange exposure of their nation's foreign banks and coordinate with parent authorities.

Supplementing the implementation of the 1975-1983 guidelines, the BIS announced in 1980 the creation of a standing Committee on Euromarkets to consider international banking statistics compiled by the BIS and other agencies, and report to the Governors at least twice a year. The latter are concerned not only with safety in the Euromarkets, but also with the impact of those markets on the effective conducting of domestic monetary policy.

Banking supervisors have other concerns with respect to the Eurocurrency market besides the solvency of the bank participants, and the impact of the Euromarkets on domestic monetary policy. These include:

1. The issue of whether the Euromarkets contribute to worldwide inflation by complicating efforts at monetary control for national authorities, or by providing a too ready source of financing for expenditures.

2. The issue of whether the Euromarkets contibute to exchange rate instability.

Aspects of the inflation issue include:

- The absence of reserve requirements in the Euromarket creating theoretically an *infinite* bank multiplier (offset by prudential reserves and leakages).
- The impact of the Euromarket on domestic monetary *velocity.*
- Whether Eurocurrencies can play the role of transactions balances (for example, it is customary for branches of U.S. banks to transfer overnight Eurodollar deposits into immediately available funds without penalty).
- Whether by increasing credit availability to deficit countries, Eurocurrency lending impedes adjustment of international payment imbalances (by displacing *conditional* IMF lending).

Finally, the issue of the impact of the Euromarkets on exchange market instability is largely derived from the proposition that they serve as a source of *finance* for exchange market speculation. Another aspect of the issue is that the Euromarkets, by expanding liquidity, magnify the exchange rate effects of other factors weakening currencies. A final criticism is that Euromarket operations, by virtue of their technical efficiency, have increased the international mobility of capital and therefore the magnitude of destabilizing capital flows.

Exhibit 8-3
PRINCIPLES FOR THE SUPERVISION OF BANKS'
FOREIGN ESTABLISHMENTS

The following is a May 1983 report by the Bank for International Settlements (Basle) Committee on Banking Regulations and Supervisory Practices

I. INTRODUCTION

The principles set out in the report are not necessarily embodied in the laws of the countries represented on the Committee. Rather they are recommended guidelines of best practices in this area, which all members have undertaken to work towards implementing, according to the means available to them.

Adequate supervision of banks' foreign establishments calls not only for an appropriate allocation of responsibilities between parent and host supervisory authorities, but also for contact and co-operation between them. It has been, and remains, one of the Committee's principal purposes to foster such cooperation, both among its member countries and more widely. The Committee has been en-

Exhibit 8-3 (con't)

couraged by the like-minded approach of other groups of supervisors, and it hopes to continue to strengthen its relationships with these other groups and to develop new ones. It strongly commends the principles set out in this report as being of general validity for all those who are responsible for the supervision of banks conducting international business and hopes that they will be progressively accepted and implemented by supervisors worldwide.

Where situations arise that do not appear to be covered by these principles, parent and host authorities should explore ways together of ensuring that adequate supervision of banks' foreign establishments is effected.

II. TYPES OF BANKS' FOREIGN ESTABLISHMENTS

Banks operating internationally may have interests in the following types of foreign banking establishment:

1. *Branches:* operating entities that do not have a separate legal status and are thus integral parts of the foreign parent bank.

2. *Subsidiaries:* legally independent institutions wholly owned or majority-owned by a bank incorporated in a country other than that of the subsidiary.

3. *Joint Ventures or Consortia:* legally independent institutions incorporated in the country where their principal operations are conducted and controlled by two or more parent institutions, most of which are usually foreign and not all of which are necessarily banks. While the pattern of shareholdings may give effective control to one parent institution, with others in a minority, joint ventures are, most typically, owned by a collection of minority shareholders.

In addition, the structure of international banking groups may derive from an ultimate holding company that is not itself a bank. Such a holding company can be an industrial or commercial company, or a company the majority of whose assets consists of shares in banks. These groups may also include intermediate nonbank holding companies or other nonbanking companies.

Banks may also have minority participations in foreign banking or non-banking companies, other than those in joint ventures, which may be held to be part of their overall foreign banking operations. This report does not cover the appropriate supervisory treatment of these participations, but they should be taken into account by the relevant supervisory authorities.

III. GENERAL PRINCIPLES GOVERNING THE SUPERVISION OF BANKS' FOREIGN ESTABLISHMENTS

Effective cooperation between host and parent authorities is a central prerequisite for the supervision of banks' international operations. In relation to the supervision of banks' foreign establishments, two principles are fundamental to such cooperation and call for consultation and contacts between respective host and parent authorities: The first principle is that no foreign banking establishment should escape supervision; the second is that the supervision should be adequate. In giving effect to these principles, host authorities should ensure that

Exhibit 8-3 (con't)

parent authorities are informed immediately of any serious problems which arise in a parent bank's foreign establishment. Similarly, parent authorities should inform host authorities when problems arise in a parent bank that are likely to affect the parent bank's foreign establishment.

Acceptance of these principles will not, however, of itself, preclude gaps and inadequacies in the supervision of banks' foreign establishments. These may occur for various reasons.

First, while there should be a presumption that host authorities are in a position to fulfil their supervisory obligations adequately with respect to all foreign bank establishments operating in their territories, this may not always be the case. Problems may, for instance, arise when a foreign establishment is classified as a bank by its parent banking supervisory authority, but not by its host authority. In such cases, it is the responsibility of the parent authority to ascertain whether the host authority is able to undertake adequate supervision, and the host authority should inform the parent authority if it is not in a position to undertake such supervision. In cases where host authority supervision is inadequate, the parent authority should either extend its supervision, to the degree that it is practicable, or it should be prepared to discourage the parent bank from continuing to operate the establishment in question.

Second, problems may arise where the host authority considers that supervision of the parent institutions of foreign bank establishments operating in its territory is inadequate or nonexistent. In such cases the host authority should discourage or, if it is in a position to do so, forbid the operation in its territory of such foreign establishments. Alternatively, the host authority could impose specific conditions governing the conduct of the business of such establishments.

Third, gaps in supervision can arise out of structural features of international banking groups. For example, the existence of holding companies either at the head, or in the middle, of such groups may constitute an impediment to adequate supervision. Furthermore, particular supervisory problems may arise where such holding companies, while not themselves banks, have substantial liabilities to the international banking system. Where holding companies are at the head of groups that include separately incorporated banks operating in different countries, the authorities responsible for supervising those banks should endeavor to coordinate their supervision of those banks, taking account of the overall structure of the group in question. Where a bank is the parent company of a group that contains intermediate holding companies, the parent authority should make sure that such holding companies and their subsidiaries are covered by adequate supervision. Alternatively, the parent authority should not allow the parent bank to operate such intermediate holding companies.

Where groups contain both banks and nonbank organizations, there should, where possible, be liaison between the banking supervisory authorities and any authorities having responsibilities for supervising these nonbanking organizations, particularly where the nonbanking activities are of a financial character. Banking supervisors, in their overall supervision of banking groups, should take account of these groups' nonbanking activities; if these activities cannot be adequately supervised, banking supervisors should aim at minimizing the risks to the banking business from the nonbanking activities of such groups.

The implementation of the second basic principle, namely that the supervision of all foreign banking establishments should be adequate, requires the posi-

Exhibit 8-3 (con't)

tive participation of both host and parent authorities. Host authorities are responsible for the foreign bank establishments operating in their territories as individual institutions, while parent authorities are responsible for them as parts of larger banking groups where a general supervisory responsibility exists in respect of their worldwide consolidated activities. These responsibilities of host and parent authorities are both complementary and overlapping.

The principle of consolidated supervision is that parent banks and parent supervisory authorities monitor the risk exposure— including a perspective of concentrations of risk and of the quality of assets—of the banks or banking groups for which they are responsible, as well as the adequacy of their capital, on the basis of the totality of their business wherever conducted. This principle does not imply any lessening of host authorities' responsibilities for supervising foreign bank establishments that operate in their territories, although it is recognized that the full implementation of the consolidation principle may well lead to some extension of parental responsibility. Consolidation is only one of a range of techniques, albeit an important one, at the disposal of the supervisory authorities, and it should not be applied to the exclusion of supervision of individual banking establishments on an unconsolidated basis by parent and host authorities. Moreover, the implementation of the principle of consolidated supervision presupposes that parent banks and parent authorities have access to all the relevant information about the operations of their banks' foreign establishments, although existing banking secrecy provisions in some countries may present a constraint on comprehensive consolidated parental supervision.

IV. ASPECTS OF THE SUPERVISION OF BANKS FOREIGN ESTABLISHMENTS

The supervision of banks' foreign establishments is considered in this report from three different aspects: solvency, liquidity, and foreign exchange operations and positions.

Solvency. The allocation of responsibilities for the supervision of the solvency of banks' foreign establishments between parent and host authorities will depend upon the type of establishment concerned.

For branches, their solvency is indistinguishable from that of the parent bank as a whole. So, while general responsibility of the host authority is to monitor the financial soundness of foreign branches, supervision of solvency is primarily a matter for the parent authority. The "dotation de capital" requirements imposed by certain host authorities on foreign branches operating in their countries do not negate this principle. They exist first to oblige foreign branches that set up in business in those countries to make and to sustain a certain minimum investment in them, and second to help equalize competitive conditions between foreign branches and domestic banks.

For subsidiaries, the supervision of solvency is a joint responsibility of both host and parent authorities. Host authorities have responsibility for supervising the solvency of all foreign subsidiaries operating in their territories. Their approach to the task of supervising subsidiaries is from the standpoint that these establishments are separate entities, legally incorporated in the country of the host authority. At the same time parent authorities, in the context of consolidated

Exhibit 8-3 (con't)

supervision of the parent banks, need to assess whether the parent institutions' solvency is being affected by the operations of their foreign subsidiaries. Parental supervision on a consolidated basis is needed for two reasons: because the solvency of parent banks cannot be adequately judged without taking account of all their foreign establishments; and because parent banks cannot be indifferent to the situation of their foreign subsidiaries.

For joint ventures, the supervision of solvency should normally, for practical reasons, be primarily the responsibility of the authorities in the country of incorporation. Banks that are shareholders in consortium banks cannot, however, be indifferent to the situation of their joint ventures and may have commitments to these establishments beyond the legal commitments arising from their shareholdings, such as through comfort letters. All these commitments must be taken into account by the parent authorities of the shareholder banks when supervising their solvency. Depending on the pattern of shareholdings in joint ventures, and particularly when one bank is a dominant shareholder, there can also be circumstances in which the supervision of their solvency should be the joint responsibility of the authorities in the country of incorporation and the parent authorities of the shareholder banks.

Liquidity. References to supervision of liquidity in this section do not relate to central banks' functions as lenders of last resort, but to the responsibility of supervisory authorities for monitoring the control systems and procedures established by their banks that enable them to meet their obligations as they fall due including, as necessary, those of their foreign establishments.

The allocation of responsibilities for the supervision of the liquidity of banks' foreign establishments between parent and host authorities will depend, as with solvency, on the type of establishment concerned.

The host authority has responsibility for monitoring the liquidity of the foreign bank's establishments in its country; the parent authority has responsibility for monitoring the liquidity of the banking group as a whole.

For branches, the initial presumption should be that primary responsibility for supervising liquidity rests with the host authority. Host authorities will often be best equipped to supervise liquidity as it relates to local practices and regulations and the functioning of their domestic money markets. At the same time, the liquidity of all foreign branches will always be a matter of concern to the parent authorities, since a branch's liquidity is frequently controlled directly by the parent bank and cannot be viewed in isolation from that of the whole bank of which it is a part. Parent authorities need to be aware of parent banks' control systems and need to take account of calls that may be made on the resources of parent banks by their foreign branches. Host and parent authorities should always consult each other if there are any doubts in particular cases about where responsibilities for supervising the liquidity of foreign branches should lie.

For subsidiaries, primary responsibility for supervising liquidity should rest with the host authority. Parent authorities should take account of any standby or other facilities granted as well as any other commitments, for example through comfort letters, by parent banks to these establishments. Host authorities should inform the parent authorities of the importance they attach to such facilities and commitments, so as to ensure that full account is taken of them in the supervision of the parent bank. Where the host authority has difficulties in supervising the

Exhibit 8-3 (con't)

liquidity, especially in foreign currency, of foreign banks' subsidiaries, it will be expected to inform the parent authorities and appropriate arrangements will have to be agreed so as to ensure adequate supervision.

For joint ventures, primary responsibility for supervising liquidity should rest with the authorities in the country of incorporation. The parent authorities of shareholders in joint ventures should take account of any standby or other facilities granted as well as any other commitments, such as through comfort letters, by shareholder banks to those establishments. The authorities in the country of incorporation of joint ventures should inform the parent authorities of shareholder banks of the importance they attach to such facilities and commitments so as to ensure that full account is taken of them in the supervision of the shareholder bank.

Within the framework of consolidated supervision, parent authorities have a general responsibility for overseeing the liquidity control systems employed by the banking groups they supervise and for ensuring that these systems and the overall liquidity position of such groups are adequate. It is recognized, however, that full consolidation may not always be practicable as a technique for supervising liquidity because of differences of local regulations and market situations and the complications of banks operating in different time zones and different currencies. Parent authorities should consult with host authorities to ensure that the latter are aware of the overall systems within which the foreign establishments are operating. Host authorities have a duty to ensure that the parent authority is immediately informed of any serious liquidity inadequacy in a parent bank's foreign establishment.

Foreign Exchange Operations and Positions. As regards the supervision of banks' foreign exchange operations and positions, there should be a joint responsibility of parent and host authorities. It is particularly important for parent banks to have in place systems for monitoring their group's overall foreign exchange exposure and for parent authorities to monitor those systems. Host authorities should be in a position to monitor the foreign exchange exposure of foreign establishments in their territories and should inform themselves of the nature and extent of the supervision of these establishments being undertaken by the parent authorities.

9

The Eurobond Market

The international capital market includes the foreign bond markets and the Eurobond market. The oldest of these is the foreign bond or *Yankee* market in New York where *foreign* and *supranational* entities issue standard *local-currency*-denominated (U.S. dollar) issues. Similar markets exist in London denominated in sterling (Bulldogs), and in Tokyo denominated in yen (Samurais). Conversely, the Eurobond market involves debt securities issued by any entity, but structured and sold so as to be outside the country of origin of the currency in which the security is denominated. Notable features include the absence of registration, generally no rating, no withholding taxes, and the absence of queing in the U.S. dollar and Canadian dollar sectors. *Fixed* rate, *floating* rate, and *convertible* issues are all offered.

The fixed rate Eurobond market was initiated in July 1963 by a dollar issue for an Italian state entity arranged by an international syndicate of banks and listed on the London Stock Exchange. That initiation was in response to America's imposition of an Interest Equalization Tax (IET) on Yankee bonds, concurrent with the need for a European medium (to complement the domestic bond markets), that was not hampered by problems of exchange control, lack of integration between the different markets, and diversity of currencies.

Encouraged by the British authorities and American capital export restrictions (1965-1973), the market grew rapidly, requiring the creation of the Euroclear and Cedel *clearing systems* in 1969 and 1970, re-

Exhibit 9-1
EUROBOND MARKET INITIATIONS

1963
Initial Eurodollar bond.

1964
Initial Euro-Deutschemark bond.

1965
Initial Euro-French franc and Euro-Dutch guilder bonds.

1970
Initial floating rate notes (FRNs). Initial Asian dollar bond (Development Bank of Singapore).

1971
Initial composite currency Eurobond (SDRs).

1977
Initial Euro-yen bond.

spectively. While the market significantly contracted in response to the weak dollar, high interest rates and the termination of balance of payments controls by the U.S. in 1973-1974, new issue volume grew rapidly in the second half of the 1970s ($17 billion per year) and virtually exploded in the 1980s—$50 billion per year in 1982-1983, $79 billion in 1984, and a further 70% jump to $136 billion in 1985. It has become a larger *new issue* market than the U.S. corporate bond market.

The Eurobond market consists largely of *public* issues listed on the Luxembourg or London Stock Exchanges, complemented by a small but growing volume of private and semi-private placements. Most issues are denominated in U.S. dollars ($94 billion in 1985), followed by the Deutschemark ($11 billion in 1985), but several other currencies (pound sterling, Canadian dollar, guilder, yen, French franc, Kuwaiti dinar, Saudi rial) and *currency cocktails* (ECU, SDR) have been used. Also, there are *multiple currency* bonds which entitle the creditor to request payment of interest and principal in other predetermined currencies at unchangeable parities. Issue size varies, but averages $50-100 million; prime issuers (big multinationals and Western governments) have raised as much as $1 billion in one issue. Maturities are generally between 5 and 15 years (3-20 is the range).

Reflecting the requirements of international investors, the bonds are *bearer* instruments with detachable coupons for the payment of interest, free of all taxes, payable at the offices of paying agents in a number of different countries. Interest is calculated on the basis of 30-day months and a 360-day year, and is usually payable *annually* in the case of fixed rate issues, and *semiannually* in the case of convertibles and floating rate notes. Denominations of securities are most commonly $1,000 (or $5,000) each, but can be larger depending on the target market (institutional vs. retail).

Eurobond Market Participants

The market includes *issuers, investors, and arrangers.* Nearly half the *issuers* are highly rated (BBB or better) western industrial companies, often seeking to finance foreign investment without exchange risk (who issue *convertibles* when their stock markets are strong such as Japan in 1983), and private financial institutions (with banks also using it as a link to their *swap* business). While most of the balance are western governments and government agencies, typically funding balance of payments deficits or financing the development of state-owned agencies. In 1985, the three leading issuers by nationality were the U.S. ($36 billion), the UK ($16 billion), and Japan ($14 billion). Finally, supranational institutions (World Bank, European Investment Bank, European Coal and Steel Community, Asian Development Bank) represent around 10% of the market.

The *investors* are largely individual private ones, most commonly through professional investment advisers and fund managers. However, institutional investors—insurance companies, pension funds, and charitable organizations—are increasingly important. Central banks and large commercial banks comprise the balance.

The *arrangers,* whose prerequisite for success is *placing power* derived from large funds under discretionary management coupled with an active calling program on investors, include American investment banks, European "universal banks," Japanese securities houses, UK subsidiaries of U.S. commercial banks, UK merchant banks, and UK consortium banks. In 1984, the principal lead managers for corporate dollar issues included Credit Suisse, First Boston, Morgan Stanley International, Goldman Sachs International and Nomura Securities. Corporate Deutschemark issues were largely lead managed by the "Big 3" German banks, while corporate sterling issues were largely lead managed by S.G. Warburg, and J. Henry Schroder Wagg. Complementing the lead

Exhibit 9-2
THE EUROBOND MARKET BY CATEGORY, CURRENCY, AND NATION-ALITY IN 1984-1985
(In billions of dollars)

Eurobond Issues by Major Category

	1984	%	1985	%
Fixed rate	43.62	54.9%	75.23	55.5%
Floating rate	31.70	39.9%	55.67	41.1%
Convertible	4.15	5.2%	4.64	3.4%
Total	79.47	100.0%	135.54	100.0%

Eurobond Issues by Currency

	1984	%	1985	%
U.S. dollars	62.04	79.3%	94.40	73.2%
West German mark	6.06	7.8%	11.18	8.7%
Japanese yen	1.10	1.4%	6.89	5.4%
UK sterling	4.27	5.5%	6.48	5.0%
European currency unit	2.74	2.5%	6.88	5.3%
Canadian dollar	1.98	2.5%	3.12	2.4%
Total	78.19	100.0%	128.95	100.0%

Leading Issuers by Nationality

	1984	%	1985	%
U.S.	21.06	40.2%	35.99	38.0%
United Kingdom	4.20	8.0%	15.63	16.5%
Japan	9.62	18.4%	14.05	14.8%
France	6.70	12.8%	11.10	11.7%
Supranational institutions	6.25	11.9%	10.69	11.3%
Canada	4.54	8.7%	7.31	7.7%
Total	52.37	100.0%	94.67	100.0%

Exhibit 9-3
THE RUSSIAN BEAR IN THE EUROZOO

When the Soviet Foreign Minister Edouard Sheverdnadze signed the London agreement in July 1986 satisfying UK claims on Russia's pre-revolutionary debt (using the principal and accumulated interest on the Czar's London bank deposits), it was viewed as a step toward Russia's issuing of Eurobonds. While the Soviet Union would of course be late in joining the growing *securitization* trend, it ranks among the initiators of the Eurocurrency market. Back in the 1950s, it was Russia's transfer of its dollar deposits from New York banks to banks it owned in Paris and London, Banque Commercial pour l'Europe du Nord (Eurobank) and the Moscow Narodny Bank that was a major step in the creation of the Eurodollar market.

Exhibit 9-3 (con't)

Currently, the Soviet Union is active in several areas of the Euromarkets, including the interbank deposit-loan market, syndicated loans (qua recipient), and modestly, Eurobond underwriting. Its presence is particularly noted in the interbank Eurodollar market, for which it uses a network of five banks it owns in international money centers, plus three banks in Moscow.

The five Western banks include the $3.4 billion (12/31/85) Moscow Narodny Bank in London (established 1921), with its branch in Singapore, the $5.3 billion (12/31/85) Banque Commercial pour l'Europe du Nord (Eurobank) in Paris (established 1921), the $493 million (9/30/85) East-West United Bank SA in Luxembourg (established 1974), the Ost-West Handelsbank AG (established 1971) in Frankfurt, and the $869 million (12/31/85) Donaubank Aktiengesellschaft (established 1974) in Vienna. The three banks in Moslow include the Soviet Bank for Foreign Trade (Vneshtorgbank), a world class institution with 2,000 correspondent banks, the twenty-four year old International Bank for Economic Co-operation (IBEC), the "IMF of Comecon", 38% owned by the Soviet Union and with TR6.3 billion in assets (a transferable rouble functions as a *unit of account* like EEC *green currencies,* and is officially worth $1.47), and the seventeen year old International Investment Bank (IIB), the "World Bank of Comecon," owned 37% by the Soviet Union, and with TR2.4 billion in assets. Another Soviet-owned bank, the Wozchod Handelbank AG (established 1966), Zurich, gained notoriety in 1984 when it lost $465 million in gold trading; it was subsequently converted into a branch of Vneshtorgbank.

According to BIS statistics as of June 30, 1986, western bank's interbank *claims* on the Soviet Union totaled $26.3 billion (of which $10 billion was short-term—less than a year), while Soviet *claims* on western banks totaled $13.4 billion, leaving *net* Soviet interbank liabilities to BIS reporting banks of $12.9 billion.

Vneshtorgbank deals Eurodollars from its headquarters in a 19th century building at 37 Plyushchika Street. There, a half-dozen traders, kept abreast of market developments by Reuters and telerate screens, and communicate by *direct* telex with the leading Eurocurrency brokers in London. Some peculiarities of Vneshtorgbank's deposit procedures include an unwillingness to deposit in Western hemisphere banks, aside from Canadian banks in Toronto (though branches of American banks, etc. in London are acceptable), and a refusal to deposit in banks of "hostile" countries, such as Taiwan, Chile, Israel or South Africa.

The Soviet Union has been very successful in expanding its syndicated borrowing from the West, while concurrently narrowing its *spread* over LIBOR. Current borrowing totals $25-35 billion (much of it is *club* loans and *bilateral* loans, with the amounts and terms undisclosed), with a projected increase to about $53 billion by 1990. The potential for expansion is reflected in the fact that Russia's current external debt *per capita* is only $\frac{1}{13}$th that of the United States, and only $\frac{1}{9}$th that of Norway.

Spreadwise, the Soviets have narrowed their margin to only $\frac{1}{8}$% over LIBOR on the first five years of a $300 million credit led by BNP in October 1986 from $\frac{5}{8}$% in 1984. Concurrently, Soviet *a forait* (trade) paper was being priced at just $\frac{1}{4}$% over LIBOR for five, and as much as ten years. (Thus far, Vneshtorgbank has not issued any Euronotes).

Vneshtorgbank's initial and thus far only participation in Eurobond underwriting was in August 1986, when it took about Y 500 million ($3 million of a Y 15 billion, $92.3 million) issue for the Nordic Investment Bank. However, that modest entree is viewed as a prelude to more ambitious underwriting in the future.

managers, large *underwriting groups* and yet larger *selling groups* take Eurobonds to market. Total commissions vary from 1.75% on a 5-year issue to 2.25% on a 10-year issue. On a 7-year issue, the split would be 0.25% for management, 0.375% for underwriting, and 1.25% for selling.

EUROBOND TERMS

Issuing a Eurobond involves selecting a lead manager and then deciding the bond's *terms and conditions* (including possibly a guarantee). The terms which becomes part of the security's documentation, include:

- The principal amount (adjustable in primary syndication).
- The final maturity (some are two tranche issues, while some give investors extendable/retractable options).
- The coupon rate and issue price (adjustable).
- A sinking fund (mandatory redemption some years after issuance of a stated amount of bonds each year at par).
- A purchase fund (required only if the bonds are discounted in the period to mid-way of maturity).
- Call options (with a sliding call premium).
- Redemption at par if withholding taxes are imposed (or alternatively a *grossing up* of payments).
- Sometimes the appointment of a trustee to look after the bondholders' rights (and protect the issuer from nuisance bondholder suits).
- A negative pledge.
- Governing law (English or New York).
- Events of default (including cross default).
- Meetings of noteholders.

Specific Eurobond *documentation* includes:

- An *offering circular* (a prospectus-type document describing the issuer and the issue, that is required by the stock exchanges).

- A summary of the latter called the *selling memorandum.*
- A *trust deed* if a trustee is selected.
- Agreements governing issuance and distribution, including a subscription agreement between the issuer and managers on behalf of the underwriters; an underwriting agreement between the managers and the underwriters; and a selling agreement between the lead manager and members of the selling group.

Ancillary agreements include those:

- Between the issuer and the fiscal agent (responsible for securities authentication and other duties).
- Between the issuer and the paying agents.
- Between the issuer and the purchase agent (if there is to be a purchase fund).
- Between the issuer and a stock exchange (*listing* payments, annual disclosures).
- In the case of floating rate *notes* (FRNs), between the issuer and the agent bank fixing the applicable interest rate.

Finally, at the closing, legal opinions are required covering all aspects of the issuance. The order to deliver securities to the lead manager for the underwriters against payment is given, and a *final closing memorandum* is prepared by the attorneys summarizing all legal actions taken.

The primary market is then initiated with a 7 to 10 day *selling period* to evaluate the issue's marketability, at the end of which the issue's final terms are fixed. The balance of the life of the syndicate includes whatever period of time the lead manager decides is necessary for the issue to be properly distributed and stabilized in the *aftermarket* (days or weeks). As Eurobonds are *not* SEC-registered, they can be sold only to U.S. investors in the secondary market 90 days after all the issue is sold.

Complementing the fixed rate bonds, which totalled $44 billion and $75 billion in 1984 and 1985, respectively, and with substantially the same types of structure and documentation, are the floating rates notes (FRNs), of which 90% are U.S.-dollar- denominated. That market opened in 1971; 58 such issues in 1983 totalled $14 billion, and it jumped 130% to $32 billion in 1984. In 1985, the market grew a further 75% to $56 billion. FRNs represented 40% of the Eurobond market in 1984, and 41% in 1985. Around 10% of FRNs are denominated in pounds sterling, ECUs, Swiss francs, Deutschemarks, and yen, the latter two only since May-June 1985.

Traditionally, there were two types of FRNs, with the first being high-quality issues bought by traditional investors, corporate treasurers, and banks as liquid, relatively high yielding defensive investments in times of rising U.S. dollar interest rates. The second type of issue, commonly wholly underwritten and subscribed by a group of about a dozen banks, was a *disguised syndicated loan,* a medium-term asset whose yield (slightly below the syndicated loan rate) was offset by a minimum rate and a secondary market in the notes. Of late, the market has been expanded by strong Japanese and southeast Asian interest, increased investment in floating rate instruments, swaps, and bank trading activity.

Characteristics of FRNs include:

- A typical principal amount of $100-250 million (largest to date, $1 billion).
- Interest payable semiannually based on a fixed spread (usually 0.25% for a prime name) over 3 or 6 month LIBOR or LI-MEAN, with a minimum rate (generally 5.35% in 1984).
- An issue price that is almost always par.
- A final maturity of 5-7 years (banks often do 10-15 years, Sweden did 40 years, and Banque Paribas and some American banks have issued perpetual notes), possibly extendable or retractable.
- Generally callable on any interest payment date after a grace period of 1-2 years.

New 1984-1985 features are *mismatch FRNs* (allowing investors in a steep yield curve environment to fund themselves at the 1-month rate but receive the 6-month rate reset monthly) and *capped FRNs* with a cap typically of 13% offset by a wider spread. Finally, a few FRNs link the floating rate and fixed markets through the attachments of *warrants* (conversion rights) into a fixed rate security.

The smallest Eurobond sector (3.4% in 1985) is the *convertible* issues, which provide the option of conversion into common stock at a price above the current market price (such as 20% higher). It enables a bondholder to share in the success of the company, while enabling the company to issue bonds at a lower coupon rate. In 1984, such issues totalled $4.15 billion, and $4.64 billion in 1985.

Euro-clear and Cedel

Trading in Eurobonds began soon after the advent of the market in 1963. By the late 1960s, the growing Eurobond market was experiencing almost constant delays in delivery of bonds, as well as risk of their loss. This was caused by the practice at that time of *physically* moving securities from seller to buyer. Moreover, there was very often a credit risk created by delay in the seller's receipt of cash payment after the bonds had been dispatched to the buyer. The market needed a simultaneous settlement procedure that was rapid, efficient and risk-free.

In response to this need, the Brussels office of Morgan Guaranty Trust launched Euro-clear in 1968, while a group of 71 banks founded Cedel (Centrale de Livraison de Valeurs Mobilieres or Securities Clearing Center) in 1970 in Luxembourg.

Today (and since 1972), Euro-clear is owned by the Euro-clear Clearance System Public Limited Company (UK registered), which itself is owned by 124 banks, brokerage houses, etc. worldwide, with no shareholder owning more than 3%. Concurrently, nearly 100 banks and brokerage houses currently are shareholders of Cedel, with no shareholder owning more than 5%.

The essence of both systems is the *immobilization* of securities, which are placed in custody in selected major banks worldwide, and the use of a book-entry system in Brussels and Luxembourg for central record-keeping. Euro-clear and Cedel accept over 8,000 security issues, with Eurobonds (straights, FRNs, and convertibles), being complemented by domestic and foreign bonds, U.S. Treasury and Agency bonds, short-term instruments (Euronotes, CDs, BAs) and international and domestic equities. Complementing securities clearance and custody, both systems offer securities lending and borrowing, and money transfer and banking.

A difference between the two systems is that all Euro-clear securities are kept on a *fungible* basis (flexibility to transfer holdings within or out of the system regardless of specific certificate numbers), while Cedel offers custody on both a fungible or non-fungible basis. The latter, rather inconvenient basis is to accommodate residents of countries that require certificates to be identified by specific numbers.

Both systems can receive instructions in a variety of ways, including their own systems (EUCLID or Euro-clear Information Distribution in the case of Euro-clear, and CEDCOM in the case of Cedel), as well as by S.W.I.F.T., telex, computer tape exchange or mail. Cedel's CEDCOM can be assessed by the General Electric Time Sharing Network, Chemlink (Banklink), Investdata/Telekurs AG, and computer-to-computer link. Finally, there is an *electronic bridge* between Euro-clear and Cedel which involves daily settlement of transactions based on an exchange of computer files.

An idea of the scope of the systems is provided by the statistics of Euro-clear. Its staff of 450, communicating in over 20 different languages, daily handle more than 30,000 securities instructions, involving 23 currencies (including the ECU and SDR composites) from its 1,800 participants. In 1985, Euro-clear settled 4.4 million transactions, held $270 billion of securities on behalf of participants, provided securities loans totaling on average nearly $1.5 billion, and was accepting 12,000 issues. Reflecting, the workload, both systems are highly computerized, utilizing in the case of Cedel, an IBM 4381 and an older IBM 4341.

The Eurobond Primary Market in 1984-1986

The profile of the Eurobond market in 1984 and 1985 is shown in Exhibit 9-2. The three categories of Eurobonds are fixed rate, floating rate, and convertible. In 1985, the overall market grew 71% to $135.5 billion amidst interest stability fostered by sluggish economic growth being reinforced by continuing deflationary fiscal and/or monetary policies. Fixed rate bonds at $75 billion in 1985 kept their 55% market share of the previous year. Concurrently, floating rate notes at $56 billion edged up to 41% of the market from 40% in 1984. Finally, convertibles at $5 billion fell to 3% of the market from 5% (while rising $500 million in issuance in a much larger market), despite generally strong stock market performances.

Reflecting the impact of the big drop in the value of the spot dollar from its February 1985 peak, the dollar share of the Eurobond market fell to 69% from a more lordly 78% in the previous bull dollar year. Conversely, the Deutschemark share increased somewhat to 8%, the fast appreciating yen catapulted to a 5% market share from a modest 1%, the pound's share declined moderately to 5% of a much larger market, and the ECUs share rose to 5% from 3% of the market.

In 1985, the U.S. was by far the leading issuer by nationality, with a 27% market share. Running closely together in second and third place were the UK and Japan with 11% and 10% shares respectively. The next two places were held by France and supranational organizations as a group, with approximately 8% shares each. A similar rank order prevailed in 1984.

In 1986, the Eurobond market grew 31% to $178.1 billion. The five leading underwriters were Credit Suisse First Boston (CSFB) (11% market share), Nomura (8%), Deutsche Bank (7%), Morgan Guaranty (5%), and Daiwa (5%).

Stable interest rates pushed up the share of the *fixed rate (straight)* sector to 61.0% or $107.4 billion; it was even larger as many of the *warrants for equity* issues, a sector representing 8.7% ($15.3 billion) of the market, were fixed as opposed to floating rate issues. The pure *Floating rate note (FRN)* sector itself represented a much reduced 26.7% share ($46.9 billion) of the market, while convertibles rose marginally to 3.6% of the market. Nomura was the leading underwriter of fixed rate issues (11% share), while CSFB was the leader in FRNs (23% share).

Reflecting the weakness of the spot dollar, the dollar share of the Eurobond market fell to 64%, while the yen share doubled to 10%, and the Deutschemark and pound shares rose marginally to 9% and 6%, respectively. Other currencies of denomination included the ECU (4%), the Canadian dollar (3%), the French franc (2%), the Australian dollar (2%), and the New Zealand dollar (0.2%).

Finally, the leading issuer was the public sector (51%), for whom CSFB was the leading underwriter (18% share). It was followed by Japanese corporates (14%, of which 31% was underwritten by Nomura), U.S. corporates (13%, of which 12% was underwritten by both Salomon Brothers and CSFB), supranationals (12%, of which 28% was underwritten by Deutsche Bank), and European corporates (10%, of which 17% was underwritten by Deutsche Bank).

The Eurobond Secondary Market

The healthy new issue market in Eurobonds owes much of its success to the well-functioning, liquid $560 billion Eurobond *secondary* market. However, that market's success has involved several serious problems as well over the past few years, including excessive (to final demand) new issue volume, negative carry in the early 1980s on bond portfolios (i.e., financing costs exceeding coupon yields as a result of an *inverse* yield curve), and the lack of a Eurobond futures contract for hedging purposes—the *basis risk* between U.S. Treasury bond futures and Eurobond cash positions can be considerable.

The secondary market began informally in London among stockbroking firms and merchant banks concurrent with the initiation of the primary market in 1963. Lists of prices in major international newspapers were derived from issuing houses and stock exchanges, especially the Luxembourg one. In 1968 some formalization of the market resulted from the formation of the standard setting Association of International Bond Dealers (AIBD). Today the AIBD has approximately 550 members.

The market is organized as an over-the-counter (OTC) market, with the dealers linked by telephone. London is the preeminant center due to the lack of interference by the authorities, the existence of a well organized infrastructure, the availability of personnel from the wide range of markets in London able to adapt to Eurobond trading, and the use of English as the language of the market.

The market in London operates in a number of tiers, topped by *professional market makers* who offer a continuous market of *two-way* quotes of reasonable size in a wide range of issues. The majority of them are European and Japanese commercial banks, U.S. and Japanese investment banks and U.S. commercial banks. Complementing those are the *fairweather firms* which disappear in difficult market conditions.

While the liquidity of the professional market makers makes them particularly sought after by secondary market participants such as market practitioners and investment fund managers, other qualities are desirable, including the willingness to make prices on infrequently traded issues and to deal in small sizes to accommodate a client; the capacity to execute transactions quickly and accurately; knowledge of the product and the ability to provide good ideas; and general helpfulness and courtesy.

A recent poll by *Eurocurrency* magazine indicates that the top-rated Eurobond secondary market firms are generally leading investment or commercial banks from the country in which the various Eurobonds are denominated. For example, the top U.S. dollar firms were CSFB Securities and Merrill Lynch for fixed bonds, CSFB for floating bonds, and Morgan Stanley International for equity-related bonds. In yen, it was Nomura International, in sterling Phillips and Drew, and in Deutschemarks, it was Deutschebank. In ECUs, it was Kredietbank Brussels, in guilders, it was Amro Bank and in Canadian dollars, it was Wood Gundy. Finally, in Australian dollars, it was Orion Royal Bank, in New Zealand dollars, it was Hambros Bank, and in French francs it was Banque Nationale de Paris.

Market makers function by offering two-way prices; the difference between them, known as the *spread,* is generally 0.5% for *straight* bonds, and 0.75% or more for the more volatile *convertible* bonds. The general strategy is to lower both the bids and offers in a declining market (to discourage sellers) and to raise them in a rising market (to discourage buyers). The other option, widening the spread, is not as useful because *excessively* wide spreads are detrimental to attracting business.

ONGOING CHANGES IN THE LONDON MARKET

The major ongoing development in the Eurobond secondary market is the application of Britain's *Financial Services Act* to the London Eurobond secondary market, the world's largest such market. (Approximately three-quarters of 1986's record $3,500 billion trading volume passed through firms there.) In particular, the *Securities and Investments Board (SIB)* is responsible for Britain's securities markets, but it is delegating supervision of the Eurobond secondary market to a *self-regulatory organization (SRO),* the *Securities Association.* That association itself was formed by a merger of the *London Stock Exchange* and the *International Securities Regulatory Organization (ISRO),* which represented Euromarket firms until last year.

However, the Securities Association remains subject to a continuing role for the *Bank of England* (i.e., dual regulation, with the commercial banks particularly supportive of the Bank of England role), which has published a discussion paper on the regulation of wholesale markets. In particular, it has proposed very high *capital ratios* for inventories of Eurobonds of 11% for those of 1-5 years maturity, and 12% for maturities over 5 years (comparable *capital adequacy* ratios for gilts are 6% and 9% of there value). Applying the 11%/12% ratios would require a virtual doubling of current bank capital dedicated to such activity, and thereby a halfing of return on equity, which in turn would lead to emigration of much Eurobond business (comparable to the shifting of some Euronote business to Luxembourg, in response, to the imposition of capital requirements in the UK). Relatedly, banks are balking at a proposal to raise their capital requirements to harmonize with those of securities firms.

Another issue is the specific rules of the expected *designated investment exchange* for Eurobonds, the AIBD, to reflect, for example, the SIB's insistence that all trades be reported and published. A related issue is a possible requirement of *firm* as opposed to *indicative* prices on the Reuters screens, etc., where such prices are posted. As the biggest Eurobond traders are opposed to *transparent markets,* the AIBD has shelved plans for a screen-based trading system (the implementation of which would reduce the edge of the biggest trading houses), and instead supports a trade confirmation and matching system (to create "audit trails") which AIBD members are expected to approve at their May 1987 annual meeting in Oslo.

Dealers make profits in three ways. First, there is realized profit from selling securities at a higher price than that for which they were bought. Second, inventory profits are realized from holding a net short book when prices are falling or a net long book when prices are rising. The last potential source of profit results from positive carry on the very predominantly financed inventory. That is, by lower interest rates on the loans than the current yield on the securities being financed (i.e., positive carry). The loans themselves are largely from Morgan Guaranty via Euro-clear and from Citibank via Cedel, with collaterization usually being 90% of the face value of straight bonds and a lower 80% of the value of more volatile convertibles.

Settlement of Eurobond transactions, to save money and time, is generally done through entries on the books of the two Eurobond clearing systems, Euro-clear and Cedel. The former was set up in 1968 by the Morgan Guaranty Trust Company and Cedel was set up in 1970 in Luxembourg. Usually fungible accounts are used instead of identifying specific securities with specific individuals. Coupon clipping and crediting of accounts with earned interest are provided. In trading, seven day delivery is normal, and for short sales a bond borrowing system has been developed, at a fee to the lender of currently 4.25% annually.

The outlook for the Eurobond secondary market is mixed. Participation in it is obviously helpful for effectiveness in the primary market (e.g., pricing, placement), and is logically viewed as part of a complete range of services to meet client needs. However, the high clearing and settlement costs, the substantial risks involved, and the cutthroat competition (related to ease of entry) have created an environment of thin margins and frequent losses.

Moreover, in the fall of 1986, the $17 billion submarket of perpetual FRNs issued by banks nearly collapsed. Provoking the debacle, with declines of up to 15 points for investors who had assumed that the price would never move far away from 100, was the shift of funds, especially by Japanese investors, from those issues into collaterized mortgage obligations of Federal agencies. Underlying the shift was the fact that CMOs were generally sold with yields of 40-60 basis points over LIBOR, while the bank FRNs generally offered a spread of only 10-20 basis points over LIBOR. A subsequent further depressant on long term floating-rate bank issues was the fees that bank regulators, wary of a kind of daisy chain in the banking system, might implement.

Association of International Bond Dealers (AIBD)
Association des courtiers internationaux en obligations

Founded in 1969 in London, the AIBD has its *secretariat* (business conducted in English) in Zurich (since 1977) and its computer center in London. Its membership of 800 institutions from over 30 countries is organized into 12 regions (America; Belgium; Far East and Australia; France, Monaco and Spain; Germany and Austria; Italy; Luxembourg; Middle East; Netherlands; Nordic; Switzerland and Liechtenstein; United Kingdom and Ireland) who meet at an annual conference (Venice 1982; The Hague 1983; Nice 1984; Nelsinki 1985; Singapore 1986; Oslo, 1987). Between the conferences, affairs are handled by a Board of 17 members, including an Executive Comittee of 7 persons, meeting 6 times a year.

The aims of the AIBD are to provide for examination and discussion of questions relating to international securities markets and issue rules governing their functions; establish and maintain close liaison between primary and secondary markets in international securities; address and resolve technical problems affecting the market; establish and enforce rules governing the orderly function of the market; foster improvements in international capital markets and enhance relations between members and related national and international markets; provide information and guidance to governments and international authorities concerned with international capital market activity; represent members' interests regarding fiscal and regulatory problems affecting the market; inform and counsel members on implications of new regulations or taxes; and maintain close contact with two international clearing systems, Euro-clear and Cedel, handling most international bond transaction settlements.

The activities of the AIBD have included promoting uniform market practices governing secondary international bond market dealings; introducing a new and standard method of calculating yield for international bonds; providing market information and statistical services; conducting annual educational seminars; and maintaining data base and information exchanges with central monetary authorities and other interested institutions.

The four publications of the AIBD include the *Weekly Eurobond Guide;* the *International Bond Manual* (annual); the *Members Register* (annual); and the *Yield Book* (biennial).

Exhibit 9-4
AIBD RULES AND RECOMMENDATIONS APPLY TO SECONDARY MARKETS IN THE FOLLOWING SECURITIES

Euro-Australian dollar bonds	Euro Kuwaiti dinar bonds
Euro-Austrian schilling bonds	Euro-lira bonds
Euro-Bahraini dinar bonds	Euro-Luxembourg franc bonds
Euro-Canadian dollar bonds	Euro-New Zealand dollar bonds
Euro-dollar bonds	Euro-Norwegian kroner bonds
Euro-French franc bonds	Euro-Saudi riyal bonds
Euro-guilder bonds	Euro-sterling bonds
Euro-Hong Kong dollar bonds	Euro-yen bonds
Euro-floating rate notes	Euro-warrants
Euro-multiple currency unit bonds	Foreign US dollar bonds

The Board

Gian-Carlo Arduino   Euromobiliare S.p.A.,
                                      Milan

James Beacham*	Wood Gundy Inc. London
Wiliam Birch	Morgan Stanley & Co., Inc., New York
Richard Bristow*	Credit Suisse First Boston Ltd., London
Osama Elansari	Burgan Bank S.A.K., Kuwait
Rene Jaquet*	Les Fils Dreyfus & Cie. S.A. Basle
Remy Kremer	Banque Generale du Luxembourg S.A. Luxembourg
Masaki Kurokawa	Nomura Securities Co. Ltd., Tokyo
John Langton	Security Pacific Hoare Govett Ltd., London
Robert Nagtzaam	Algemene Bank Nederland N.V., Amsterdam
Christoph Niemann	Trinkaus & Burkhardt, Dusseldorf
Pier-Luigi Quattropani* Treasurer	HandelsBank N.W., Zurich
Elie Saouaf	Bank Paribas Capital Markets, Paris
Arthur Schmiegelow* Chairman	Privatbanken A/S, Copenhagen
David Watkins*	Goldman Sachs International Corp., London

Committee Chairman

Gian-Carlo Arduino	Committee of Regional Representatives
James Beacham	Committee of Reporting Dealers
Rene Jaquet	Education Committee
Richard Bristow	Market Practices Committee

*members of the Executive Committee

Secretariat

ZURICH: John Wolters
                                        Secretary General

                                        Erwin Fluckinger
                                        Finance Manager

                                        Hedi Keller
                                        Erika Schjorring
                                        Junko Greber

LONDON: Royston Lambert
                                        General Manager

AIBD (Systems and Information) Limited

LONDON: Stephen Burry
                                        Systems Manager

                                        David Self
                                        Data Manager

Exhibit 9-5
THE FIRMS IN THE EUROBOND SECONDARY MARKET*

Akroyd & Smithers
London, United Kingdom

Algemene Bank Nederland
Amsterdam, Netherlands

Amsterdam-Rotterdam Bank
Amsterdam, Netherlands

Andelsbanken Danebank
Copenhagen, Denmark

Arab Banking Corp.
Manama, Bahrain

Arab Investment Co.
Manama, Bahrain

Arnhold & S. Bleichroeder
New York, NY

BA Asia
Hong Kong

Bache Securities (UK)
London, United Kingdom

Banca Commerciale Italiana
Milan, Italy

Bank of America International
London, United Kingdom

Bank Van der Hoop Offers
Amsterdam, Netherlands

Bank of Tokyo International
London, United Kingdom

Bankers Trust International
London, United Kingdom

*Banque Arabe et Internationale
d'Investissement*
Paris, France

Banque Bruxelles Lambert
Brussels, Belgium

Exhibit 9-5 (con't)

Banque Generale du Luxembourg
Luxembourg, Luxembourg

Banque Gutzwiller, Kurz, Bungener
Geneva, Switzerland

Banque Indosuez
Paris, France

Banque Internationale a Luxembourg
Luxembourg, Luxembourg

Banque Internationale de Placement
Paris, France

Banque Nationale de Paris
Paris, France

Banque Paribas Capital Markets
London, United Kingdom

*Banque de la Societe
Financiere Europeene* Paris, France

Banque de l'Union Europeene
Paris, France

Baring Brothers & Co.
London, United Kingdom

*Bayerische Hypotheken-Und
Wechsel-Bank*
Munich, West Germany

Bergen Bank
Bergen, Norway

*Berisford Cresvale
International*
London, United Kingdom

Bondpartners
Lausanne, Switzerland

James Capel & Co.
London, United Kingdom

W.I. Carr, Sons & Co.
(Overseas)
London, United Kingdom

Charterhouse Japhet
London, United Kingdom

Chase Manhattan, Ltd.
London, United Kingdom

Chemical Bank International
London, United Kingdom

Christiania Bank og Kreditasse
Oslo, Norway

CIBC
London, United Kingdom

Citicorp Investment Bank
London, United Kingdom

Commerzbank
Frankfurt/Main, West Germany

Copenhagen Handelsbank
Copenhagen, Denmark

County Bank
London, United Kingdom

Credit Commercial de France
Paris, France

Credit Suisse
Zurich, Switzerland

*Credit Suisse First
Boston Securities*
London, United Kingdom

Creditanstalt-Bankverein
Vienna, Austria

Creditanstalt-Bankverein
(London branch)
London, United Kingdom

Cresvale International
New York, NY

Dai-Ichi Kangyo International
London, United Kingdom

Dean Witter Capital Markets
(Asia)
Singapore

*Dean Witter Capital Markets
International*
London, United Kingdom

Deltec Securities (U.K.)
London, United Kingdom

Den Norske Creditbank PLC
London, United Kingdom

Exhibit 9-5 (con't)

Deutsche Bank (Dusseldorf)
Dusseldorf, West Germany

Deutsche Bank (Frankfurt)
Frankfurt/Main, West Germany

Deutsche Bank (Mannheim)
Mannheim, West Germany

Deutsche Bank Capital Corp.
New York, NY

Deutsche Bank Capital Markets
London, United Kingdom

*Development Bank of Singapore
(DBS Bank)*
Singapore

Dewaay Luxembourg
Luxembourg, Luxembourg

Dillion, Read Ltd.
London, United Kingdom

Dominion Securities Pittfield
London, United Kingdom

Dresdner Bank
Frankfurt/Main, West Germany

Drexel Burnham Lambert Securities
London, United Kingdom

EBC Amro Bank
London, United Kingdom

Enskilda Securities-Skandinviska Enskilda
London, United Kingdom

First Chicago, Ltd.
London, United Kingdom

First Interstate Capital Markets
London, United Kingdom

Robert Fleming Securities
London, United Kingdom

Fuji International Finance
London, United Kingdom

*Girozentrale und Bank der
oesterrichischen Sparkassen
(Girozentrale Vienna)*
Vienna, Austria

*Gironzentrale und Bank der
oesterrichischen Sparkassen
(Girozentrale Vienna London Brance)*
London, United Kingdom

Goldman Sachs International Group
London, United Kingdom

Grieveson, Grant & Co.
London, United Kingdom

Hambros Bank
London, United Kingdom

Handelsbank
Zurich, Switzerland

Hill Samuel & Co.
London, United Kingdom

Hongkong Bank
London, United Kingdom

*E.F. Hutton and Co.
(London)*
London, United Kingdom

IBJ International
London, United Kingdom

Indosuex Asia (Singapore)
Singapore

Investment Bank of Ireland
Dublin, Ireland

*Istituto Bancario San Paolo
di Torino*
Turin, Italy

Italian International Bank
London, United Kingdom

Jardine Fleming (Securities)
Tokyo, Japan

Kansallis-Osake-Pankki
Helsinki, Finland

Kidder, Peabody Securities
London, United Kingdom

Kitcat & Aitken
London, United Kingdom

Exhibit 9-5 (con't)

Kredietbank
Brussels, Belgium

Kredietbank Luxembourgeoise
Luxembourg, Luxembourg

F. van Lanschot Bankiers
Amsterdam, Netherlands

Lloyds Merchant Bank
London, United Kingdom

London & Continental Bankers
London, United Kingdom

LTCB International
London, United Kingdom

Mabon Nugent International
London, United Kingdom

Manufacturers Hanover Ltd.
London, United Kingdom

McLeod Young Weir International
London, United Kingdom

Merill Lynch International & Co.
London, United Kingdom

Merill Lynch International & Co.
(Money Markets)
London, United Kingdom

L. Messel & Co.
London, United Kingdom

Midland Doherty
London, United Kingdom

Mitsubishi Finance International
London, United Kingdom

Mitsui Finance International
London, United Kingdom

Morgan Grenfell & Co.
London, United Kingdom

Morgan Guaranty Ltd.
London, United Kingdom

Morgan Stanley International
London, United Kingdom

National Bank of Abu Dhabi
Abu Dhabi, United Arab Emirates

Nederiandsche Middenstandsbank
Amsterdam, Netherlands

Nikko Securities Co. (Europe)
London, United Kingdom

Nomura International
London, United Kingdom

Orion Royal Bank
London, United Kingdom

Paine Weber International Trading
London, United Kingdom

Philips & Drew
London, United Kingdom

Pierson, Heldring & Pierson
Amsterdam, Netherlands

PK Christiania Bank (UK)
London, United Kingdom

Postipanski
Helsinki, Finland

Provinsbanken
Copenhagen, Denmark

Purcell Graham & Co.
London, United Kingdom

Quadrex Securities
London, United Kingdom

L.F. Rothschild, Unterberg
Towbin International
London, United Kingdom

Salomon Brothers International
London, United Kingdom

Sanwa International
London, United Kingdom

Saudi International Bank
(Al-Bank Al-Saudi Al-Alami)
London, United Kingdom

J. Henry Schroder Wagg & Co.
London, United Kingdom

Shearson Lehman Brothers
International
London, United Kingdom

Exhibit 9-5 (con't)

Simon & Coates
London, United Kingdom

Smith Barney, Harris Upham
International
London, United Kingdom

Societe General
Paris, France

Societe General Merchant Bank
London, United Kingdom

Societe Generale Strauss Turnbull
London, United Kingdom

Sparekassen SDS
Copenhagen, Denmark

Standard Chartered Merchant Bank
London, United Kingdom

Sumitomo Finance International
London, United Kingdom

Svenska Intrernational
London, United Kingdom

Swiss Bank Corp.
Basel, Switzerland

Swiss Bank Corp. International
London, United Kingdom

Thomson McKinnon Securities
London, United Kingdom

Toronto Dominion International
London, United Kingdom

Union Bank of Norway
Oslo, Norway

Union Bank of Switzerland
Zurich, Switzerland

Union Bank of Switzerland
(Securities)
London, United Kingdom

Vereins-und Westbank
Hamburg, West Germany

S.G. Warburg & Co.
London, United Kingdom

Westdeutsche Landsbank—
Girozentrale
Dusseldorf, West Germany

Wood Gundy
London, United Kingdom

Yamaichi International
(Europe)
London, United Kingdom

*More detailed information, including firm data, instrument specializations, etc. is available in the complete list in the May 1986 issue of *Institutional Investor,* prepared by its Associate Editor Lisa Halliday.

Appendixes

Appendix 1: Glossary

Acceptance House. Financial institution in the U.K. lending money on the security of bills of exchange. Acceptance houses often lend money to an exporter to cover the gap between the production of goods and the receipt of proceeds from their sale.

Accepting Houses Committee. The 17 leading London merchant banks. Bills of exchange drawn on them are discountable at fine rates. The Committee also ensures policy coordination between its members, the Treasury, and the Bank of England.

Agency Bank. A foreign bank in the U.S. market, authorized to grant loans, but not to accept local deposits.

AIBD. The Association of International Bond Dealers, with offices in Zurich and London.

All-In Costs. Total costs, both explicit and others (for issuing CDs, etc.).

Arbitrage. Simultaneous purchase and sale of a security or other financial interest to take advantage of price/yield differentials.

Asian Currency Units (ACUs). Special department of local and foreign banks in Singapore authorized to conduct Eurocurrency operations.

Asian Dollar Bonds. Eurobonds issued in Singapore.

Asian Dollar Market. The Eurocurrency market centered in Singapore.

Bank for International Settlements. *See* BIS.

Bank of England. The U.K. central bank, founded in 1694 and nationalized in 1946, as result of which it is controlled by the Chancellor of the Exchequer.

Bank of France. The French central bank, founded in 1800 and nationalized in 1946, with 233 branches throughout France.

Bank of Japan. The Japanese central bank, founded in 1882 and rein-
stituted in 1942, with 45% private shareholders but under complete government control.

Bardepot. A West German regulation which requires a percentage of
foreign borrowings by German residents (corporations) to be deposited in cash in a noninterest-bearing account with the Bundesbank.

Basis Point. One hundredth of a percentage point (i.e., 0.01%).

Bid. The highest price/yield that a dealer is prepared to pay for a sec-
urity/deposit.

BIS. The Bank for International Settlements, located in Basle, Switzerland, is an intergovernmental financial institution, originally
founded in 1930 to assist in transferring World War I reparations
among central banks. Now it functions as a "central bank for central banks," with activities including collecting and disseminating
information on the Eurocurrency market.

Branch Bank. A branch of a foreign bank, authorized to make loans
and take local deposits.

Bundesbank. The Deutsche Bundesbank, the German central bank,
was founded in 1957. Controlled by a 16 member Central Bank
Council which meets every other Thursday, it is totally independent of the federal government.

Call Money. Money that is immediately available, generally accruing
interest at the overnight rate.

Call Option. Contract giving the holder the right to buy a financial future or other underlying interest at a specified price until an expiration date.

CD. *See* Certificate of Deposit.

CEDEL. Centre de Livraison de Valeurs Mobilieres, Luxembourg. A
computerized clearing system for Eurobonds and other securities.

Central Bank. The major regulatory bank in a nation's monetary system, generally government-controlled. Its role normally includes
control of the credit system, the note issue, supervision of commercial banks, management of exchange reserves, and the national
currency's value, as well as acting as the government's bank.

Central Rate. Exchange rate against the European currency unit (ECU) adopted for each currency within the European Monetary System. Central rates are used to tie members' currencies together in a grid of fixed parities. Similar parities are calculated via the ECU central rate between all member states' national currencies.

Certificate of Deposit (CD). Interest-bearing negotiable time deposit of fixed maturity, but of fixed or variable interest rate, at a commercial bank.

Chicago Mercantile Exchange (CME). The exchange housing the International Monetary Market, where Eurodollar futures and options are traded.

CHIPS. The Clearing House Interbank Payments System, the international private clearing system in New York City for Euromarket transactions, with 142 bank participants, including 21 "settling participants."

Closing Out. Action offsetting a long or short position.

Closing Price. Price recorded by an exchange at the close of a trading session.

Co-Manager. In security issues, an invitee on an ad hoc basis by the lead manager or at the request of the issuer, who shares responsibility for pricing and placing the issue.

Commercial Paper. Promissory note of a corporation, government agency, or bank holding company, usually unsecured, but with bank backup lines, normally with a maturity of up to 270 days and sold at a discount from face value.

Commitment Fee. Fee charged by banks on the unused portion of a loan.

Composite Currency. Also known as a "currency cocktail," a unit composed of several currencies, such as ECU and the SDR, or a customized unit created by a central bank for foreign exchange management purposes.

Concordat. The 1975 statement of guidelines by the so-called Basle Committee of the Group of 10 plus Switzerland central bank supervisors (outgrowth of the Cooke Committee) under the auspices of the BIS, providing for the supervision of banks' foreign establishments.

Convertible Eurobonds. Straight bonds with option to convert into equity shares of issuing company; bonds and shares may be denominated in different currencies.

Corset. Limitation on the growth of bank lending in the UK where banks had to make a noninterest-bearing deposit with the Bank of England if the limit was exceeded (abandoned in 1980).

Country Risk. Risk of lending funds or making an investment in a particular country.

Coupon. Interest rate payable on bonds (also the corresponding detachable certificate).

Cross Default. Clause in a loan agreement stipulating that default by borrower on any other loans will be regarded as a default on the one governed by that clause.

Creditor Nation. Country with a balance of payments surplus.

Credit Rating. Overall creditworthiness of borrower. (Moody's and Standard & Poor's are rating agencies).

Current Account. The balance of payments account including trade in goods and services plus unilateral transfers.

Debenture. A bond secured by a general guarantee.

Debtor Nation. Country with a balance of payments deficit.

Debt Service Ratio. Cost to a country of servicing the annual principal and interest payments on its debt relative to exports (20% is generally an acceptable maximum).

Discount Houses. London financial institutions dealing in money market instruments, twelve of which have a special relationship with the Bank of England.

Discount Securities. Money market instruments issued at discount and redeemed at maturity for full face value.

Drawdown. Drawing down of funds made available from a financial institution.

Droplock Loan. Medium-term floating rate facility that automatically becomes a fixed rate bond if interest rates fall to a predetermined level.

Dutch Auction. Auction where the lowest price needed to sell the entire offering is the price at which all the securities being offered for sale are sold.

ECU. European currency unit, a composite currency, created in 1979 by the EEC, and composed of the German mark, the French franc, the British pound, the Italian lira, the Dutch guilder, the Belgian and Luxembourg francs, the Danish krone, the Irish punt, and the Greek drachma; worth approximately $1.15 (4/87).

Either Or Facility. Arrangement allowing a U.S. corporation to borrow Eurodollars from a foreign bank (at LIBOR plus spread) or dollars (at prime) from the bank's head office.

EMS. European Monetary System, the 1979 successor to the European Joint Float, is composed of West Germany, France, Italy, Netherlands, Belgium, Luxembourg, Ireland, and Denmark; 4.5% wide bands are utilized, aside from Italy (12%).

Entrepôt. A major international trading center to which goods are shipped for re-export elsewhere (literally, a warehouse).

Equivalent Bond Yield. The true annual yield on a discount instrument.

Eurobond. Bonds denominated in a currency other than that of the country in which the bond is sold.

Euro-Clear. A computerized system in Belgium for Eurobonds and other securities.

Eurocommercial Paper. Short-term (generally three or six months) promissory notes issued in the Euromarket on a *nonunderwritten* basis.

Eurocredit. Medium-term Eurocurrency credits.

Eurocurrency. A currency on deposit outside its country of origin; also called "external currencies," "xenocurrencies," "international currencies."

Euronotes. Short-term (generally three or six months) promissory notes issued in the Euromarket on an *underwritten* basis.

Fedwire. The preeminent U.S. domestic bank clearing system, managed by the Federal Reserve System and utilizing depository accounts at Fed banks and branches.

Fiscal Agent. The bank-appointed agent for a Eurobond issue.

Floating Rate Note (FRN). A 5-7 year Eurosecurity, with generally a six-month rollover rate and a minimum rate.

FOMC. The Federal Open Market Committee is composed of 12 voting members, including the Fed Chairman (Chairman), the President of the New York Fed (Vice Chairman), the other six Governors and four of the remaining eleven Fed presidents on a one-year rotational basis. Meetings are held every six weeks.

Foreign Bonds. Bonds issued in foreign domestic capital markets (in the domestic currency); defined as international bonds but not as Eurobonds (Yankees, Bulldogs, Samurais).

Foreign Exchange Premium/Discount. The difference between the spot and outright forward rates.

Forward Forward. The future delivery of a deposit maturing on a further forward date.

Gearing. The capital: debt ratio.

Gen-Saki Market. The repo market conducted by Japan's security houses.

Gilts. UK government securities.

Grace Period. Length of time before which loan repayments are due (also before which the commitment fee is applied).

Group of Ten (G-10). The principal industrial countries within the framework of the IMF, composed of the Belgium, Canada, France, Great Britain, Italy, Japan, Netherlands, Sweden, the U.S., and West Germany. Switzerland is associated with most G-10 meetings. (G-3 includes the U.S., Japan and Germany, while G-5 adds France and the UK, and G-7 adds Italy and Canada.)

Hot Money. Sensitive short-term speculative or arbitrage funds moving in very rapid response to exchange rate pressurbs or yield differentials.

IMF. International Monetary Fund, which provides temporary balance of payments assistance and is actively involved in resolving international debt problems.

IMM. *See* International Monetary Market.

Institute of International Finance. Composed of major banks throughout the world and located in Washington, D.C., it monitors conditions in borrowing countries.

Interest Basis. Usually 360 days, but 365 in the case of the British and Irish pounds, Kuwaiti dinar, and sometimes the Belgian franc.

Interest Equalization Tax. A U.S. tax of up to 15% from 1963-1974 on most foreign securities (stocks and bonds).

International Monetary Fund. *See* IMF.

International Monetary Market (IMM). The CME division that trades Euro-dollar futures and options.

Joint Venture Bank (Consortium Bank). A bank owned by several other banks.

Kiwi Paper. Securities denominated in New Zealand dollars.

Lead Manager (Lead Underwriter). Manager who leads a Euroissue.

LIBOR. London Interbank Offered Rate, being the interest rate at which a sample of reference banks in the London Euromarket offer funds for deposit in the interbank market. The rate depends on the currency selected (generally U.S. dollars, unless designated otherwise) and the maturity (usually three or six months); Euroissues generally utilize the average rate of selected reference banks at 11 a.m. two days before the rollover date for resetting the interest rate.

LIFFE. The London International Financial Futures Exchange, where Eurodollar futures and options on the futures are traded.

Limit Up and Down. Maximum price advance or decline from the previous day's settlement price permitted in one trading session.

Listing. Listing an issue on a stock exchange, representing the latter's approval for trading.

London Dollar CD. A Eurodollar certificate of deposit (CD) issued by a bank in London.

Long Funding. Liability maturity exceeds corresponding asset maturity (that is, ARBL or asset repriced before liability).

Merchant Bank. An investment bank, especially in London (e.g., the acceptance houses).

Money Supply. Monetary aggregates including M-1, M-2, and M-3.

Net Accessible Interest Differentials. The difference between two Eurocurrency deposits of the same maturity, being *net* (free of withholding taxes) and *accessible* (available to all market participants as opposed to the restricted availability of many domestic markets).

NIF. Note issuance facilities are underwriting commitments of as long as ten years for short-term note issuance.

Nostro Account. Bank's account held with a foreign bank.

Odd Dates. Deals for periods other than regular market periods which are generally one, two, three, six, nine, and twelve months.

Offer (Asked). The lowest price/yield that a dealer will accept for a security/deposit.

Offshore Banking Units (OBUs). Special departments of banks in Bahrain, Manila, and Taipei authorized to conduct Eurocurrency operations.

Option Eurobonds. Straight bonds with option to receive interest and/or principal in a different currency.

Perpetuals. A debt issue, generally at a floating rate, with no maturity.

PHIL. The Philadelphia Stock Exchange, which offers European style options on Eurodollar deposit rates.

Reference Banks. A group of banks whose interbank lending rates to prime banks are used to determine the interest rate on floating rate securities and loans.

Rescheduling. Renegotiation of terms and conditions of existing borrowings.

Round Turn. A completed futures transaction of purchase and subsequent sale (or vice versa).

SDRs. Special drawing rights are IMF currency units, composed of U.S. $.54, DM. 46, £.071, FFr. 74 and Y 34; worth approximately $1.29 (4/87).

Secondary Market. The market for seasoned securities (cf. primary market).

SFE. The Syndney Futures Exchange, where Eurodollar futures are traded.

Short Dates. Standard Eurodeposit periods from overnight up to three weeks.

Short Funding. Asset maturity exceeds corresponding liability maturity (that is, LRBA or liability repriced before asset).

SIMEX. The Singapore International Monetary Exchange, where Eurodollar futures and options are traded.

SNIF. Short-term note issuance facility (same as NIFs)

Sovereign Risk. Risk resulting from government action (such as freezing assets) or nonaction (failure to pay direct or guaranteed loan).

Split Spread. Different spreads over LIBOR for different periods of the credit.

Spread (Margin). The margin over LIBOR charged a borrower.

Squeeze. To dry up a Eurodeposit market to support the spot currency.

Straight Bond. A bond not convertible into equity (plain vanilla).

Subsidiary Bank. An independent legal entity owned by another bank.

Subordinated Debt. Junior debt, as opposed to senior debt.

Swiss National Bank (SNB). The Swiss Central bank, founded in 1905 with its legal/administrative headquarters in Berne and its directorate in Zurich.

Syndicated Eurocredit. A medium-term loan denominated in a Eurocurrency granted by a group of banks, at a spread over a floating rate of interest (LIBOR).

Straight Eurobonds. Fixed coupon with a maturity of up to 25 years.

Tap CD. Certificates of deposit (CDs) written on an ad hoc basis.

TED Spread. A Eurodollar futures strategy involving the changing differential between the Treasury bill future and the Eurodollar future.

Tombstone. Advertisement of a syndicated credit issue.

Tranche CDs. Large certificate of deposit (CD) issues sliced into tranches for retail marketing.

Two-way Market. Market where dealers quote both buying and selling rates.

Warrants. Warrant provides option to purchase shares of issuing company; may be traded separately from the related bonds.

World Bank. The International Bank for Reconstruction and Development, traditionally a project lender, but becoming involved in global debt solutions.

Zero Coupon Bond. A discount basis instrument redeemed at par value.

Appendix 2: Eurocurrency Market Chronology

1947 Post-World War II monetary system (Bretton Woods) gives the dollar a central role (gold exchange system), requiring central banks to hold dollar reserves (hence pool of investible dollars) to maintain fixed parities (within 1%); post-World War II exchange controls (lasting until 1958) give dollar central role in international trade.

September 1949 30.5% devaluation of the pound ($4.03 to $2.80) enhances dollar role.

Early 1950s Chinese/Soviet/East European banks, advised by Chase, transfer dollar deposits from U.S. to Moscow Narodny Bank (London) and Banque Commerciale pour l'Europe du Nord (Paris), creating Eurodollar market.

Italian banks begin to bid for dollar deposits for competitive local lending due to fixed interest rate structure on lira loans.

1956 U.S. freezing of belligerent (United Kingdom, France, Israel, Egypt) assets in the Suez War of 1956 inclines Arabs to transfer dollar deposits from U.S. to Europe.

1957 U.K. government due to balance of payments pressures, prohibits UK banks from financing of nonresident (third country) trade, leading to dollar financing.

1958(end) Termination of most West European foreign exchange controls substantially boosts Eurocurrency operations.

1960-1968 Creation/duration of Gold Pool (U.S., UK, Belgium, Italy, Netherlands, Switzerland, Germany) to stabilize the dollar:gold relationship ($35/troy ounce).

February 1961-February 1965 "Operation Twist" combination of high short-term rates to protect spot dollar, and low long-term rates to foster investment.

Mid-1963-January 1974 Introduction/duration of the Interest Equalization Tax (IET) to equate U.S. and European yields on U.S. sales of foreign securities (15% on stock; 0-15% on bonds) — promotes Eurodollar financing by European companies.

February 1965-January 1974 Introduction/duration of the Voluntary Foreign Credit Restraint Program (guidelines to U.S. banks limiting their acquisitions of foreign assets) — encourages European companies to do Euro-dollar financings.

Bahamas passes Bank and Trust Companies Regulation Act to enhance the integrity of its banking system.

1966 Citibank-London creates negotiable Euro-dollar CD (negotiable domestic CD created in 1961); White Weld simultaneously creates secondary market in Euro-dollar CDs.

Cayman passes the Banks and Trust Companies Regulations Law, creating "Class A" and "Class B" banking licenses.

November 1967 Pound devaluation of 14.3% ($2.80 to $2.40) enhances dollar role.

January 1968-1974 Introduction/duration of Mandatory Foreign Investment Program — encourages U.S. multinationals to use Eurodollar market for foreign investments.

1968 Initiation of two-tier gold price (official transactions; private sector transactions), replacing Gold Pool.

October 1968 Bank of America initiates Asia Dollar market in Singapore, becoming first Asian currency unit (ACU).

September 1969 U.S. bank Euro-dollar borrowings subjected to reserve requirement by Regulation M (10% marginal reserve requirement on any increase in borrowings from their foreign branches above May 1969 level).

November U.S. bank Euro-dollar borrowings peak at $15 billion.

June 1970 Interest rate ceilings suspended on "large CDs" with maturities of less than 90 days (Regulation Q), to enhance competitiveness of domestic market.

Panama's Cabinet Decree No. 238 reestablishes the integrity of its banking system.

Failure of Asia dollar CD market in Singapore because of lack of secondary market.

January 1971 U.S. bank Euro-dollar borrowing marginal reserve requirement raised to 20% from 10% (Regulation M).

August 1971 U.S. suspends dollar-to-gold convertibility; import surcharge imposed (10%).

September 1971 Largest deviation of Euro-dollar rate from arbitrage tunnel: 241 basis points.

Central banks from Group of 10 and Switzerland agree to abstain from making further Euro-dollar deposits to reduce speculation against the dollar.

November 1971 Export credits freed from the Mandatory Foreign Credit Restraint ceilings.

December 1971 Smithsonian dollar devaluation of 8.6% ($38 gold); DM/yen revalued; import surcharge terminated.

March 1972 Germany imposed a *Bardepot* 40% cash deposit on foreign borrowing by German firms.

July 1972 Switzerland imposed a negative interest rate on nonresident Swiss franc deposits.

September 1972 Japanese Minister of Finance gives permission to Japanese banks to issue London dollar CDs, boosting CD market growth.

February 1973 Dollar devaluation of 11.1% ($42.22 gold).

U.S. bank Euro-dollar borrowing sink to under $700 million — lowest level since the early 1960s.

May 1973 Interest rate ceilings suspended on "large CDs" with maturities of more than 90 days (Regulation Q).

June 1973 U.S. agencies/branches of foreign banks subjected to reserve requirements on Euro-dollar borrowings.

U.S. bank Euro-dollar borrowing reserve requirement reduced to 8% from 20% (Regulation M), while CD reserve requirement raised to 8% from 5%.

September 1973 U.S. CD reserve requirement raised to 11% from 8%.

Autumn 1973 Jump of oil price from $3.92/bbl to $6.49/bbl (later to $12) by OPEC leads to large scale petrodollar recycling.

Failure of U.S. National Bank of San Diego (Arnholt Smith, President, friend of President Nixon) upsets banking system.

December 1973 U.S. CD reserve requirement reduced to 8% from 11%.

January 1974 U.S. balance of payment controls abolished, including Interest Equalization Tax, Voluntary Foreign Credit Restraint Program, and Mandatory Foreign Investment Program; spot dollar subsequently fell sharply.

May-June 1974 Franklin National Bank (Sindona) mismanagement involving large foreign exchange losses required merger into European American Bank.

Bankhaus Herstatt-Cologne collapsed with over $600 million in foreign exchange losses (June).

Considerable foreign exchange losses at Lloyd's Bank-Lugano, Bank of Belgium, and Westdeutsche Landesbank lead to increased risk: Eurocurrency market contraction/tiering of rates (prime banks, secondary Italian, Japanese), and general increase in margin over LIBOR on loans.

September 1974 Germany abolished the Bardepot.

Autumn 1974 Total yield to lenders on blended average of *medium-term* corporate/government credits reached historic high of 1.60% over LIBOR.

December 1974 U.S. CD reserve requirement reduced to 6% from 8%.

April 1975 European unit of account approved; forerunner of ECU.

May 1975 U.S. banks' Euro-dollar borrowing marginal reserve requirement reduced to 4% from 8% (Regulation M).

Spring 1975 Total yield to lenders on blended average of medium-term corporate/government credits declines to 1.40% over LIBOR.

August 1975 BIS Concordat on central bank cooperation re: Euromarket.

November 1975 New York City fiscal crisis triggered start of extensive dollar decline.

Autumn 1976 Total yield to lenders on blended average of *medium-term* corporate/government credits declines to 1.20% over LIBOR.

November 1977 Bank of Japan imposed a 50% marginal reserve requirement on inflows into yen.

December 1977 Bundesbank increased the marginal reserve requirement on inflows into DM to 100%.

December 1977 U.S. banks' reserve requirements on foreign branch loans to U.S. borrowers reduced to 1% (Regulation M).

March 1978 Bank of Japan raised the marginal reserve requirement on inflows into yen to 100%.

August 1978 U.S. banks' reserve requirements on foreign borrowing from their foreign branches and other foreign banks reduced to zero from 4% (Regulation M); Fed began raising the U.S. discount rate in stages from 7.25%. Successful reopening of Asia-dollar CD market.

November 1978 Carter/Fed dollar defense measures include 2% increase on large CD reserve requirement (to 8%), encouraging Euro-dollar borrowing; Fed raised the discount rate 1% to 9.5%; U.S. mobilized $30 billion in credits and announced $10 billion of foreign security issuance.

October 1978 Fed institutes marginal reserve requirements of 8% (above banks' end-September borrowing level) on managed liabilities including Euro-dollar borrowings and large CDs.

May 1979 Mrs. Thatcher elected UK prime Minister; emphasis on monetary control; interest rates raised sharply.

July 1979 Carter appointed Volker Fed Chairman; U.S. discount rate raised to 10%.
UK terminates foreign exchange controls on the pound sterling.

February 1980 Switzerland allowed interest payments on nonresident Swiss france deposits.

March 1980 Switzerland and Germany raised bank rates 1%.

March 1980 Fed increases marginal reserve requirement to 10% from 8%, while decreasing exempt base (end-September borrowing level) by 7%; triggered recession and corresponding U.S. interest rate fall from 20% to 8.75% by June.

May-June 1980 In response to below-target monetary growth and a rapidly deteriorating economy, the Fed increased the exempt base on "managed liabilities" by 7.5% and later reduced the marginal reserve requirement to 5% from 10%.

July 1980 In response to the severe recession, the Fed canceled the marginal reserve requirement on "managed liabilities," and the CD reserve requirement was reduced to 6% causing increased growth in the monetary aggregates.

November 1980 The Monetary Control Act imposed an ultimate 3% reserve requirement on Eurocurrency borrowings — to be phased in over a three-year period (1980-1983).

August 1981 The Bank of England terminates its Minimum Lending Rate.

October 1981 Beginning of same-day clearing for Euro-dollar transactions, eliminating one-day lag for clearing house funds (Thursday-Friday dollars, weekend dollars, and the like).

December 3, 1981 Inauguration of international banking facilities (IBFs), authorizing U.S. banks to create special divisions (set of books) to accept Eurocurrency (dollar, Deutsche mark, yen, etc.) deposits from abroad to be lent abroad (or to other IBFs or the parent) free of reserve requirements (except when lent to parent), insurance fee, Regulation Q requirements, and so on, but subject to $100,000 transaction minimum (deposits/withdrawals) and two-day notice for nonbanks (O/N for banks).

April 1982 UK freezes all of Argentina's assets in the UK such as bank deposits in response to its seizure of the Falkland Islands.

July 1982 Penn Square Bank failed.

Fed began discount rate reductions in stages from 12% to 8.5% by December.

Hong Kong terminates 15% withholding tax on nonresident foreign currency deposits.

Banco Ambrosiano Holdings, SA (Luxembourg) loses $400 million, causing failure of owner; Italy's eleventh largest bank.

May 1983 BIS revision of 1974 Concordat' *Principles for the Supervision of Banks' Foreign Establishments.*

August 1983 Schroder Munchmyer, Heugst & Co. (Hamburg), Germany's largest private bank requires a DM 420 million rescue package due to losses of its Luxembourg subsidiary.

A Florida grand jury forces relaxation of Cayman/Nassau's banking secrecy laws.

Failure of Banco Ultramar (Venezuela) in Panama.

May 1984 Run on Continental Illinois Bank required $7.5 billion rescue package.

Taipei initiates Euromarket by granting five OBU licenses.

September 1984 Intervention by Bundesbank held strong dollar at DM 3.18, setting an effective dollar ceiling for four months.

February 1985 Concerted intervention by European central banks to depress dollar after sterling hit $1.035 all-time low; UK interest rates up 4 percentage points; dollar fell by over 6% from DM 3.48 and yen 264 peaks.

April 1985 Australian dollar hit $0.6320, an all-time low.

July 1985 Italian lira devalued unilaterally by 8% in EMS.

September 1985 The Group of 5 (G-5 or U.S., UK, Germany, France, Japan) finance ministers and central bank governors agree at the New York Plaza Hotel and subsequent Seoul meeting to orchestrate a spot dollar depreciation, especially versus yen; dollar fell 8%.

January 1986 Freely negotiated commissions replace the fixed rate commission system in the UK Eurocurrency deposit market.
The G-5 at a London meeting agrees on the desirability of lower interest rates.

March 1986 Coordinated 0.5% discount rate cuts by Japan, U.S., and Germany.
Canadian dollar reached C$1.45/$, an all-time low, in wake of budget statement perceived as inadequately addressing fiscal deficit.

April 1986 Coordinated 0.5% discount rate cuts by U.S. (to 6.5%) and Japan (to 3.5%).
General EMS realignment DM, +3%; DG, +3%; BFr, +1%; DK, +1%; FFr, −3%.

July 1986 U.S. cuts discount rate by 0.5% to 6% without Japan/Germany also cutting rates.

August 1986 Irish pound unilaterally devalued 8% in EMS.
U.S. cuts discount rate 0.5% to 5.5% without similar cuts by Japan/Germany.
OPEC agrees to production quotas for September-October, raising the price of oil from $10 to $15/barrel.

September 1986 A jump of over $50 in the gold price to more than $400 per troy ounce raises fears of inflation and higher interest rates.

October 1986 The "Big Bang" in London considerably advances the deregulation of UK financial markets.
OPEC agrees to maintain production quotas during November–December stabilizing the higher oil prices and raising inflationary expectations.

November 1986 Japan cut its discount rate 0.5% to 3.0%.

January 1987 General EMS realignment DM: +3%; DG: +3%; BFr: +1%.

February 1987 G-6 agrees at Paris meeting to stabilize exchange rates. Japan cuts discount rate 0.5% to 2.5%.

March 1987 Brazil's suspension of interest payments on its medium and long-term debt raises perceptions of risk in the Eurocurrency market.

Appendix 3: Three-Month
Eurocurrency Rates (Weekly) 1984-1986
Levels and Differentials with the U.S.: Tuesday Rates

	U.S.	Canada		Japan		Germany		France		Italy		U.K.		Belgium		Netherlands		Switzerland	
	Euro	Euro	Diff	Euro	Diff	Euro	Diff	Euro	Diff	Euro	Diff	Euro	Diff	Euro	Diff	Euro	Diff	Euro	Diff
1984																			
Jan 31	9.63	9.69	6	6.31	-332	5.81	-382	13.00	337	16.88	725	9.38	.25	10.81	118	5.88	-375	3.44	-619
Feb 28	10.13	9.88	-25	6.63	-350	5.75	-438	17.30	700	17.50	737	9.25	.88	12.44	231	6.00	-413	3.63	-650
Mar 27	10.56	10.44	-12	6.25	-431	5.50	-506	14.88	432	16.38	582	8.88	.168	11.88	132	6.06	-450	3.69	-687
Apr 24	10.94	10.63	-31	6.13	-481	5.50	-544	13.00	206	15.38	444	8.81	.213	11.25	31	5.94	-500	3.69	-725
May 29	11.69	11.38	-31	6.38	-531	5.94	-575	13.31	162	15.38	369	9.56	.213	11.94	25	6.06	-563	3.94	-775
Jun 26	12.06	11.75	-31	6.19	-587	5.88	-618	12.25	19	15.00	294	9.44	.262	11.56	-50	6.13	-593	4.56	-750
Jul 31	11.81	12.81	100	6.31	-550	5.75	-606	11.69	-12	14.75	294	12.31	50	11.50	-31	6.38	-543	4.88	-693
Aug 28	11.88	12.00	12	6.31	-557	5.44	-644	11.25	-63	14.00	212	10.81	.107	11.13	-75	6.19	-569	5.13	-675
Sep 25	11.50	11.88	38	6.31	.519	5.44	-606	11.25	-25	15.38	388	10.81	.69	11.00	-50	6.13	-537	5.44	-606
Oct 30	10.00	11.31	131	6.31	-369	5.75	-425	10.69	69	15.38	538	10.56	56	10.88	88	6.06	-394	5.19	-481
Nov 27	9.13	10.50	137	6.31	-282	5.56	-357	11.00	187	14.50	537	9.75	62	10.56	143	5.75	-338	4.94	-419
Dec 18	8.56	10.31	175	6.25	-231	5.44	-312	10.63	207	14.25	569	9.75	119	10.63	207	5.69	-287	5.00	-356
1985																			
Jan 29	8.44	9.44	100	6.31	-213	5.88	-256	10.50	206	14.88	644	14.19	575	10.69	225	6.06	-238	5.50	-294
Feb 26	9.25	11.00	175	6.38	-287	6.13	-312	10.94	169	14.25	500	14.19	494	10.81	156	7.13	-212	6.13	-312
Mar 26	9.19	11.00	181	6.31	-288	5.94	-325	10.81	162	14.63	544	13.56	437	10.75	156	6.94	-225	5.81	-338
Apr 30	8.69	9.81	112	6.25	-244	5.75	-294	10.31	162	12.75	406	12.75	406	10.38	169	7.00	-169	5.19	-350
May 28	7.81	9.38	157	6.25	-156	5.56	-225	10.06	225	12.88	507	12.56	475	9.00	119	6.88	-93	5.25	-256
Jun 25	7.81	9.56	175	6.25	-156	5.50	-231	10.25	244	13.63	582	12.44	463	8.69	88	6.63	-118	5.44	-237
Jul 30	8.13	9.00	87	6.31	-182	4.75	-338	11.38	325	12.50	437	11.19	306	8.94	81	6.00	-213	4.75	-338
Aug 27	8.00	8.88	88	6.31	-169	4.44	-356	10.94	294	12.25	425	11.63	363	9.44	144	5.69	-231	4.63	-337
Sep 24	8.06	8.69	63	6.38	-168	4.38	-368	10.13	207	12.63	457	11.25	319	9.06	100	5.63	-243	4.44	-362
Oct 29	8.13	8.50	37	7.63	-50	4.94	-319	9.75	162	13.13	500	11.31	318	8.75	62	6.19	-194	4.56	-357
Nov 26	8.06	8.81	75	7.88	-18	4.63	-343	9.13	107	13.50	544	11.56	350	8.50	44	5.81	-225	3.94	-412
Dec 31	7.88	9.00	112	6.63	-125	4.75	-313	13.00	512	16.25	837	11.81	393	9.63	175	5.81	-207	3.94	-394

Date																		
Jan 7	7.88	9.38	150	6.50	-138	4.56	-332	11.88	400	16.25	837	12.50	462	9.81	193	5.63	-225	3.94	-394
14	8.25	9.88	163	6.81	-144	4.69	-356	11.75	350	17.25	900	13.06	481	9.81	156	5.75	-250	4.19	-406
21	8.06	10.06	200	6.88	-118	4.56	-350	12.00	394	17.88	982	13.38	532	9.81	175	5.69	-237	4.06	-400
28	7.94	10.50	256	6.19	-175	4.50	-344	13.31	537	19.13	1119	12.69	475	9.75	181	5.69	-225	4.19	-375
Feb 4	7.88	11.06	318	6.06	-182	4.50	-338	16.00	812	18.50	1062	13.13	525	9.88	200	5.69	-219	4.06	-382
11	7.94	11.50	356	6.06	-188	4.44	-350	15.00	706	18.75	1081	12.75	481	9.75	181	5.69	-225	3.88	-406
18	7.88	11.81	393	5.88	-200	4.69	-319	14.00	612	17.50	962	12.56	468	9.75	187	5.69	-219	3.69	-419
25	7.81	11.44	363	6.00	-181	4.44	-337	14.13	632	17.75	994	12.19	438	9.69	188	5.75	-206	3.94	-387
Mar 4	7.88	11.06	318	6.06	-182	4.50	-338	16.00	812	17.50	962	13.13	525	9.88	200	5.69	-219	4.06	-382
11	7.94	10.88	294	5.38	-256	4.38	-356	14.00	606	16.00	806	11.81	387	9.63	169	5.50	-244	3.81	-413
18	7.38	10.25	287	5.38	-200	4.38	-300	11.00	362	15.75	837	11.63	425	9.63	225	5.44	-194	3.94	-344
25	7.44	10.38	294	5.56	-188	4.63	-281	12.50	506	15.75	831	11.44	400	9.63	219	5.44	-200	4.13	-331
Apr 1	7.19	10.00	281	5.06	-213	4.44	-275	12.50	531	15.13	794	11.38	419	9.63	244	5.38	-181	3.94	-325
8	6.88	9.25	237	4.81	-07	4.31	-257	7.63	75	11.75	487	10.56	368	8.75	187	5.25	-163	3.94	-294
15	6.69	9.44	275	4.69	-200	4.38	-231	7.50	81	11.75	506	10.19	350	8.25	156	5.19	-150	4.13	-256
22	6.63	9.13	250	4.63	-200	4.44	-219	7.44	81	12.38	575	10.13	350	7.94	131	5.19	-144	4.13	-250
29	6.75	8.75	200	4.69	-206	4.50	-225	7.44	69	11.75	500	10.38	363	8.31	156	5.50	-125	4.06	-269
May 6	6.69	8.50	181	4.50	-219	4.50	-219	7.44	75	11.63	494	10.31	362	8.06	137	5.44	-125	4.13	-256
13	6.94	8.50	156	4.56	-238	4.50	-244	7.25	31	11.63	469	10.19	325	7.94	100	5.94	-100	4.25	-269
20	7.06	8.38	132	4.75	-231	4.63	-243	7.06	0	11.88	482	10.25	319	7.94	88	5.94	-112	4.69	-237
27	6.94	8.13	119	4.69	225	4.50	-244	7.38	44	11.25	431	9.88	294	7.44	50	5.81	-113	4.44	-250
Jun 3	7.06	8.81	175	4.63	-243	4.56	-250	7.44	38	11.13	407	9.69	263	7.31	25	5.94	-112	4.75	-231
10	7.00	8.50	150	4.63	-237	4.50	-250	7.31	31	11.50	450	9.63	263	7.25	25	5.88	-112	4.75	-225
17	6.78	8.31	153	4.63	-215	4.44	-234	7.25	47	11.50	472	9.69	291	7.25	47	5.78	-100	5.00	-178
24	6.88	8.44	156	4.69	-219	4.50	-238	7.19	31	11.38	450	9.75	287	7.19	31	6.00	-88	5.50	-138
Jul 1	6.69	8.06	137	4.56	-13	4.50	-219	7.38	69	11.38	469	9.75	306	7.13	44	6.00	-69	5.00	-169
8	6.63	8.19	156	4.44	-219	4.50	-213	7.25	62	11.00	437	9.94	331	7.00	37	6.00	-63	4.69	-194
15	6.50	8.06	156	4.50	-200	4.44	-206	7.13	63	11.00	450	9.94	344	7.13	63	5.50	-100	5.00	-150
22	6.44	8.13	169	4.56	-188	4.50	-194	7.13	69	11.38	494	9.94	350	7.13	69	5.63	-81	4.81	-163
29	6.50	8.75	225	4.63	-187	4.56	-194	7.19	69	11.13	463	9.94	344	7.25	75	5.44	-106	4.81	-169
Aug 5	6.38	8.31	193	4.69	-169	4.56	-182	7.19	81	10.75	437	9.75	337	7.25	87	5.44	-94	4.38	-200
12	6.19	8.38	219	4.69	-150	4.38	-181	7.00	81	10.75	456	9.81	362	7.25	106	5.38	-81	4.25	-194
19	6.06	8.31	225	4.69	-137	4.44	-162	7.13	107	10.63	457	9.69	363	7.19	113	5.38	-68	4.31	-175
26	5.88	8.25	237	4.69	-119	4.31	-157	7.31	143	11.50	562	9.88	400	7.31	143	5.06	-82	4.06	-182

Source: Foreign Exchange Advisory Service, Chemical Bank, *Comparative Economic Indicators* (July - August 1986).

Appendix 4: Chronology of Policy and Economic Events Affecting Eurodollar Arbitrage

Date	Event	Comments
March 1965	Voluntary foreign credit restraint (VFCR) program introduced	Voluntary ceiling on banks' foreign lending
January 1968	Federal Reserve given authority to make VFCR mandatory	Authority never used
October 1970	CD reserve requirement changed	Reduced from 6 to 5%
January 1971	Eurodollar reserve requirement changed	Increased from 10 to 20%
August 1971	Gold window closed; wage-price controls imposed	Largest deviation of Eurodollar rate from tunnel follows in September: 241 basis points
February 1973	Eventual abolition of VFCR announced	
August 1975	Concordat proclaimed by Bank for International settlements	Evidence of central bank cooperation; reassuring effect on international financial markets
August 1978	Eurodollar reserve requirement changed	Reduced from 4 to 0%
November 1978	Dollar "rescue" package; CD reserve requirement changed	2% supplemental increases CD reserve requirement to 8%
October 1979	Federal Reserve operating procedures changed; marginal reserve requirements imposed	8% marginal requirement added to managed liabilities aggregates, including Eurodollar borrowings and large CDs

March 1973	Collapse of Bretton Woods system	End of fixed exchange rate system
June 1973	Reserve requirements changed	CD reserve requirement increased from 5 to 8%; Eurodollar reserve requirement reduced from 20 to 8%
September 1973	CD reserve requirement changed	Increased from 8 to 11%
October 1973	First oil price shock	Price of oil increased from $3.92/bbl. to $6.49/bbl.
December 1973	CD reserve requirement changed	Reduced from 11 to 8%
January 1974	VFCR abolished	
March 1980	Federal Reserve implements special credit restraint program; marginal reserve requirements increased	Marginal reserve requirement on managed liabilities increases from 8 to 10%; exempt base amounts decrease
June 1980	Marginal reserve requirements changed	Marginal reserve requirement on managed liabilities reduced from 10 to 5%
July 1980	Marginal reserve requirements eliminated; supplemental CD reserve requirement eliminated	Marginal Eurodollar reserve requirement reduced to 0%; CD reserve requirement reduced to 6%

Appendix 4 (con't)

Date	Event	Comments
June 1974	Herstatt Bank fails; Franklin National on verge of collapse	Increased risk in international financial markets
December 1974	CD reserve requirement changed	Reduced from 8 to 6%
May 1975	Eurodollar reserve requirement changed	Reduced from 8 to 4%
November 1980	Monetary Control Act of 1980 takes effect	Phase-in of ultimate 3% reserve requirements on CDs and Eurodollars begins
October 1981	Change to same-day settlement	Eurodollar transaction settled in immediately available funds as opposed to one-day lag
August 1982	Mexican debt crisis	Discouraged Eurodollar arbitrage because of enhanced perception of risk in inter-bank market

Source: Federal Reserve Bank in New York, *Quarterly Review*, (Summer 1982), with author's addition subsequent to October 1981.

Appendix 5: Directory of Major International Financial Advisory Services *

Barnes and Co. Financial, Board of Trade Building, 141 West Jackson Boulevard, Suite 1240 A, Chicago Illinois 60604, U.S.A. Tel: (312) 341-4500. Cost: $1,500 pa in the US and $4,500 overseas.

Best & Associes SARL, 46 Rue de Provence, 75004 Paris, France. Tel: 45.25.81.79. Telex: 640384. Cost: Ffr 90,000-120,000 pa by negotiation.

A.G. Bisset and Co. Inc, Five Mile Landing, 71 Rowayton Avenue, Rowayton, Connecticut 06853, U.S.A. Tel: (203) 866-3540. Cost: $15,000 pa basic fee.

Chase Econometrics, 52 Avenue des Arts, 1040 Brussels, Belgium. Tel: (322) 511-1144. Cost: $12,000 pa.

Chemical Bank, 277 Park Avenue, New York, N.Y. 10172 U.S.A. Tel: (212) 310-4730. Cost: $25,000-100,000 pa according to the amount of consultancy advice required.

Commodity Management Service Corporation, 327 South LaSalle Street, Suite 800, Chicago, Illinois 60604, U.S.A. Cost: basic service $1,000 per month.

Chemifco SA, Avenue des Arts/Kuustlaan 46, B 1040 Brussels, Belgium. Tel: 322-512-3647. Cost: according to the amount of consultancy advice required.

Compucon Research Inc, 60 Madison Avenue, Suite 1217, New York, New York 10010, U.S.A. Tel: (212) 889-5890. Cost: $30,000 pa.

Forexia (UK) Ltd, 46 Limerston Street, London SW 10 OHH. Tel: (01) 351-0350. Remuneration: via a share of brokerage fees.

Freedberg Commodity Management Inc., 347 Bay Street, Suite 207, Toronto, Ontario, MH5 2R7, Canada. Tel: (416) 364-1171. $295 pa for the market letter plus fees for other services.

FX Concepts, 26 Broadway, New York, N.Y. 10004, U.S.A. Tel: (212) 269-4440. Cost: $25,000 pa.

Goldman Sachs, 5 Old Bailey, London EC2, United Kingdom. Tel: (01) 248-6464. Cost: approximately $10,000 pa to non-Goldman clients.

Hanseatic Group, 1110 Pennsylvania NE, Albuquerque, New Mexico 87110, U.S.A. Tel: (505)262-1981. Telex: 660834. Cost: Basic package: $10,000 semiannually.

Henley Centre for Forecasting, 2 Tudor Street, London EC4, United Kingdom. Cost: *Currency Profiles* $600 pa plus other publications, services.

Interfinance SA, 222 Avenue de Tervueren, Box 2, 1150 Brussels, Belgium. Tel: (322) 763-0960. Cost: Sfr 40,000 pa for basic service, Sfr 60,000 pa for two models.

International Treasury Consulting Inc., (ITC) and Fintech International SARL, 26 Broadway, New York, N.Y. 10004. Tel: (212) 809-1400 or Fintech International SARL, 49 Boulevard Royal, L-2449, Luxembourg. Tel: (352) 47-55-05 Cost: $5,000-35,000 pa.

International Treasury Management, Hong Kong Bank Ltd, Wardley House, 7 Devonshire Square, London EC2M 4HN. Tel: (01)626-0566. Cost: $10,000-50,000 pa.

Investment Research, 28 Panton Street, Cambridge CB2 1DH. Tel: (0223) 356-251. Cost: £525.

Brian Marber & Co., 16 Charles II Street. London SW14 4QU, United Kingdom. Tel: (01) 930-8532. Cost: $18,000 pa.

Multinational Computer Models Inc, 605 Blomfield Avenue, Montclair, New Jersey 067042, USA. Tel: (201) 746-5060. Cost: $15,000-40,000+ pa.

NP Record Ltd, George V Place, 4 Thomas Avenue, Windsor, Bershire, United Kingdom. Cost: negotiated.

Predex, 3 East 54 Street, New York, N.Y. 100022-3108, U.S.A. Tel: (212) 319-6400. Cost: $20,000 pa.

Preview Economics Inc, 6623 Deer Gap Court, Alexandria, Virginia 22310, U.S.A. Tel: (703) 971-4736. Cost: $11,400 pa.

Stoll Momentum System, Pretiosa Enterprises Ltd, 50 Teddington Park Avenue, Toronto, Ontario M4N 2CG, Canada Tel: (416) 488-2181. Cost: $15,000-60,000 pa.

Valuta Economics, Hojleddet 12, DK 2840 Holte, Copenhagen, Denmark. Tel: (02) 804-151. Cost: $12,000 pa + .

Waldner & Co., 2301 West 22 Street, Suite 201 Oak Brook, Illinois 60521, U.S.A. Tel: (312) 574-0770. Telex: 206241. Cost: $20,000 pa + .

---

*These companies provide Eurocurrency and/or foreign exchange forecasts utilizing a variey of judgemental, econometric, and technical (both charting and momentum oscillators) methodologies. More detailed information is available in the August issues of *Euromoney*. Services and prices are, of course, subject to change.

Appendix 6: Calendar of Statistical Information Pertaining to Eurocurrencies

(monthly releases available the *following* month
unless otherwise indicated)

United States
Reserves: weekly on Thursdays.
Consumer Price Index: fourth week.
Wholesale Price Index: latter part of second week.
Money Supply (M-1): weekly on Thursday afternoons (4:30 p.m.).
Money Supply (M-2; M-3): second Thursday afternoon of the following month.

West Germany
Cost of Living Index: middle of third week.
Wholesale Price index: usually fourth Tuesday (sometimes Monday).
Producer Price Index: usually 20th day (unless that day is on a weekend.)

Switzerland
Consumer Price Index: usually on the eigth or ninth day.
Wholesale Price Index: usually second Friday.
Retail Price Index: usually second Friday
Money Supply: first week.

Japan
Consumer Price Index: first part of first week.
Wholesale Price Index: usually on or close to 20th day.
Money Supply: first week.

United Kingdom
Retail Price Index: usually third Friday (sometimes fourth).
Base Wage Rate Index/Average Earnings: third Wednesday.
Money Supply: Five Week Banking Period: usually third week.

France
Retail Price Index: last Thursday or Friday.
Money Supply: first week.

The Netherlands
Wholesale Price Index: end of first week to end of second week.
Cost of Living Index: end of first week to middle of second week.

Belgium
Wholesale Price Index: third week
Consumer Price Index: fourth week

Italy
Producer Price Index: third week of *second* month following.
Consumer Price Index (950 items): first week of *third* month following.
Cost of Living Index (350 items): last week of same month.
Money Supply: third week of *second* month following.
Total Domestic Credit: third week of *second* month following.

Canada
(information is available usually in the late afternoon)
Reserves: usually first Monday.
Money Supply: weekly on Thursday.
Wholesale Price Index: usuall beginning of second week.
Consumer Price Index: (release dates vary).

Australia
Consumer Price Index: last week.
Money Supply (M-2): first week (Monday-Tuesday).
Articles Produced by Manufacturers Price Index: quarterly - first week
of following quarter.

Appendix 7: Directory of Euromarket Institutions

Central Banks/Monetary Authorities

Bahrain Monetary Agency, P.O.Box 27, Manama, State of Bahrain; tel. 241241; telex BN8295 BAHMON.

Banco Nacional de Panama,
Apartado 5220, Panama 5; tel. 69 2111; telex COMSA WU1 368773.

Bank for International Settlements, Centralbahnplatz 2, Postfach, CH-4002, Basle, Switzerland; tel. 061/208111; telex 962487.

Bank of Canada, 324 Wellington Street, Otawa K1A 069; tel. 782-8111; telex 053-4241.

Bank of England, Threadneedle Street, London EC2R 8AH, England; tel. 01-601-4444; telex 885001.

Bank of Japan, C.P.O. Box 203, Tokyo 100-91 (No. 2-1, 2-Chome, Hongoki-Cho, Nihonbasni, Chuo-ku); telex J 22763.

Bank Van de Nederlandse Antillen, Breedestraat 1 (P), Willemstad, Curacao; tel. 613600; telex 1155.

Banque de France, F 75049 Paris Cedpx 01, Boite Postal 140-01; 39, rue Croix-des-Petits-Champs; tel. 1/42-924292; telex 220932.

Banque National de Belgique, S.A., Boulevard de Berlaimont 5, B-1000 Bruxelles; tel. 2/219 4600; telex 21-105-bnbsg b.

De Nederlandsche Bank N.V., Westeinde 1, 1017 ZN Amsterdam; tel. 524-9111; telex 11355.

Bermuda Monetary Authority, Government Administration Building, Parliment street, Hamilton 5-24; tel. (809-29) 5-5278; telex; 3567 BEEMA BA.

Central Bank of the Bahamas, Frederick Street, P.0. Box N-4868, Nassau, Bahamas; tel. 322-2193; telex 20115.

Federal Reserve Bank of New York, 33 Liberty Street, New York, N.Y. 10045; tel (212) 530-1874

Federal Reserve System, Board of Governors, Washington, D.C. 20551; tel (202) 452-3000.

Financial Secretary of Cayman Islands (Thomas C. Jefferson), Cayman Islands, British West Indies.

Guernsey Banking Supervisor (Richard Whitford), St. Peter Port, Guernsey, Channel Islands.

Institut Monetaire Luxembourgeois, (Director General Pierre Jaans), 63 ave de la Liberte, 2983 Luxembourg-ville, Luxembourg, tel. 47-88-68; telex 2766.

Jersey Banking Supervisor, St. Helier, Jersey, Channel Islands.

Monetary Authority of Singapore, SIA Building, 77 Robinson Road, Singapore 0106, Republic of Singapore; tel. 225-5577; telex RS 28174 ORCHID.

Clearing Houses and Related Institutions

CEDEL, *67,* Bd Grande-Duchess Charlotte, 1010 Luxembourg, P.O. Box 1006 Luxembourg; tel. (352) 44 9921; telex 27911u); **London Representative Office** (Elain Meyers, Representative) 77, London Wall, London EC2N IBU; tel. (01) 588-4142; telex 894 628; **New York Representative Office** (Philippe Humbert, Representative), One World Trade Center, Suite 8351, New York, N.Y., 10048; tel. (212) 775-1900; telex 324 172.

CHIPS (Clearing House Interbank Payments System), 450 West 33rd Street, New York, New York; operated by the New York Clearing House Association, 100 Broad Street; New York, N.Y. 10004; tel. (212) 943-2200.

Euro-clear, (Peter Culver, Vice President and General Manager), Rue de la Regence, 4, B-100 Brussels, Belgium; tel. 32- 2-5191211; telex 61025 MGTEC B.

S.W.I.F.T., 81 Avenue Ernest Solvay, 13-1310 La Hulpe, Belgium; **New York Representative Office** SWIFCO US Inc. (Carl Brickman, Area Manager), One World Trade Center, Suite 1429, New York, N.Y., 10048; tel. (212) 938-0544; telex 233744; **Rio de Janiero Representative Office** (Fred Jordi, Area Manager), Av. Almirante Barrozo

63-203-4 Rio de Janeiro CEP20031; tel. 55-21- 2403730; telex 391-2133891; **Hong Kong Representative Office** (Neil Ferris, Area Manager), 1306, 13F, Exchange Square, Central Hong Kong; tel. 852-5-2521241; telex 78064344; **United Kingdom Representative Office** (Ray Towner, Area Manager), 7th Floor, Winchester House, 77 London Wall, London, EC2N lBE, England; tel. 441-628-8691; telex 0518954761.

Futures/Options Exchanges

Chicago Mercantile Exchange (CME) **International Monetary Market (IMM) Division,** 30 South Wacker Drive, Chicago, Illinois 60606; tel. (312) 930-1000; **New York office** (Ira Kawaller, Vice President-Director), 67 Wall Street, Suite 1610, New York, N.Y. 10005; tel. (212) 363-7000; **London office** (Keith Woodbridge, Vice President), 27 Throgmorton Street, EC2N 2AN, London, England; tel. 01-920-0722; telex 892577.

London International Financial Futures Exchange (LIFFE) Royal Exchange, London, England EC3V EPJ; tel. 01-623- 0444.

Singapore International Monetary Exchange (SIMEX), 1 Maritime Square, No. 09-39, World Trade Centre, Singapore 0409; tel. 65-2786363.

Sydney Futures Exchange (SFE), 13-15 O'Connell Street, Sydney, NSW, Australia 2000; tel. (612) 233-7633.

Other Institutions

Association of International Bond Dealers, (AIBD) Rigistrasse 60, Postfach, CH,-8033 Zurich, Switzerland; Tel. (01) 363-4222; telex 815 812; telefax (01) 363-7772; **London Office,** International House, 1 St. Catherine's Way, London E19UN, England; tel. 011-441-488-0521; telex 8813069; fac. no. 01- 4805500.

International CD Market Association, c/o Wood Gundy Ltd., 30 Finsbury Square, London, EC2A 1SB.

Reuters, 85 Fleet Street, London EC4P4AJ, England; tel. 011-441-250-1122; **New York Office:** 1700 Broadway, New York, NY 10019; tel. (212) 603-3300.

Telerate, One World Trade Center, New York, NY 10048; tel. (212) 938-5200; **London Office:** APDJ Telerate, Winchmore House, 1215 Fetter Lane, London EC4A 1BR; tel. 011-441-583- 0044.

The Institute of International Finance, Inc., 2000 Pennsylvania Avenue, N.W., Washington, D.C. 20006; tel. (202) 857-3600.

Annotated Bibliography

Books

Bell, Geoffrey, *The Euro-dollar Market and the International Financial System.* New York: John Wiley & Sons, 1973.

Bhattacharya, Anindya K., *The Asia Dollar Market: International Offshore Financing.* New York: Praeger Publishers, 1977.

Clendenning, E. Wayne, *The Euro-Dollar Market.* Oxford: Clarendon Press, 1970.

Davis, S.I., *The Eurobank: Its Origins, Management and Outlook.* New York: Macmillan, 1976.

Deak, Nicholas L. and Joanne C. Celusak, *International Banking.* New York: New York Institute of Finance, 1984.

Particularly relevant are Chapter 2, "International Banking Entities", and Chapter 8, "Eurodollar Lending."

Delamaide, Darrell, *Debt Shock.* New York: Anchor Press/Doubleday, 1985.

Dufey G. and I.N. Giddy, *The International Money Market.* Englewood Cliffs, N.J.: Prentice Hall, 1978.

Federal Reserve Bank of Chicago, *Readings in International Finance,* 2nd Ed. Chicago, 1984.

Especially relevant is Part V entitled "The Eurodollar."

Fisher G.G. III, *The Eurodollar Bond Market.* London: Euromoney Publications, 1979.

George, Abraham M. and Ian H. Giddy, eds., *International Finance Handbook,* Vol. 1. New York: John Wiley & Sons, 1983.

Particularly relevant is Part 3, "The Eurocurrency Markets" which includes "The Eurocurrency Market" by Ian H. Giddy, "Eurocurrency Dealing" by Julian Walmsley, "Eurocurrency Interest Rates and Their Linkages" by Ian H. Giddy, "Syndicated Eurolending-Pricing and Practice" by Laurie S. Goodman, "Legal Aspects of Syndicated Eurocurrency Lending" by Philip R. Stansbury, and "Eurocurrency Centers" by Maximo Eng and Francis A. Lees.

Also recommended is Part 5, "The International Bond Market," which includes "The Eurobond and Foreign Bond Markets" by Morris Mendelson, "Issuance of Eurobonds: Syndication and Underwriting Techniques and Costs" by Antoine W. Van Agtmeal, "Legal Aspects of International Bonds" by Daniel Magraw, and "The Eurobond Secondary Market" by Brian Scott Quinn and Perry Aldred.

Hewson, J. and E. Sakakibara, *The Eurocurrency Markets and Their Implications.* Lexington, Massachusetts: Heath, 1975.

Hogan, W.P. and I.F. Pearce, *The Incredible Eurodollar.* London: George Allen and Unwin, 1982.

Johnston, R.B., *The Economics of the Euro-Market: History, Theory and Policy.* New York: St. Martins Press, 1982.

Lees F. and M. Eng., *International Financial Markets.* New York: Praeger, 1975.

Little, Jane Sneddon, *Euro-Dollars: The Money Market Gypsies.* New York: Harper & Row, 1975.

Lomax, D.F. and P.T.G. Gutmann, *The Euromarkets and International Financial Policies.* New York: John Wiley and Son, 1981.

McKinnon, R.I., *The Eurocurrency Market.* Princeton Essays in International Finance No. 125 Princeton: Princeton University, 1977.

Quinn, B.S., *The New Euromarkets.* New York: Macmillan, 1975.

Stigum, Marcia, *The Money Market.* Rev. Ed. Homewood, Illinois: Dow Jones-Irwin, 1983.

Particularly relevant are Chapter 6, "The banks: Euro operations," and Chapter 16, "The Euro time deposit market."

Official Publications

Banco Nacional de Panama, *Informacion Economica y Financiera de la Republica de Panama* (Annual).

Baharain Monetary Agency, *Annual Report.*

Bahrain Monetary Agency, Directorate of Economic Research, *Quarterly Statistical Bulletin.*

Bank for International Settlements *Annual Report* April - March.

Especially recommended is Chapter V, "International Financial Markets."

Bank of England *Quarterly Bulletin.* Especially recommended is the March issue with its international banking analysis by country.

Board of Governors of the Federal Reserve System, *Federal Reserve Bulletin* (monthly).

Section 3.14, Foreign Branches of U.S. Banks Balance Sheet Data (Asset Account/Liability Account) includes a section aggregating Bahama and Nassau data.

Institute Monetaire Luxembourgeois, *Bulletin Trimestriel*(Quarterly).

Periodicals

Euromoney (monthly)

Financial Times (daily)

Institutional Investor (monthly).

Institutional Investor - International Edition (monthly).

International Financing Review (weekly).

The IFR is especially useful source of information on the Euro-securities market.

Morgan Guaranty Trust Company of New York, *World Financial Markets* (monthly). Especially relevant is the statistical appendix which includes "Eurocurrency deposit rates," "International bond issues by country of borrower," "International bond yields," "Eurocurrency bank credits by country of borrower," and "Eurocurrency market size."

The Economist (weekly).

Articles

A Correspondent, "Fall-out from the Manakh Disaster," *The Banker,* December 1983.

A Special Correspondent, "Baharain Loses Some of its Allure," *The Banker,* December 1983.

Berg, Eric, "U.S. Banks Swap Latin Debt," *The New York Times,* 11 September 1986.

Bernauer, Kenneth, "The Asian Dollar Market," *Economic Review,* Federal Reserve Bank of San Francisco, Winter 1983.

Chicago Mercantile Exchange, "The CME-SIMEX Trading Link," *Market Perspectives,* September 1984.

—, "CME-Singapore Trading Link: Around-the-World, Around- the- Clock Trading," *Market Perspectives,* September, 1983.

"CHIPS: Goodby to Next-Day Settlement," *Business Week,* 23 March 1981.

Curtin, Donald, "Are the Euromarkets Ready for Financial Futures," *Euromoney,* March 1982.

Federal Reserve Bank of Chicago, "Eurodollars - An Important Source of Funds for American Banks," *Business Conditions,* June 1986.

Fine, Edward, P., "Recent Developments in the Canadian Dollar Sector of the Eurocurrency and Eurobond Markets," *Bank of Canada Review,* January 1978.

French, Martin, "Spring is Better Late Than Never" (Luxembourg), *Euromoney,* July, 1986.

Frydl, Edward J., "The Debate Over Regulating the Eurocurrency Markets," *Quarterly Review,* Federal Reserve Bank of New York, Winter 1979-1980.

Garwin, Larry, "Luxembourg: Where Banking is Still King," *Institutional Investor,* July 1985.

Goodstadt, Leo, "How Hongkong Came of Age as a Euromarket Centre," *Euromoney,* February 1982.

Hector, Gary, "Money and Markets: A Foreign Fuse for Mexico's Debt Bomb," *Fortune,* 7 July 1986.

—, "Third World Debt: The Bomb is Defused," *Fortune,* 18 February 1985.

Hewson, Margot, "Arab Banks in the Euromarkets," *The Banker,* December 1983.

Key, Sidney, J., "Activities of International Banking Facilities: The Early Experience,"*Economic Perspectives,* Federal Reserve Bank of Chicago,Fall, 1982.

Kreicher, Lawrence L., "Eurodollar Arbitrage", *Quarterly Review,* Federal Reserve Bank of New York, Summer 1982.

Naylor, Bartlett, "International Finance Institute Aims for Active Role in Fighting Debt Crisis," *American Banker,* 10 October 1986.

Osborn, Alan, "Banking: Backbone of the Economy (Luxembourg)," *Europe,* January/February 1984.

Preston, Samuel, "New York CHIPS Goes Over to Same-Day Settlement," *Euromoney,* March 1981.

Rafferty, Kevin, "The Debate Over Hongkong Bank Regulation," *Institutional Investor,* March 1986.

Schmerken, Ivy, "Telerate vs. Reuters: Get Ready for Battle," *Wall Street Computer Review,* February 1986.

Sobol, Dorothy Meadow, "The SDR in Private International Finance," *Quarterly Review,* Federal Reserve Bank of New York, Winter 1981-1982.

Van Waesberghe, Igno, "Borrowers Queue Up Quietly in the Euroguilder Notes Market," *Euromoney,* May 1977.

Weinert, Richard S., "Swapping Third World Debt," *Foreign Policy,* Number 65, Winter 1986-87.

Reports

Brittain, Bruce, "U.S. Dollar Offshore Markets: Neglected Dimensions of Dollar Credit Flows," *Bond Market Research,* Salomon Brothers, August 1982.

Chemical Bank, Foreign Exchange Advisory Service, *Foreign Exchange Market Report* (monthly).

—, *Comparative Economic Indicators* (monthly).

Hanna, Jeffrey, "Domestic LIBOR-Based Floating-Rate Notes- Opportunities in an Emerging Market," *International Bond Market Analysis,* Salomon Brothers, 4 September 1984.

—, and Peter Niculescu, "Eurodollar Floating Rate Notes: Determinants of Price Behavior," *Bond Market Research,* Salomon Brothers, September 1981.

Hung, Tran Q. and Karen A. Johnson, "Eurodollar Zeros'-Locking in High Rate of Return," *Institutional Bond Market Analysis,* Salomon Brothers, 26 May 1982.

Patrick Paradiso and Marsha Nosworthy, "1985 International Bond Issuance," Special Report No. 8, Merrill Lynch Capital Markets, December 1985.

Parente, Gioia M., "An Anatomy of the Eurodollar Floating-Rate Note Market," *Bond Market Reserach,* Salomon Brothers, March 1984.

Sargen, Nicholas and Susan Bodyna, "Determinants of the LIBOR-Treasury Bill Spread," *Bond Market Research-International Values,* Salomon Brothers, 29 October 1984.

Index